STUDENT-ASSISTED TEACHING

STUDENT-ASSISTED TEACHING

A Guide to Faculty-Student Teamwork

Judith E. Miller
Worcester Polytechnic Institute

James E. Groccia
University of Missouri-Columbia

Marilyn S. Miller
University of Missouri-Columbia

EDITORS

ANKER PUBLISHING COMPANY, INC.
Bolton, Massachusetts

Student-Assisted Teaching
A Guide to Faculty-Student Teamwork

ISBN 1-882982-42-8

Composition by Deerfoot Studios
Cover design by Vicki Czech

Anker Publishing Company, Inc.
176 Ballville Road
P. O. Box 249
Bolton, MA 01740-0249

www.ankerpub.com

God made the bees,

The bees make honey,

We do the work,

The teacher gets the money.

Traditional school yard chant

As Cicero has written: The authority of those who teach

is often an obstacle to those who want to learn.

(Montaigne, 1588)

About the Editors

JUDITH E. MILLER is Director of Educational Development, Technology, and Assessment, and Professor of Biology and Biotechnology at Worcester Polytechnic Institute. She has published and presented extensively in the areas of cooperative learning and educational productivity. She received the Outstanding Undergraduate Science Teacher award from the Society for College Science Teachers and Kendall-Hunt Publishers in 1997.

JAMES E. GROCCIA is Director of the Program for Excellence in Teaching, Adjunct Associate Professor in the Department of Psychology, and a member of the Graduate Faculty in Educational Leadership and Policy Analysis at the University of Missouri-Columbia. His teaching and research interests center on student-assisted learning, college teaching, educational innovation and productivity, and cross-cultural psychology.

MARILYN S. MILLER is Assistant Director of the Program for Excellence in Teaching, and Adjunct Professor in the Department of Educational Leadership and Policy Analysis at the University of Missouri-Columbia. She has presented nationally on issues of communication across linguistic and cultural lines, and the role of interactive learning in compensating for linguistic difficulties of foreign instructors and students.

Contents

Part II: Undergraduate Students Assisting with Difficult Courses

Part III: Undergraduate Students Assisting with Special Groups

Part IV: Undergraduate Students Assisting in Courses and Programs for All Students

Part V: Undergraduate Students Assisting in Faculty Development

Appendices

Appendix A: Hiring Documents

Appendix B: Training Syllabi

Appendix C: Teaching Materials

Appendix D: Evaluation Procedures

Foreword

Research conducted over 40 years ago and replicated many times in later years demonstrates that one of the most effective methods for achieving both cognitive and attitudinal goals of education is undergraduates teaching other undergraduates (Carpenter, 1959; Davage, 1958; Johnson & Johnson, 1975; Webb & Grib, 1967). Yet, it is only in the past few years that student-assisted teaching has become widely used, and what research could not achieve, economic stresses did.

Politicians no longer see public higher education as an unchallenged common good. Prisons are a higher priority than universities, and most public institutions have been forced to teach larger numbers of students with diminished support from tax dollars. The pressure to teach more students with less funding has hit many private colleges as well. Because peer-assisted learning is cost effective as well as educationally effective, student-faculty partnerships are experiencing a resurgence of interest.

As class sizes increase, faculty members require less writing from their students, and there is less opportunity for them to participate in discussion, resulting in more one-way communication and student passivity. Yet if students are to remember and use learning later, if they are to develop critical thinking skills, they need to have opportunities to bring misconceptions into the open. They need to have opportunities to practice the skills for learning and thinking that are among the most important objectives of higher education. The chapters in this book illustrate how a varied group of institutions and faculty members have solved this dilemma by instituting student-assisted teaching and learning.

Student-assisted teaching is not a panacea. Like other methods, it can be done well or badly, and it can be helpful for some students but not so helpful for others. Nonetheless, it is certainly one of the most important tools in a teacher's workbox. Even those who are not confronted with the problems of larger class sizes should pro-vide opportunities for peer-assisted learning. As this book demonstrates, it produces educational outcomes that are seldom achieved with other methods of teaching and learning.

Thus, *Student-Assisted Teaching: A Guide to Faculty-Student Teamwork* comes at a time when a number of peer learning models have been developed and tried, and have produced promising results. The authors of the chapters that follow represent a wide range of disciplines and peer-assisted teaching and learning approaches. They recognize some of the difficulties facing first-time users of this approach, and offer informative and practical suggestions and advice in order to implement it.

The concluding chapter provides a nice summary of the benefits of these models to students who are taught, students who are teaching or tutoring, graduate students who are involved, and faculty members who create peer-assisted teaching and learning models.

This book should be disseminated by every faculty development center, read by every academic administrator, and discussed by every faculty member—it is a rich resource whose approach places learning into the hands of the students, where it will grow and flourish.

Wilbert J. McKeachie
Professor of Psychology
University of Michigan

REFERENCES

Carpenter, C. R. (1959). *The Penn State pyramid plan: Interdependent student work study grouping for increasing motivation for academic development.* Paper presented at the 14th National Conference on Higher Education, Chicago, IL.

Davage, R. H. (1958). *The pyramid plan for the systematic involvement of university students in teaching-learning functions.* University Park, PA: Pennsylvania State University, Division of Academic Research and Services.

Johnson, D. W., & Johnson, R. T. (1975). *Learning together and alone: Cooperation, competition and individualization.* Englewood Cliffs, NJ: Prentice Hall.

Webb, N. J., & Gribb, T. F. (1967, October). *Teaching process as a learning experience: The experimental use of student-led groups* (Final Report, HE-000-882). Washington, DC: Department of Health, Education and Welfare.

Preface

Creative faculty, faculty developers, and administrators know from firsthand experience that educational innovation in general, and student-centered learning in particular, almost always demands more work from the faculty member, not just for start-up, but on an ongoing basis. When the cost of innovation, in both time and money, is higher than that of the traditional alternative, willingness of faculty to initiate change, and of their institutions to support that change, almost always suffers. This problem is exacerbated by the tendency of innovators to attempt, or even permanently adopt, new educational models with scant evidence of their potential or actual effectiveness.

THE BOOK'S PURPOSE

Providing a range of models for undergraduate student-faculty teams, or partnerships, to help faculty, faculty developers, and administrators make learning more student-centered, more effective, and more productive, is the purpose behind this book. Each model in this volume is supported with concrete, practical details, and focuses on four main aspects of student-assisted teaching: 1) implementation, 2) evidence of effectiveness and learning benefits, 3) details of time and cost expenditures (or in some cases, savings) needed for implementation, and 4) specific suggestions for replication to save those wishing to emulate the model from experiencing the setbacks of the original designers.

THE BOOK'S ORGANIZATION

The chapters included in this book represent a range of approaches, applications, disciplines, institutions, and contexts. We have attempted to demonstrate that student-faculty teams can be adapted to meet diverse needs in a variety of situations. Therefore, the chapters have been organized based on target populations:

- Chapters 1–12 focus on models dealing specifically with first-year students.

- Chapters 13 and 14 describe models that support first-year students in dealing with difficult courses.

- Chapters 15–18 focus on difficult courses with no restriction on level of student.

- Chapter 19 focuses on adult students in a distance education context.

- Chapters 20 and 21 primarily highlight honors students.

- Chapter 22 describes a model that is remedial in focus.

- Chapters 23–28 are more general as the target audience includes all students.

- Chapters 29–31 describe models in which students provide instructional feedback and support for faculty development programs.

ACKNOWLEDGMENTS

The editors wish to acknowledge the Davis Educational Foundation, whose support of a peer-assisted learning project at Worcester Polytechnic Institute ultimately inspired this volume. The chapters in this book would not exist but for the adventurous spirit of the many faculty and administrators worldwide who have experimented with, reflected upon, and so ably written about new models of student-centered learning, and the foresight of the institutions that have supported their endeavors. Most importantly, we express our continuing gratitude to the peer assistants and the students who make it both possible and important to continually reexamine how we do higher education, and who inspire and guide us in doing it better.

Judith E. Miller
James E. Groccia
Marilyn S. Miller

Introduction

USING STUDENT-ASSISTED TEACHING TO ENHANCE TEACHING AND LEARNING

The motivation for this volume, and for the creation of the student-faculty teamwork models that it describes, is twofold. The first objective is to improve educational effectiveness for peer assistants and the students they work with by increasing student involvement in learning. Student-centered learning models are widely accepted as catalysts for improved learning and psychosocial outcomes, and their use is especially important in the critical early years of an undergraduate education. Much of higher education is still, however, reliant on teacher-centered, lecture-based, large class instruction, and student-centered approaches, while attractive, may seem unfeasible to many instructors.

Enter the second motive for this volume: increased cost effectiveness. The use of relatively inexpensive undergraduate peers to assist in the learning enterprise can make interactive learning approaches feasible and affordable in almost all learning settings. The purpose of this book is to explicate student-assisted teaching approaches so that educators can harness the potential of higher education's hidden learning resource—the undergraduates themselves—to improve the college learning experience.

HISTORICAL BACKGROUND

A student helping other students learn is not novel; however, its power and usefulness has been largely ignored in the higher education community. Peer teaching can be traced back at least to Aristotle's use of student leaders to guide younger students (Wagner, 1982). It experienced resurgence in England in the late 18th and early 19th centuries where the practice of utilizing children as teachers for other children was an essential aspect of the Bell-Lancaster educational system (Allen, 1976; Bell, 1797; Lancaster, 1803). Bell describes older students tutoring younger students and the teaching of an entire class by an older student with younger student assistants. Lancaster developed a "monitorial" system in which he claimed that up to 1,000 students could be taught by only one adult teacher, and in 1816 around 100,000 students were being taught by this system in England and Wales alone (Allen, 1976). In the latter part of the 19th century through the early part of the 20th century, teachers in one-room schoolhouses in the rural US, out of necessity as much as pedagogical principle, regularly enlisted older children to teach younger children.

While the power of peer influence on human behavior had been recognized as early as the 1950s (Newcomb, 1962), there was little mention of peer-assisted teaching in the educational literature until the 1960s. Early literature reviews (Ehly & Larson, 1980; Goldschmid & Goldschmid, 1976) reveal few empirical studies that assess the impact of peer teaching until the 1960s (Whitman, 1988). While a few of the models described in this book originate from the mid-1960s and early 1970s, the majority are relatively recent and owe their origins to movements of the 1980s and 1990s in active and cooperative learning, supplemental education, first-year experience, and learning communities.

DEFINITION OF STUDENT-ASSISTED TEACHING

The term used in this book, student-assisted teaching, refers to an instructional process where undergraduates are given responsibility by faculty for portions of their fellow undergraduates' learning experience. The degree of responsibility can vary from incidental assistance on a specific in-class problem or project, to full control over content selection, delivery, and assessment. We use the terms student-assisted teaching, or peer teaching, in a generic functional sense and they include traditional (tutor, mentor, etc.) peer roles as well as nontraditional ones (instructional consultant, technology preceptor, etc.).

THEORETICAL AND EMPIRICAL JUSTIFICATION

The reasons for adopting student-assisted teaching strategies are grounded in theory and research emanating from education and the social sciences. Employing undergraduate students increases student responsibility. Traditional educational methods, according to Jerome Bruner (1972) impose a moratorium upon students' vocational development by forcing them to assume the role of student. As an antidote to this forced student role, which retards the development of self-efficacy and responsibility for one's own learning, Bruner strongly advocates "...that we use the system of peer-assisted learning from the start in our schools" (p. 63). Learning should be a community activity, and by giving students some responsibility for helping other students, they can gain a sense of purpose and useful participation that is often lacking in their lives.

In a similar vein, James Coleman (1974) states that students should have an opportunity to take on responsibilities that affect the lives of other persons: "Only with the experience of such responsibilities can youth move toward the mutually responsible and mutually rewarding involvement with others that constitute social maturity" (p. 3), an outcome that could be safely stated to be a goal of higher education. Coleman suggests that the role of peer teaching is one way to accomplish this end.

While the influence of peers has received less attention than that of teachers and parents (Newcomb & Wilson, 1966; Ryan, 2000), peer groups play an important role in influencing adolescent academic motivation, beliefs, engagement, and achievement. Peers exert influence through socialization processes involving information exchange, modeling, and reinforcement of peer norms and values both inside and outside the classroom. While the impact of peers may be most profoundly felt on personality development, they also influence attitude and intellectual change (Brown, 1972). Channeling peer influence into teaching and learning processes enables educators to harness some of this social energy for academic growth.

Student-faculty teamwork in teaching and learning capitalizes on student ability to be powerful role models and agents of change in the classroom. People tend to ascribe power and the ability to influence behavior, attitudes, and beliefs to others they perceive to be similar to them in appearance, background, and attitudes but dissimilar in competence level (Scott, 1990). Due to their current student status, special training, and prior academic success, undergraduate students are ideally suited to overcome the resistance and apathy toward learning that may confront older faculty. Peer-student similarity also facilitates development of a shared sense of communicative meaning. Teachers want students to understand what they are saying and to share in the intended meaning of their messages. Shared meaning is most easily attained between people who are similar in culture, language, education, and values (Scott, 1990).

A review of the active and cooperative learning research (Bonwell & Eison, 1991; Chickering & Gamson, 1987; Johnson, Johnson, & Smith, 1991; Sutherland & Bonwell, 1996) reveals empirical and practical support for students actively working together in college learning environments. This research echoes "...an old, old truth which we are all of us a little apt to forget. LEARNING IS A SOCIAL ACT: it is best carried on under social conditions" [capitals in original] (Meiklejohn, 1882, p.177). College students are, as anyone who has spent time on a college campus can attest, social creatures. The process of adolescent identity formation occupies a prominent place in the lives of college age students (Erikson, 1959) and is solidified through social interactions with others. College students often define who they are through a process of attachment with or separation from others that relies on interpersonal interaction. Use of student-faculty teamwork and peer teaching facilitates interpersonal relationships centered around learning and teaches social skills necessary for teamwork and negotiation, skills that help students succeed in future classes as well as in the working world after graduation (American Society for Training and Development, 1988; National Society of Professional Engineers, 1992).

Student-assisted teaching has been shown to have both positive cognitive and affective effects upon both the peer teacher (Devin-Sheehan, Feldman, & Allen, 1976; Ehly & Larson, 1980; Gartner, Kohler, & Riessman, 1971) and the students taught (Cohen, Kulik, & Kulik, 1982; Fuchs, Fuchs, Mathes, & Simmons, 1997; Gartner, Kohler, & Riessman, 1971; Goldschmid & Goldschmid, 1976; Rubin & Hebert, 1998). Greenwood, Carta, and Hall (1988) report that peer tutoring results in academic gains "equivalent to and even greater than conventional procedures involving lecture and student discussion" (p. 262). To teach is to learn twice or as the ancient Latin dictum states, "Qui docet discit," he who teaches, learns (Allen, 1976).

Student-assisted teaching models serve to personalize education and can be an antidote to the disconnectedness and atomization that often characterizes higher education. The competitive atmosphere that exists on many college campuses can alienate students from faculty, other students, and even from the institution itself (Johnson,

Johnson, & Smith, 1991; Massy, Wilger, & Colbeck, 1994; Palmer, 1998). Student-faculty partnerships can facilitate the creation of a true cooperative community of scholars—a cherished but infrequently attained goal of higher education—where students and faculty share responsibility for teaching and learning, resulting in improved student satisfaction, success, and retention (Astin, 1975). Student-teacher roles are transformed and traditional hierarchical structures are replaced with more mentoring and equality between faculty and peer teacher. These new relationships can lead to a renewed sense of connectedness for faculty as well as students.

A final justification for the use of these models relates to the vitality of the professoriate and of the institutions themselves. Student-faculty partnerships in teaching can provide an opportunity for the renewal of the professoriate thorough first-hand exposure of peer teachers to the world of academe. With the "graying" of the professoriate and the projected shortage of college teachers in the not too distant future (Magner, 1999), these partnerships may offer lifelines to faculty renewal through the recruitment of new faculty and contact with energetic peer teachers.

PRODUCTIVITY

Student-assisted teaching approaches are a practical and productive means of improving educational quality. Educational and counseling research indicates that peers with basic minimal training can effectively change the behavior of others, and peers can be as effective as professionals in facilitating positive change in short periods of time (Brown, 1965; Carkhuff & Truax, 1965; Fuchs, Fuchs, Bentz, Phillips, & Hamlett, 1994; Zunker & Brown, 1966). As the chapter authors in this volume demonstrate, faculty can, without excessive time investment, prepare undergraduate students to assume instructional helping roles.

Faculty benefit when their time is used better, and more parsimoniously, for tasks such as course design and management that really require faculty skills and perspective. Frequent close interaction with undergraduate assistants also gives faculty the opportunity to see their courses through a new lens, and to rethink their educational objectives and strategies. And most faculty agree that teaching with active and cooperative learning strategies is far more fun than lecturing! If graduate teaching assistant (GTA) roles are carefully redesigned when a course begins to incorporate undergraduate students, GTAs can benefit enormously. They can gain first-hand experience with student-centered models of education that will serve them well in future faculty careers. Insofar as student-

faculty partnerships and the student-centered approaches they enable improve student learning, the institution benefits from reduced failure rates in courses (thus necessitating fewer sections to accommodate repeating students), reduced student attrition from the institution (especially important since the number of transfer students is generally insufficient to fill the slots vacated by unsuccessful students), and improved student and parent satisfaction that results in increased institutional reputation.

Many of the benefits of student-assisted teaching, admittedly, do not lend themselves to easy assignment of a dollar value; however, preliminary attempts to conduct cost-benefit analyses of peer-assisted college teaching methods (Catterall, 1998) are promising. In earlier research in precollege settings, Levin and colleagues (Levin, Glass, & Meister, 1984; Levin & Meister, 1986) found that cross-age tutoring among students or adults was most cost effective in comparison to three other reform strategies—reduced class size, computer-assisted instruction, or a lengthened school day. The benefits of using peer assistants appear to overwhelmingly outweigh the costs in faculty and staff time (Churchill & John, 1958) (much of which is front-end loaded) and money (generally for salaries for additional faculty, staff, and peer assistants).

OVERVIEW

Our goal has been to make this volume a practical resource for individual faculty, educational innovators, and those responsible for instructional development. The models described demonstrate an array of student-assisted teaching approaches. The model matrix located at the end of the introduction has been constructed to provide the reader an easy-to-use guide for identifying the important characteristics of each model. The matrix allows the reader to search for models meeting their needs by looking at variables such as institution size, target audience, subject area, and model logistics such as peer responsibilities, training, and compensation sources, and go to these chapters.

Most chapters follow a standardized format—model, outcomes, productivity, and suggestions for replication—to facilitate comparison and practical application. We hope that this organization will help the reader to better determine which model or combination of models of student-assisted teaching is most appropriate for their needs and institutional realities. Each chapter introduction briefly describes the institutional context and genesis or historical development of the model. This is followed in the "model" section by a discussion of the key features of the approach such as how the undergraduate students are selected, trained, and compensated, what role the undergraduate students and faculty play, and other program logistics. The next section of each chapter provides results or outcomes and demonstrates variation in assessment approaches and data. Following Groccia and Miller's (1998) focus on educational productivity, each chapter then attempts to present evidence that the model reduces costs while maintaining or increasing benefits or effectiveness. Finally, each chapter concludes with suggestions for replication, a discussion of lessons learned, pitfalls to avoid, and guidance for future success.

REFERENCES

Allen, V. L. (1976). *Children as teachers: Theory and research on tutoring*. New York, NY: Academic Press.

American Society for Training and Development. (1988). *Workplace basics: The skills employers want*. Washington, DC: The US Department of Labor, Employment and Training Administration.

Astin, A. W. (1975). *Preventing students from dropping out*. San Francisco, CA: Jossey-Bass.

Bell, A. (1797). *An experiment in education made at the male asylum of Madras: Suggesting a system by which a school or family may teach itself under the superintendence of the master or parent*. London, England: Cadell and Davis.

Bonwell, C. C., & Eison, J. A. (1991). *Active learning: Creating excitement in the classroom* (ASHE-ERIC Higher Education Report No. 1). Washington, DC: The George Washington University, School of Education and Human Development.

Brown, R. D. (1972). *Student development in tomorrow's higher education: A return to the academy*. Washington, DC: American College Personnel Association.

Brown, W. F. (1965). Student-to-student counseling for academic adjustment. *Personnel and Guidance Journal, 3* (8), 811-817.

Bruner, J. (1972, October 27). Immaturity—its uses, nature and management. *The Times Educational Supplement*, 62-63.

Carkhuff, R. R., & Truax, C. B. (1965). Training in counseling and psychotherapy. *Journal of Consulting Psychology, 29*, 333-336.

Catterall, J. S. (1998). A cost-effectiveness model for the assessment of educational productivity. In J. E. Groccia, J. E. Miller (Eds.), *Enhancing productivity: Administrative, instructional, and technological strategies* (pp. 61-84). New Directions for Higher Education, No. 103. San Francisco, CA: Jossey-Bass.

Chickering, A. W., & Gamson, Z. F. (1987). Seven principles for good practice. *AAHE Bulletin, 39*, 3-7.

Churchill, R., & John, P. (1958). Conservation of teaching time through the use of lecture classes and student assistants. *Journal of Educational Psychology, 49* (6), 324-27.

Cohen, P. A., Kulik, J. A., & Kulik, C. (1982). Educational outcomes of tutoring: A meta-analysis of findings. *American Educational Research Journal, 19*, 237-248.

Coleman, J. S. (1974). *Youth: Transition to adulthood*. Chicago, IL: University of Chicago Press.

Devin-Sheehan, L., Feldman, R. S., & Allen, V. L. (1976). Research on children tutoring children: A critical review. *Review of Educational Research, 46*, 355-385.

Ehly, S., & Larson, M. (1980). *Peer tutoring: References from the educational and psychology literature*. Iowa City, IA: The University of Iowa.

Erikson, E. H. (1959). *Identity and the life cycle*. New York, NY: International Universities Press.

Fuchs, D., Fuchs, L. S., Mathes, P. G., & Simmons, D. C. (1997). Peer-assisted learning strategies: Making classrooms more responsive to diversity. *American Educational Research Journal, 34*, 174-206.

Fuchs, L. S., Fuchs, D., Bentz, J., Phillips, N. B., & Hamlett, C. L. (1994). The nature of student interactions during peer tutoring with and without training and experience. *American Educational Research Journal, 31*, 75-103.

Gartner, A., Kohler, M., & Riessman, F. (1971). *Children teach children: Learning by teaching*. New York, NY: Harper & Row.

Goldschmid, B., & Goldschmid, M. L. (1976). Peer teaching in higher education: A review. *Higher Education, 5* (1), 9-33.

Greenwood, C. R., Carta, J. J., & Hall, R. V. (1988). The use of peer tutoring strategies in classroom management and educational instruction. *School Psychology Review, 17,* 258-275.

Groccia, J. E., & Miller, J. E. (Eds.). (1998). *Enhancing productivity: Administrative, instructional, and technological strategies.* New Directions for Higher Education, No. 103. San Francisco, CA: Jossey-Bass.

Johnson, D. W., Johnson, R. T., & Smith, K. A. (1991). *Active learning: Cooperation in the classroom.* Edina, MN: Interaction Book.

Lancaster, J. (1803). *Improvements in education as it respects the industrious classes of the community.* London, England: Darton and Harvey.

Levin, H., Glass, G. V., & Meister, G. R. (1984). *A cost-effectiveness analysis of four educational interventions* (Project Report No. 84-A11). Stanford, CA: Stanford University, Institute for Research on Educational Finance and Governance.

Levin, H., & Meister, G. (1986). Is CAI cost-effective? *Phi Delta Kappan, 67,* 745-749.

Magner, D. K. (1999, September 3). The graying professoriate. *Chronicle of Higher Education, 46* (2), A18-A19.

Massy, W. F., Wilger, A. K., & Colbeck, C. (1994, July/August). Overcoming "hollowed" collegiality. *Change, 26* (4), 10-20.

Meiklejohn, J. M. D. (1882). *Dr. Andrew Bell: An old educational reformer.* London, England: Blackwood.

National Society of Professional Engineers. (1992). *Report on surveys of opinions by engineering deans and employers of engineering graduates on the first professional degree* (Publication No. 3059). Alexandria, VA: National Society of Professional Engineers.

Newcomb, T. M. (1962). Student peer group influence. In N. Sanford (Ed.), *The American college* (pp. 469-488). New York, NY: Wiley.

Newcomb, T. M., & Wilson, E. K. (Eds.). (1966). *College peer groups: Problems and prospects for research.* Chicago, IL: Aldine.

Palmer, P. J. (1998). *The courage to teach: Exploring the inner landscape of a teacher's inner life.* San Francisco, CA: Jossey-Bass.

Rubin, L., & Hebert, C. (1998). Model for active learning: collaborative peer teaching. *College Teaching, 46* (1), 26-31.

Ryan, A. M. (2000). Peer groups as a context for the socialization of adolescents' motivation, engagement, and achievement in school. *Educational Psychologist, 35* (2), 101-111.

Scott, M. D. (1990). *Agents of change: A primer for graduate teaching assistants.* Chico, CA: Trustees of the California State University.

Sutherland, T. E., & Bonwell, C. C. (Eds.). (1996). *Using active learning in college classes: A range of options for faculty.* New Directions for Teaching and Learning, No. 67. San Francisco, CA: Jossey-Bass.

Wagner, L. (1982). *Peer teaching: Historical perspectives.* Westport, CT: Greenwood.

Whitman, N. A. (1988). *Peer teaching: To teach is to learn twice* (ASHE-ERIC Higher Education Report No. 4). Washington, DC: Association for the Study of Higher Education. (ERIC Document Reproduction Service No. ED 305 016)

Zunker, V. G., & Brown, W. F. (1966). Comparative effectiveness of student and professional counselors. *Personnel and Guidance Journal, 44* (7), 738-743.

Model Matrix

Chapter key: 1 Adams et al. · 2 Chidester et al. · 3 Gittleman & Woolf · 4 Henscheid · 5 Larson et al. · 6 Wood et al. · 7 Stover et al. · 8 Miller et al. · 9 Murray · 10 Thompson et al. · 11 Warner & Farris · 12 Wright & Barton · 13 Custer & Dourmashkin · 14 Garvin & Snyder · 15 Paredes et al. · 16 Poulton & Kemeny · 17 Streveler · 18 Zaritsky · 19 Couchman · 20 Coppola et al. · 21 Mickel · 22 Paoli & Hobson · 23 Allen & White · 24 Golden & McMorris · 25 Lebduska · 26 Sarquis et al. · 27 Stelzner et al. · 28 Thibodeau · 29 Cox · 30 Kinland et al. · 31 Sorenson

Function	Group	Item	1	2	3	4	5	6	7	8	9	10	11	12	13	14	15	16	17	18	19	20	21	22	23	24	25	26	27	28	29	30	31
Function	Working with	Individuals					X	X	X	X			X		X	X	X	X	X	X	X	X		X			X				X		X
		Small groups		X			X	X	X	X	X		X											X	X			X					
		Conf/lab section	X			X	X	X	X					X															X	X			
		Whole class			X	X	X	X	X			X			X											X			X	X		X	
Responsibilities		Course logistics	X		X		X		X			X			X	X	X	X			X	X	X						X	X			
		Grading	X		X							X			X														X				
		Office hours		X			X	X	X						X		X	X												X			
		Homework help		X			X	X	X	X			X		X									X			X						
		Review old material		X		X					X	X			X				X	X	X	X	X					X	X				
		Intro. new material	X	X	X	X						X							X	X	X	X				X		X	X				
		Skills development	X		X		X	X	X	X	X	X	X	X		X	X	X				X	X				X	X		X		X	
		Mentoring	X		X		X	X	X		X		X	X																X			
		Facilitation	X				X	X	X		X			X		X									X			X			X		
		Feedback to prof.	X		X	X	X											X			X	X				X			X	X	X	X	X
		Curriculum develop.	X		X	X	X								X			X											X		X		
		Socialization		X																													
		Tutoring								X			X			X			X					X			X			X			
		Training tutors																	X	X				X									
Context	Target Audience	Remedial											X											X									
		1st year students	X	X	X	X	X	X	X	X	X	X		X	X	X	X	X				X	X	X	X	X	X	X	X	X			
		Gen. ed. courses					X	X	X																								
		All students	X										X		X	X	X	X							X	X	X	X	X	X			
		Difficult courses																													X	X	
		Faculty																													X	X	X
		Adult students																			X		X										
		Honors																				X	X										

xx

Chapter #	Author	In-class	Out-of-class	Attached to course	Unattached to course	Distance education	Volunteer	Service	Academic credit	Pay	Pre-semester	During semester	Designated course	Internal	External	Former student	Concurrent student	No connection	Institution Type*	Subject Area*
		Connection					**Logistics — Compensation**				**Training**			**Funding/Support**		**Peerness**				
1	Adams et al.	X		X	X				X		X	X	X	X				X	R	F
2	Childester et al.	X	X	X					X		X	X	X	X		X	X		R	L
3	Gittleman & Woolf	X	X	X					X			X	X	X		X	X		R	F
4	Henscheid	X	X	X						X		X	X	X					R	F
5	Larson et al.	X	X	X					X			X	X	X		X	X		R	G
6	Wood et al.	X	X	X					X			X	X	X		X	X		R	G
7	Stover et al.	X	X	X						X		X	X	X	X	X	X		R	G
8	Miller et al.	X	X	X							X	X	X	X	X				R	D
9	Murray		X	X							X	X	X	X	X				N	T
10	Thompson et al.	X							X	X		X		X		X			R	F
11	Warner & Farris		X		X				X			X			X			X	B	G
12	Wright & Barron	X		X					X				X	X			X	X	N	D
13	Custer & Dournashkin	X	X		X				X		X	X	X	X		X	X	X	R	T
14	Garvin & Snyder		X						X		X	X		X		X	X		D	T
15	Paredes et al.		X	X					X		X	X		X	X				M	M
16	Poulton & Kemeny		X	X				X				X		X	X				R	GT
17	Streveler		X	X					X		X	X	X	X			X		R	MT
18	Zaritsky		X	X					X		X	X		X	X				D	D
19	Couchman		X	X			X		X		X	X		X					N	D
20	Coppola et al.		X	X					X		X	X		X	X				R	T
21	Mickel		X	X		X			X			X		X	X		X		C	F
22	Paoli & Hobson	X	X	X		X	X		X		X	X		X			X		M	D
23	Allen & White	X	X	X					X		X	X		X		X	X		R	D
24	Golden & McMorris	X	X	X					X					X			X		B	S
25	Lebduska		X	X		X					X			X	X		X		D	D
26	Sarquis et al.		X	X							X	X		X	X	X			N	T
27	Stelzner et al.		X	X					X		X	X	X	X	X	X	X		B	S
28	Thibodeau		X	X					X		X	X		X					R	S
29	Cox	X	X	X				X	X	X	X	X		X	X	X			R	D
30	Kinland et al.	X	X	X			X		X		X	X		X			X		R	D
31	Sorenson		X		X				X	X		X	X	X			X		R	D

*Institution Type and Subject Area use the following coding:

Institution Type (based on Carnegie classifications):

R = Research I & II
D = Doctoral I & II
M = Master's I & II
B = Baccalaureate I & II
A = Associate of Arts
P = Professional & Specialized
N = Not Applicable

Subject Area:

M = Mathematics
T = Science, Engineering, Technology
H = Humanities
S = Social & Behavioral Sciences
F = First Year Seminar
L = Learning Communities
G = General Education Courses
D = Multiple Disciplines

Part I

Undergraduate Students Assisting with Programs for First-Year Students

Chapter 1

Establishing a Common Ground: A Conjoint Training Model for Instructors and Peer Educators

Eve M. Adams, Susan C. Brown, and Terry L. Cook

New Mexico State University is a land-grant university in southern New Mexico with an undergraduate enrollment of 15,500, many of whom are first generation college students from small towns. Since 1990, we have offered a first-year seminar (UNIV 150) through the Center for Learning Assistance (CLA) to help students adjust to college life. UNIV 150 significantly increases one-year retention rates for minority students (77.3% retention for those enrolled in UNIV 150 versus 72.9% for those not enrolled), students with average high school academic achievement (74% versus 64.2%), and students without a declared major (77.4% versus 70.4%).

The UNIV 150 course is taught by professional staff (predominantly academic advisors, CLA staff, and student affairs professionals), and at times by faculty from various academic departments. Although the course is not required, approximately 250 (15% of all full-time first-year students) enroll each fall. The seminar is a three-credit, graded course, meets for two and one-half hours a week, and has a maximum enrollment of 25 students per section. Course content includes orientation to the university, study skills, values clarification, research skills, campus resources, career planning, appreciation of diversity, and building a support network. Most of these topics are covered in multiple class sessions.

◼ MODEL

Inspired by the peer leader program at the University of South Carolina (Berman, 1996), and recognizing the impact that peer mentoring can have on first-year students, we decided to add a peer education component to the UNIV 150 seminar. We felt that first-year students would be more motivated to learn new study skills with a more advanced, successful peer encouraging these habits (Bandura, 1986), and that upper-class students would enhance their self-awareness and acquire new skills by teaching what they had learned to less experienced students (Fry & Kolb, 1979).

Selection of Peer Educators (PEs)
Students interested in becoming PEs for UNIV 150 must be juniors or seniors and have a GPA of 3.0. Nominations can come from department heads, advisors, student affairs personnel, or students themselves. Students apply for this opportunity not only because the associated three-credit course fulfills a general education requirement, but also because it provides a leadership experience that enhances the students' resumes, and because students anticipate that it will develop their communication and teaching skills in preparation for being graduate assistants.

In the first stage of selection, the applicants are rated on written answers to questions about their involvement in extracurricular activities, their interest in being PEs, and their experience in providing academic assistance to others (Appendix A-3). Next, an interview is used to assess their oral communication skills, maturity, responsibility, and ability to serve as role models, particularly in the academic realm (Appendix A-4). Approximately 12 students out of a typical pool of 25 applicants are selected for the ten sections of UNIV 150.

Peer Education Course (UNIV 350) Requirements
The CLA developed a course, UNIV 350 "Peer Education," to train upper-class students to cofacilitate the UNIV 150 class. The UNIV 350 course requirements include two days of presemester training. The training agenda includes team building activities, the demographics of first-year students, reflections on their first year in college, assessment of teaching and learning styles (Kolb, 1976), an overview of Perry's (1970) model, assessment of

cognitive development (Fago, 1995), how to design a workshop and make an effective presentation, classroom management and group listening skills, case scenario role plays on professionalism and ethics, and an overview of CLA resources (Appendix B-3). Training also includes making a brief presentation with another PE on a topic related to the UNIV 150 curriculum, and then receiving feedback. After the two-day training, students write a paper in which they assess their strengths and areas of growth as a PE.

The course requirements during the fall semester include participation as a PE in their assigned UNIV 150 course. Their duties are negotiated with their instructor; however, a major requirement is that PEs plan and teach two entire class periods in which they are observed and evaluated by the UNIV 350 instructor. Writing assignments during the semester are a weekly journal and a self-assessment paper at the end of the semester.

PEs meet for an hour a week for the first half of the semester, and an hour every other week the second half. During the first half of the semester, the UNIV 350 instructor (a CLA staff member) models sample classroom activities that the PEs can utilize in their UNIV 150 classes, and facilitates discussion on issues brought up by PEs. Topics addressed in the UNIV 350 class include time management, listening and note taking, textbook reading, test preparation and test taking, appreciating cultural diversity, and student development theory. As the semester progresses and the UNIV 350 classes meet every other week, students discuss their experiences, provide suggestions to one another, and critique the learning and teaching process in their own and others' classes. During the alternating weeks the UNIV 350 instructor visits each PE's class. PEs are evaluated by the instructor of UNIV 350 (written and oral feedback), by the UNIV 150 instructor with whom they are paired (numerical rating), and by the students in their UNIV 150 class (Likert-type teacher rating form).

Need for Conjoint Training Model

In class discussions and journal entries, approximately half of the PEs complained about being under- or over-utilized. The instructors had been told to include the PEs in every class period, even in such simple ways as asking the PEs to relate their personal experience after the instructor had talked about a topic. The instructors also knew that the PEs needed two entire classes to deliver presentations that would be observed and evaluated by CLA staff. Beyond these guidelines, the UNIV 150 instructor and PE were expected to negotiate their roles during their class planning time.

Negotiation proved difficult for two reasons—a power imbalance between the PE and the UNIV 150 instructor, and the UNIV 150 instructors' lack of experience in coteaching. The power imbalance stemmed not only from the instructor being a professional and the PE a student, but also from the fact that the PE had no previous experience with teaching the course (there are no returning PEs), whereas over half of the instructors had taught the course numerous times. Because these instructors had already fine-tuned their course curriculum, it was difficult to integrate another person's ideas into their lesson plans, and joint planning did not always occur.

The UNIV 150 instructors were surveyed after the second year of utilizing PEs. Those who responded felt comfortable with and appreciative of having a PE assigned to their course. However, when instructors listed the roles and responsibilities of their PEs, we discovered great variability in the degree to which PEs were integrated into class instruction. Listed roles ranged from monitoring homework and observing the students to helping with reviews and presenting a topic for a whole class period. Part of the variability might have been because, as one instructor explained, "I didn't know how much to delegate."

The comments from the PEs and the survey of the UNIV 150 instructors made us realize that UNIV 150 instructors needed more guidance in integrating PEs, and PEs needed guidance in negotiating their roles with instructors. Initially, we had assumed that coteaching would happen naturally. When it didn't, we realized that in order for the PEs and instructors to function as a team, they needed to be trained as a team and given a structured opportunity to define their partnership and learn cofacilitation skills. Thus, the conjoint model of training was developed.

PE MODEL WITH CONJOINT TRAINING COMPONENT

Conjoint training for teaching partnership occurs just before the semester begins, within the context of the PEs' and UNIV 150 instructors' separate training experiences. UNIV 150 instructor training lasts two days, PE training one and a half days, and conjoint training one evening. Since the PE-instructor pairs have already been determined, they go through the conjoint training as a team. The training focuses on areas that promote ongoing negotiation—definition of roles, planning and feedback, integrating PEs into the course curriculum, and communication. Repeated use of the words "team" and "cofacilitation" reinforces the collaborative model.

Activities for Learning How to Cofacilitate

The first activity gets the instructors and PEs to define their individual roles and their identity as a team. The team brainstorms possible roles of the instructor and the PE. Instructors introduce issues that might prevent them from fully utilizing PEs, and PEs discuss what might keep them from being fully involved as PEs. This discussion identifies some underlying fears for both parties and increases communication. Finally, each team develops some ideas of how to present themselves as a team to their students, and shares these ideas with the entire group.

The second activity is team discussion of a handout on the advantages and potential disadvantages of class-

Figure 1.1 ADVANTAGES AND POTENTIAL DISADVANTAGES OF CLASSROOM COFACILITATION

Advantages of Cofacilitation

1) One of the most compelling reasons to cofacilitate is to complement each other's styles.

2) One of the ways students learn is by studying facilitators/instructors as behavioral models. Cofacilitating presents two models of interacting and presenting information.

3) Cofacilitators can help each other grow professionally by giving and receiving feedback.

4) With two instructors, the class student-teacher ratio is smaller. Students are less dependent on one person. This reduces the pressure on the instructor.

5) Cofacilitating allows each individual to be both observer and teacher, an opportunity that instructors rarely have.

6) Peer educators can often explain things in a way that is clear to students.

7) Peer educators can serve as sounding boards.

8) Two individuals can vary the pace of the class and make it more interesting.

Potential Disadvantages of Cofacilitation

1) Individuals who have extremely different styles or contradictory goals may have a negative effect on students receiving information.

2) Cofacilitation requires extra time in planning, organizing, and debriefing.

3) Students may prefer to talk to the peer educator instead of the instructor.

4) The instructor may feel that he/she has less control or may be left out.

Adapted from Pfeiffer and Ballew (1988)

room cofacilitation (Figure 1.1). The purpose of this activity is to help the UNIV 150 instructors see the value in having a coinstructor. By also discussing the disadvantages, the instructors can own their hesitations and be encouraged to resolve them.

One challenge to cofacilitation is blending two different teaching styles. In the third activity, each team member is asked to list ten characteristics of how they learn a difficult subject, considering senses, environment, instructor style preference, time, and technique. They discuss their learning styles in pairs, and then they assess their teaching styles using use the Trainer Type Inventory (TTI) (Wheeler & Marshall, 1986), which is based on Kolb's (1976) Learning Styles Inventory.

After completing the TTI, the team discusses their results using the following stimulus questions:

- What similarities do you have in the way you teach?

- What are your differences?

- What do you think is the best way to communicate ideas and strategies to first-year students?

- What kinds of classroom activities will you each feel most comfortable with? Least comfortable with?

- Based on your teaching and learning styles, and the different learning styles of your students, how will you make sure that you will include some of those least comfortable activities?

Then all teams join a more general discussion of teaching and learning styles. This activity allows the partners to acknowledge that they have differences in teaching and learning, and realize that their unique strengths will make for a stronger team. It also impresses upon each person the need to invest energy to negotiate his or her differences.

The fourth activity asks the teaching partners to discuss their classroom communication styles (Appendix B-4). Rather than addressing stylistic differences in how course content will be presented, this activity focuses on how the team can establish a classroom community. In this activity, the team practices the type of planning activities in which they will regularly engage and looks at the class feedback and planning form that they will use each week (Appendix C-3).

A challenge for the instructor in UNIV 150 is to understand and provide for the different developmental needs of both the PEs and the first-year students. In the next activity, we present Perry's (1970) model of intellectual and ethical development of college students, which provides the team with another layer of understanding to add to the teaching and learning styles they already know. The PEs complete an instrument based on Perry's model (Fago, 1995). The model and the feedback from the instrument help both PEs and instructors to be more attuned to the developmental aspects of teaching a first-year seminar, and help instructors to structure experiences to facilitate the growth of both first-year students and PEs.

Finally, the teams must figure out how to integrate the PE into classroom activities. We provide guidelines on the appropriate amount of PE involvement in the course, based on a developmental timeline of PE participation. Discussing this timeline helps UNIV 150 instructors understand that they are expected to provide a quality learning experience for the PEs as well as for the UNIV 150 students. In addition, the guidelines provide instructors with suggestions for class activities that could potentially broaden their own teaching style.

■ OUTCOMES

Every year UNIV 150 instructors are asked to rate the value of the PEs on a scale of 1-5, with 1 being "very valuable." All of the instructors who responded to the fall 1998 survey (N = 6, for a 60% response rate) rated their PEs a 1 or a 2 (M = 1.5), and found coteaching to be an effective addition to the UNIV 150 students' experience. Comments following these ratings indicated a general appreciation for what the PEs add to the course. For example, "They are essential to the success of the course. Their input is taken very seriously by students." "There are topics that are best heard from your peers (i.e., time management and diversity)." "They can often supplement class discussion from a seasoned student's perspective." "It is important for students to have a role model (successful student) to relate to." When the same survey was completed in fall 1999 after the first conjoint training, the instructors (N = 10, for a response rate of 100%) continued to be very satisfied (M = 1.55).

Informal evaluation of conjoint training by the training staff, PEs, and instructors has been very positive. Teams were so actively engaged during the training that the training staff frequently had to stop conversations in order to move on to the next topic. The six instructors who responded to the fall 1999 survey all indicated that they found the conjoint training valuable because it enhanced both communication between the instructor and the PE and the feeling of being a team. When asked, "How was the training helpful?" their narratives expressed appreciation of finding common ground on teaching styles, and laying the groundwork for productive communication with their PEs. All of the instructors indicated that their PEs had attained or exceeded the minimum level of integration laid out in the guidelines for classroom integration.

As expressed in a 1999 survey (Appendix D-6), all (N = 9, response rate = 82%) PEs were pleased with the training, and four of them specifically appreciated the joint training. They enjoyed getting to know their coinstructor before the class began, and beginning the planning process right away. One felt the entire training should be conjoint. Based on a survey at the end of the semester (Appendix D-7), all agreed (average rating of 1.5 on a 1-5 Likert scale) that they had sufficient opportunities to participate in the UNIV 150 class. Comparing this rating to the previous year's (preconjoint training) rating of 2.5, it appears the revised training program has resulted in more effective utilization of PEs.

The UNIV 150 students felt they had benefited as illustrated by their response to the statement, "My PE helped facilitate my learning." In fall 1998, prior to conjoint training, the UNIV 150 students (N = 166) answered this question with 76% strongly agreeing, 22% slightly agreeing, and 2% disagreeing. In fall 1999, after the first conjoint training, the UNIV 150 students (N = 169) answered the question with 86% strongly agreeing, 12% slightly agreeing, and 2% disagreeing.

In addition, as a result of their participation in the peer education program, the PEs become ambassadors for the CLA, advocating that students outside the UNIV 150 classes attend study skills workshops and classes.

■ PRODUCTIVITY

The use of PEs requires increased personnel time and cash outlays for delivering UNIV 150. Most notably, instructors spend more time planning when working with a PE. A typical comment in the annual instructor survey has been: "This requires more work on my part to ensure that (the PEs) are receiving a quality experience." However, these costs have been virtually unchanged by the addition of conjoint training (Table 1.1). The large amount of training time that the CLA provides is offset by a decrease in the provision of study skills outreach presentations to the UNIV 150 classes. Prior to the peer education program, the CLA provided at least 18 study skills presentations per semester to the UNIV 150 classes. The number has now dropped to an average of eight as a result of training the PEs to provide these presentations. The addition of the conjoint training reduced duplication between the separate UNIV 150 instructor training and the PE training, and so did not increase training time.

SUGGESTIONS FOR REPLICATION

The conjoint training model is transferable to most universities and to other programs, including first-year orientation classes, supplemental instruction programs, and graduate assistant training, that involve collaborative teaching. The most important key to success is to select PEs and instructors who want to learn as they teach others to learn.

It is worth expending as much time as possible on the PE selection process. Because the peer education program is largely presentation oriented, we would recommend that their selection include a strong emphasis on previous public speaking experience. In addition, choosing PEs who model good study habits is important. Some of the PEs have been bright but undisciplined, and that can create a mixed message for the UNIV 150 students.

Instructors should be recruited for their interest in assisting first-year students and PEs, and for their ability to commit the time necessary to work with them. This may involve negotiation with their supervisors for additional release time.

The conjoint training undergone by the UNIV 150 instructors and the PEs is essential to the heightened success of the PE program. We recommend that at least half a day should be spent in the conjoint training; more reinforcement of the team concept would be even better. Ideally, we would have several meetings of all PEs and UNIV 150 instructors throughout the semester to showcase outstanding examples of innovative classroom activities and collaborative teaching practices. At the end of the semester the best of the best could be given an award.

CONCLUSION

We never tell the PEs or UNIV 150 instructors that team teaching is going to be easy. But we do emphasize that it's guaranteed to be rewarding. Those involved in this mul-

Table 1.1 COSTS OF PE AND CONJOINT TRAINING

Resource	Activity	UNIV 150 no PE		With PE		With PE and Conjoint Training	
		Hr/Yr	Cash Outlays	Hr/Yr	Cash Outlays	Hr/Yr	Cash Outlays
CLA Staff (2)	PE Selection	0	0	25	0	25	0
	PE Training	0	0	28	$250	22	$250
	Instructor Training[1]	48	$350	48	$350	48	$350
	Conjoint Training	0	0	0	0	6	$100
	Study Skills for UNIV 150	36	0	14	0	14	0
UNIV 350 Instructor (1)	UNIV 350 Teaching	0	0	45	0	45	0
UNIV 150 Instructors (10)	Instructor Training	160 (16 each)	0	160 (16 each)	0	160 (16 each)	0
	Weekly Planning	600 (60 each)	0	750 (75 each)	0	750 (75 each)	0
	UNIV 150 Teaching	450 (45 each)	0	450 (45 each)	0	450 (45 each)	0
Total		1,294	$350	1,520	$600	1,520	$700

[1]One staff member meets with UNIV 150 instructors throughout the semester.

tilayered endeavor must be willing to embrace the complexity that comes with the territory of collaboration in a system that does not often model such practices.

◼ REFERENCES

Bandura, A. (1986). *Social foundations of thought and action: A social cognitive theory.* Englewood Cliffs, NJ: Prentice Hall.

Berman, D. (1996). *University 101 peer leaders program information packet.* Unpublished manuscript, University of South Carolina. (Available from National Resource Center for the First-Year Experience and Students in Transition, http://www.sc.edu/fye/, phone 803-777-6029).

Fago, G. C. (1995). *A scale of cognitive development: Validating Perry's scheme.* Collegeville, PA: Ursinus College. (ERIC Document Reproduction Service No. ED 393 862)

Fry, R., & Kolb, D. (1979). *Experiential learning theory and learning experiences in liberal arts education.* New Directions for Experiential Learning: Enriching the Liberal Arts through Experiential Learning, No. 6. San Francisco, CA: Jossey-Bass.

Kolb, D. A. (1976). *Learning style inventory: Technical manual.* Boston, MA: McBer.

Perry, W. (1970). *Forms of intellectual and ethical development in the college years: A scheme.* New York, NY: Holt, Rinehart, and Winston.

Pfeiffer, J. W., & Ballew, A. C. (1988). *Presentation and evaluation skills in human resource development* (University Associates Training Technologies (UATT) Series, Vol. 7). San Diego, CA: University Associates.

Wheeler, M., & Marshall, J. (1986). Trainer type inventory. In J. W. Pfeiffer & L. D. Goodstein (Eds.), *The 1986 annual: Developing human resources* (pp. 93-97). San Diego, CA: University Associates.

◼ AUTHORS

EVE M. ADAMS is a College Assistant Professor in the Counseling and Educational Psychology Department at New Mexico State University.

SUSAN C. BROWN is the Director of the Center for Learning Assistance at New Mexico State University.

TERRY L. COOK is the Associate Director of the Center for Learning Assistance at New Mexico State University.

Chapter 2

Lessons from Peers:
The Design Exchange

Mark J. Chidister, Frank H. Bell, Jr., and Kurt M. Earnest

The Design Exchange is a residential learning community for new undergraduate students entering Iowa State University's College of Design, created in collaboration with the Department of Residence. Participating students have regular contact with in-residence, upper-class design students who serve as peer mentors. Participants also share a common studio space and computer lab in the residence hall and enroll in a required companion course each semester.

The College of Design is one of seven colleges at Iowa State University, a Carnegie Research I land-grant university that enrolls over 25,000 students. The College of Design enrolls over 1,800 students in six disciplines: architecture, community and regional planning, graphic design, interior design, landscape architecture, and studio arts. Most new undergraduate students begin their course of study in a one-year, preprofessional program. At the end of that year, these students apply to the professional program in their chosen discipline. Because demand for these programs exceeds the college's capacity, a fixed number of students are admitted each year and selected according to faculty evaluation of their academic performance, an essay, and a portfolio of work. These circumstances and an environment where new students are not fully engaged in their disciplinary community add to the stresses that all first-year students face.

Two focus groups with College of Design freshmen supported these observations and also revealed that this situation is exacerbated because new students rarely find support from other design students living on their residence hall floor (the college enrolls 7% of the university's total undergraduate population). Not surprisingly, the college has a low first-year retention rate. Of the 480 freshmen and transfer students who constituted the fall 1997 first-year class, 60.7% returned to the College of Design for the second year, and 20.0% transferred out of the college but stayed at the university. This 80.7% retention rate is below the 82.3% of the 1997 new undergraduate cohort for the entire university.

◼ MODEL

The catalyst for the development of this model was an interaction of the college's efforts to better understand persistence and the first-year experience, and the Department of Residence's interest in assisting colleges in accomplishing the academic mission of the university. The result of this interaction was the creation of a new learning community, the Design Exchange. Cross (1998) has defined learning communities as "groups of people engaged in intellectual interaction for the purpose of learning" (p. 4). The Design Exchange learning community was created to foster intellectual interaction and acclimation to the university through proximity, place, peers, and a two-semester course. Clustering design students together in the residence hall and providing a studio space nearby employs both proximity and place for discussions between peers outside of scheduled class times on class assignments and academic challenges. Students form a support community to learn from and encourage one another.

A key element in this model is the upper-class peer mentor who provides his/her perspectives on university life, the College of Design, and university resources. Peer mentors also work with college faculty and staff to facilitate a two-semester seminar sequence created for the Design Exchange. The constellation of these elements is intended to promote academic success, persistence and ultimately graduation, help students confirm their chosen major or select one appropriate for their interests and aptitudes, prepare them for application to their respective professional program, and prepare them for university life and studies.

In its inaugural year (1997–1998), residential and studio space was set aside for 50 new students in two houses, one each for men and women, located in one residence hall. Each house also included students from the university's other colleges to provide an environment where design students were with others who shared their academic interests as well as allowing them to meet students from other disciplines. All students offered enrollment to the College of Design were invited to participate in the Design Exchange, and assignments to the program were made on a first-come, first-served basis. One hundred fifteen applications were received in the first year, suggesting a strong demand for this living option.

Approximately 120 applications—50 from men and 70 from women—have been received in each of the subsequent years, one-fourth of the new undergraduate students who enter the College of Design each fall. The distribution of majors has roughly approximated enrollment in each of the college's degree programs. The Design Exchange has since been doubled in size to approximately 100 students yearly, and is located in two different residence halls.

Since the second year, the Design Exchange has been supported by a required course, two semesters in length. Students receive one course credit each semester and are graded on a satisfactory/fail system. The course is facilitated by an instructional team comprised of a faculty member, student services specialist from the College of Design, and the peer mentors. The course takes a holistic view of student learning through topics focused on student acclimation and development and the study of design. Class sessions are held on the students' turf in studio spaces located in the residence halls. Topics include learning styles, time management, finances, substance abuse, diversity, relationships, and stress management, as well as topics that detail the different design disciplines and career options (portfolio development, sketchbooks, presenting work, creativity, internships, community service, and study abroad opportunities). Many of these topics are elaborated on during a two-day trip to Minneapolis to visit professional offices, significant built work, and galleries. Class assignments facilitate clarification of personal and career goals.

The Design Exchange learning community employs four peer mentors selected from the ranks of junior and senior design students who serve as programmers, peer educators, and community builders. From the moment that the new class of design students arrives on campus, the mentors are actively engaged in establishing one-on-one relationships, responding to questions, and facilitating the development of supportive communities of peers.

The mentors live on the same floor as the entering design students, play a key role in the required orientation course, and coordinate out-of-class experiences. They share examples of their portfolios and recount how study abroad experiences have influenced their program of study. Mentors also find other upper-class students who are leaders in their field of study to make presentations and lead class discussions.

Peer mentors also provide feedback to the program coordinators in a manner that does not violate confidentiality. Because the mentors live with the students, they are available to students in ways and at times not normally possible for faculty and staff. Peer mentor contact with students in both their academic and living environments allows the mentors to increase students' time on task. Thus, the role of the peer mentors is crucial.

Each peer mentor must possess a thorough understanding of the principles that govern design-related fields, an ability to make associations across design disciplines, and an ability to articulate design concepts to a broad range of constituents. In addition, the successful mentor must be an effective communicator, resourceful at building and maintaining social networks, and creative in structuring and facilitating out-of-class experiences which reinforce students' in-class learning.

In February of each year, a letter and job description explaining the philosophy of the Design Exchange learning community and mentor responsibilities are mailed to College of Design juniors and seniors with a grade point average of at least 2.25 on a 4-point scale (Appendices A-1 and A-2). Faculty members, academic advisers, and current mentors are asked to identify students who would excel as mentors.

Interested students are required to complete an application and provide recommendations from two College of Design staff members. Applicants must also respond to open-ended questions that measure their ability to discuss design concepts. Students who are selected for an interview are asked to articulate their understanding of disciplines within the college, and demonstrate their knowledge and experience as student leaders.

A panel, comprised of the faculty member and student services specialist who facilitate the course, and a representative from the Department of Residence, screens the written applications and interviews the candidates. The panel selects the candidates on their knowledge of the discipline, leadership ability, and communication ability.

Mentors are invited to campus prior to the opening of the fall semester for a required, two-day training session (Figure 2.1) designed to provide the knowledge base and skills they will need in performing their mentor role.

For efficient use of staff time and campus resources, the initial training session is conducted with mentors from other learning communities at Iowa State and includes many aspects of the training that resident assistants receive. Every effort is made to make the training as interactive as possible. Role playing, minilectures, case study approaches, multimedia activities, and panels are used to help mentors grasp concepts and develop skills. Presenters representing a number of university offices and colleges facilitate sessions. On the closing day of training, mentors meet with the resident assistants and hall directors assigned to their building and begin to establish relationships with residence hall personnel who will assist in the development of an effective learning environment. Both staffs define their roles and develop plans of interaction to enable them to work together effectively. Additional training is conducted throughout the year on an as-needed basis.

Program coordinators have found it essential to meet weekly with peer mentors. These meetings, held in the College of Design, help gauge the well being of peer mentors and student participants, as well as reveal issues needing attention. When needed, portions of the meetings are used to conduct in-service training and coaching. The meetings enable coordinators to assess mentors' decisions and affect their decision-making processes. Mentors also use these meetings to discuss course progress, share student feedback, and explore transition and adjustment issues experienced by the first-year students. In fall 1998, this feedback and subsequent conversations resulted in a major revision of the course, increasing the focus on design-specific topics and issues. Students responded positively to the changes as demonstrated by improved quality of participation in studio discussions, increased attendance, and expressions of higher satisfaction with the course and the learning community.

Peer mentors also meet with Department of Residence staff twice a semester to keep all partners informed about developments in the learning community, to discuss initiatives to enhance learning, and to strengthen the relationship between the College of Design and the Department of Residence.

Throughout the academic year, coordinators use a number of evaluation methods to track mentor effectiveness. Weekly meetings provide coordinators with an opportunity to evaluate mentor progress. In addition, Design Exchange students are periodically involved in focus group interviews to gather student perceptions about mentor functioning. At the conclusion of the spring semester, a peer mentor evaluation instrument is distributed to all Design Exchange students. These data are analyzed and used to assist in the ongoing development of the peer mentor position and Design Exchange learning community.

Figure 2.1 PEER MENTOR TRAINING CURRICULUM

Topic	Description
First-Year Experience	Defining the population to be served, identifying key issues and types of assistance needed.
Peer Mentors	Research on peer mentors, effective peer mentoring, and specific duties and responsibilities.
Learning Communities	Defining learning communities and establishing social networks.
Interpersonal Communication	Effective listening, conflict resolution, interviewing, and facilitating large group discussions.
Programming	Role of programming as well as designing, advertising, and facilitating effective programs.
University Resources	Identifying academic resources on campus and referring students.
Tracking Student Progress	Role of assessment and assessment strategies.
Working with Residential Staff	Enforcing conduct policies, establishing positive relationships with hall directors and resident assistants, and working with house governments.
Confidentiality	Handling sensitive information and establishing trust.

■ OUTCOMES

In general, peer mentors have instant credibility with first-year design students. They are able to draw upon their knowledge of the college's culture, opportunities, and pitfalls that may plague unwary students. They are seen as role models and valuable resources because of their first-hand experiences with handling success and overcoming setbacks. Students are comfortable sharing important academic, personal, and developmental issues with their peer mentors.

The Design Exchange program was developed with the expectation that participants would perform better than nonparticipants in at least five ways: 1) exhibit greater satisfaction with their first-year experience, 2) interact more frequently with faculty and staff from their department, 3) have a better academic standing at the end of the first year, 4) persist into the second year, and 5) graduate at higher rates than nonparticipants with similar backgrounds.

Participants were compared with a control group of new design students who were living in the residence halls but not participating in the Design Exchange. The two groups were matched by gender, ethnicity, high school rank, entering ACT composite score, and, when possible, major. Reliable comparative data were obtained for academic standing and persistence. Low survey return-rates from students in the control groups prevented reliable comparisons on dimensions of satisfaction and interaction. However, qualitative data obtained from focus groups and course evaluations shed some light on participant satisfaction. As the first group of Design Exchange students began in fall 1997, graduation data will not be available until after spring 2001.

For the fall 1997 cohort, there were no patterns of statistically significant differences between the grade point averages (Table 2.1) and persistence (Table 2.2 and Table 2.3) of the Design Exchange and control groups. While extracurricular enrichment activities were offered most

Wednesday evenings of the academic year for the fall 1997 cohort, only about one-third of the Design Exchange students consistently participated. Low student participation and lack of program refinement due to its newness, likely affected the first-year outcomes.

Patterns of statistically significant differences in grade point averages and persistence in original major were observed between the fall 1998 participant and control group (Tables 2.4 and 2.5).

Table 2.1 SEMESTER GRADE POINT AVERAGES (4-POINT SCALE) FOR THE FALL 1997 COHORT

	Fall 97		Spring 98		Fall 98		Spring 99	
	M	SD	M	SD	M	SD	M	SD
Design Exchange	2.98	.53	2.84	.71	2.89	.65	3.02	.67
Control Group	2.67	.82	2.83	.74	2.91	.65	2.90	.60
Difference	.31		.01		(.02)		.12	
t-test (df)	$t(96) = 2.24*$		$t(91) = .09$		$t(84) = -.17$		$t(812) = .81$	

M = Mean, SD = Standard deviation
* Significant at .05 level

Table 2.2 PERSISTENCE IN ORIGINAL MAJOR OF THE FALL 1997 COHORT. REPORTED AS PERCENT OF STUDENTS IN ORIGINAL MAJOR AT THE END OF EACH SEMESTER

		Spring 98	Fall 98	Spring 99	Fall 99
Design Exchange	(n = 49)	79.6 %	65.3 %	59.2 %	57.1 %
Control Group	(n = 49)	79.6 %	59.2 %	46.9 %	38.8 %
Difference		0.0	6.1 %	12.3 %	18.3 %
X^2 (df = 1)		0.0	.39	1.48	3.31

Table 2.3 PERSISTENCE AT ISU OF THE FALL 1997 COHORT. REPORTED AS PERCENT OF STUDENTS STILL AT ISU AT THE END OF EACH SEMESTER

		Spring 98	Fall 98	Spring 99	Fall 99
Design Exchange	(n = 49)	93.9 %	85.7 %	81.6 %	83.7 %
Control Group	(n = 49)	95.9 %	89.9 %	87.8 %	77.6 %
Difference		(2.0) %	(4.1) %	(6.2) %	6.1 %
X^2 (df = 1)		.21	.38	.71	.59

Table 2.4 SEMESTER GRADE POINT AVERAGES (4-POINT SCALE) FOR THE FALL 1998 COHORT

	Fall 98		Spring 99	
	M	SD	M	SD
Design Exchange	2.95	.57	2.90	.65
Control Group	2.67	.70	2.65	.79
Difference	0.28		0.25	
t-test (df)	$t(175) = 2.93**$		$t(167) = 2.21*$	

* Significant at .05 level
** Significant at .01 level

Table 2.5 PERSISTENCE IN ORIGINAL MAJOR OF THE FALL 1998 COHORT. REPORTED AS PERCENT OF STUDENTS IN ORIGINAL MAJOR AT THE END OF EACH SEMESTER

		Spring 99	Fall 99
Design Exchange	(n = 89)	84.3 %	74.2 %
Control Group	(n = 89)	69.7 %	50.6 %
Difference		14.6 %	23.6 %
X^2 (df = 1)		5.36*	10.56**

* Significant at .05 level
** Significant at .01 level

While no significant differences were found in overall persistence at ISU with the fall 1998 cohort, the Design Exchange students show a better retention pattern (Table 2.6).

The major difference between the cohorts that entered ISU in fall 1997 and fall 1998 was the introduction of the two-semester companion course. The extracurricular activities offered to the fall 1997 cohort were refined and elaborated in the courses introduced to the fall 1998 cohort. These courses brought a new level of rigor and accountability that appears to have a positive affect on academic performance and persistence. In addition, the peer mentor training was refined and several Design Exchange alumni remained on the residence hall floor, extending the circle of peers available to the new freshmen. Assessment of future cohorts will reveal whether the differences observed were the result of the enthusiasm surrounding the first-year of this experiment or whether the program has similar effects for future Design Exchange students.

The Department of Residence conducted a focus group with students who participated in the Design Exchange during 1998–1999. Students commented that the peer mentors were extremely helpful and were not perceived as authority figures. They appreciated the opportunity to get to know other design students early in the semester and valued having students from other majors living on the same floor. They found that the Design Exchange helped them confirm their choice of major or helped them make an informed change of major. Students valued the relationships they developed with other design students, the peer mentors, and the course instructors. The studio space was an integral part of making the program a success as well as special events like the field trip. The studio provided the setting for student participants to interact with and learn from each other. It also was the venue for bringing learning experiences into the residence hall. The field trip gave students an inside view of several professional offices and was instrumental in shaping their career and educational goals. Overall, focus group participants perceived that participating in the Design Exchange improved their grades and their adjustment to the college and university, and they expressed their desire that the program be continued.

■ PRODUCTIVITY

Our data support Astin's (1984) conclusion that students who become involved with academic and social support systems are more likely to persist, and that these increases in persistence have definite fiscal implications for the institution. Eighty-six of the fall 1998 Design Exchange participants returned to ISU in spring semester 1999, 28 from out of state. Only 83 from the control group returned, 23 from out of state. During spring 1999, Design Exchange participants generated $211,638 in tuition, $20,579 more than students in the control group. In the fall of 1999, 82 Design Exchange participants returned to ISU compared to only 77 of those in the control group. Assuming that all students who returned in fall 1999 will complete their degree programs, the Design Exchange participants will generate $1,275,222 in tuition between fall 1999 and graduation, $213,970 more than student in the control group (Table 2.7).

When added to the additional tuition generated in spring 1998, the tuition income resulting from increased persistence has the potential of totaling $234,549. Thus, the data collected to date indicates that the learning community contributed to higher rates of persistence, resulting in the generation of tuition dollars that would have otherwise been lost.

The costs associated with the Design Exchange are approximately $43,000 for each cohort. This covers $20,000 for faculty and staff salary expenses, $20,000 of room and board expenses for the peer mentors ($5,000 each), and $3,000 for program and course expenses. When compared to the anticipated tuition generated by increased persistence, it appears to be a very productive investment of resources.

■ SUGGESTIONS FOR REPLICATION

Peer mentors' effectiveness is dependent on their own academic ability, experience, personality and attitude, and the extent to which program coordinators have engaged them appropriately in program planning and implementation. The suggestions that follow elaborate on these observations to aid others who desire to use peer mentors to enhance undergraduate learning.

Table 2.6 PERSISTENCE AT ISU OF THE FALL 1998 COHORT. REPORTED AS PERCENT OF STUDENTS STILL AT ISU AT THE END OF EACH SEMESTER

		Spring 99	Fall 99
Design Exchange	(n = 89)	96.6 %	92.1 %
Control Group	(n = 89)	93.3 %	86.5 %
Difference		3.3 %	5.6 %
X^2 (df = 1)		1.05*	1.47**

Learning community coordinators can easily devote most of their attention to pedagogy, curriculum needs, and budgets. However, it is also important that peer mentors be included in the planning process. Our experience has been that mentors desire meaningful involvement in structuring the learning environment, syllabus and course design, and in the development of interactive activities. They can draw upon their experiences as students and provide examples of effective teaching methods. They are also helpful in gathering feedback from students—peer mentor involvement produced higher than average return rates for almost every survey used in the Design Exchange program.

A well thought-out recruiting and selection process holds the best potential of yielding a good group of peer mentor candidates with a mix of diverse backgrounds, experience, maturity, leadership qualities, and characteristics that will contribute to desired learning and developmental outcomes. Current mentors are excellent recruitment sources because they interact formally and informally with other students and have unique perspectives on the qualities and skills that their peers could contribute.

Providing comprehensive initial and ongoing training for peer mentors is essential. The initial training sessions help peer mentors become aware of their roles, our expectations, and prepare them for their work with students. We have found that much of the training resident assistants receive is appropriate for peer mentors, but that training needs to be augmented with material specific to the peer mentor's role and the goals of the learning community. After a few weeks, successive training should include opportunities for mentors to contribute to the course content. Training fosters the mentors' personal growth and development, improves their morale and co-operation with learning community coordinators, and provides mentors with an actual and perceived sense of readiness.

Appropriate incentives to attract quality peer mentor candidates can be as important as selection and training. Provision of a single room and board has been a viable incentive on our campus. The single room is especially important because it allows a place for mentors to interact with students in confidence. On other campuses, the appropriate incentive may be earning course credit or satisfying a capstone or service-learning requirement.

Finally, we believe it is important to promote the peer mentor position as a prestigious opportunity and seek the finest students the campus has to offer

■ CONCLUSION

Qualified peer mentors are a vital component of residential learning communities, particularly when they are well trained, engaged in the academic preparation received by new freshmen, and in a position to spend in-class and out-of-class time with these students. Their involvement is one of a handful of key factors that result in increased academic performance, persistence, and student satisfaction with the first-year experience.

Table 2.7 PROJECTED TUITION INCOME RESULTING FROM ONE-YEAR PERSISTENCE OF FALL 1998 DESIGN EXCHANGE PARTICIPANTS AND CONTROL GROUP MEMBERS

	Design Exchange		Control Group	
	Number of Students	Projected Tuition Income	Number of Students	Projected Tuition Income
In-State Five-Year Program Four Years Left, $2,786/Year	12	$133,728	6	$66,864
Out of State Five-Year Program Four Years Left, $9,346/Year	9	$336,456	5	$186,920
In-State Four-Year Program Three Years Left, $2,786/Year	46	$384,468	53	$442,974
Out of State Four-Year Program Three Years Left, $9,346/Year	15	$420,570	13	$364,494
Total	82	$1,275,222	77	$1,061,252

REFERENCES

Astin, A. (1984). Student involvement: A developmental theory for higher education. *Journal of College Student Personnel, 25* (4), 297-308.

Cross, K. P. (1998, July/August). Why learning communities? Why now? *About Campus, 3* (3), 4-11.

AUTHORS

MARK J. CHIDISTER is Associate Dean for Academic Programs and Associate Professor of Landscape Architecture at Iowa State University, College of Design.

FRANK H. BELL, JR. is Student Services Specialist and Minority Liaison Officer at Iowa State University, College of Design.

KURT M. EARNEST is a Department of Residence Academic Program Coordinator at Iowa State University.

Chapter 3

Peer Teaching
in the Experimental College

Robyn Gittleman and Howard Woolf

At Tufts University, a private research institution of 4,700 undergraduate and 3,200 graduate and professional students in Massachusetts, small, peer-taught seminars for entering students provide supportive learning communities to help students acclimate to the academic and social aspects of the undergraduate experience.

In 1962, then-president Nils Wessell formed a committee of Tufts administrators and faculty to investigate and facilitate institutional innovation. This led to the establishment of the Experimental (Ex) College in 1964. The Ex College became a place where new ideas could be entertained, new subjects introduced, and new teaching methods tested. In 1966, the oversight board of the Ex College was expanded to contain an equal number of students and faculty—a tradition of faculty/student collaboration that continues to this day.

Giving students this degree of power in 1966 was both groundbreaking and risky, particularly at a time when most schools in the country were clinging to conventional curricula and student/teacher roles. Students have responded to this shared authority by taking leadership roles in a variety of university initiatives, including peer teaching.

Peer teaching at Tufts originated in 1968 with an orientation program where upper-level students volunteered to discuss a set of books assigned as summer reading to incoming students. This orientation program continued for three years and led to peer-taught freshman seminars offered by the Ex College. A study done in 1969–1970 concluded, "independent of the subject taught, a [freshman] seminar fosters confidence and eases discussion. It also exposes [students] to a teacher of their own generation who is more experienced and knowledgeable and therefore an excellent role model" (Trefethen, 1970, pp. 36-37).

These peer-taught freshman seminars evolved into two programs, Explorations and Perspectives, both of which are administered by the Ex College. Table 3.1 contains a detailed comparison of the two programs. The objectives of Explorations and Perspectives are to give students an opportunity to make new friends, be part of an interactive learning experience, have their previously held assumptions challenged, and get a good start at Tufts.

Explorations

In 1972, student members of the oversight board felt that the Ex College could adapt the model of freshman seminars and use it to establish a personal, more responsive premajor advising system. Named Freshman Explorations, this new program began with teams of undergraduates and faculty members from the Ex College board working together to design and teach a seminar for entering students. Rather than offering a "learn about college" seminar, these initial teams decided that a class covering politics, media, popular culture, international affairs, and business would be more effective. The seminar used interactive learning and collaborative teaching techniques to further break down traditional classroom structure and help establish a supportive, small community. Furthermore, although Explorations was to be a first-semester program, each faculty member would remain the premajor academic adviser for the first-year students in his or her group.

Explorations was so successful that the board enthusiastically elected to expand the program with one major modification: The responsibility for teaching was shifted to a team of undergraduates. Faculty served as mentors to the peer teachers and continued in the role of premajor adviser.

This basic structure has not changed significantly since the mid-1970s. An average of 20 interactively taught, subject-based seminars has been offered every fall, led by peer teachers who have taken a level of expertise that they have acquired—either through coursework, cocurricular activities, or personal experience—and built a course on it (see Table 3.2 for a sample of Explorations titles).

Perspectives

In 1988, due to overflow demand on the part of entering students for placement in Explorations, the Ex College added a second peer-taught seminar program, called Perspectives. Perspectives originally employed an "umbrella" topic so that peer teachers did not have to provide their own subject and course materials. It incorporated a weekly, program-wide talk or film that formed the basis for discussion in the separate group meetings. Furthermore, it initially ran for only half of the first semester, awarding students half-course credit and peer teachers one-course credit.

Table 3.1 EXPLORATIONS AND PERSPECTIVES: A SIDE-BY-SIDE COMPARISON

	Explorations	Perspectives
Peer Teacher Application Process	• applications available February 1st • due mid-March • apply as a team • choose their own topic • submit a working syllabus and supporting materials • secure a faculty participant	• applications available February 1st • due mid-March • apply as a team • no content required other than suggesting possible subtopics under general umbrella of "the movies"
Criteria for Selection of Peer Teachers	• a minimum 3.0 GPA • two acceptable recommendations from faculty (one from the major adviser) • demonstrate—through application and interview—a solid grasp of subject	• a minimum 3.0 GPA • two acceptable recommendations from faculty (one from the major adviser) • ability to think and write critically, based on answers to application questions
Program Structure	• fall semester only • seminars for 12–14 entering students • led by two upper-level peer teachers • weekly three-hour meetings • interactive teaching and learning stressed • topics vary from group to group, chosen by peer teachers • syllabi designed by peer teachers • faculty participant attends class, acts as premajor adviser to first-year students, mentors peer teachers	• fall semester only • seminars for 12–14 entering students • led by two upper-level peer teachers • weekly three-hour meetings • interactive teaching and learning stressed • all groups studying "the movies" as art and industry • all groups follow a program–wide syllabus • peer teachers create their own approaches and decide on their own materials • adviser assigned to group, has no role in the seminar
Student Credit and Grading	• one course credit • graded pass/fail	• one course credit • graded pass/fail
Student Workload	• moderate reading and writing assignments • 15 pages of short writing • ten-page research paper	• moderate reading and writing assignments • film screenings • 15 pages of short writing • ten-page research paper
Peer Teacher Credit and Grading	• 1.5 course credits • graded pass/fail	• 1.5 course credits • graded pass/fail
Peer Teacher Workload	• three–six hours of preparation a week • leading a three-hour seminar • taking a one-hour methods seminar	• three–six hours of preparation a week • leading a three-hour seminar • taking a one-and-one-half hour methods seminar

Over the next half-dozen years, Perspectives underwent major changes. While committed to the umbrella topic as the basis for providing an alternative path to peer teaching, the large lecture/small discussion group format and the half-semester, half-course credit structure were dropped in favor of a seminars only, full-semester, full-credit format—one much more closely aligned to that of Explorations.

In its present form, Perspectives ranges from 15 to 18 seminars each fall and uses the movies as art and industry as its signature subject area. Peer teachers lead groups through a three-month curriculum, the first of which is how to "read" a film, the second, the business of movies, and the final month, a topic of their own choosing.

■ THE PEER TEACHING MODEL

With both Explorations and Perspectives, pairs of upper-level undergraduates teach seminars for 12–14 first-year students who receive one course credit that counts as an elective toward graduation and are graded on a pass/fail basis. Peer teachers plan and lead the weekly, three-hour seminars, evaluate student performance, attend a weekly teaching seminar, and serve as personal and academic resources for their students. Peer teachers in both programs receive one-and-one-half course credits, on a pass/fail basis. While it is rare, one or two students each year find the experience of teaching, as juniors, so compelling that they do it again in their senior year, but for only one course credit. The two programs require a year-long process to select, train, and support a cohort of 60 peer teachers.

While peer teachers in both seminars are given latitude in choosing the specific approaches they will employ, all rely heavily on participatory and collaborative peda-

Table 3.2 SAMPLE EXPLORATIONS TITLES

- Adolescent Fiction
- Who is John Galt? The Literature and Philosophy of Ayn Rand
- The Gay Civil Rights Movement: Success or Failure?
- Violence in Film
- From Buddha to Bob Marley
- Bioethics: Medical Science in the Face of Religious and Cultural Diversity
- Beyond BeBop: Miles and Coltrane
- *Nuestros Vecinos*: Issues in Latin American Development
- The Flip Side of Disney: Beyond Euphoria

gogical techniques (e.g., brainstorming, small group work, role playing, and simulations). Freshmen are required to complete weekly reading and writing assignments, oral presentations to promote public speaking, and a ten-page library research paper. Finally, each seminar includes community-building activities (e.g., brief check-in sessions, values-clarification exercises, and visits from representatives of campus organizations).

Selection and Training

Recruitment for each year's peer teachers starts in the preceding November with an initial information session, followed by a larger meeting in February, at which point applications are made available.

Peer teachers are expected to be juniors or seniors when they teach, and get two recommendations from faculty, one specifically from their adviser. Students applying to Explorations must immediately indicate and justify their choice of individually designed subjects and their potential for successfully teaching in this area. They must supply a 13-week course syllabus, a class reading list keyed to the syllabus, and an annotated bibliography of scholarly and critical sources that they propose to read over the summer in preparation for teaching. In marked contrast, and for the expressed purpose of attracting peer teachers who otherwise would likely not take advantage of the opportunity, the Perspectives application process is very streamlined. Would-be Perspectives peer teachers simply complete a series of background questions to demonstrate how well the applicant writes and thinks.

Explorations peer teachers are required to partner with a faculty member who will be the premajor adviser for their group. This can become a complex and difficult task for the peer teacher as the advising functions for Explorations far exceed those that full-time faculty at Tufts are asked to perform. Explorations faculty come to each class meeting and stay through the first hour of the three-hour weekly seminar meeting to help break down barriers between adviser and advisee. Recently, to acknowledge the added time commitment, a small financial incentive, $500, to be used for academic development, is provided each faculty member working with Explorations.

Each May, all new peer teachers attend a brief training session that includes an introduction to the philosophy of small group, participatory learning, and receive a teaching manual with concrete methods and activities to put this philosophy into practice. The Perspectives peer teachers also meet separately with the program administrator and are given required readings on film history and an annotated list of 40 films. They are encouraged to see as many of these films as they can. Six of the films are mandatory, and 12 are strongly recommended.

Peer teachers for Explorations read their source materials and refine their syllabi during the summer. Perspectives peer teachers, along with background reading and viewing, receive a set of suggestions for building a sequence of four classes on how to read a film. In addition, they get a detailed list of texts that can be used to support any approach a teaching team decides to try.

In July, all peer teachers receive the names and addresses of the students assigned to their groups and write a letter of welcome to each one. In August, one week before first-year students arrive for orientation, peer teachers participate in an intensive six-day training session. The administrators of both programs offer pedagogical suggestions and model teaching exercises, especially mock teaching. Then, using guidelines in the teaching manual, peer teachers develop workable lesson plans for the first two classes. In addition, strategies for dealing with personal, social, and campus issues are discussed by student service staff. Finally, one session is devoted to academic advising as, in spite of the fact that faculty advisers work with both programs, students inevitably seek their peers for advice.

During the fall, peer teachers in each program participate in a weekly methods support seminar. Here campus information is discussed so that it can be channeled to first-year students, teaching problems and issues related to group dynamics are shared, new pedagogical techniques are practiced, and relevant educational/ethical issues are examined. In weekly seminars, Perspectives peer teachers go through the process of selecting an approach for the next subtopic. Allowing each team to choose and shape its own teaching approach encourages autonomy. In this way, the experience of Perspectives peer teachers realigns itself with the experience of Explorations peer teachers who are making similar choices throughout the semester and are recording them in a required weekly journal—along with problems, observations, and insights. Both program administrators have an open door policy for peer teachers as a forum for resolving grievances and problems.

Teaching Methodology

Building on existing facilitation skills, peer teachers are encouraged to create highly participatory classroom environments. Peer teachers in Explorations and Perspectives are asked to facilitate critical thinking skills, not just provide in-depth information. They do this by framing key questions to get at the complexity of issues and then to engender independent thought, discussion, and research in an attempt to guide students in the search for answers.

Each Explorations or Perspectives seminar meets one evening each week for three hours. Peer teachers work from a lesson plan which breaks the time down into segments, each one keyed to an exercise planned out in advance (right down to which peer will take the lead, what materials or equipment, if any, are needed, why it's being done, and how long it should take).

Each seminar session begins with a 20-minute group check-in period during which announcements about campus events are made, discussion of "pressure points" in the semester takes place (e.g., parents' weekend, mid-semester exams, or the deadline for dropping courses), and perhaps most importantly, personal concerns are aired. Peer teachers are trained to be alert to what they hear during these times and, if they feel the need, to consult with their program administrator or with a liaison person from the counseling center.

Academically oriented activities follow. These might include, along with numerous class discussions, formally researched, forensic-style debates with the class split into two teams; the viewing and discussion of clips from a film that was screened as homework; role playing exercises based on characters in a reading; work with an ongoing, web-based simulation; the presentation of a few one-page papers written in response to an assigned article; two minutes of in-class writing as a prelude to a discussion about newspaper clippings which had been circulated during class; or reports of findings from small groups that had completed short fieldwork assignments.

At an appropriate point in the seminar, peer teachers signal time to socialize, have a snack, or talk with one of the peers (or, if this is an Explorations meeting, with the faculty participant, who is there during class). While this may seem trivial, such moments are important to building the sense of community that gives Explorations and Perspectives seminars their special character.

A key function of the peer teachers is guiding students through the library research paper project. Peers take their students through a week-by-week, step-by-step process involving thesis statement, creation of an annotated bibliography, development of an outline, draft writing and revisions. Once a final version is accepted, peer teachers provide extensive comments as a way of completing the semester-long dialog between teacher and student.

◼ OUTCOMES

Attainment of program objectives is assessed with end-of-semester evaluations (see Figure 3.1 for student responses for fall 1998). In addition to these questions, students were asked, "Would you recommend the program to incoming students?" Of the 424 students in the two programs in 1998, all but five said they would recommend the program to incoming students. (Two of those five said it was too much work!) Most of the answers echoed the following comments: it was a great experience; it was a chance to meet people right away; I got to know about Tufts; it was great fun, yet I was surprised by the work load; it was enjoyable both academically and socially.

For peer teachers, the experience offers a different set of outcomes. From their evaluations—submitted at the end of the semester as a short narrative assessing the experience they just completed—it's clear that they feel the experience added to their self-knowledge, helped them to make choices about the future, and enabled them to understand their education better. The following comments, taken from fall 1998 evaluations completed by peer teachers, represent the consensus that continues to emerge.

> It was without question the hardest, most tiring, but also the most rewarding thing I have ever done... Teaching is not something that can be learned out of a book. Each class and each student is so different that a teacher has to adjust and readjust him or herself without losing his or her stability. To see a student's eyes glow with passion made the hours of preparation worthwhile.

> Teaching a real class for a whole semester taught me more than any class I ever took as a student... It showed me how to compromise with a partner when I disagreed,... how to be a student's friend and yet never lose his or her respect as a teacher,... how to inspire and stimulate a young person's intellect.

Figure 3.1 STUDENT REPONSES ON FINAL EVALUATIONS IN 1998

Question	Percent Response			
	Strongly Agree	Agree	Neutral	Disagree
1) My peer-taught seminar helped provide me with a good start	61	28	10	1
2) Small group learning was a positive experience	60	30	9	1
3) My peer-taught seminar helped build new relationships	48	32	18	2
4) Class discussions encouraged critical thinking	46	40	13	1

I gained a new respect for my professors at Tufts during my own teaching experience and began to notice the nuances of good teaching.

Peer teachers also speak about the value of the organizational, relational, and communications skills that they develop—skills that, as alumni who were peer teachers constantly tell us, have translated well in any number of professions.

It is instructive to see what one faculty member had to say about peer teachers in the Explorations program:

> The real value of peer teaching lies in the opportunities it gives for growth in leadership... First, the learners learn how to collaborate with each other from the very first day of planning through to the end of the semester. Secondly, each of the leaders has a back up, to take over when things slow down or go wrong. Leaders, I have noticed, tend to learn more from their peers than they could ever receive in instruction....

> Most students arriving in college have never been responsible for a group endeavor. They have been responsible for themselves but not for something greater than themselves, something to which they have made a commitment that demands their attention... This sense of responsibility to a commitment is perhaps the greatest lesson gained from the Explorations experience.

While no empirical investigation of the impact of these programs has ever been conducted, we feel confident of its positive value. Very few Explorations or Perspectives students ever come up for placement on academic probation. Perhaps the best evidence of how these programs impact students' success is that the overwhelming majority of students who become Explorations and Perspectives leaders were in the programs as first-year students.

■ PRODUCTIVITY

The only direct costs, other than the aforementioned $500 subsidy given to faculty participants in Explorations, are a small budget of $50.00 put aside for seminars in both programs to support the creation of group cohesiveness and $600–700 for the kick-off dinner. This is to be used for such community-building activities as buying snacks, having a pizza party, going as a group to the movies, or taking a trip into Boston. In terms of instructional energies, because of the almost total autonomy of the peer teachers, the vast percentage of time required to make the programs work is put in by the student teachers. Furthermore, because they receive academic credit for this endeavor, the program becomes part of their regular semester course load and, consequently, is very cost effective.

The cost related to the program administrator's salary is difficult to parse out because it is embedded in salary as part of regular job responsibilities. It would be appropriate to say, therefore, that the costs involved would be equivalent to one-fourth of a full-time administrative or faculty salary.

The heavy commitment to these programs on the part of the peer teachers translates into a fairly limited use of faculty resources. The baseline for faculty involvement consists of being responsible for first-year students' premajor advising. (Because advising is one of the contractual responsibilities assumed by faculty, advising time is explicitly included in their regular compensation process.) For faculty in Explorations, add to that a one-and-one-half-hour weekly commitment to attend class, plus time spent meeting with the peer teachers to discuss pedagogy.

We have found that each program requires at least ten hours a week of a person's focused attention. This individual, be it a professional administrator or a faculty member, will be responsible for preparing and teaching a weekly seminar for the peer teachers, reading journals, and being on call for any and all problems relating to class preparation, the emotional trials of team teaching, and the difficulties of first-year adjustment. In addition, because each seminar has copying and budget expenditures as well as AV and room requests, a support staff person needs to be available for the program.

■ SUGGESTIONS FOR REPLICATION

In thinking about replicating one or both of our programs a number of recommendations come to mind. First, as they themselves have told us, peer teachers must feel passionate about their subject. If not, they advise, "you will quickly get bored with the subject and that can turn a very valuable nine-month experience—including a summer of preparation—into something you dread."

Second, programs such as Explorations and Perspectives need staff to oversee all the details. At Tufts, the Associate Director and Director of the Experimental College administer Perspectives and Explorations respectively; we believe that any administrator who feels comfortable training and supervising a cohort of peer teachers could do the job. With a program such as Perspectives, the administrator should have an academic background in the umbrella subject area.

With Perspectives, we initially attempted to farm out the academic responsibilities for the program to people who were only peripherally involved. A welter of logistical problems ensued and taught us that any such program must be the sole responsibility of a single professional staff person (or faculty member splitting an appointment). Realistically, it should be a year-round position, at least half time.

Third, start small. By proceeding in this manner, the administrator in charge has a better chance of choosing the best peer teachers, can have time to monitor things closely, engage in frequent debriefing with the peer teachers, and do a careful assessment of the experience. A successful beginning means that peer teachers and first-year students alike will become evangelists for the program.

Finally, peer-teaching programs such as Explorations and Perspectives live or die on the energy, commitment, and passion of all involved. Any school where such commodities are in good supply should have no trouble implementing its own versions.

■ CONCLUSION

Ultimately, the beauty of these programs is that they have special benefits for everyone involved. The first-year students receive sustained support and a genuine sense of community throughout their all-important first semester. The upper-level student teachers get a chance to understand academic life from "the other side of the desk" and to "battle test" their organizational, interpersonal, and intellectual skills. And the academic advisers get to know the students as individuals—their advisees and the student teachers. Finally, with Explorations, the faculty mentors get a rare opportunity to observe other teachers and are exposed, perhaps for the first time, to a participatory teaching style. In the final analysis, employing peer-taught first-year seminars for advising and acclimation purposes is a model that works.

■ REFERENCE

Trefethen, L. (1970). *The Trefethen report*. Medford, MA: Tufts University.

■ AUTHORS

ROBYN GITTLEMAN is Director of the Experimental College and an Associate Dean of the Colleges at Tufts University.

HOWARD WOOLF is Associate Director of the Experimental College at Tufts University.

Chapter 4

Peer Facilitators as Lead Freshman Seminar Instructors

Jean M. Henscheid

Washington State University (WSU) is the state's land-grant institution serving some 16,500 residential students at its main campus, and 2,000 students at its three branch campuses. WSU, known for its strong general education, writing-across-the-curriculum, agriculture, business, and veterinary programs, and a well-developed extended degree program, has also established seven learning centers throughout the state.

The university's Freshman Seminar Program is an outgrowth of a general commitment to preparing the university's students for both for the rigors of academic life and for life after graduation. The specific impetus for creation of the program came in 1996 when faculty members lamented that first-year students coming directly from high school were entering higher education either ill-prepared for this experience or lacking the serious attitude required of successful academic members. Drawing on learning community success stories (Gabelnick, MacGregor, Matthews, & Smith, 1990), the Washington Center for the Improvement of Undergraduate Education, and the freshman seminar models adapted from the University of South Carolina (Upcraft, Gardner, & Associates, 1989), WSU designed a program to coenroll groups of 15 to 20 residential first-year students in two courses, one an entry-level general education course or beginning major course, and the other a two-credit, peer-facilitated freshman seminar. The central notion that continues to drive the program is that coenrollment and freshman seminars would help students and faculty members build a community where they could share knowledge about and enthusiasm for learning. Content from the course linked with the freshman seminar is used to illustrate learning in a discipline and as a contrast to the learning processes required in other disciplines. The mission of the program is to bring together new and continuing students and faculty members in a collaborative, intellectually challenging environment where new students are supported as they become successful members of the academic community, continuing students serve as peer facilitators providing academic mentoring, and instructors of the linked courses serve as intellectual role models.

Each fall semester since 1996, some 300 to 400 students have voluntarily enrolled in 20 to 25 sections of the seminar and their linked courses. Between 100 and 150 students, many of whom have experienced first-semester academic difficulty, have participated in the program each spring. The number of students served and funding for the program have remained constant over the years.

■ MODEL

The most distinctive characteristic of the WSU Freshman Seminar Program is its undergraduate peer facilitators, who are chiefly responsible for day-to-day instruction in the seminar course. Each peer facilitator is assigned to lead a section of the seminar. Program designers chose to hire undergraduates in 1996 because they are less expensive than other instructors and because of the solid evidence (as described in this volume) favoring this approach. This decision has served as the foundation for all others, including enrollment numbers in each section, use of new computer technologies, and content selection for the seminar. Initially, section enrollment was limited to 20 students, and then decreased to 15 in 1999. Each academic assignment is designed by a faculty and student syllabus committee and written into a web-based course management system before the semester begins, and the content of the seminar is strictly intellectual to guard against the course becoming a forum for socializing or personal counseling facilitators are not qualified to provide. Socializing, naturally, still occurs but as a valued informal adjunct to the formal course content. The syllabus includes a several-week section on learning to design and research viable academic topics, followed by sections on the analytical and presentational traditions of various academic disciplines.

In a typical 50-minute seminar session, a peer facilitator records attendance and leads the day's activities, which usually involve a group reading, discussion, research, and writing assignment. The web-based course management system details the assignments and is accessed on computers located in the seminar's three classrooms, where most seminar sessions are held. These three classrooms were intentionally built with round tables, movable chairs, and no discernable "front" to encourage interactive learning and peer facilitation, and to minimize lecture.

As of fall 1999, each peer facilitator was paid $8 per hour to work ten hours per week. Applications are accepted for the coming year during a spring recruitment campaign, which includes announcements on the university electronic bulletin board, letters to high achieving students, nomination solicitations from faculty members, and flyers. Candidates are selected for interviews based upon their understanding of and experience with facilitating learning, leadership skills, academic performance, references, experience with new technologies, and commitment to active learning approaches. Facilitators enroll in a for-credit, semester-long course where they learn about issues related to classroom management, leadership, responding to academic writing, and the uses of new technologies. In this course, facilitators give program designers feedback on the student response to the assignments and negotiate assignment adjustments. The peer facilitators also attend the linked course, the entry-level class in which members of their seminar group are coenrolled. They attend to serve as in-class role models, build a working relationship with the instructor, and gather content to use as examples in their seminar. Graduate teaching assistants with significant college teaching experience directly supervise the peer facilitators. While undergraduate facilitators function as teachers in their sections, they are actually members of a team of instructional staff who ensure smooth functioning of the program.

In theatrical terms, the first-year students and the peer facilitators are the lead actors in the WSU freshman seminar drama. Using this same analogy, the supporting actors are the Hypernauts, undergraduate learning-through-technology consultants who provide regular assistance to seminar students and facilitators as they use web-based computer conferencing, create multimedia compositions, and build computer-based projects. Hypernauts receive ongoing, for-credit instruction on issues related to facilitation, learning, and educational technologies and are paid at the same rate as the peer facilitators.

Several times during the semester, faculty from the linked course are invited to participate in the seminars as discussants, consultants, and learning role models. They are the equivalent of veteran actors making cameo appearances, as are the reference librarians who assist in research activities. Classroom faculty and librarians receive a $250 stipend per semester.

The central task of this team is to develop activities related to the five units of the syllabus: 1) students as members of an academic community, 2) students as critical pursuers of information, 3) students as producers of information, 4) students as contributors to knowledge, and 5) review and reflection on the college academic experience. The assignments in each unit focus on honing the students' abilities to organize academic information for the purposes of conducting original research and improving their abilities as academic writers. In the web-based course management system, individuals and groups of students participate in discussions about their assignments and experiences and access resources germane to the seminar syllabus. They have the opportunity to converse with students, faculty members, and other individuals across seminars, across the state, or around the world.

■ OUTCOMES

Checking progress toward the goal of integrating new students into the WSU academic community is a central component of the freshman seminar. The directors of General Education, the Honors College, the Student Advising and Learning Center, the Freshman Seminar Program, and the Center for Teaching, Learning, and Technology (CTLT) meet regularly to discuss measurements of success along both attitudinal and behavioral dimensions. The results of quantitative and qualitative program evaluations are analyzed and changes recommended as necessary. Evaluation results are shared with facilitators in their weekly meetings.

In terms of attitudes, students report that the seminars are helpful academically and socially. Compared to nonseminar students, those who take the seminars perform academically as well or better, and persist from freshman to sophomore year at a higher rate. It is notable that students who select to enroll in the seminars represent an academic preparedness distribution similar to the overall first-year student population.

A comparison of data collected in 1996 in the seminars (using the active learning approaches described above), and a media-enhanced class relying almost exclusively on lectures revealed that students in the seminars were more likely to feel they had learned to manage large complex tasks, work through a process to solve problems, ask for clarification about academic work, exercise creativity, gain confidence in attaining academic goals, better understand subject matter, perform tasks to be faced in their professions, and experience diversity of opinions and cultures. Every year since, the majority of students taking the seminars have reported similar gains in most of these areas.

The impact of the freshman seminar upon fall 1998 students was assessed in a number of ways. Student perceptions of the impact of the seminar on their learning are presented in Table 4.1. The overwhelming majority report positive outcomes.

Students view the web-based course management system component of the seminar, the WSU-designed Speakeasy Studio and Cafe, as helpful to successful completion of course requirements (Table 4.2).

During this same period, seminar students indicated that their ability to complete multimedia research projects in the freshman seminar had a positive impact relative to more traditional course experiences (Table 4.3).

Students indicated that the seminar requirement to create multimedia materials (including morphs, web pages, and online audio and video products) throughout the semester enhanced their educational experience (Table 4.4).

Student attitudes were also measured using the College Student Experience Questionnaire (CSEQ) (Pace, 1990), a questionnaire administered to second-semester, first-year students. A *t*-test procedure used to analyze the responses revealed that seminar participants were significantly ($p<.05$) more likely to read more than other students, read basic references or documents, gain familiarity with computers, and gain specialization to further their education. These students also recorded strong but not statistically significant differences in being actively engaged in their learning, cooperating with other students, making

Table 4.1 FALL 1998 WSU FRESHMAN SEMINAR SELF-REPORT LEARNING DATA FROM THE FLASHLIGHT CURRENT STUDENT INVENTORY (N = 317)

I am more comfortable participating in discussions in this course than I am in other courses.	86%
The emphasis on working in groups in this course has helped me to understand the ideas and concepts being taught.	83%
This course has taught me how to work in a team/group to complete a project.	80%
This course helped me learn to manage large, complex tasks.	66%
This course helped me learn to work through a process to solve problems.	66%
Assignments for this course encouraged me to exercise my creativity.	67%

Table 4.2 FALL 1998 WSU FRESHMAN SEMINAR SELF-REPORT ON THE IMPACT OF THE SPEAKEASY STUDIO AND CAFE

(Because of the use of Speakeasy Studio and Cafe) how likely were you to work on assignments with other students?	60%
How likely were you to ask other students for comments on your course work?	54%
How likely were you to complete assignments on time?	47%
How likely were you to receive [instructor] comments on assignments quickly?	53%

Table 4.3 FALL 1998 WSU FRESHMAN SEMINAR SELF-REPORT ON THE IMPACT OF MULTIMEDIA PROJECT

(Because of my experience creating multimedia projects I am better able to) produce one or more versions of an assignment before producing the final product.	49%
Work on assignments with other students.	59%
Discuss the ideas and concepts taught in this course with the instructor.	54%
Apply what you are learning to real world problems.	45%

Table 4.4 FALL 1998 WSU FRESHMAN SEMINAR SELF-REPORT OF IMPACT OF CREATING MULTIMEDIA MATERIALS

(Because of my experience creating multimedia materials) I am better able to communicate my ideas to others.	78%
I am better able to understand the ideas and concepts taught in this course.	76%
I am encouraged to exercise my creativity.	79%
I am more confident that I can reach my academic goals.	61%

contact with faculty, and gaining the capacity to become lifelong learners.

A third type of measurement, focus groups and individual interviews, have been administered over the life of the seminars. Findings from these suggest that students perceive the seminar syllabus as challenging and academically useful, peer facilitators as supportive, and the exposure to learning technologies as valuable. Students believe they are learning research skills, how to work with other students, and key concepts for improving their research and writing.

The freshman seminar has also impacted freshman to sophomore retention. Students enrolled in the 1996 and 1997 seminars had a 5% higher retention rate than nonseminar students. For 1998, the last year for which figures were available prior to this writing, retention was 4% higher. In fall 1996, academically at-risk seminar students (defined as those who enrolled at WSU with academic records predicting a 25% or higher likelihood that they will fail) earned cumulative grades that were nearly a full grade point higher (p = .003) than their nonseminar cohort. Similar findings were reported for fall 1997 at-risk students. This group of students were slightly less well academically prepared (based upon a combination of the high school grade point averages and college entrance examination scores) than their nonseminar peers, yet still earned better grades and, as noted above, were retained to their sophomore year at a higher rate. Qualitative comments from students support these quantitative data. Students report that they value working with other students, learn research skills, and feel comfortable asking a broad range of questions related to the college transition.

Since the program's inception, peer facilitators have received approval ratings from their students in the 80%-90% range. These positive attitudes are consistent with those noted by other researchers and practitioners about paraprofessionals and peer teachers (Carns, Carns, & Wright, 1993; Schwenk & Whitman, 1984; Whitman, 1988). An explanation for these high approval ratings might be found in a statement by a newly graduated peer facilitator: "I think that the students are going to be a lot more honest and real with people their own age. No matter how comfortable a professor is, it's still intimidating. In the seminars, they're learning the same things that they would learn in a 'regular' class. I just don't have a PhD. We are learning together."

■ PRODUCTIVITY

The cost of offering peer-facilitated freshman seminars to WSU's new students is less than it would be if professional faculty or staff were hired to provide the same instructional services, even including wages for graduate facilitator supervision of the peer facilitators. For example, during the fall 1999 semester, each of 20 peer facilitators taught one 15-student freshman seminar and was paid $8 per hour to work ten hours per week for 16 weeks, for a total of $1,280 or $25,600 in total wages. The cost for graduate facilitator supervision over these peer facilitators was $1,500 per section. These combined costs were less than the cost of two other instructional alternatives considered by program designers, i.e., employing assistant professors on an overload basis or hiring adjunct faculty using a pay schedule similar to that used by the WSU College of Education. As noted in Table 4.5, for all three alternatives, additional direct costs would remain constant and include Hypernaut wages, linked course faculty and librarian stipends, maintenance and upgrade on 30 computers, and supplies. Salaries of four full-time staff members who work part-time in the program were then and continue to be paid through other budgets. As Table 4.5 demonstrates,

Table 4.5 COMPARISON OF WSU FRESHMAN SEMINAR INSTRUCTIONAL COSTS FOR EACH SEMINAR SECTION OVER A 16-WEEK SEMESTER

All Other Fixed Costs	Peer Facilitator/ Graduate Facilitator	Assistant Professor	Adjunct Instructor
	$1,280/$1,500 = $2,780	$,5040 (Based on estimated overload salary + 26% benefits.	$3,000 (Salary, no benefits)
Hypernaut	$640	$640	$640
Linked Course Faculty Stipend	$250	$250	$250
Librarian Stipend	$250	$250	$250
Supplies and Materials	$250	$250	$250
Total	$4,170	$6,430	$4,390

the argument that the students are our best asset (Wrigley, 1973) held great sway with designers of the WSU freshman seminars.

Cost was also a factor in the decision to design a template web forum or course management system (the Speakeasy Studio and Cafe) to house the seminar assignments and online discussions. The online environment, originally designed to meet the needs of students in the freshman seminars, was serving more than 100 courses throughout the world by the spring of 1999. A cost-benefit analysis reported in a recent issue of *Change* (Ehrmann, 1999) suggested that the software developed for WSU's freshman seminars is less expensive than a stand-alone computer-based instructional module, and requires less faculty (or facilitator in the case of the seminars) expertise than the conversion by that faculty member or facilitator of their individual course materials into an online format. Brown and Henderson, authors of the analysis, concluded that dividing the cost of a technological innovation by student use per week is an appropriate gauge when determining an acceptable cost threshold for the integration of new technologies into courses. Using this formula, the Speakeasy Studio and Cafe cost $8 per student-week to develop, compared to the instructional module price tag of $1,400 per student-week.

And finally, while student motivation, goal orientation, and other factors not measured by grades may help explain the difference in retention rates between equally prepared seminar and nonseminar participants, the fact remains that over the lifetime of the program, 4%-5% more students involved have remained in school after their freshman year. Conservatively, this translates into tuition revenues from 100 additional students per year. Even if only the Freshman Seminar Program can explain a percentage of this difference, the financial impact appears to be powerful.

■ SUGGESTIONS FOR REPLICATION

The following seven axioms are offered as guiding principles for those working in an environment such as the WSU freshman seminars which combines peer facilitation and heavy reliance on new technologies.

Axiom 1. Be willing to change your vision. The pace at which knowledge is generated and information is accessed in the academy is changing so rapidly that a stagnant vision may do more harm than good. When adding to this mix the unorthodox, new approaches often proposed by peer facilitators, the best vision might be one that accepts metamorphosis.

Axiom 2. Expect to work with top administrators with budgetary authority who may not have the background to completely understand centrally important components of your program. While this axiom was originally developed to address the difficulties inherent in understanding courses or programs that incorporate new technologies, peer facilitation as an innovation can be just as foreign.

Axiom 3. Expect to encounter a high percentage of faculty members who will be suspicious of, if not hostile toward, your efforts. Just as new technologies pose a challenge to traditional teaching methods, peer facilitation calls into question the value added by a faculty member. Be prepared to provide data to prove the quality of the program content, process, and outcomes.

Axiom 4. Be willing to go where few have gone before. This axiom is helpful to those offering undergraduates instructional responsibilities comparable to duties usually saved for graduate students and full-time faculty members. Peer instructors with primary responsibility for facilitating assignments, grading, and managing a for-credit class of up to 20 students are more rare nationally than cofacilitators and peer tutors who either follow a strict script or work in close collaboration with faculty members.

Axiom 5. Beware of overplanning. Leadership experts typically recommend that administrators move into an activity with a solid plan in hand. In the ever-changing landscape of a peer-facilitated, technology-rich learning enrichment program, however, a better alternative may be to make concurrent the process of planning and the process of doing. A forum, such as the weekly peer facilitator training course, is one method of doing this.

Axiom 6. Be willing to accept that, on a regular basis, you may be the least qualified member of your team to take charge. Seasoned instructors may have an edge over undergraduates on facilitation, but, by their very nature, they are not peer facilitators. However messy, the process of peer facilitation belongs to the undergraduates. Also, these individuals may be your resident experts on new technologies.

Axiom 7. Plan to fail. A peer-facilitated, technology-rich learning enrichment program sets up a situation for success, failure, or both. The paradox inherent in the phrase peer facilitator results in occasional confusion for the students and some amount of stress for the facilitators. Anticipate that there will be uncertainty and some degree of disagreement in roles, responsibilities, and outcomes, and that problems will develop along the way. People who are characterized as problem minimizers and avoiders may find this approach uncomfortable.

■ CONCLUSION

The Washington State University Freshman Seminar Program recently entered its fourth year, with its first waiting list of incoming students wishing to enroll, a peer facilitator corps selected from the best undergraduates, and faculty members and librarians enthusiastically renewing their participation. The university now entrusts peer facilitators to acculturate hundreds of new students to the WSU learning community.

■ REFERENCES

Carns, A. W., Carns, M. R., & Wright, J. (1993). Students as paraprofessionals in four-year colleges and universities: Current practice compared to prior practice. *Journal of College Student Development, 34,* 358-363.

Ehrmann, S. C. (1999). Asking the hard questions about technology use and education. *Change, 31* (2), 25-29.

Gabelnick, F., MacGregor, J., Matthews, R. S., & Smith, B. L. (1990). *Learning communities: Creating connections among students, faculty, and disciplines.* San Francisco, CA: Jossey-Bass.

Kouzes, J. M., & Posner, B. Z. (1995). *The leadership challenge.* San Francisco, CA: Jossey-Bass.

Pace, C. R. (1990). *College student experiences questionnaire* (3rd ed.). Los Angeles, CA: University of California, Center for the Study of Evaluation. (Available from the Center for Postsecondary Research and Planning, Indiana University.)

Schwenk, T. L., & Whitman, N. (1984). *Residents as teachers.* Salt Lake City, UT: University of Utah School of Medicine.

Upcraft, M. L., Gardner, J. N., & Associates. (1989). *The freshman year experience.* San Francisco, CA: Jossey-Bass.

Whitman, N. A. (1988). *Peer teaching: To teach is to learn twice* (Report No. 4). College Station, TX: Association for the Study of Higher Education.

Wrigley, C. (1973, March). Undergraduate students as teachers: Apprenticeship in the university classroom. *Teaching of Psychology Newsletter,* 5-7.

■ AUTHOR

JEAN M. HENSCHEID is the Associate Director of the National Resource Center for The First-Year Experience and Students in Transition at the University of South Carolina.

Chapter 5

The Teaching Teams Program:
A "Just-in-Time" Model for Peer Assistance

**Harold P. Larson, Reed Mencke, Stacy J. Tollefson,
Elizabeth Harrison, and Elena Berman**

The University of Arizona was founded in 1885 as a land-grant college. Its 34,300 students, 71% of whom are Arizona residents, include 26,200 undergraduates. In 1998, the University of Arizona introduced a new general education curriculum that adhered closely to the recommendations made by the Boyer Commission Report (1998) for reinventing undergraduate education in Research I universities. The university's new general education courses are taught by ranked faculty in technology-rich, collaborative learning environments that emphasize the development of writing, communication, and critical thinking skills. These sweeping changes presented us with an opportunity to extend into the general education curriculum a model based on teaching teams

which had been offered for many years by individual faculty and in a few departmentally sponsored programs. Our teaching teams program (TTP) encourages faculty, graduate teaching assistants (GTAs), and preceptors (undergraduate peer assistants) to work together both inside and outside the classroom to provide a multilevel support system for undergraduate students. By empowering highly motivated undergraduates to perform a variety of instructional tasks in exchange for academic credit in training courses, we offer a comprehensive approach to undergraduate education reform in which responsibilities are shared among all participants (Figure 5.1).

■ THE TEACHING TEAMS MODEL

Table 5.1 describes representative courses from each of the university's three general education strands: Individuals and Societies (INDV), Natural Sciences (NATS), and Traditions and Cultures (TRAD). Student-to-team ratios are 10:1 or less in these courses, all of which have more than 100 students. The teaching teams of these preceptored courses provide more attention to individual students, and conduct more group activities, than could the same number of instructors and GTAs in traditionally taught classes.

The TTP has grown substantially (Table 5.2). Participating faculty must recruit and train several hundred preceptors each semester to populate teaching teams in dozens of courses throughout the general education curriculum. We meet this need by allowing preceptors, even first-semester freshmen, to be concurrently enrolled in the courses served by their teaching teams. Preceptors concurrently enrolled in a course must complete their assignments on accelerated schedules ("just-in-time" preparation), in order to be ready to provide true peer assistance with course work.

Figure 5.1 THE TEACHING TEAMS PROGRAM

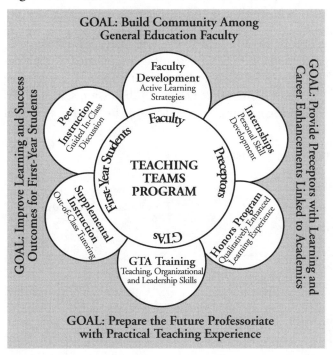

The Special Role of the Preceptor

The central feature of our model is the preceptorship, which engages an underutilized and annually renewable resource available at every institution of higher learning: self-motivated undergraduates and their vested interest in acquiring a quality education. Preceptors facilitate collaborative learning exercises and group discussions in class; serve as writing consultants, technology experts, and assistants for hands-on research projects outside class; and hold office hours. They attend weekly team meetings with faculty and GTAs, where they provide feedback and help plan class activities. During these team meetings, preceptors catalyze curriculum development as they educate their instructors and GTAs about student life, attitudes, and cross-disciplinary connections. Being undergraduates themselves, preceptors are sympathetic to the frustrations and problems of their classmates, and their status as peer learners makes them approachable. Preceptors are trained to recognize the warning signs of academic or personal distress and to refer students to appropriate campus support personnel for professional attention.

Preceptor Recruiting

Methods for recruiting preceptors depend on the instructors' goals and preferences. Students currently enrolled in a course usually volunteer after listening to the instructor's presentation of the teaching team model. Honors students may be offered a preceptorship to earn honors credit for the course. Students who did well previously in a course may be contacted directly by the instructor and offered a preceptorship. The selection process is completed during the first few weeks of classes. Most faculty conduct interviews in the spirit of placing, rather than weeding out, candidates to determine how each can best contribute to their team. Acceptance depends on the instructor's impressions of a candidate's motivation, reliability, work ethic, prior leadership experience, attitude toward the subject matter, and academic record. Many instructors use contracts to emphasize the mutual commitment of time and effort in a preceptorship, and to allow a probationary period during which either party may terminate the relationship.

Many students volunteer for preceptorships in succeeding semesters. These experienced preceptors assume lead roles in organizing and conducting class activities, especially in courses using teaching teams for the first time. Some returning preceptors interested in acquiring technology skills are trained as student technology preceptors (STPs) to work with faculty in developing and preparing class materials, troubleshooting technology problems, serving as technology resource experts for students in a class, and being webmasters for class web sites.

Preceptor Rewards

Preceptors earn academic credit in workshop training courses carrying a university-wide code, UNVR (Table 5.3). Faculty decide during interviews which UNVR course best suits each candidate. First-time preceptors usually enroll concurrently in UNVR 197a and in the class in which they precept. Students who volunteer for subsequent preceptorships enroll in one of the UNVR 397 courses; they need not be concurrently enrolled in the supervising instructor's course. A student may use the UNVR courses for four or more preceptorships, which could be completed with a single course and instructor or be distributed among multiple faculty in different disciplines. Students receive grades in the UNVR courses from the instructors who lead their teaching teams. Grades reflect performance in the instructor's class (e.g., attitude, preparedness, attendance at office hours and weekly team meetings) and attendance at the training workshops, which is monitored and reported to supervising faculty.

New Roles for Graduate Teaching Assistants

Traditionally, GTAs are financially supported by their departments in exchange for grading papers, proctoring exams, holding office hours and discussion sessions, and delivering lectures when supervising instructors are out of

Table 5.1 EXAMPLES OF TEACHING TEAMS IN GENERAL EDUCATION COURSES

Course	Teaching Team	Enrollment	Student-to-Team Ratio
INDV 101 Language	Instructor, four GTAs, two experienced preceptors, one student technology preceptor, ten first-time preceptors	132	7:1
NATS 102 The Universe and Humanity: Origin and Destiny	Instructor, three GTAs (two in science, one in higher education), two experienced preceptors, five first-time preceptors	113	10:1
TRAD 101 Confucian Asia	Instructor, two GTAs, five experienced preceptors, 16 first-time preceptors	183	8:1

town. Formal training in pedagogy, to prepare GTAs to teach independently in the future, rarely augments these experiences. Some GTAs evolve into innovative instructors in tune with modern interactive trends in higher education, often through trial and error at the expense of their students; others seem never to consider teaching beyond the traditional lecture-only mode.

The TTP intervenes early in the career development of GTAs by shifting their attention away from being academic laborers to developing as apprentice faculty (see Chapter 6 in this volume for the GTA perspective on TTP). One programmatic requirement that drives this shift is that GTAs on teaching teams are strongly encouraged to attend the program's training workshops, and may elect to receive academic credit in the graduate-level training course. Also, instructors on teaching teams usually present their GTAs with options to extend traditional GTA roles such as mentoring preceptors, organizing and leading collaborative group activities, and introducing new projects and technology into the curriculum. In interdisciplinary environments, GTAs may assume the role of coinstructors when their expertise complements that of their supervising instructors, thus replacing the token GTA lecture with a more "honest" usage of GTAs based on their skills and subject matter knowledge. In all of the above, the significant new element is that motivated GTAs on a teaching team can display initiative that will enrich the classes they serve, develop their knowledge about learning and teaching, and make their teaching portfolios more compelling.

Teaching Team Training Workshops

All teaching team participants attend special training workshops consisting of an all-day Saturday session early in the semester and a half-day Saturday session at mid-semester. Presenters include faculty, GTAs, returning preceptors, and experts from support units such as the learning center, the teaching center, assessment and enrollment research services, and the library. Plenary sessions feature keynote speakers and team building activities for all teaching team members. First-time and experienced preceptors, STPs, GTAs, and faculty attend parallel sessions that focus on issues specific to their experience and roles on teaching teams. Topics include collaborative learning, learning styles, dealing with difficult students, peer review of writing assignments, academic integrity issues, and guidance on incorporating preceptorships and other academic experience into portfolios and résumés. The effectiveness of a teaching team is ultimately dependent on the instructor, who is likely to have experienced an academic environment where lecture-only courses were the norm. The workshops, therefore, include sessions for faculty to discuss their experiences with their teaching teams, and to expose them to new ways of incorporating technology and active learning strategies in their courses.

Administration of the Teaching Teams Program

A coordinating council meets year-round on a weekly basis to plan and assess all aspects of the TTP. The council's membership includes ten faculty and staff who have direct interactions with undergraduates in courses or in campus support units. Undergraduate and graduate student coordinators who assume lead roles for classroom liaison, workshop support, database management, publications, recruiting, and program representation assist the council. Coordinator positions are filled through competitive reviews of applicants with extensive prior experience in preceptoring, tutoring, and related skills. The number of coordinators has evolved to an average level of six undergraduates and three GTAs, each working 10–20 hours per week. This student-powered approach to program implementation has been remarkably effective in promoting teaching teams among students and faculty, and the coordinators themselves acquire valuable communication and management skills.

Table 5.2 PARTICIPATION IN THE TEACHING TEAMS PROGRAM

Preceptored Courses	Fall 1998	Spring 1999	Fall 1999
Number of Courses	9	21	29
Participating Faculty	9	18	26
Participating GTAs	18	21	40
Preceptors	86	181	217
Total Enrollment in Courses	1,309	2,936	3,682

Table 5.3 TRAINING COURSES FOR TEACHING TEAM PARTICIPANTS

Course	Target Group	Credit Hours	Repeatable[1]
UNVR 197a	First-time preceptors	2	No
UNVR 397a	Experienced preceptors	2–3	Yes
UNVR 397b	Student technology preceptors	2–3	Yes
UNVR 397c	Student technology preceptors	6–9	No
UNVR 597a	Graduate teaching assistants	1–3	Yes

[1] Repeatable up to a total of 9 credit hours

The council promotes university-wide visibility for the TTP. Publications, mostly student-produced, include three newsletters per semester, a start-up kit for faculty new to the program, a web site (TTP, 2000) for current program information, and brochures for prospective students, GTAs, and faculty. Undergraduate coordinators explain the benefits of enrolling in preceptored classes to incoming students during freshmen orientation sessions, and graduate student coordinators make similar presentations at GTA orientation workshops. Each semester the council invites all teaching team members to an end-of-semester showcase event at which teaching teams use posters, videos, and computer presentations to present accomplishments in their classes.

The council awards about 12 curriculum development grants annually, averaging $4,000 each, to teams led either by faculty or by GTAs with undergraduates as mandated partners. The product of such a grant, typically the development of a collaborative learning activity or the introduction of some aspect of technology, must show up in a specific general education course within one or two semesters, thus enhancing the university's transformation of its general education curriculum.

■ OUTCOMES

We surveyed all four participant groups (faculty, GTAs, preceptors, and students) during TTP's first year (AY 1998–1999) using questionnaires, focus group discussions, and interviews (Table 5.4). The preliminary assessments reported here and in Chapters 6 and 7 provide useful formative insight into the initial acceptance of teaching teams among faculty and students, the mechanics of implementing them, and the problem areas that need attention as the program evolves.

Faculty Experience with Teaching Teams

All responding faculty liked having preceptors in their classes, as indicated by their enthusiasm during the interviews and the fact that all of them declared that they would repeat the experience. Many faculty reported that because of their teaching team, they were able to work closely with students in a large class where it is typically difficult to get to know any students. They noted that preceptors offered constructive advice about their courses and teaching that had never emerged from written evaluations at the end of the semester. Many faculty adopted teaching teams because of enthusiastic recommendations from colleagues who had previously worked with preceptors. About 70% of the surveyed faculty redesigned their courses at least somewhat around preceptors in order to meet the university's new general education guidelines.

Some faculty were not satisfied with their efforts to identify suitable preceptor candidates, especially from among freshmen during the first few weeks of classes. These faculty were determined to be more selective in the future by looking specifically for students who are computer literate and competent in math, writing, and communication skills. They will also attempt to recruit at least a few experienced preceptors to mentor first-time preceptors.

GTA Experience on Teaching Teams

Approximately half of the GTAs were satisfied with their experience and thought that preceptors worked out quite well in the classroom. Interestingly, those GTAs who were most involved with preceptors were the most positive about their usefulness in the class. Dissatisfied GTAs expressed concern about the indistinct boundaries between GTA and preceptor roles, in some cases because preceptors took students' attention away from them. They also perceived preceptors as having inadequate knowledge and skill levels, or having unfair advantages over other students in the class. The GTA comments reveal much uncertainty about what it means to be a preceptor, and little appreciation of potential GTA roles in mentoring them. The GTA experience on teaching teams, and what could be done to improve it, are discussed in detail in Chapter 6.

Table 5.4 EVALUATION FOR FALL 1998-SPRING 1999 SEMESTERS

Participant Group and Method	Number Surveyed	Number of Responses	Response Rate (%)
Faculty			
Interviews (fall 98)	9	7	78
Questionnaires[1] (spring 1999)	18	14	78
GTAs			
Questionnaires[2]	39	26	67
Focus groups	39	5	13
Email commentary	39	7	18
Preceptors			
Questionnaires[3]	267	150	56
Focus groups	56	44	79
Students			
Questionnaires	3,686	1,316	36

[1]Appendix D-11
[2]Appendix D-10
[3]Appendix D-9

Preceptor Experience on Teaching Teams

Preceptors were the most satisfied participant group, both in terms of their own classroom experience and their overall impressions of the TTP. Most reported that these experiences developed their self-confidence and improved their teamwork, leadership, and communication skills. They also reported becoming more organized with their time and course work, and they enjoyed getting to know their classmates. Some preceptors wanted even more active participation in their classes, such as planning and delivering a lecture and having more opportunities to peer review student work.

Preceptors were not an elite group in terms of their academic profile. Their ACT/SAT scores and high school grades were about average, so their college grade distribution should have resembled that of the general student body. Preceptors actually did far better academically than would have been expected from their ACT/SAT scores and high school GPAs. Preceptors concurrently enrolled in general education courses received more than twice the number of As and less than half the Cs of their peers enrolled in similar, but nonpreceptored, general education courses, and they were much less likely to do poorly (Ds and Es) or withdraw from the course (Figure 5.2). We attribute their persistence and academic achievement to their motivation to learn, close interactions with instructional personnel, discussing their assignments in small groups, and articulating what they learned to other students. In principle, this preceptor experience could be shared by all motivated students who adopt similar study and time management habits. The preceptor experience in the TTP is discussed in detail in Chapter 7.

Student Reactions to Teaching Teams

Approximately 42% of all students surveyed had regular contact (at least two to four interactions per month) with preceptors. About 80% of these students said that preceptors contributed a moderate to exceptional amount to their understanding of the course material. About 54% of all students surveyed stated that if given a choice they would prefer to take preceptored courses.

About 27% of the students in preceptored classes had only one or two personal or electronic contacts with preceptors during the entire semester, and another 31% of these students made no contact at all. One probable factor in low student-preceptor contacts in some classes is that many faculty are still figuring out how to integrate preceptors into their courses. Some preceptors felt that the students in their classes were not given enough information about who the preceptors were, what their roles were, and how they could help students. Some GTAs noted that preceptors were merely "tacked on" to an existing class structure to provide extra office hours, which inevitably were as poorly attended as those of the instructor and GTAs. Many faculty realized that their preceptors were underutilized by their students, a situation which they planned to remedy by giving their preceptors more visibility in the classroom and giving the class more

Figure 5.2 ACADEMIC PERFORMANCE OF PRECEPTORS AND NONPRECEPTORS ENROLLED IN THE SAME CLASSES

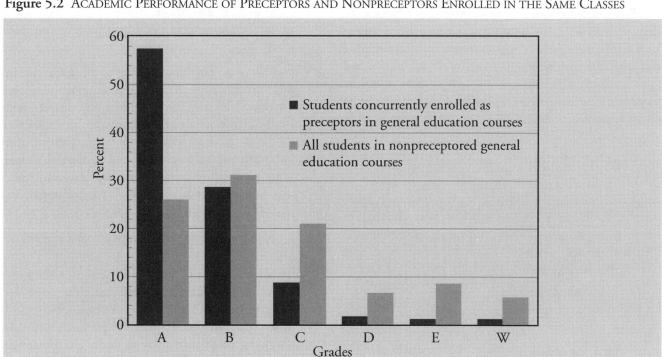

assignments that required interacting with preceptors during office hours.

PRODUCTIVITY

The key ingredients of the teaching teams program exist at many universities: large numbers of motivated students, faculty with innovative ideas drawn from their research programs, and academic support units responsive to student needs. Our major expenses are associated with coordinating these resources and investing in curriculum development (Table 5.5). We provide financial support only for our student coordinators. Faculty and staff who serve on the council associate their involvement with service to the university community. The project director is a full-time faculty member whose time commitment is credited to research in science education. We have therefore minimized our administrative overhead costs by engaging existing resources, a strategy that should make it easier to institutionalize the program when our external funding ceases. One measure of the cost of running TTP for one year is to divide the coordinators' wages, stipends, and workshop expenses by the number of preceptors in the program and by the number of students enrolled in preceptored courses. These costs are about $190 per preceptor and $10 per enrolled student.

Participating faculty agreed unanimously that preceptored courses required more work than traditional lecture courses. Still, all responding faculty planned to repeat their experience because the frequent interactions with motivated students made teaching a more satisfying experience. Moreover, part of the increase in work load is directly attributable to the university's new general education curriculum, whose requirements for collaborative learning, intensive writing practice, critical thinking, and (in science courses) hands-on research projects, represent more work for instructional personnel regardless of how they choose to conduct their classes. If all team partici-

Table 5.5 TEACHING TEAMS PROGRAM ADMINISTRATIVE EXPENSES (FALL 1998-SPRING 1999)

Item	Annual Expenditure
Wages for faculty and staff on the coordinating council	0
Wages and stipends for student coordinators	$52,000
Training workshops	$10,000
Curriculum development grants	$55,000

pants explore new roles in which the new larger workload is appropriately shared, the faculty workload could remain unchanged or even decrease. For example, papers should be easier to grade after preceptors conduct peer reviews of student writing assignments. When GTAs share mentoring and curriculum development tasks, they save the instructor time while they enhance their own professional development. Finally, the instructor spends less time preparing and delivering lectures when preceptors and/or GTAs lead in-class activities.

SUGGESTIONS FOR REPLICATION

Any instructor can set up a teaching team in a class using standard collaborative learning strategies, but it is a much more challenging endeavor to extend the practice throughout a large university. Below, we offer suggestions to guide the set-up of a TTP elsewhere. Our web site (TTP, 2000) contains training course syllabi, sample contracts, lists of preceptored courses, and workshop schedules that are adaptable for use elsewhere.

- Identify faculty already providing peer-assisted learning experiences and bring them together to share their ideas and experience. We asked ten such faculty to share their vision and methods in a meeting with others who were attracted to the idea, but were not sure how to proceed.

- Keep your participants active in administering and running your program. Our program's founding group chose a council of faculty who taught preceptored general education courses, representatives of key academic support units, and student coordinators.

- Define your program broadly to preserve the instructor's flexibility to innovate at the classroom level. We provide practical information (e.g., a start-up kit and how to stay out of trouble) and offer assistance during the formation of teaching teams, but we minimize our presence once the teams are established. Initially, coordinators attended weekly team meetings, but we discovered that many faculty preferred to stay in contact with the program via email.

- Procure funding for your program. We applied for external support to build program visibility (T-shirts for all participants, an end-of-semester showcase event), to fund faculty-student curriculum development grants, and to provide a reasonable period (three years) in which to test the program before attempting to institutionalize it. In circumstances where funding is unavailable, a bare-bones budget might suffice to cover the indispensable elements (in our case, student coordinator wages and training workshop expenses).

- Include students on your planning team and give them high visibility and lead roles in program promotional activities. Our student coordinators are the program's most articulate and compelling ambassadors.

- Use preceptors to recruit new preceptors. Experienced preceptors can provide information about the benefits of their role.

- Be selective in recruiting faculty for your program. Overzealous recruiting of faculty participants produced some with only marginal commitments to making teaching teams work. We moved to becoming more selective in accepting new faculty and we are particularly insistent that they meet the program's expectations for student participation in the training workshops.

- Incorporate assessment and evaluation expertise into your program. Assessment is usually required by external funding agencies, but competent program evaluation should be conducted even for local funding. Our council includes staff members from several units charged with the evaluation of teaching and learning.

- Link your program to the vision documents and educational objectives of your institution. The acceptance and growth of our TTP have been aided by a supportive university administration which was aggressively promoting undergraduate education reform. We kept key academic administrators aware of the linkage between our program and the university's new general education guidelines.

■ CONCLUSION

As a consequence of the open atmosphere for communication and change at the University of Arizona, the teaching teams program has acquired elements of a grassroots movement in which the participants themselves, not just a distant administration, believe that they are actually transforming the educational system. The teaching team has emerged as a natural structure for channeling this enthusiasm, which contributes to making the University of Arizona a student-centered research university in the spirit of the Boyer Commission report.

■ ACKNOWLEDGMENTS

We gratefully acknowledge encouragement and support of the TTP at all levels in the University of Arizona's Office of Undergraduate Education, especially from Dr. Michael Gottfredson, Provost; Dr. Randall Richardson, Vice President for Undergraduate Education; and Dr. Saundra Taylor, Vice President for Campus Life. The teaching teams program is supported with grants from the US Department of Education's Fund for the Improvement of Post-Secondary Education (FIPSE) and the W. K. Kellogg Foundation.

■ REFERENCES

The Boyer Commission on Educating Undergraduates in the Research University. (1998). *Reinventing undergraduate education: A blueprint for American research universities* [Online]. Available: http://notes.cc.sunysb.edu/Pres/boyer.nsf

TTP. (2000). *Teaching teams program* [Online]. Available: http://www.LPL.arizona.edu/teachingteams

■ AUTHORS

HAROLD P. LARSON is a Professor in the Department of Planetary Sciences at the University of Arizona at Tucson.

REED MENCKE is Associate Director of the University Learning Center at the University of Arizona at Tucson.

STACY J. TOLLEFSON is a doctoral candidate in the Department of Teaching and Teacher Education at the University of Arizona at Tucson.

ELIZABETH HARRISON is Associate Director of the University Teaching Center and Adjunct Assistant Professor in the Department of East Asian Studies at the University of Arizona at Tucson.

ELENA BERMAN is an Assessment and Faculty Development Specialist in Assessment and Enrollment Research at the University of Arizona at Tucson.

Chapter 6

The Teaching Teams Program: Transforming the Role of the Graduate Teaching Assistant

David A. Wood, Jr., Jennifer L. Hart, Stacy J. Tollefson,
Dawn E. DeToro, and Julie Libarkin

Graduate Teaching Assistants (GTAs) have played important roles in undergraduate education for years, but the role of the GTA must be reviewed as the focus of higher education shifts toward increased undergraduate involvement in the teaching and learning process. Traditionally, GTAs have served as instructors of record, lecturers, lab instructors, graders, discussion leaders, and informal advisors for a wide variety of courses and faculty. Graduate students receive financial compensation and the institution receives inexpensive academic labor. Often overlooked, however, is the fact that the GTA position can also serve as an apprenticeship for future faculty. If carefully guided, GTAs can redefine their roles in undergraduate education while enhancing not only their own educational experiences, but those of their students as well.

In the 1998–1999 academic year, the University of Arizona implemented a comprehensive, multilevel general education curriculum. The teaching teams program (TTP), described in detail in Chapter 5, evolved to provide undergraduates with personal attention in large classes while supporting the university's general education reform efforts. Teaching teams operate on the premise that undergraduate preceptors, drawn from motivated students concurrently enrolled in general education classes, can actively help not only themselves, but other students as well. Typically, preceptors lead small group discussions, hold office hours, assist with projects, and peer review writing assignments. In some classes, preceptors conduct homework or review sessions, perform demonstrations, provide technology support, or carry out other tasks as appropriate to the course.

With preceptors assuming important roles both inside and outside the classroom, GTAs find themselves increasingly displaced from their traditional roles. For example, the university eliminated a traditional GTA assignment by restructuring independent lab classes formerly taught by GTAs into combined lecture/lab classes taught by ranked faculty with the assistance of GTAs or preceptors. However, the TTP model offers GTAs new opportunities to develop the teaching skills they will need as they ultimately move into faculty positions.

Through the TTP, GTAs have the opportunity to work closely with faculty who recognize the importance of teaching. Since many faculty allow GTAs to decide the extent to which they will participate in the program, GTAs may choose simply to grade papers and hold office hours, or they may opt to explore new areas of pedagogy such as collaborative learning, mentoring preceptors, course and curriculum development, and interdisciplinary teaching (Table 6.1). For GTAs who choose to expand their roles, the wide array of opportunities available to them has the potential to revolutionize the GTA experience to better serve faculty, GTAs, undergraduates, and the university as a whole.

■ OUTCOMES

Since its inception in fall 1998, the TTP has offered a series of workshops to all teaching team members. Although GTAs were specifically encouraged to attend, only 11%-27% did so in AY 1998–1999. In spring 1999, only three GTAs attended the first of four scheduled forums to discuss their TTP experiences, prompting the cancellation of the remaining forums. The unanticipated apathy demonstrated by GTAs signaled the deeper problem that GTAs were being left behind by general education reforms.

Therefore, feedback from GTAs was sought through questionnaires (Appendix D-10), focus group discussions, and comments sent to evaluators by email. All of the GTAs who responded reported performing a variety of traditional GTA duties including grading student work, substitute lecturing, leading discussion and review sessions, and developing quizzes and projects. Sixty percent of GTAs indicated that they supervised preceptors in ways such as training them as project assistants and debriefing them after homework assignments.

GTA attitudes toward teaching teams were more varied that those of any other participant group. A substantial majority (84%) of GTAs who returned questionnaires indicated satisfaction with their teaching assistantships, with more contact between GTAs and preceptors correlating with more positive GTA experiences. Among the GTAs who supervised preceptors, 60% thought that working with preceptors enhanced their GTA experience; only 20% of the GTAs who did not supervise preceptors believed that working with preceptors was beneficial. Many GTAs enjoyed working with a small group of students. They believed that programs like the TTP were necessary in large general education classes. Some GTAs even found that preceptors lightened their workloads by assisting students and by handling administrative details (e.g., returning papers in class).

However, GTAs expressed concerns about the TTP philosophy that were not echoed either by the participating faculty or by the students. Among the many reservations voiced by GTAs was concern that preceptors were usurping GTA positions as the primary student mentors. One GTA recommended, "Ensure that student interaction with preceptors does not interfere with student interactions with GTAs." Some instructors may have exacerbated this issue: One instructor admitted, "[B]ecause preceptors were new, I put a lot of emphasis on the preceptors and the GTAs got jealous."

Some GTAs believed that preceptors were given too much authority in the classroom. As expressed by one GTA: "It seems inappropriate to have students *in the same class* [her emphasis] in a position of authority over other students in the class." Additionally, approximately

Table 6.1 GTA Roles on Teaching Teams

Course	Teaching Team	Collaborative Teaching	Mentoring Preceptors	Course/Curriculum Development	Interdisciplinary Teaching
INDV 101 Language	Instructor, four GTAs, 13 preceptors	The instructor identifies activities that GTAs can develop. GTAs then prepare the preceptors for their classroom roles. For some activities, the GTAs may take the lead inside the classroom.	GTAs interact with subgroups of preceptors, modeling the interaction between GTAs and the instructor.	One GTA developed a peer evaluation by studying various pedagogical approaches beyond her linguistics training. She created a system of feedback that was incorporated into class. The instructor is planning to use this new system in her future classes.	One GTA is from the second language acquisition and teaching program. Another is an anthropology/linguistics student. All bring breadth of academic experience, culture, and age, using their diversity to enhance the classroom and team experience.
NATS 102 The Universe and Humanity: Origin and Destiny	Instructor, three GTAs, seven preceptors	Fifteen minutes in each class is devoted to an activity developed, organized, and run by GTAs and the preceptors. Both GTAs and preceptors perform demonstrations in class.	GTAs organize and run weekly preceptor meetings, train preceptors to assist their classmates, and guide preceptors through a peer review of class journals.	GTAs develop and present lectures on course topics. One GTA received a $4,000 curriculum development grant to create, with the assistance of undergraduate students, the infrastructure for a new general education course in planetary science that simulates a spacecraft mission.	One GTA is a higher education student who brings an education philosophy and innovative pedagogical techniques into a natural science classroom. The three GTAs come from backgrounds in geology, physics, mathematics, planetary science, higher education, and political science.
TRAD 101 Confucian Asia	Instructor, two GTAs, 21 preceptors	The course is structured by dividing the class into teams. GTAs supervise group interactions and assist the teams by answering questions.	Preceptors lead small groups. The instructor supervises preceptors. GTAs provide additional assistance to groups.	Each GTA plans and gives a lecture, but course and curriculum development opportunities are still very limited in this strand of general education.	One GTA is a Japanese literature student and the other is a Chinese language student whose perspective and expertise are a natural fit to an East Asian studies general education course.

40% of the GTAs who provided qualitative feedback believed that concurrently enrolled preceptors, especially freshmen, did not possess a sufficient grasp of the course material to assist other students, even when they completed assignments ahead of time. GTAs also expressed concern that preceptors received an unfair advantage over their classmates. A few GTAs point to extra help that preceptors obtained from the instructor and the GTAs at team meetings. One GTA stated: "Anything that isolates a small group out of the whole class and gives them extra help in that class is fundamentally wrong. All the students pay the same to come here; wide-eyed freshmen have the same expectations and should expect to have that [same attention]."

Many of these negative attitudes can be explained by the fact that most TTP classes were being taught for the first time in this format, and the role of GTAs in teaching teams was not well developed. Many GTAs were unfamiliar with the TTP and its philosophy. Over both the fall 1998 and spring 1999 semesters, 40% of the GTAs did not know in advance that the course to which they were assigned implemented a teaching team approach. The "format shock" may account for some of their views about the program. However, as the program became more established, GTAs became increasingly negative (Table 6.2). Discontent was most evident among GTAs who were least involved in teaching teams. We hypothesize that lack of information and understanding about changing roles continued to cause resistance to change.

Table 6.2 SELECTED RESPONSES FROM THE GTA QUESTIONNAIRE

Item and response options	Total (N = 26)	Fall 1998 (N = 13)	Spring 1999 (N = 13)
How familiar was the term "preceptor" to you?			
Very familiar or had an idea of what it was	57%	31%	85%
Heard of it but didn't know what it was	12%	8 %	15%
Never heard of it	31%	61%	0%
No response	0%	0%	0%
What kind of effect do you think preceptors and GTAs had on each other?			
Overall positive	50%	62%	38%
Neither positive nor negative	27%	15%	38%
Overall negative	11%	8%	16%
Mixed	4%	0%	8%
No response	8%	15%	0%
How did working with preceptors affect your experience as a GTA?			
Made it better	42%	46%	38%
Made no difference	11%	8%	16%
Made it worse	16%	8%	23%
Made it better in some ways, worse in others	23%	23%	23%
No response	8%	15%	0%
If given a choice, would you work with preceptors again?			
Definitely yes	42%	46%	38%
Probably yes	15%	23%	8%
Uncertain	4%	0%	8%
Probably not	27%	23%	31%
Definitely not	8%	0%	15%
No response	4%	8%	0%
Overall, how satisfied were you with your teaching assistantship this semester?			
Highly satisfied	38%	31%	46%
Moderately satisfied	46%	61%	31%
Minimally satisfied	8%	0%	15%
Not at all satisfied	4%	0%	8%
No response	4%	8%	0%

A New Model for GTAs

GTA positions can no longer be viewed as a means of providing financial support in exchange for academic labor. GTAs must see themselves as learners in the classroom, not simply as teachers; they must begin to consider teaching as a learning experience. By reassessing assumptions concerning the role of GTAs in teaching and learning, the academy can better prepare its future faculty while simultaneously improving the quality of undergraduate education (Angelo & Cross, 1989; Association of American Colleges, 1985; Boyer Commission, 1998).

Perhaps the greatest obstacle to the professional development of GTAs is the pressure (emanating from the faculty reward system and reinforced by the lack of faculty interest in GTA development) to emphasize research over teaching, especially in Research I universities. Teaching beginner level courses is often perceived by faculty and GTAs as a distraction from the GTAs' true goal of becoming experts in their fields. It is understandably difficult to convince GTAs that becoming skilled teachers who value learning is as important as becoming skilled and published researchers (Nyquist et al., 1999). Current faculty need to ensure that as their proteges move into faculty positions, they will be ready for a new definition of faculty that values teaching as well as research, so that the momentum that has been built by current undergraduate reform efforts will continue to grow.

Trying to force uncooperative GTAs into a program based upon collaborative learning and teamwork is at best an exercise in futility, and at worst a recipe for disaster. Two alternative approaches for dealing with uncooperative GTAs within the TTP have met with partial success. The first minimizes the GTAs' interaction with students by limiting their duties to grading papers or giving an occasional lecture. In this scenario, GTAs can comfortably retain their traditional duties while the remainder of the team participates in a more collaborative teaching experience. These GTAs, however, may feel isolated from both the students and the instructor, and they are the ones most likely to criticize the program. The second approach requires significantly limiting the responsibilities of preceptors to projects that do not overlap with GTA responsibilities (e.g., holding office hours, conducting review sessions). While this is a comfortable arrangement for GTAs, preceptors become little-used resources in a program that was designed to make personal instruction and peer-to-peer interactions more readily accessible. While these approaches address the symptoms of the problem, collaborative teaching suffers. Thus the question

remains: What alternative approaches address the issue of uncooperative GTAs, yet remain true to undergraduate reform efforts like the TTP?

In the most successful TTP models, faculty seize the opportunity to mentor GTAs for their new roles as apprentice faculty by actively recruiting interested GTAs to join their teaching teams. GTAs are encouraged to collaborate with their teaching teams to develop and assess class demonstrations, group projects, lab experiments, and a variety of other course-enhancing activities. GTAs may serve as principal investigators or may assist instructors in applying for small grants to develop or improve particular general education courses, providing them with an opportunity to develop professional skills that include grant writing, grant administration, and course/curriculum development. Also, as interdisciplinary general education courses become more common, GTAs can create nontraditional development opportunities by teaching in fields outside their specialty. Faculty have actively recruited GTAs from other fields to complement their course content or teaching style. Refer to Table 6.1 for specific examples of ways that GTA roles have been redefined within the TTP.

Finally, a university course (UNVR 597a, "Teaching Teams Graduate Assistant Training") was established to assist GTAs participating as members of teaching teams. This course is offered at no additional cost to many GTAs in return for the additional workload they may incur by working within the teaching team structure. Those enrolled in the course attend three functions (a training workshop, a team-building workshop, and a teaching team showcase) and must participate fully in the planning and implementation of their teaching team's activities.

At an evaluation retreat in May 1999, the teaching teams coordinating council restructured the training workshops to meet the specific needs of preceptors, GTAs, and faculty. During the 1999-2000 academic year, the TTP required all GTAs enrolled in UNVR 597a, and strongly encouraged all other GTAs participating in teaching teams, to attend three functions: a one-day, conference-style training near the beginning of the semester that emphasizes GTA responsibilities and professional development; a half-day workshop addressing common issues facing all teaching teams, at mid-semester; and a teaching team showcase celebration at the end of the semester. For the fall 1999 training workshop, the 30% attendance among all GTAs affiliated with teaching teams marked a slight, but encouraging rise over the previous year's attendance. Still more encouraging was a doubling in the number of

GTAs who enrolled in UNVR 597a, and a 90% attendance among UNVR 597a students at the fall 1999 training workshop.

In an effort to actively engage more GTAs in teaching teams, the TTP is focusing on two major objectives: to assist GTAs established within teaching teams through training workshops and academic credit, and to obtain feedback from GTAs concerning their experiences within teaching teams by performing qualitative and quantitative assessment. Ultimately, by emphasizing the positive aspects of teaching teams, while identifying and then improving the negative aspects, it is hoped that more GTAs will request assignments to teaching teams, rather than avoiding or compromising them.

■ CONCLUSION

GTAs are a critical component of undergraduate education, and their concerns about undergraduate education reform must be addressed. If GTAs are receptive to the changes occurring around them and become involved in professional development programs such as the TTP, they will be uniquely positioned to serve both as mentors to their students and as apprentices to their instructors. In contrast, if they are unwilling to adapt, GTAs can threaten both the immediate effectiveness of individual teaching reforms, such as the TTP, as well as the long-term stability of undergraduate education reform as a whole. For institutions that want to make a smoother transition, we recommend that undergraduate education reforms include graduate student input. Then, even before the reforms are implemented, graduate students should be encouraged to seek GTA experiences that promote their professional development.

The nationwide shift toward improving undergraduate education has caused Research I universities to weigh the teaching credentials of faculty candidates much more heavily than at any time in the recent past. The most competitive candidates for tenure-track positions blend a strong research background with a well-developed teaching portfolio that includes innovations like collaborative learning and curriculum development. Models like the TTP encourage GTAs to experience the full range of fundamental faculty responsibilities: teaching, learning, mentoring, developing curricula, conducting research, and engaging in service. The expansion of the GTA experience beyond the traditional roles increases the quality of undergraduate education as well as the quality of the future professoriate. Universities can only benefit by shifting the role of the GTA from academic laborer to faculty apprentice.

■ ACKNOWLEDGMENTS

We gratefully acknowledge the support of the TTP, the University Learning Center, and the Office of Assessment and Enrollment Research at the University of Arizona. Beth Harrison, Hal Larson, and Cecile McKee provided valuable information about their courses; Elena Berman assisted with assessment; and Lacey Stover reviewed multiple drafts of the manuscript. The TTP is supported with grants from the US Department of Education's Fund for the Improvement of Post-Secondary Education (FIPSE) and the W. K. Kellogg Foundation.

■ REFERENCES

Angelo, T. A., & Cross, K. P. (1989). Classroom research for teaching assistants. In J. D. Nyquist, R. D. Abbott, & D. H. Wulff (Eds.), *Teaching assistant training in the 1990s* (pp. 99-108). San Francisco, CA: Jossey-Bass.

Association of American Colleges. (1985). *Integrity in the college curriculum: A report in the academic community.* Washington, DC: Author.

The Boyer Commission on Educating Undergraduates in the Research University. (1998). *Reinventing undergraduate education: A blueprint for American research universities* [Online]. Available: http://notes.cc.sunysb.edu/Pres/boyer.nsf

Nyquist, J. D., Manning, L., Wulff, D. H., Austin, A. E., Sprague, J., Fraser, P. K., Calcagno, C., & Woodford, B. (1999, May/June). On the road to becoming a professor: The graduate student experience. *Change, 31* (3), 18-27.

■ AUTHORS

DAVID A. WOOD, JR. is a doctoral student and Graduate Associate in the Department of Planetary Sciences at the University of Arizona. He is also a Graduate Student Coordinator with the TTP.

JENNIFER L. HART is a doctoral student in the Center for the Study of Higher Education at the University of Arizona. She is also a Graduate Teaching Associate in the Department of Planetary Sciences and a Graduate Student Coordinator with the TTP.

STACY J. TOLLEFSON is a doctoral student in the Department of Teaching and Teacher Education at the University of Arizona. She works in conjunction with the Office of Assessment and Enrollment Research as the Graduate Research Assistant responsible for program evaluation of the TTP.

DAWN E. DETORO is a doctoral student in the Center for the Study of Higher Education and a Graduate Student Coordinator with the TTP at the University of Arizona.

JULIE LIBARKIN is a National Science Foundation Post-Doctoral Fellow in Science, Mathematics, Engineering, and Technology Education working with the University Learning Center at the University of Arizona.

Chapter 7

The Teaching Teams Program: Empowering Undergraduates in a Student-Centered Research University

Lacey A. Stover, Kirstin A. Story, Amanda M. Skousen,
Cynthia E. Jacks, Heather Logan, and Benjamin T. Bush

The University of Arizona is undertaking an ambitious restructuring of the undergraduate experience with the goal of creating a student-centered university, of which a defining characteristic is that its undergraduates are actively engaged in their education. However, this engagement cannot be accomplished solely by restructuring core program requirements and individual course curricula. Meaningful involvement can be achieved by incorporating undergraduate students in the teaching process and by offering them roles in course and curriculum development.

To further undergraduate students' engagement in their own learning and that of their peers, the University of Arizona created the teaching teams program (TTP), described in detail in Chapter 5. Teaching teams consist of faculty, GTAs, and undergraduate peer leaders working together to facilitate collaborative learning experiences in large general education classes. In this chapter, we discuss the experience of the undergraduate members of the team, the preceptors.

■ PRECEPTOR ROLES IN THE CLASSROOM

Preceptors are an integral part of the teaching team along with faculty and GTAs. The specific duties of preceptors are dependent on the goals of the instructor and on the structure of the class. However, all preceptors assist students with course material, act as liaisons between students and instructors, hold office hours, and attend training workshops (Table 7.1). Course syllabi (TTP, 2000), created by the TTP with substantial input from its undergraduate coordinators, formalize this standard. Instructors are free to supplement these activities with additional responsibilities that they consider necessary for their courses. Approximately 75% of preceptors in 1998–1999 assisted with in-class activities, 50% acted as discussion leaders, and 25% helped develop class projects or activities.

The presence of preceptors is beneficial to everyone in the classroom when they assume roles in the teaching process that their classmates readily embrace. An obvious benefit of this is that preceptors increase opportunities for

Table 7.1 PRECEPTOR DUTIES

Obligatory Duties of Preceptors	Examples of Additional Preceptor Responsibilities
• Finish assignments on an accelerated schedule when concurrently enrolled in the course. • Hold one to two office hours per week to assist students with projects and coursework. • Attend TTP training workshops. • Attend weekly meetings with instructor and GTA(s) • Give instructor constructive feedback on student progress and concerns. • Refer students to instructor or GTA(s) when uncomfortable with material.	• Help create in-class activities for small group discussions. • Develop and deliver in-class presentations. • Facilitate in-class group discussions and collaborative learning activities. • Facilitate hands-on laboratory experiments or projects. • Conduct study sessions to assist students with exam review or with homework problems. • Conduct peer writing review. • Assist the instructor with class field trips or other special events.

help in the course by expanding the number of office hours available per week, and by conducting out-of-class help sessions. In "Traditions and Cultures: Confucian Asia" (TRAD 103), preceptors discussed Confucian virtues with small groups of students. Preceptors were able to answer student questions because they had completed the work ahead of time. Preceptors in the TRAD course also performed practical tasks such as taking attendance, monitoring student activity, and answering students' questions.

Preceptors provide the resources necessary for instructors to include hands-on activities in high-enrollment science courses. For example, preceptors allowed the instructor of "Natural Sciences: The Universe and Humanity: Origin and Destiny" (NATS 102) to implement a model-building activity based on student-defined experiments using a Crookes' radiometer. This project required a great deal of out-of-class, hands-on activity, so there was a need for supervision beyond what the instructor and the GTAs could provide. The preceptors on the teaching team in this course readily provided the extra supervision after having conducted and analyzed their own observations prior to the rest of the class. Preceptors then peer reviewed the final drafts of the radiometer experiment reports.

Preceptors provide the facilitation necessary for collaborative learning activities in large lecture classes. In "Individuals in Society: Language" (INDV 101), a large, lecture-oriented linguistics course, preceptors monitored small group discussions and assisted with class discussion of group presentations. In a special project, preceptors polled students about their linguistic backgrounds, then created and presented a map based on this information.

We discovered early in our program that giving preceptors high visibility in classes could generate negative reactions among students, GTAs, and faculty. One major risk of giving undergraduates leadership roles in the classroom is that their peers may assume that these positions bring preferential treatment, such as access to privileged information. When students feel that preceptors are receiving special treatment, trust between the two groups suffers, and benefits from student-preceptor interactions diminish. In order to head off such problems, instructors should describe the qualifications for a preceptor position and emphasize that all students are eligible. Also, instructors should make clear that preceptors are neither privy to confidential information, nor permitted to dispense answers to students. In our experience, accusations of special treatment rarely emerge when these two points are established and reiterated throughout the semester.

The fact that preceptors, when concurrently enrolled in the same course, tend to achieve higher grades than their peers can compound the perception of privilege (see Chapter 5). Faculty need to explain that preceptors achieve higher grades because they spend extra time reviewing assignments and because they explain the assignments repeatedly to other students, an action that any student wishing to improve his or her study skills can engage in independently. Also, preceptors receive assistance from instructors during weekly team meetings, and such attention is available to all students during faculty office hours.

PRECEPTOR ROLES IN COURSE AND CURRICULUM DEVELOPMENT

We believe that it is important for undergraduates to be involved in course and curriculum development if they are to take an active role in their education. Traditionally, undergraduates have had difficulty giving feedback to their instructors during the semester because evaluations were not available for inspection by faculty until after the semester was completed, and they have rarely had any role in the planning of their courses. Through the TTP structure and the curriculum development grants offered by the TTP, undergraduates can provide timely feedback to their instructors and take part in curriculum development.

Because preceptors tutor their classmates, they can observe the students' progress and inform their instructor about areas of confusion. This method provides more immediate opportunities for course adjustment than relying on exam results or end-of-semester evaluations to judge the progress of the students. The most successful teaching teams hold weekly meetings in which preceptors feel free to voice their concerns about the course.

TTP awards curriculum development grants for the creation of new student-centered general education courses. The requirement that one third of the budget must be used to support undergraduate members of the project team gives undergraduates a very unique and powerful role in transforming the curriculum to a student-centered one. Principal investigators of TTP grants have employed undergraduates to assist in adding technology to existing general education courses, creating experiments for natural science courses, and designing new courses.

ENDOWING STUDENTS WITH THE SKILLS NECESSARY FOR SUCCESS

Preceptors work with faculty and GTAs to create unique collaborative learning environments in large lecture classes. Preceptors benefit from this interaction because they must understand the course material in order to help design an activity that will help the students, and as a consequence their course performance improves. In addition, preceptors benefit from the opportunity to develop communication skills, practice critical analysis, and reflect on their educational and life goals.

Serving as a preceptor while concurrently enrolled in the course is unquestionably beneficial to the preceptors themselves. Although earning better grades is not overemphasized as a benefit during preceptor recruiting, in the questionnaire data collected in spring 1999, 71% of respondents cited earning a better grade in the course as either a "strong" or a "moderate" influence in their decision to become preceptors. Similarly, 61% of respondents stated that they expected to earn higher grades by serving as preceptors. Preceptor grades were indeed higher than would be expected from their high school GPA and SAT/ACT scores (see Chapter 5). We know that many preceptors are highly motivated and would likely outperform the group average whether they served as preceptors or not. On the other hand, we also know that many preceptors improved their study and time management skills through their experience. In our opinion, these students almost certainly earned higher grades because of their preceptorship.

One of the most difficult transitions to university life is the change in student-teacher relationships. Students in large research universities are often too intimidated to approach instructors who are renowned experts in their fields. Before a university can call itself student-centered, this intimidation must be overcome by instilling in students the self-confidence necessary to approach and to communicate successfully with their faculty. TTP requires frequent, extended interaction between preceptors, GTAs, and faculty, thus allowing preceptors to get to know their instructors personally early in the semester. Often, this familiarity helps preceptors in their other courses, as it gives them the self-confidence necessary to approach their other instructors. In addition, the TTP structure allows nonpreceptors to develop self-confidence by providing them peer resources to approach for help, and by providing them with role models who interact regularly with faculty. Helping undergraduates develop these skills diminishes the impersonal nature of the research university and allows students to feel comfortable speaking openly with other members of the university community.

Every semester, the TTP collects assessment data from preceptors (Appendix D-9). Of the 101 respondents to the spring 1999 evaluation, 78% of preceptors "strongly agree" with the statement, "being a preceptor has allowed me to get to know the professor better." Similarly, 88% of respondents stated that they either "strongly

agree" or "somewhat agree" with the statement, "being a preceptor has improved my ability to explain complicated ideas to others." These data clearly indicate that students involved in TTP feel that they acquire communication skills that are vital to their professional development and to the creation of a student-centered academic culture.

We see general education as an opportunity for students to integrate their major area of study with other disciplines and, in doing so, to improve their critical thinking and problem solving skills. TTP provides opportunities for interdisciplinary study because preceptors are rarely majors in the disciplines in which they serve as preceptors, and therefore bring knowledge of other fields into their preceptorships. For example, in the NATS course, two political science majors prepared a presentation and facilitated a discussion on the effect on the upcoming presidential race of the debate on evolution. In another presentation, a psychology major facilitated a class discussion about the public fear of irradiated food and prompted students to consider the complex reasons why such fears are sustained. In each case, both preceptors and nonpreceptors were able to realize the value of interdisciplinary study, and the process of integrating the disciplines was valuable to improving reasoning skills, obtaining active involvement, and making informed decisions.

Attending college is a life-changing experience in which students are exposed to new points of view and new potential careers. We have observed our peers changing their majors and future plans frequently throughout their academic careers. In a spring 1999 survey, 55% of responding preceptors agreed that they had an increased interest in the teaching profession as a result of their preceptorships, suggesting that a preceptorship is an opportunity to evaluate new educational and career paths.

CONFLICTING POINTS OF VIEW ABOUT THE PRECEPTOR ROLE

Some perceptions of the program's strengths and weaknesses are at odds with GTA opinions. A sometimes contentious issue has been the delegation of roles between preceptors and GTAs. In assessment feedback, GTAs have expressed concern that preceptors are usurping duties traditionally reserved for GTAs, such as holding office hours (see Chapter 6). As preceptors, we do not perceive a problem with role definition, so long as the instructor clearly defines roles at the beginning of the semester and takes steps to isolate nonteam players.

Our perception is reinforced by preceptor evaluation data. Sixty-four percent of respondents in spring 1999 felt that their instructors were "completely clear" and another

28% felt that their instructors were "somewhat clear" in defining roles between preceptors and GTAs. In a related question, 85% of respondents indicated that the word "team" is a "very good" or "good" descriptor of the interaction between the instructors, GTAs, and preceptors on their teams (compared with 75% of the faculty and 70% of the GTAs). These data indicate that the majority of preceptors in the spring 1999 semester did not perceive a conflict between GTA and preceptor roles. However, the sharp contrast between GTA and preceptor opinions on role definition cannot be discounted (see Chapter 6).

GTAs have also expressed reservations about the ability of preceptors concurrently enrolled in a course to help classmates without disseminating false information (see Chapter 6). We do not share their view. We believe that concurrent enrollment is actually beneficial to both preceptors and nonpreceptors. In our classroom experience, preceptors who are concurrently enrolled in the class provide their peers with moral support. By observing preceptors master and teach material, nonpreceptors may acquire more confidence in their ability to comprehend the same material. Moreover, in our experience as coordinators, we have never heard participating faculty raise the issue of the dissemination of false information.

We believe that allowing students to serve as preceptors while concurrently involved in the course is vital to affording undergraduates control over their education. In our opinion, if students had to wait to serve as preceptors until they had completed courses, they would miss opportunities to obtain the valuable skills that come from learning and teaching material simultaneously. In addition, students miss opportunities to participate in course and curriculum development and, in so doing, to provide feedback on the future of a course in which they are enrolled.

■ CONCLUSION

Empowering undergraduates is a necessary step in creating the student-centered research university. In addition to placing students in leadership roles within the classroom, the teaching teams program allows them to seek out interdisciplinary opportunities and to participate in course and curriculum development. Only when undergraduates take active roles in their education, and have real control over their undergraduate experience, can a university truly become student-centered.

■ ACKNOWLEDGMENTS

We would like to thank the TTP coordinating council for advocating undergraduate empowerment at the University of Arizona. Dr. Hal Larson, Dr. Cecile McKee, Dr. Elizabeth Harrison, and Stacy Tollefson contributed to this chapter, and Jennifer Hart, Cari Copeland, and Dr. Reed Mencke assisted with revisions. The TTP is supported with grants from the US Department of Education's Fund for the Improvement of Post-Secondary Education (FIPSE) and the W. K. Kellogg Foundation.

■ REFERENCE

TTP. (2000). *Teaching teams program* [Online]. Available: http://www.LPL.arizona.edu/teachingteams

■ AUTHORS

LACEY A. STOVER is a political science major and a preceptor in the Department of Planetary Sciences at the University of Arizona.

KIRSTIN A. STORY is an English and creative writing major and a preceptor in the Departments of Planetary Science, English, and Latin American Studies at the University of Arizona.

AMANDA M. SKOUSEN is a graduate of the University of Arizona with a degree in political science. She was a preceptor in the Department of Planetary Sciences.

CYNTHIA E. JACKS is a business management major and a preceptor in the Departments of Astronomy and Classics at the University of Arizona.

HEATHER LOGAN is a speech and hearing sciences and elementary education major and a preceptor in the Department of Mining and Geological Engineering at the University of Arizona.

BENJAMIN T. BUSH is a political science major and a preceptor in the Department of Planetary Sciences at the University of Arizona.

All have served as TTP coordinators.

Chapter 8

Peer-Assisted Cooperative Learning: An Experiment in Educational Quality and Productivity

Judith E. Miller, David DiBiasio, John Minasian, and James S. Catterall

Worcester Polytechnic Institute (WPI), the nation's third oldest engineering college, enrolls about 2,500 undergraduate and 1,000 graduate students, mostly majoring in engineering, management, and natural sciences. In a major departure from typical terms, WPI's academic year consists of four seven-week terms, in which students take three courses in a term. In the early 1970s, prescribed lists of courses were radically replaced with the outcomes-based WPI Plan. The plan required that students develop and demonstrate their competency for real world challenges by carrying out independent projects in their junior and senior years. However, traditional lecture-based teaching, which remained the norm, did little to prepare students for the type of projects they would encounter at WPI and later in the professional world.

Fortuitously, in 1992, the Davis Educational Foundation challenged colleges to develop ideas to increase educational quality and faculty productivity. The model WPI proposed, and which the Davis Foundation funded, addressed educational quality with minigrants to faculty to restructure their large introductory courses from a traditional to a cooperative learning (CL) format. Many studies have shown that CL improves educational outcomes (Cooper et al., 1990; Johnson & Johnson, 1989; Johnson, Johnson, & Smith, 1991); however, in our experience, using the traditional CL model often increases demands on faculty time. WPI addressed this issue by employing undergraduate peer learning assistants (PLAs) to facilitate CL groups. PLAs are a support resource to facilitate small group problem solving both within and outside the classroom, and are very useful in large classes where the instructor cannot monitor or support all CL activities. PLAs are neither peer tutors nor peer teaching assistants, though they may occasionally provide educational guidance and limited academic instruction. Primary responsibility for teaching remains with the instructor and graduate teaching assistants, and primary responsibility for learning rests with students themselves. In this model, the instructor becomes the manager of, instead of the sole performer in, an educational process that relies on contributions from many participants.

The model incorporating PLAs was called peer-assisted cooperative learning (PAC). Faculty were invited to apply for $20,000-$40,000 course redevelopment PAC grants. The grants typically covered summer salary for the faculty member, plus some combination of teaching assistant (TA) salary and PLA salary for the duration of the course, and small amounts for supplies and travel. A faculty committee reviewed proposals and made funding decisions. From 1993 to 1997, 11 courses in seven disciplines were converted to the PAC model with Davis Foundation funds, and more faculty later adopted the model without funding.

From the PAC model, three different variations of PLA use developed. We describe here these three models of PLA use, their implementation, and their effects on learning, attitudes, and productivity. All three models resulted in improved student learning and none had any consistent effect on student attitudes. Two of the three yielded savings in faculty time, and all three models incurred slight additional costs due to the cost of paying PLAs. But in the ultimate test of an externally funded project—sustainability—all eleven initiatives have been continued by the departments involved once grant funding expired.

■ MODEL

Model I: PLAs Facilitate Small Groups

The first model, typical of the science and engineering courses, utilized PLAs to facilitate group process and problem solving in small CL groups in large class settings of 80 to 150 students. The courses implementing this model included introductory courses in biology (Groccia & Miller, 1996; Miller & Groccia, 1997), chemical engineering (DiBiasio & Groccia, 1995), civil engineering (Hart & Groccia, 1994), computer science (Wills & Finkel, 1994), and materials science (Demetry & Groccia, 1997). In a typical course, the entire class met in small CL groups within the large class setting two to three times per week. At these sessions, PLAs circulated to assist groups with short in-class problems or activities. One class meeting per week was typically used for each CL group to meet with its PLA. The task for this meeting might be group work on the current project, homework set, or programming assignment, revision of a group-written draft, or preparation for a laboratory exercise. Facilitation of group process was the primary role of PLAs, with communication of course content secondary. Group facilitation involved tasks such as assisting students in planning an approach to an open-ended problem, and mediating the inevitable disagreements and miscommunications among group members. In most cases, each PLA was assigned to three to five groups and would have several in-class meetings scheduled per week, in addition to optional out-of-class meetings with groups.

PLAs enabled the replacement of passive lecture with active, real-life, group-oriented learning experiences. In introductory biology, the use of open-ended group projects on current hot topics had been implemented when the course enrolled 40 students. PLAs made it possible to continue group projects even as student numbers grew. In a new team-taught course, "Introduction to Civil Engineering," students worked in PLA-assisted teams on weekly computer projects that simulated real-life engineering projects. In "Techniques of Programming," PLAs assisted students with group programming projects similar to those encountered in the working world as a replacement for smaller, individually completed assignments. The integration of PLAs into "Introduction to Chemical Engineering" enabled the addition of two new projects to the course and the continuation of an important laboratory project, in spite of an increase in class size.

Model II: PLAs Facilitate Large Group Review and Problem Solving Sessions

Courses using this model included all four courses in an introductory calculus sequence, and courses in linear algebra and differential equations (Davis, 1994). PLAs employed in this model served primarily as conference or recitation session leaders, somewhat like undergraduate TAs. They supervised cooperative learning sections where students worked in small groups on problems related to

lecture material. Cooperative learning conference sections that met once or twice per week were subsets of a much larger lecture class that met three times per week. A typical class might have two PLAs working with 25 students divided into teams of three. PLA activities included group building exercises, homework reviews, discussion questions, and facilitation of group processing in project groups. Some sessions involved computer labs with students working on group projects using mathematics software. Unlike Model I, PLAs also served as graders, evaluating homework and individual student group contribution.

Using PLAs as undergraduate TAs was not the original ideal model. However, its application in very large courses found widespread use in the mathematical sciences department. It allowed faculty to introduce cooperative learning into these large courses and make more efficient use of the graduate student TAs. Math faculty were faced with the simultaneous problems of dealing with large classes and instituting calculus reform. PLAs allowed a reduction in the number of large lecture sections and an increase in the number of smaller discussion sections. The end result was that passive, large lecture time was reduced in favor of smaller group-based, active, technology-driven activities.

Model III: PLAs Mentor One-on-One for Theatre Production and Writing

In an exciting departure from the course-based PLA model, the professor who runs the drama program pioneered the use of PLAs in the advising of the theatre sufficiency (one Humanities Sufficiency). The Humanities Sufficiency is an independent study/project experience, required of all students, culminating in the study of five thematically related courses or projects in humanities. A theatre sufficiency integrates five courses related to theatre, acting, or play analysis. The sixth course, the sufficiency, is a capstone project, and usually involves working on a drama production. Theatre sufficiencies are particularly demanding of drama faculty effort due to high student interest, limited faculty numbers, and the fact that peak sufficiency project activity coincides with peak demands in the staging of theatre productions.

In a theatre sufficiency, a student both participates as cast or crew in a production and writes a paper about the experience. In a typical seven-week production term, each student is involved in the rehearsal or production process for 40-250 hours. The student is expected to meet once a week with the advisor and other students, keep a journal of the production activity, organize a bibliography of plays she/he has studied, and, once the performance has closed, write a final essay reflecting on the experience. During the same term, the professor simultaneously oversees up to 200 people working on a theater festival and advises 20–30 students on their sufficiency papers. Each student needs individual tutoring by the advisor on a rough draft, and the advisor must spend time reading and writing comments on the papers.

PLAs were added to the staff to guide students through the production process and advise them on written drafts of their sufficiency reports. For example, a PLA helping students work on a publicity sufficiency might work with advisees on a calendar of deadlines or help advisees brainstorm on publicity gimmicks. A PLA helping students with acting sufficiencies could advise group members on approaches to learning lines or devising ways of reading the script to learn more about the characters. In one case, the PLA assisting a directing sufficiency mediated disputes between a new student playwright and a first time director.

All theatre sufficiencies require submission of a written report. PLAs work with students in both group and individual meetings on all aspects of the report, assisting with the bibliography and the appendices, reviewing drafts, etc. Their charge is to see that each advisee has a final working draft to the professor by a specific date. Once the professor has reviewed the draft, PLAs advise students on how to respond to comments and corrections.

Hours and Pay

PLAs worked for a maximum of ten hours per week, and were paid between $5.50 and $6.50 per hour, depending on experience. This rate of pay was somewhat above both minimum wage and prevailing rates for unskilled on-campus employment. They typically spent two to three hours attending lectures or TA-led conferences, three to six hours meeting with assigned groups both in and out of class, one hour in staff meetings, and the rest in preparation (e.g., reading the text and reading draft student work) and miscellaneous voluntary course activities (e.g., running quiz review sessions, monitoring computer lab work, and sorting and returning student assignments).

Selection and Training

Students who had earned As or high Bs in previous course offerings were invited to apply for open PLA positions. Applicants were screened using both group and individual interviews (Appendix A-4). All PLAs received about ten hours of paid training prior to the start of PAC courses. Additional information is available from the authors (Groccia & Miller, 1996).

■ OUTCOMES

Evaluation Methods

Faculty investigators involved in PAC initiatives were required by the grant to write final reports. Each initiative used assessment tools specific to the discipline and course, but most employed some type of student survey. Learning outcomes in individual initiatives were measured by a variety of tools, including student grades on exams, group project reports, group oral presentations, and homework. In some cases PAC-taught students could be compared to non-PAC students taught in a traditional lecture format by the same professor involved in the PAC course. In comparison studies, every effort was made to minimize differences between comparison and PAC courses so that learning differences could be assessed. The primary question in each project was, "What was the educational impact on students in courses taught in the PAC format?"

Standard WPI course evaluation summaries were analyzed for all individual initiatives. When comparison courses were available, we compared student responses on course evaluations and looked for statistically significant differences. We also compared composite scores of the 14 questions on the evaluation form that are generally taken as indicative of overall student satisfaction with the course and the instructor.

We used the registrar's student record database to determine the impact of PAC courses on student grades in upper-level courses. We also explored the impact of PAC courses on retention and the probability that students would graduate in four years. Our assessment consultant interviewed all faculty involved in Davis-funded initiatives, and conducted a cost-effectiveness analysis of each disciplinary initiative. Details of tools and methodologies have been published (Catterall, 1998; Miller, DiBiasio, Minasian, & Catterall, 1998).

Learning Outcomes

Improved student performance was observed in nearly every initiative. Several implementations resulted in statistically significant gains in student learning compared to traditionally taught courses, as measured on common exams. Based on student performance on tests and assignments, and on student perceptions as reported in surveys, faculty reported improvements in student skills that transcended factual knowledge, such as team skills, ability to find information on their own, oral and written communication, and learning at higher levels of Bloom's taxonomy (Bloom, 1956).

On a more global level, taking a PAC course positively affected GPA in later courses. The database we used contained about 1,200 students in the graduating classes of 1996 and 1997 who had taken between zero and five PAC courses, thus enabling us to do regression analysis of the effects of PAC courses. In the analyses, we controlled for the effects of math SAT score, percentile rank in high school class, and different grading in major departments at WPI. Details of methods and results have been published (Catterall, 1998; Miller et al., 1998). In summary, taking one or more PAC courses resulted in statistically significant ($p<.05$) grade improvement (more As and Bs, fewer failing grades) in later class years, with additional improvement accruing for each additional PAC course taken. Students who took one PAC course in their first academic year had 5% more As and Bs in their second year. Taking one PAC course in the first or second year resulted in 3% more As and Bs in the students' third and fourth years. Results were proportionately better for students who took additional PAC courses.

Taking one PAC course resulted in a dramatic 20% improvement in both retention (measured as completion of the junior year after satisfactory completion of the first year) and four-year graduation rates. It is intriguing and noteworthy that taking one PAC course had a large positive effect on both retention and graduation, and additional PAC courses had no added value with respect to increased retention or graduation rates. One explanation is that taking a single PAC course is sufficient for students to learn teamwork and communication skills that make later courses easier. Another is that taking just one PAC course lets students develop the social support network that is crucial to persistence. Additional analysis is required in order to identify whether particular PAC courses, or particular groups of students are primarily responsible for these results. Self-selection into courses was not a factor because, in most cases, students had no choice of course formats.

Attitude Outcomes

Data from WPI course evaluations and from our own surveys revealed no significant differences in student satisfaction between PAC and traditional modes of teaching. Interpretation of these results should be tempered by the realization that in most cases student satisfaction with both PAC and traditional courses was quite high (around 90% positive). A common theme across initiatives was a tendency for A students to be less satisfied with team-based work than average students, a tendency not uncommon in cooperative learning formats. In general, student satisfaction with PLAs was quite good, and was directly connected to careful selection, proper training, and continuous monitoring of PLAs.

■ PRODUCTIVITY

With course redevelopment efforts prorated over eight course offerings, all science and engineering faculty who implemented Model I reported spending the same or less time teaching in the PAC mode than they had in the traditional lecture mode. Savings in faculty time were attributed primarily to reduced time spent in office-hour, "drop-by," and email consultations. The PLAs handled most student questions, and less faculty intervention was required for group dynamics problems. Other significant savings in faculty time resulted from decreased time preparing and delivering lectures, and decreased time spent in laboratory supervision. Like faculty, TAs spent less time answering student questions. Also, PLA-supervised group projects resulted in fewer and better-quality projects for faculty and TAs to grade. In a case of second-order improvement in productivity, the computer science department was able to allocate one less TA to the PAC course than would normally be the case, and that TA was allocated to assist with other courses.

In general, in the Model II math courses, however, productivity gains realized by reducing lecture time from four sessions per week to three were more than offset by a work load caused by using PLAs. Increased demands on faculty time included meeting weekly with PLAs to ensure that they understood the course content well enough to convey it accurately, and course development activities, such as generating group projects, expanding the syllabus, and creating in-class exercises. Even though the large-class PAC model required more faculty time than the large-class traditional lecture model, it still reduced costs relative to a small class lecture model with which the department had previously experimented. Since improvement of math education was a priority, a return to the traditional (ineffective) large lecture model was not an option.

The use of PLAs allowed the drama professor to accept a greater number of sufficiencies in a term, thus increasing her productivity by an estimated 36%.

Throughout the project, we paid considerable attention to cost effectiveness. A course ingredients survey was developed that allowed an inventory of development and delivery costs of each PAC course and an appropriate traditionally-taught comparison course. The survey included faculty, clerical, and student assistant time, course preparation and PLA training time, office hours, email, and lecture time, and one-time course development and recurring course development time. Costs were associated with each item. All PAC faculty completed the survey and were subsequently interviewed. The details of this process are found in Catterall (1998).

This cost analysis showed us that on average PAC courses cost $5,000-$7,000 more per offering than comparison courses taught without PLAs. The main cost differentials were attributed to $2,400 for PLA salaries and $2,600-$4,600 worth of added faculty time. Cost ranges are reported to account for two different methods of valuing faculty time: a typical salary rate and an average consulting fee rate. The positive cost in faculty salary was surprising since we had expected a net reduction in faculty time. A closer look at the survey results indicated a significant difference in faculty costs by type of implementation model. Faculty teaching Model II (math) courses generally spent more time with PAC course development and maintenance than any other model. When these cases were removed from the analysis, the net additional cost for PAC courses was reduced to $1,000–$2,000. Costs of $2,400 for PLAs were still incurred but $400–$1,400 of faculty time was saved. We attribute the increased faculty time demands in the Model II courses to the following factors. Since math PLAs were called upon to convey course content, they had to be exceptionally well qualified and well prepared with respect to content knowledge. Due to the large number of math courses that utilized PLAs, and to the relatively small number of math majors, the demand for qualified PLAs came close to outstripping the supply. For these two reasons, faculty needed to spend considerable time training and monitoring PLAs on course content.

Linking costs and benefits is problematic and extremely difficult at best. Our project showed that the PAC model resulted in a net increase in costs. However, the PAC model also resulted in significantly improved learning in PAC courses, higher grades earned by PAC-taught students in upper division courses, improved retention and graduation rates, and in some cases reduced faculty time input. Even in Model II math courses where use of the PAC model imposed increased demands on faculty time, the learning gains were such that the mathematical sciences department continues to employ more PLAs than the rest of the campus put together. Faculty time liberated by the delegation of peer-appropriate tasks to PLAs is available for new course development, professional development, and scholarship that ultimately should yield benefits to the department and to the university.

■ SUGGESTIONS FOR REPLICATION

PLAs were essential to the success of the PAC model, and we have identified the following keys to their successful use.

Selection: Look for those students who show potential as facilitators, rather than as group leaders, who are people-oriented, and who are interested in the teaching and learning process.

Training: Plan on spending about ten hours over two days before the course begins, focusing heavily on group facilitation skills.

Support: Provide ongoing support, with a weekly one-hour meeting involving all course staff, and frequent email or face-to-face communication between professor and PLAs.

Course design: Develop the course around carefully structured group tasks that are PLA-appropriate.

PLA recruitment, interviewing, and training are critical, and resources are available from the authors for those who are interested.

Faculty clearly took liberties in adapting the original PAC model to their own courses. Virtually all experienced success, indicating the flexibility of the PAC model. The model could be replicated at any campus where interest in cooperative learning is increasing. The PAC model was designed for first- and second-year courses where large enrollment courses are a norm, but it is very flexible as is demonstrated by the success faculty experienced even when they liberally adapted the model to their own courses.

■ CONCLUSION

Education is a labor-intensive industry that has changed very little in its basic mode of delivery in several centuries. Educational productivity is a controversial topic, but one with which institutions of higher learning must grapple if they are to survive. We have described a model in which productivity is not antithetical to quality. Increased student responsibility for learning, facilitated by caring and competent peers, benefits each participant and the institution as a whole. The PAC model successfully allows the instructor to become the manager of, rather than the lead performer in, the learning process.

■ ACKNOWLEDGMENTS

This work was supported by a grant from the Davis Educational Foundation, established by Stanton and Elisabeth Davis after his retirement as chairman of Shaw's Supermarkets, Inc.

■ REFERENCES

Bloom, B. S. (Ed.). (1956). *Taxonomy of educational objectives.* New York, NY: David McKay.

Catterall, J. S. (1998). A cost-effectiveness model for the assessment of educational productivity. In J. E. Groccia & J. E. Miller (Eds.), *Enhancing productivity: Administrative, instructional, and technological strategies* (pp. 61-84). New Directions for Higher Education, No. 103. San Francisco, CA: Jossey-Bass.

Cooper, J. L., Prescott, S., Cook, L., Smith, L., Mueck, R., & Cuseo, J. (1990). *Cooperative learning and college instruction: Effective use of student teams.* Carson, CA: California State University Foundation.

Davis, P. (1994). Asking good questions about differential equations. *College Mathematics Journal, 25* (5), 395-400.

Demetry, C., & Groccia, J. E. (1997). A comparative assessment of student experiences in two instructional formats in an introductory materials science course. *Journal of Engineering Education, 86* (3), 203-210.

DiBiasio, D., & Groccia, J. E. (1995). Active and cooperative learning in an introductory chemical engineering course. *Proceedings of the Frontiers in Education 25th Annual Conference, Engineering Education for the 21st Century, Institute of Electrical and Electronics Engineering, USA, 2,* 19-22.

Groccia, J. E., & Miller, J. E. (1996). Collegiality in the classroom: The use of peer learning assistants in cooperative learning in introductory biology. *Innovative Higher Education, 21* (2), 87-100.

Hart, F., & Groccia, J. E. (1994). An integrated cooperative learning oriented freshman civil engineering course: Computer analysis in civil engineering. *Proceedings of the 19th International Conference on Improving College Teaching, USA,* 318-327.

Johnson, D. W., & Johnson R. T. (1989). *Cooperation and competition: Theory and research.* Edina, MN: Interaction Book.

Johnson, D. W., Johnson, R. T., & Smith, K. A. (1991). *Active learning: Cooperation in the college classroom.* Edina, MN: Interaction Book.

Miller, J. E., DiBiasio D., Minasian J., & Catterall, J. (1998). *More student learning, less faculty work? The WPI Davis experiment in educational quality and productivity.* Worcester, MA: Worcester Polytechnical Institute, Center for Educational Development. Retrieved May 18, 2000 from the World Wide Web: http://www/wpi.edu/Academics/CED/reports.html#davis

Miller, J. E., & Groccia, J. E. (1997). Are four heads better than one? A comparison of cooperative and traditional teaching formats in an introductory biology course. *Innovative Higher Education, 21* (4), 253-273.

Wills, C., & Finkel, D. (1994). Experience with peer learning in an introductory computer science course. *Computer Science Education, 5* (2), 165-187.

■ AUTHORS

JUDITH E. MILLER is Professor of Biology and Biotechnology and Director of the Center for Educational Development, Technology, and Assessment at Worcester Polytechnic Institute.

DAVID DIBIASIO is Associate Professor of Chemical Engineering at Worcester Polytechnic Institute.

JOHN MINASIAN is Director of the School of Industrial Management at Worcester Polytechnic Institute.

JAMES S. CATTERALL is Professor at the Graduate School of Education and Information Studies at University of California, Los Angeles.

Chapter 9

Students: Managing to Learn
Teachers: Learning to Manage

Martin H. Murray

Freshman engineering students in a course at Queensland University of Technology (QUT) are enjoying their study more, their grades have improved, their attrition from the degree program is reduced, and it is costing less to run the course.

Now, that sounds a little bit like finding the Holy Grail, but it is true, and peer mentoring/learning has been the key. Before describing the peer model that has wrought these apparent wonders, I would like briefly to describe the context in which this model has been applied.

QUT is an inner-city, multicampus university with 35,000 students across all the major disciplines except medicine. The institution has existed in various forms for 150 years. Freshmen are drawn primarily from the state capital Brisbane, with about 50% coming straight from high school.

The four-year professional engineering degree at QUT has a first year, one semester course in engineering science, which is compulsory for the 400 or so freshman students from civil, mechanical, electrical, medical, computing, and avionics engineering. The course is four hours per week and is an introduction to difficult but vital concepts central to the work of professional engineers. Until 1994, it was taught to groups of 80 students using a two-hour lecture repeated six times per week, together with one-hour tutorials (drill-and-practice sessions) taught by graduate students. Failure rates at times exceeded 40% of the class, leading to low student satisfaction, high attrition rates, and pressure to artificially reduce the failure rate by lowering pass marks.

The course was reconstructed starting in 1995, with supplemental instruction (SI) included as a key peer-facilitated scheme for supporting student learning. SI was created at the University of Missouri Kansas City (Martin & Arendale, 1994) in the 1970s and was introduced to QUT in 1992 to help reduce large failure rates in a freshman nursing course. SI has been featured more recently in QUT courses as diverse as architecture, media studies, law, psychology, and information technology; the engineering SI scheme is currently one of the largest and longest standing here.

My role as teacher in the reconstructed course has changed, requiring me to learn how to manage students rather than just lecture to them, and the students have had to adopt a new role in which they manage the new physical and human resources to support their learning.

◼ MODEL

Course Structure

In order to reduce failure rates, address student dissatisfaction, and contain increasing costs, a new approach was needed which would make the students the focus of the learning process rather than the teacher. Figure 9.1 compares the preSI and SI course structures.

Under the preSI system, the two-hour, one-way lecture was the student's primary and sometimes sole contact with the course. Untrained tutors in poorly attended drill-and-practice sessions (tutorials) provided students with minimal interaction with each other. In the SI system, students are surrounded by and work with printed and computer-based resources; their learning has strong support from SI sessions, and from lectures which are now based on a new interactive format (Mazur, 1997). The tutors are trained to make them more sensitive to students' needs. The focus of both students and teacher is now their use of the printed, computer, and human resources to help learn and understand the material. The teacher lecturer now manages and sustains the whole structure.

The study guide mentioned in Figure 9.1(b) is a cheap, 90-page home-grown guide to and supplementation of the commercial textbook, and is an organizer of the semester's study program. Students are exposed to the course content primarily through these printed materials rather than through the new one-hour interactive lectures. The latter are now used for setting the context of content, for exploring concepts, for motivation, for managing the whole structure, and to satisfy students' need for regular contact with the teacher. The computer exercises are proprietary software modules from book publishers mounted with permission on the university's server for free use by students at different points during the semester. The email listserv facility allows the 400 or so students good access to the teacher and to each other; all students automatically receive a copy of anything posted to the listserv by anyone, which includes questions, responses, tidbits of information, etc.

Simply providing students with the various printed and computer resources, and expecting them to use these resources to learn, did not improve students' grades, however, though it did not harm them either (Murray, 1994). It was the progressive inclusion of the SI components in Figure 9.1(b) between 1995 and 1997 that made the new structure a success.

SI leaders are trained to run their sessions first and foremost as opportunities for participants to work cooperatively and to learn from each other, with guidance only from the leader. It is made very clear to students and leaders, and emphasized repeatedly throughout the semester, that leaders are not experts. They are trained to redirect students' questions back to the group, but nevertheless to be aware when the group is missing the point or going off on a tangent. SI sessions are not remedial in nature but are intended to benefit all students. The leaders construct sessions in which the students find the answers from each other, with quicker students both learning and contributing through explaining their ideas to those not quite as quick.

A leader usually commences a session with some friendly chat, then might use a short quiz generated by the leader to review work from the previous week's session with questions framed to start the students participating and debating. The bulk of a session is dependent upon the leader's energy and creativity in constructing enjoyable activities that will drive students to explore concepts rather than numerical problems. Contests based on current TV shows are often the most popular with students, with simple prizes (cheap candy) to stimulate involvement.

In the best SI sessions, the students run the process and the leader appears, to the casual observer, to be just one of the students. It is vital that the students see the leader as a partner and peer, and as one who has experienced the course and conquered it. Leaders act therefore as role models, as good students who can work well with others, and not as all-knowing experts who will correct students' mistakes individually. This is different from the tutorials that are specifically designed to be drill-and-practice periods where students work on weekly textbook problems, and the tutor is very much an expert and a teacher.

Recruiting and Training

I assemble a list of students about to enter their sophomore year who have been identified as high achievers and able to work with others, and offer them the opportunity to be new SI leaders. Those who accept sign contracts (Appendix A-5) and receive training before the academic year commences, and again halfway through the semester. The initial training comprises a full day of

Figure 9.1 (A) PreSI and (B) SI Course Structures

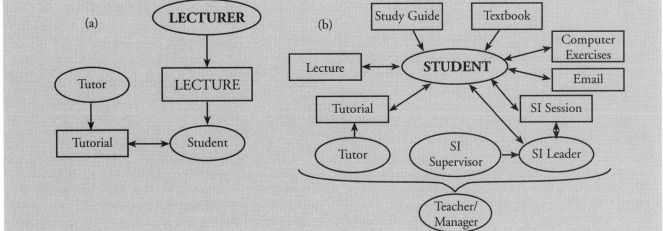

workshops and discussion sessions focusing on the principles of SI; the facilitation, management and motivation of small and large groups; redirecting questions; and creating a friendly atmosphere (Appendix B-1). In the last part of the day, trainees run mock SI sessions in which they practice the skills they've observed. The number of trainees varies from year to year, but is usually around 15 to 20 students, comprising leaders and supervisors.

Each leader is then assigned a group of 25 freshmen for a one-hour session per week throughout the semester; attendance of the freshmen is strongly encouraged, but is nonetheless voluntary. Typically, over 95% of students attend at least one session in a semester, and over 60% attend more than half of the sessions.

Because good facilitation skills are hard to develop, leaders who do not have close regular supervision and feedback tend to drift away from being a collaborating guide toward becoming a teacher. An important innovation in SI at QUT is the use of junior year students who developed well as leaders in the previous year to assist the new leaders in learning how to conduct friendly, productive sessions. These supervisors help train the new leaders and receive training themselves from senior year students who are experienced supervisors. A supervisor acts as guide, mentor, overseer, and helper to three leaders. Supervisors sit in on the sessions, observing the leader, the atmosphere in the session, and the interaction between the students; the extent to which they become involved in running a session depends upon the individual leader and

upon the success or otherwise of a given session. Supervisors conduct a weekly one-hour group meeting with their leaders to review, swap ideas, solve problems, and plan the next sessions. Supervisors all meet together with the teacher for one hour per week for similar reasons, and for reasons of quality assurance.

■ OUTCOMES

Students' responses in surveys about the new structure, and about the SI scheme specifically, have been almost unanimously positive. Table 9.1 summarizes their views on what is useful about SI.

Rows 1 and 2 in Table 9.1 comprise 39% of respondents, and show that a bit over one-third of the students stated SI was best at helping them to grapple with the content of the subject. Only 4% found no use in the SI sessions (row 8).

However, the remaining rows (3-7) in Table 9.1, comprising 57% of respondents, deal with what might be called the human aspects of the scheme. Over half the respondents believed that the aspects of SI most helpful to their studies were those involving the leader and the ways in which the leader constructed the sessions: the atmosphere, the interaction, the cooperative aspects, and the perceived empathy of the leader who is seen as "one of them."

Table 9.1 STUDENTS' VIEWS OF USEFUL ASPECTS OF SI

Most Useful Aspect of SI	Percentage of Respondents
1) Developed greater understanding	21%
2) More helpful than tutorials or lectures	18%
3) Appreciated having a leader of similar age who'd recently done the course	16%
4) Enjoyed the discussion in the session	14%
5) Developed greater confidence in self, to study, and to ask questions	10%
6) Enjoyed the group work	9%
7) Enjoyed the relaxed atmosphere	8%
8) Nothing helpful (i.e., did not attend SI)	4%

Note: Data were taken from students' responses to one question in a survey asking them to "List the thing about SI that you think has been most useful or helpful to you." Each of the responses was found to fit into one of the categories listed. The survey was conducted in class at the end of each semester over a two year period from 1997 to 1999 inclusive; all students were surveyed, with an 85% response rate.

Figure 9.2 EFFECT OF SI ON STUDENTS' FINAL COURSE SCORES

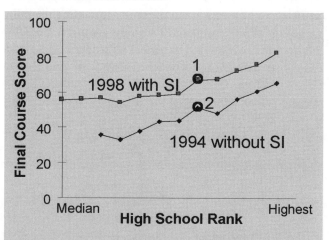

Note: Each point on the graph was obtained by taking the final scores of all freshmen with a particular high school rank in the indicated year, and plotting their mean scores against the associated ranks. Comparisons should be made between the performances of students with an equal high school rank, e.g., comparison between data point "1" from the 1998 data and data point "2" from the 1994 data. The differences between the two years' data for each high school rank are statistically significant at (p≤.01), using a *t*-test analysis.

Affective variables are important, but the effect of SI and the new structure on the students' grades speaks even more strongly to administration. Figure 9.2 shows students' final scores out of 100 in the course, against high school rank from 1994 (before SI was put in place) and 1998 (three years after SI was installed). The frequency, style, and degree of difficulty of grading items were kept as similar as possible in every year from 1994 to 1998. However, in 1994, four different teachers gave parallel lectures to 80 students at a time, but in 1998, only one teacher gave a single lecture to all 400 or so students at once.

Figure 9.2 shows that students' performance in the course was generally higher among those with better high school rankings, as might be expected. However, it also shows that all ranks of students performed significantly better under the new structure with SI included, than without SI. In fact, students with a median level high school rank in 1998 (with SI and the new structure) achieved scores similar to those for students in 1994 with upper level high school ranks (without SI, and under the preSI structure). In addition, course scores improved with more frequent SI attendance (Figure 9.3).

SI also has a significant effect upon attrition rates. A study of 811 freshman engineering students completing the course in 1995 and 1996, and their progression into their sophomore year in 1996 and 1997 respectively, showed that SI attendance was related to improved mean scores and decreased attrition rates (Table 9.2).

Each year, surveys are taken of students' opinions of the program at the beginning of their following semester, after the sobering experience of sitting their examinations (exams in Australia usually occur in the first few weeks immediately following the end of a teaching semester). Table 9.3 shows some results from those surveys. More than half the students nominate the SI scheme as the single component in the program of greatest use to them in their study. The values in Table 9.3 do not reflect the number of students using that component or finding it useful, just the proportion of students nominating that component as "most" useful.

What about the effects of SI on the students themselves? There is a wealth of literature on the contribution of collaborative learning experiences like SI to students' development in many transferable attributes, including teamwork, self-evaluation, motivation, and the like (Kagan, 1994), though no data is available as yet for this engineering course.

For the leaders and supervisors, however, the effect of SI on developing their transferable attributes has been one of the less quantifiable but greatly satisfying outcomes of the scheme. In surveys of SI leaders, they freely comment on how they enjoy their role in conducting SI sessions and the personal development they gain. Surveys of the supervisors on their own role include comments on development of their organizational skills and leadership, self-confidence, sense of professional responsibility,

Table 9.2 EFFECT OF SI ATTENDANCE ON MEAN SCORES AND ATTRITION RATES FOR 811 STUDENTS (1995 AND 1996 COURSE DATA)

SI Attendance	# Students	Mean Final Score	Attrition Rate
Attended at least one SI	691	52	17%
Didn't attend SI	120	42	32%

Table 9.3 MOST USEFUL PROGRAM COMPONENTS

Program Component	Percent Nominating Component Most Useful
Aspects of SI Scheme	53%
Lecture/Lecturer	22%
Textbook	16%
Study Guide	13%
Tutorials/Tutors	9%

Note: Data were tabulated from students' responses to a question, in a survey at commencement of following semester, asking them to nominate "What person/item/thing/session/manner of teaching, was most useful/helpful to you." The total percentage adds up to more than 100% due to some students nominating two components as being of equal "most use."

Figure 9.3 EFFECT OF SI ATTENDANCE ON FINAL COURSE SCORES

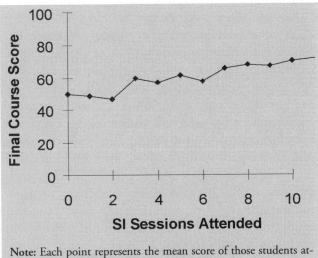

Note: Each point represents the mean score of those students attending a given number of sessions (1998 course data).

and interpersonal skills. These are the ones who become leaders and managers of the annual civil engineering freshman camp, and of undergraduate student bodies on the campus. A more complete discussion is given in Murray (1999).

PRODUCTIVITY

Since there are typically 400 freshman students doing this course, the difference in attrition rates in Table 9.2 means that the SI scheme could influence up to 55 freshmen to continue studying, who might otherwise have not progressed into their sophomore year. Considering the follow-through effect of this number into the junior and senior years of the program, SI has clear and important impacts on funding for departments, whose viability usually depends upon numbers, and retention helps the numbers. The University of Missouri-Kansas City (UMKC) web site (http://www.umkc.edu/cad/si/) has more comprehensive studies of the substantial financial benefits of SI in reducing attrition of students from institutions.

An additional and important outcome is that all these gains have been achieved while reducing the actual cost of providing the course. In 1994, there was a mix of full-time and part-time teachers and tutors; in 1998, there was one full-time teacher with part-time tutors, SI leaders, and supervisors. The simplest way of comparing the real costs of running the course is to assume all teachers/tutors/leaders were part-time in both years, and to use the hourly pay rates of part-time persons to calculate the total cost. In this analysis, the preSI model cost about $33 (in 1998 US$) per enrolled student in 1994, and the SI model about $28 (in 1998 US$) per student in 1998. The savings were obtained by reducing the amount, and therefore, the cost of lecturing hours (tutoring hours remained constant); this more than compensated for the additional cost of the SI scheme. This cost analysis is based on using 12 leaders for one session per week each, plus four supervisors; the leaders were paid $13 per week, the supervisors $20 per week, giving a total of $3,068 (US$) to run the scheme for one 13-week semester.

The SI model has brought a changed role for me as teacher/lecturer, as I have moved from being a knowledge guru to manager of the whole program. This change has meant a reevaluation of my workload as follows. Initial preparation of the study guide required teaching relief from one three-credit course in 1994. Annual editing of the guide takes about one day. Selection and training of new SI leaders and supervisors requires about three days' work over the summer break. I provide a weekly suggestion sheet for the SI sessions, and meet for one hour a week with the supervisors and/or leaders. Combining all these activities means that the ongoing commitment to running the SI scheme is equivalent to about one to two hours per week of formal teaching. Under the SI course structure, however, the students receive only one hour per week of formal lecture instead of two hours per week under the preSI structure, so that the reduction in lecturing load balances much of the increased time in managing the course. The Center for SI (1998) provides a detailed approach to determining establishment and ongoing costs for a new SI scheme in a more traditional North American three credit hour course.

SUGGESTIONS FOR REPLICATION

Reducing teacher driven lecturing and providing, instead, quality resources for learning is something proficient faculty can achieve, particularly with help from instructional designers. Most universities have personnel who can provide advice on the preparation of printed guides. Furthermore, existing guides for correspondence courses can serve as models.

Having decided to begin an SI scheme, it is best to have someone experienced in SI to initially guide and train leaders, and to help oversee operation of the scheme. It is usual for such a person to charge a fee for their services, and this would have to be factored into the initial set up costs in the budget. If SI or a similar peer facilitation scheme already exists at one's institution and funds are very tight, however, it may be that there is a generous "old hand" there who's prepared to help bring a new scheme into existence for the enjoyment of it (such people do exist!).

There is excellent help available through the Center for Academic Development at UMKC where SI originated. This center's web site (http://www.umkc.edu/cad/si/) has a very comprehensive list of publications drawn from the 1,000 or so degree programs in which the scheme has been implemented internationally. In addition, the center has a listserv, accessible through its web site, to which faculty, supervisors, and leaders (both experienced and new to SI) post contributions, questions, and ideas. UMKC also runs comprehensive courses for training faculty in how to train leaders and how to run an SI scheme.

Having obtained support from an experienced person, an inexperienced faculty member can partner with them in the training sessions, and in the meetings during the semester. In this manner, the novice can prepare to run the scheme solo the next time. It is best, however, for the novice to receive training via a three-day SI supervisor workshop available through UMKC.

In case funding is near or at zero, faculty at some institutions have developed ways in which students become SI leaders at no cost (for example through leaders obtaining credit for a course). Some institutions have SI schemes funded by annual sponsorship from private companies.

◼ CONCLUSION

Whichever approach is taken to incorporate SI, the essence and value of a new SI scheme is to start providing students with sessions in which the leader is seen as a peer who will show students how to find the answers among themselves, how to network, and how to study better. Any faculty member who takes this on, however, must understand that it will require both students and teacher to change their roles, as suggested in the title to this chapter: Students will take more responsibility for their own learning, and the teacher will change to be more of a manager of students' learning. But isn't this the better way anyway?

◼ REFERENCES

Center for SI. (1998). *Review of research concerning the effectiveness of SI from the University of Missouri-Kansas City and other institutions from across the United States* [Online]. Available: http://www.umkc.edu/cad/si/sidocs/sipubindex.htm#overview

Kagan, S. (1994). *Cooperative learning.* San Clemente, CA: Kagan Cooperative Learning.

Martin, D.C., & Arendale, D. (Eds.). (1994, Winter). *Supplemental Instruction: Increasing achievement and retention.* New Directions for Teaching and Learning, No. 60. San Francisco, CA: Jossey-Bass.

Mazur, E. (1997). *Peer instruction.* Upper Saddle River, NJ: Prentice Hall.

Murray, M. H. (1994, December). Integrating internal and distance education. *Proceedings of the 6th Annual Conference of the Australian Association of Engineering Education, Sydney, Australia.*

Murray, M. H. (1999, October). Building networks through peer interaction. *ASCE Journal of Professional Issues in Engineering, 125* (4), 1-4.

◼ AUTHOR

MARTIN H. MURRAY is Senior Lecturer and Director of Teaching and Learning in Civil Engineering at Queensland University of Technology, Brisbane, Australia.

Chapter 10

Undergraduates Teaching in a Collaborative Learning Paradigm

Samuel B. Thompson, Sarah B. Westfall, and Christine Reimers

In the fall of 1997, Indiana University initiated a freshman interest groups (FIGs) program with the first cohort entering in fall 1998. A large (36,000 students), residential, public Research I institution, the Bloomington campus of Indiana University received a five-year grant from the Lilly Endowment to increase the retention of students from freshman to sophomore year, and ultimately to improve the university's graduation rate. Sister institutions, including the Universities of Oregon, Washington, and Missouri, have longstanding successful FIG programs. Our goal was to adapt the concept to the Indiana campus.

A FIG is defined as a group of about 20 first-semester students who are coenrolled in three or four courses, usually centered on a theme or topic (e.g., popular culture and the modern age). In most cases, figsters (local campus parlance for these students) live near each other in residence halls. The FIG enables students to establish a close academic and social community within the larger university.

An integral part of the FIG program is the FIG seminar, a required, one-credit pass-fail course designed to help figsters make a successful academic transition to the university. Junior or senior peer instructors (PIs) teach the FIG seminar.

■ MODEL

The FIG seminar includes study skills enhancement and out-of-class experiences designed to acquaint figsters with campus cultural, intellectual, academic, and service resources. PIs are responsible for every aspect of teaching this course—planning and writing syllabi and lesson plans, developing class attendance and evaluation policies, teaching the course, organizing out-of-class experiences, grading students, and serving as role models. They are the instructors of record and have similar administrative responsibilities to graduate teaching assistants and faculty. In addition, they usually reside near their figsters and interact informally with them outside of class.

PIs are selected for proven academic success, leadership potential, and interpersonal skills. An essay-based application, grade transcript review, faculty recommendations, and interviews comprise the selection process. Students must have a junior or senior standing during the semester they teach, must be enrolled full-time, and must have a GPA of 3.0 or above. During the first two years of the program, PIs had group GPAs of 3.54 and 3.76 respectively. PIs receive a stipend of $1,000 during their teaching year ($500 in the fall and $500 in the spring) and receive a single residence hall room as additional compensation.

To prepare PIs for the dual role of peers and instructors, we conduct an intensive leadership seminar on seven Saturdays during spring semester and three days in August before the PIs first teach their course. The entire seminar comprises 41 hours of training that is explicitly learner-centered and aimed toward effective classroom practice.

Traditionally, the principal teaching preparation for university instructors—whether undergraduate teaching interns, graduate students, or faculty—has been their own experience as successful students. Each generation of instructors teaches with the values, norms, and models of the last generation. In an era of greater student diversity and evolving social and economic forces, traditional perspectives and models are increasingly problematic. For those future teachers who do receive formal training in theory and practice of teaching and learning, instruction is usually conducted by faculty within their academic departments, and the focus is on content presentation rather than the learning process. Many faculty initiatives to improve teaching and learning amount to little more than revision of curriculum or presentation methods.

The initial focus of the PI seminar is on the process of learning and how it can be enhanced, something to which all of the PIs can relate due to their full-time undergraduate status. We segue from learning to teaching, with teaching treated as an activity whose purpose is to improve learning. The PI seminar exposes PIs to a critical analysis of traditional pedagogy and to contemporary methods in teaching and learning. Perhaps most important, the seminar is designed to model these methods for PIs and gives them the chance to practice with the methods. PIs do readings on teaching and learning, design lesson plans, teach microlessons to their peers, and design their syllabi during the seminar (Appendix B-2).

An assumption underlying the FIG program is that PIs are most effective if they have full ownership of courses and are not regarded simply as assistants or trainees. The newness of the program and lack of local precedent for working with PIs (as distinct from undergraduate teaching assistants) provides us considerable latitude in allowing PIs to chart their own courses. Our collective experience working with faculty and with undergraduate students guided our decision to conceive of the PI position as autonomous with a high level of responsibility. We trust PIs as colleagues to make decisions even when problems arise. We are available should PIs ask for guidance as they teach, but in each case, we stress that they make final decisions about students in their course.

A cornerstone of the PI seminar is collaboration. The seminar is team-taught and we three carefully plan the content and activities, and at least two of us participate in every session. Therefore, collaboration by their seminar teachers is continuously modeled to the PIs. In contrast to courses taught by a single teacher, PIs note a higher level of organization and efficiency in the seminar. They feel that activities are more consistently on target in meeting student needs and achieving intended goals. By conducting the seminar in this way, we model the strengths of collaboration, including consideration of a broader spectrum of knowledge, values, and perspectives, and accommodation of a broader range of teaching and learning styles.

PIs practice collaboration from the beginning of the seminar, organizing themselves into permanent teams and establishing unique names and identities as they meet seminar requirements. Each session uses collaborative activities, sometimes requiring PIs to work with groups other than their permanent teams. The collaborative spirit proves infectious; PIs have lunch for further discussion after seminar sessions and establish electronic networks for collaboration regarding teaching experiences. The collaborative nature of their training helps them gain confidence, value new ways of teaching and learning, and address the emotive and motivational aspects of collaborative learning that will later inform their own teaching.

A collaborative spirit persists through the teaching semester. A few PIs have team-taught their freshman seminars and found the experience positive. In addition to the required weekly meetings of PIs during the teaching semester, PIs meet voluntarily in small groups. These seem mostly social but also have a support group feel. Two to three comments about teaching issues are posted on a listserv by PIs each week, and PIs share instructional materials and successful activities.

■ OUTCOMES

Impact on Peer Instructors

Originally, we imagined only outcomes for figsters, but we were surprised and gratified by an unexpected transformation in the PIs during their leadership training and their first experiences as teachers.

Outcomes for 21 peer instructors were assessed over a period of nine months via reflective statements, focus groups and questionnaires, weekly meetings during the teaching semester, and continuous informal dialog. Reflective statements provided particularly useful assessments because PIs wrote freely and without prompts about the outcomes most salient in their own minds. The transformation we observed and documented in PIs was independent of their backgrounds or major fields of study.

The collaborative model of the seminar provided PIs with a cohort of trusted colleagues who could help them troubleshoot problematic situations or simply act as sounding boards for new ideas about teaching.

> We have worked well together to help each other reach goals and get work done . . . I usually do not like doing so much group work, but I have actually found it enjoyable through the seminar. I tend to be the one who does all the work, but in my group, I have noticed that this is not the case. Everyone works equally hard at the task put before us, and we all want to do well at what we do as a group. Along with this, I have learned to give up control of the group and let others share in the responsibility. It is a nice change from what I usually encounter in class.

> I've really enjoyed working with the other peer instructors as well. I'm amazed at the thoughtfulness behind the group's critiques . . . . I think it

helps us to feel that we've got a solid support group to which we can turn in times of need.

By the midpoint of the leadership seminar all PIs commented in unstructured reflective statements that they were learning a great deal about teaching, would feel well prepared when they entered their own classrooms, and were enthusiastic and confident about doing so.

For me the most valuable lessons have been those dealing specifically with how to be deliberate in communicating with students... This taught me the important lesson that even those things which I take for granted might tell students something about my attitude. Teachers, because they occupy a position of such authority and potential respect are under the close scrutiny (conscious or subconscious) of their students....

Near the end of the semester, more than half of PIs wrote that their primary teaching focus had been on active engagement of students; making material relevant, and adjusting for learning styles.

In the leadership seminar, students were asked to attend simultaneously to the seminar content and to the teaching and learning processes occurring in the classroom. Unexpectedly, about a quarter of the PIs reported carrying this metacognition outside the FIGs program to apply it in their regular classes. Table 10.1 summarizes PI change in awareness of the pedagogical process.

These PIs wrote that they became more expert as critical consumers of their own education, more aware of how teaching and learning styles affect one another, and more discerning and evaluative of the instructional processes in which their professors engaged or failed to engage students in classrooms. In our conversations with PIs, it was clear to us that the heightened critical consumerism of their own education provided a useful frame of reference for productive reflections on their new roles as teachers.

A second transformation in the PIs was their increased understanding of themselves as learners. PIs wrote of "learning different approaches to studying," and "viewing my worst habits as a student and [being encouraged] to view them as opportunities for change within myself." Table 10.2 summarizes changes in PI learner perspectives.

In helping figsters improve their study skills, PIs improved their own. To the survey item administered toward the end of the teaching semester, "Has being a PI helped you gain more from your academic experience at IU?," 88% of respondents answered yes, 12% not sure, and 0% no.

Third, PIs gained an appreciation and understanding of the value of interpersonal processes to both personal and professional development. To many PIs, these

Table 10.1 CHANGES IN PI VIEWS OF FACULTY ROLES AND RESPONSIBILITIES

PIs were asked:

In your April reflective statements, you mentioned that you'd become more critical of teaching methods in other courses. Has anything more "leaked out" from your teaching this semester? (Asked in November in focus groups)

PIs responded that they:

• Expect more of professors in teaching style, personal attention to students, answering questions

• Notice boring classes and student attention spans, especially during noninvolving lectures

• Wonder about the teaching styles they see, critique them internally

• Critique testing strategies and classroom mechanics

• Are more aware of mixed signals professors send and how they might confuse fellow students

• Notice "wait time" and perceive it more negatively when professors don't give students the chance to answer questions; this is perceived as an incivility

Table 10.2 CHANGES IN PI VIEWS OF THEIR ROLES AND RESPONSIBILITIES AS STUDENTS

PIs were asked:

In April you mentioned that you'd become more sophisticated as students. Has any further sophistication resulted from your teaching this semester? (Asked in November in focus groups)

PIs responded that they:

• Pay more attention to syllabi

• Go to office hours more often

• No longer skip class or arrive late—these are newly perceived as disruptive, embarrassing public actions

• Ask more and better questions in class—do not hesitate to ask "dumb" questions—are more involved in their classes, understand that professors want them to ask questions

• Are more aware of their own behavior in class, and how it might look to the professor

• Hold themselves to higher standards of responsibility to their classes—spend more time evaluating themselves as students

processes seemed a revelation. They most often cited as important the value of peer relations, collaborative approaches to problem solving, and emerging personal friendships. PIs wrote of learning "to give up control," "to think in a different perspective," "to cherish the individuality of others," "of strengths in others I'd like to cultivate in myself," and of "skills with people that are relevant to my life." More than 50% mentioned the value of collegiality or support from peers as among the greatest personal gains from the PI experience. Ninety percent of PIs indicated that increased confidence as teachers and public speakers was an important outcome of the program. PIs also described improvement in leadership, communication, time management, organization, and study skills, and they rated their overall experience as "positive, rewarding, great, valuable."

A fourth benefit was increased feelings of enfranchisement and efficacy. Our confidence and trust in PIs fueled a sense of empowerment that, in turn, induced loyalty to and responsibility toward the institution. More than half of the PIs wrote of the pride they felt in their roles. Late in the teaching semester, feelings of enfranchisement were broader and deeper. PIs spoke of feeling more connected to the institution, more credible as instructors, and more confident and freer in approaching professors and staff members regarding other campus resources.

Enfranchisement was reinforced by a new empathy for faculty. As PIs gained greater awareness of the realities of teaching, the variability and unpredictability of student behavior, and the complexities of logistical and scheduling issues, their comments showed a growing appreciation and respect for faculty. In focus groups during the teaching semester, they spoke of noticing and appreciating syllabi more now that they understood the difficulty of constructing one.

In our observation of and communication with PIs over nine months, we noted significant gains in their knowledge of and enthusiasm for teaching and learning, self-confidence in teaching, recognition of challenges presented by diversity in students, and appreciation of the perspectives of faculty and administrators. Much insight is embodied in their statements, and we clearly saw parallels between them and the most effective faculty we know at the university.

PIs also emerged with feelings of greater enfranchisement within the university community, a greater sense of responsibility for the success of the university's teaching mission, and a greater tolerance of university enterprises that fall short of their own ideals.

We propose that learning-centered seminars such as the leadership seminar will produce a generation of faculty better prepared to deviate from traditional epistemology and adapt to changing challenges of university teaching. Having undergraduates analyze traditional pedagogy and consider contemporary teaching methods, and at a formative stage, may affect them profoundly and permanently. The potential long-term outcomes of such early teacher training do not seem as yet to be fully appreciated.

Impact on Freshmen in FIGs

The 217 figsters entering the university in the first year of our program ranked, on average, significantly lower in percentile of their high school graduating class than the entering freshman class at large. Enrollment in the FIG seminar elevated the average number of credit hours for figsters (15.7) relative to the entering class at large (15.1). Despite these differences, figsters' grade point average at the end of the first semester was 2.76, not significantly different from the freshman class average of 2.84.

As the university's goal for the FIGs program is retention, in assessing outcomes, retention rate is of primary interest. The retention rate of figsters from first to second semester and from first to third semesters did not differ significantly from the freshman class at large (81.6% for figsters and 84% for the freshman class). This result seems particularly encouraging because the figsters were a little weaker than their overall class in criteria used to project academic success, and because institutional research within our university shows that the largest number of students who do not graduate leave between the freshman and sophomore years.

Data from the College Student Experiences Questionnaire (Pace & Kuh, 1998), which was administered to all 217 figsters and a comparison group of nonfigsters, indicate that figsters spend more out-of-class time on academic work than their nonFIG peers—28% of figsters spent 21 hours or more on out-of-class academic work compared to 13.2% of a comparison group of nonfigsters. Fifty-two percent of figsters completed their assigned readings "very often" compared to 45.6% of nonfigsters. Perhaps most compelling, from an institutional perspective, is that figsters had a higher level of overall satisfaction with their experience at the university than nonFIG students—86% of figsters would make the decision to come to Indiana University again, compared to 79% of their nonFIG peers. To the degree that satisfaction enhances retention, students participating in the FIG program may have a higher chance of being retained than their peers.

Table 10.3 summarizes other indications of end of the semester student satisfaction with the FIG seminar and PI performance.

While assessment of the FIG program is extensive, it is important to view these data in the appropriate context: We have solid data but a short history.

■ PRODUCTIVITY

In our view, the cost of preparing undergraduates to be effective classroom teachers is minimal, given what looks like early success in this program. We must stress, of course, that this program is still in its infancy, so future changes may create additional costs.

The overall direct yearly cost of the FIG program at Indiana University ranges from $95,000 to $150,000 as summarized in Table 10.4. This reflects the growth orientation of the grant that funds the program—20 FIGs were offered the first year and the number will increase by ten each year of the grant until a total of 50 FIGs are offered. The costs for other items, such as marketing materials, equipment, and the like will vary, depending upon how a given learning community is funded, where it is situated in the organization, and prevailing costs for computers, labor, and materials.

The benefit that is most difficult to represent quantitatively this early in the program is the financial savings to the university that accrues from retained students. Nearly everyone in higher education understands that it is cheaper

to retain a student than to recruit a new one, to say nothing of lost human potential associated with dropouts.

It is also important to remember that the FIG seminar is a revenue-generating course, just as any other course is. Therefore, any cost benefit analysis must factor into the assessment the additional revenue generated by these added course enrollments. Since campuses differ, a calculation of this kind can be made using local tuition and fee structures.

Finally, and perhaps the most important but impossible outcome to quantify, programs like FIGs tend to develop a significant amount of good will toward the institution and a perception of institutional caring. This can assist with admissions, with residence life occupancy, and with policy makers demanding that undergraduate education receive more attention.

■ SUGGESTIONS FOR REPLICATION

We believe, first of all, that it is essential for faculty developers to be involved in the training of PIs. Those who prepare PIs to teach must be able to act as content experts and model teachers during the seminar, and as teaching consultants throughout the year. The team that designs and teaches the leadership seminar must therefore know the literature about learning and teaching, be experienced classroom teachers, and have the consulting experience that is common in faculty development personnel.

Second, the seminar instructors must do more than just talk about good teaching. They must 1) model teaching strategies for metacognitive discussion, 2) give PIs hands-on practice of being a classroom instructor (e.g., designing lesson plans, developing syllabi, teaching a microlesson and giving feedback), 3) provide consistent feedback and support during the seminar and throughout the PIs' teaching tenure, and 4) be willing to step back and give PIs, autonomy in the classes they teach.

Third, we found that undergraduates, no matter how talented and successful, do not initially expect to be treated as colleagues by faculty. While all of our PIs have risen to the challenge of independent decision-making and appreciate the autonomy over their own courses, this level of responsibility initially produced anxiety in some. We have found it is necessary to anticipate sources of anxiety as PIs move into their new role as university instructors. For example, we found that many PIs initially resisted the instructor label to minimize the risks of alienation from their peers. When considering the use of undergraduates to assist teaching and learning, this resistance should be expected and plans made to help students adjust to their new instructional responsibilities.

Table 10.3 END OF FIG SEMINAR EVALUATION RESULTS

Recommend FIGs to other entering freshmen	80%
FIG helped ease academic transition to the university	77%
Recommend that the PI teach a FIG seminar again	88%
PI covered useful topics in the seminar	80%
PI was easy to approach	89%
PI was well organized and prepared for class	86%
PI presented information in a clear and interesting manner	80%

Table 10.4 FIG COSTS PER ANNUM

Factor	Number of Persons	Amount
Staff Hours	3	500 Hours
PI Compensation	20	$94,000
Copies and Supplies	23	$1,000

Fourth, the emphasis on collaboration in the PI preparation seminar was key to the early success of our program. Collaboration is a hallmark of learning communities, and its high profile in PI preparation led to collaboration among PIs and helped PIs create a collaborative community among figsters in their classes.

Fifth, designing a new program and shepherding it into reality takes more time than putting revisions into place in later years; therefore, expect long hours during program development. We now know that the cost of the first year in terms of hours put in by the authors was much higher than in the subsequent year.

Finally, since a learning community is usually not housed in a department or school, replication of this model requires "buy-in" from important partners on campus, including faculty development offices, powerful departments that provide pan-campus service courses for freshmen, and student services and student advising offices.

■ CONCLUSION

Within the context of the Indiana University FIGs Program, both peer instructors and figsters demonstrated a high level of satisfaction, learning, and growth as a result of their work together. The investment of time, trust, and human and financial resources described herein has the potential to fundamentally change the way new generations of teachers teach.

■ REFERENCE

Pace, C. R., & Kuh, G. D. (1998). *College student experiences questionnaire* (4th ed.). Bloomington, IN: Indiana University, Center for Postsecondary Research and Planning.

■ AUTHORS

SAMUEL B. THOMPSON is an Instructional Consultant with the Freshman Interest Groups Program at Indiana University at Bloomington.

SARAH B. WESTFALL is Director of the Freshman Interest Groups Program and Adjunct Assistant Professor of Higher Education at Indiana University at Bloomington.

CHRISTINE REIMERS is an Instructional Consultant with the Freshman Interest Groups Program at Indiana University at Bloomington.

Chapter 11

Peers at Work:
Tutors at Spelman College

Anne B. Warner and Christine K. Farris

Spelman College, a small, historically Black liberal arts college for women, supports a spectrum of peer tutoring programs. All are predicated upon goals for 1) student-client empowerment for learning, 2) student success and retention, 3) faculty productivity, and 4) enhancement of learning opportunities for undergraduate peer tutors. Each program has training activities designed to meet the needs of each tutor group, and all emphasize the goal of reinforcing and empowering students so that they will be more disciplined and more independent in handling assignments. The peer tutorial programs also feature thorough, ongoing development of the peer tutors as professionals, and extensive efforts to teach undergraduate clients that tutoring is not for deficient students, but instead is an opportunity for all students, from advanced to beginning, to become less dependent learners. Spelman peer tutors and their supervisors try to shape tutoring programs which work toward true, long-term empowerment rather than a quick fix. Every semester at Spelman, about 70 peer tutors assist undergraduates in four main programs:

The Learning Resources Center	10 peer tutors
The Comprehensive Writing Program	10 peer tutors
The Language Laboratory	9 peer tutors
The Freshman Success Program	40 peer tutors

Thus, Spelman College, with a student body of 2,000, supports tutors in a 1:29 ratio of tutors to full-time students. Many student-clients come for their tutorials through the recommendation of faculty, but the majority come on their own initiative.

In the largest program, the Freshman Success Program, the 40 tutors are further divided among the departments of biology, chemistry, computer information science, math, and physics, making no single group of tu-

tors larger than ten. These small groups create a manageable community of peer tutors who can work together, compare notes, and benefit from each other's experiences. Each tutorial group is located within programs that address specific needs of the student-clients, allowing the tutorial group to offer services on a highly accessible small scale and to emphasize the interactive nature of tutorial conferences. Because each is housed separately and has evolved to meet the specific needs of their student-clients, each has a slightly different organization and delivery system. For example, the language laboratory supports language instruction in Spanish, French, and Japanese, and the nine tutors in the lab work with groups of students in each language in a variable schedule to fit peak and slow usage of the language lab. The Comprehensive Writing Program (CWP) employs ten tutors, who staff the center from 10:00 a.m. to 5:00 p.m. one weekday, 10:00 a.m. to 9:00 p.m. on three other weekdays, and 10:00 a.m. to 2:00 p.m. on Friday. The CWP offers student workshops with groups and also one-on-one peer tutorial conferences. The Learning Resources Center is staffed with ten tutors who usually work one-on-one, but can also work with students in the classroom. These peer tutoring programs have existed for at least three years (far longer in CWP), and undergo regular assessment from the various participants in the programs.

■ TWO SPELMAN MODELS

In this description of the peer tutorial programs at Spelman, we will focus on two programs, the Learning Resources Center (LRC) and the CWP in the writing center. Together, they represent one of the newest and one of the oldest peer tutorial programs at Spelman. In our description of these two programs, we will present the structure of the peer tutor program, explain the selection process, examine the training techniques, review tools of assessment, survey the institutional adjustments that resulted from these activities, and make suggestions for those who would like to replicate our programs.

Tutors in the Learning Resources Center: Duties, Selection, and Training

LRC, which has been in operation for more than five years, provides an advisement and tracking program for provisional or probationary students, peer tutorial services, online tutorials, and student workshops on enhancing performance. The ten peer tutors in this program constitute a substantial part of LRC's student-support system. The center was designed through workshops at a Kellogg Foundation Institute. The planner used a number of models, adhering to the standards set out by the National Association of Tutorial Services, and closely following a process-approach model known as The Tutor Cycle (MacDonald, 1994). LRC's tutorial services focus particular attention on the first-year core curriculum, especially the required interdisciplinary course, "The African Diaspora and the World."

LRC tutors follow the tutoring cycle outlined in MacDonald (Table 11.1), but have leeway to adapt the procedure for individual situations.

Empowering student-clients to understand and utilize their dominant learning style is also a goal of LRC. In their training sessions, peer tutors were exposed to various measurements of learning styles, and, in tutoring sessions, they use these instruments to help each student-client

discover her own learning style and the best study strategies to work with that style. In this process, the peer tutor is more a collaborator than a teacher. In fact, in a section on diagnosing student needs in the LRC tutor handbook, tutors are cautioned to "avoid the urge to 'teach'" (Roberts, 1998, p. 9). At the end of each semester, the peer tutors also host "Success Secrets," a session for their student-clients on learning styles and related study habits and strategies. When client activity is low, LRC tutors create "tip sheets" and assist center staff with various tasks.

LRC peer tutors are either nominated by department chairpersons and faculty or invited to self-nominate if they are members of the Honors Program or Alpha Lambda Delta, the first-year honor society. LRC sends a letter to nominated candidates and to members of the Honors Program and Alpha Lambda Delta in the spring for tutoring positions for the following fall. Interested candidates contact LRC to complete the application process. They must complete an application form, provide two letters of recommendation (from their department chair and an instructor in their designated subject), schedule and complete an interview, and submit a one-page essay expressing their interest in becoming a peer tutor. The LRC staff specialist makes selections. However, because the application process is so extensive, most of those who complete it become peer tutors.

LRC requires all peer tutors to attend an intensive, one-day fall workshop, a mid-semester review session, and a January organizational meeting. In addition to an introduction to the routine procedures of the program, students receive training in diagnosis of student learning styles, strategies for textbook reading and analysis, and "The Twelve Steps of the Tutoring Cycle" (MacDonald, 1994). Particular emphasis is placed on the helping relationship of peer tutors, especially in helping the student-client learn how to learn. In the workshop, which is guided by the staff specialist and senior tutors, tutors are shown a 20-minute student-produced video of tutorial situations, along with other videos of model tutorials. The peer tutors receive materials they need in the specially designed LRC tutor handbook. The most extensive workshop segment focuses on collaborative and role playing activities that explore situations in the tutor-student dynamics and train tutors in listening techniques. The training includes a discussion of the effects of disciplinary differences on tutorial activities, an exploration of tutoring ethics, and an introduction to major professional organizations for tutors (the College Reading and Learning Association and the National Tutoring Association). Because of the thorough training agenda, LRC has applied for and received certification for tutoring at Level 1 through the College Reading and

Table 11.1 TUTORING CYCLE USED BY LEARNING RESOURCE TUTORS AT SPELMAN COLLEGE

Beginning Steps	1) Greeting and climate setting
	2) Identification of task
	3) Breaking the task into parts
	4) Identification of thought processes which underlie task
Task Steps	5) Set the agenda for the session
	6) Addressing the task
	7) Tutee summary of content
	8) Tutee summary of underlying process
Closing Steps	9) Confirmation
	10) What next?
	11) Arranging and planning the next session
	12) Closing and goodbye

(From The Master Tutor: A Guidebook for More Effective Tutoring *by Dr. Ross B. MacDonald, copyright 1994. Reprinted by permission of Cambridge Stratford, Ltd.)*

Learning Association. The tutor program certification includes documentation on the amount, duration, modes, and content of training, the required tutoring experience, the selection criteria, and criteria for tutor evaluation.

Tutors in the Comprehensive Writing Program: Duties, Selection, and Training

The comprehensive writing program (CWP) was founded in 1980 as a faculty and student program for writing-across-the-curriculum, as well as a peer tutorial program. A computer classroom was incorporated into the CWP in the 1990s. In 1996, when the program moved into a new facility with two computer classrooms, it expanded to include help with faculty and student multimedia projects and writing technology. After the 1996 move, CWP developed a fuller reporting system for tutors and clients, which produced better reports of peer tutor activities and outcomes. The activities and quality of the CWP program have been sustained with interim leadership during the past two years, which demonstrates the strong foundation and well-established procedures of the program. With a staff of ten peer tutors, each working five hours per week, CWP has sustained its commitment to offering the best possible writing tutorial services to students in all majors.

The overarching commitment of the tutorial program is to empower student-clients as writers and thinkers. In CWP, the tutor-client conference is interactive and emphatically collaborative. Above all, it aims to develop the client's ability to make meaningful decisions about her own work. In sessions, tutors must regularly emphasize that they are neither proofreaders nor teachers; they are agents for student discovery and reflection. As one tutor put it, "I now understand that I must make [the student-clients] work harder to come up with their own ideas. By doing so, I will help them to develop the critical thinking and analytical skills necessary to become better writers."

The design of the center has always functioned to give student-clients respect and privacy and minimize any stigma that may be attached to seeking assistance. The empowerment focus of the writing program provides a collaborative, nonhierarchical environment that reduces the notion that students come to writing tutors for remediation. The openness of the setting and its multiple functions further enhance this goal. In the day, instructors bring their classes to the two computer classrooms for software training, Internet research, and writing sessions. In working with faculty on course design and classroom activity projects that utilize writing technology and multimedia, specially trained student teaching assistants cre-

ate the same interactive, collaborative mode for the faculty. After hours, students come in to attend small evening workshops, use the typewriters for application forms or the computers for homework, or work in the lab under supervision by student monitors. The multiple activities, collaborative modes, and atmosphere of respect for individual skills regardless of position or title, work together to subvert the standard hierarchies.

CWP peer tutors are recruited most often through first-year core instructors who teach writing-intensive courses. The selection process for CWP peer tutors closely resembles the process in LRC. The assistant director requests student nominations, screens applicants, and conducts interviews. Particular attention is given to students who plan to pursue a career in secondary or post-secondary teaching. Ideally, peer tutors represent a variety of majors and student classifications.

Peer tutor training for CWP usually begins in late August with a daylong workshop introducing new peer tutors to practical issues of procedures and scheduling, as well as to various writing pedagogies appropriate for student conferences. Experienced tutors participate as student mentors for this training workshop.

In addition to the presemester workshop, CWP offers a one-credit, pass/fail course for new CWP peer tutors. The course meets twice monthly for two semesters for presentations and discussion of course readings, and ensures ongoing training and interaction of the peer tutors. *The St. Martin's Sourcebook for Writing Tutors* (Murphy & Sherwood, 1995), as well as articles on the writing process, pedagogy, tutorial paradigms, and ethics of the tutorial process constitute the course readings. Among the assignments for the course is the creation of tutor-initiated writing aids which are posted in a rotating file. Course material is adapted to meet the concerns and requests of peer tutors, though there is a consistent emphasis on materials and presentations that will support first-year students in the core course, "The African Diaspora and the World." Students are evaluated on four equally weighted components: development of writing aids, student evaluations, class participation, and a self-assessment essay. In the second semester of this course, tutors have chosen to explore methods of electronic tutoring, using external consultants as well as student assistants in the multimedia program. Though the peer tutors are paid for their student-client conferences, academic credit for their training and preparation has increased their awareness of the intellectual value of their efforts and given incentives for fuller preparation.

Learning Resources Center

For LRC, overall program assessment is multifaceted: The center monitors participation in large student workshops, advising of provisionally admitted and probationary students, and uses of electronic tutorials, as well as keeping monthly totals of initial tutorial registrants. The large student workshops, with multiple faculty and staff presenters, always end with evaluation forms. Peer tutors also participate substantially in the assessment process.

The tutor evaluation and self-assessment tool (TESAT) is a substantive qualitative assessment which offers an informal self-evaluation for tutors in their fulfillment of the 12 steps of the tutoring cycle (MacDonald, 1994). Further assessment of tutors occurs as the peer tutors are tracked through their accomplishments at Spelman. In 1998–1999, all seniors who had been peer tutors graduated with honors, two were inducted into Phi Beta Kappa, some were accepted into Mortar Board, and others received departmental honors. Finally, student-clients fill out an evaluation form on their tutoring session. Reports of client progress are anecdotal, coming mainly from repeat visits. Periodic meetings of the tutors with supervising staff, including a review of all evaluations, also offer opportunities for assessment and revision.

The strengths-weaknesses-opportunities-visions (SWOV) analysis is a substantive assessment measure that offers a broader view of the peer tutorial activities, including tutors' suggestions for revisions in the program. The SWOV analysis has helped LRC identify and correct weaknesses, for example the need to increase subject specialties offered for tutorials, and the need to publicize the center for greater recruitment of student-clients.

The Comprehensive Writing Program

At the conclusion of each semester, the director of the CWP reports student visits to the writing center, log-ons for the computer laboratories, course activities in the computer laboratories, and numbers of students attending the workshops and the peer tutoring conferences. After each peer tutoring conference, tutors create a computer record that includes a description of the student-client and the particular services sought. Tallies of these responses are made each semester to evaluate the amount and kind of services provided and the needs of both students and instructors.

For instance, of the 148 tutor-client conferences in fall 1999, 66% served first-year students, 16% sophomores, 4% juniors, and 11% seniors, and most were from biology, economics, English, political science, and psychology. Of the types of assignments addressed, 71% pertained to course essay assignments. The course-subject areas most frequently addressed were "The African Diaspora and the World" and English. The specific type of tutorial help sought depended on whether the student was developing her draft or revising it (Table 11.2).[1]

Such data allow the program to reflect upon what tutorial skills are in most demand and what subject areas are most important for tutor preparation. In addition, the assistant director may draw some conclusions about the increasing specificity of tasks performed on revisions.

At the end of each semester, peer tutors write about their tutoring experiences, discussing their own learning, self-evaluation of their work and experience, ways to maximize their usefulness, suggestions for program improvement, and views of clients' evaluations of them. These commentaries allow the tutors and their supervisor to examine the relationship between theory and practice. For example, they confirmed the goal of peer tutors learning from the tutoring experience: "Working with other students has influenced the quality of my writing," and, "Each day I learn more about the writing process as I assist students in expressing their ideas clearly and effectively."

Student-client evaluations supply an additional source for assessment. Clients complete a form at the conclusion of a session, giving a numerical rating for their peer tutor's performance and indicating from a list of 20 characteristics those that apply to their tutor. They may also write comments in a free response space. Client satisfaction has been high, with all but a few (five) ratings in

Table 11.2 TYPE OF TUTORIAL HELP STUDENTS SOUGHT

Type of Tutoring Help Sought	Number of Students Who Sought Help	
	Developing a Draft	Revising
Formulating a thesis	25	27
Development of ideas	43	33
Sentence structure	12	14
Paragraph structure	16	23
Essay organization	33	49
Summarizing information	6	13
Analyzing information	7	11
Synthesizing information	10	19

the highest category, and tutor assistance being described as "appropriate," "clear," "effective," and "helpful." The most common descriptions selected for tutors have been "approachable," "good listener," "effective," and "patient." After the assistant director collects and computes scores for each tutor, he incorporates them into the end-of-the-semester tutor evaluations, which become part of the pass/fail scoring for the course.

These multiple assessments provide opportunities for improving both the structure and substance of the tutoring program. Through this feedback, we have adjusted our schedule to meet students' study hours, emphasized our reporting system, changed the course content of the training to meet tutors' requests, improved the communication gaps between supervisor and tutors, and improved our program publicity and recruitment of clients.

Student-Client Empowerment for Learning

The client free-responses in both programs directly express that the college's goal of empowerment was attained: "I feel a lot more confident now." "The tutoring I received from the LRC helped me change my opinion about mathematics and helped improve my grade from a potential C to an A." "The friendliness, concern, and encouragement from the staff make me feel as if I am among people who care." "I was able to see [my] own mistakes after a while."

Enhancement of Undergraduate Peer Tutor Learning

In both LRC and CWP, peer tutors almost invariably communicate that they have gained intellectually and personally from the tutoring experience. Their comments convey the seriousness with which they view their tasks, and their focus for satisfaction covers three main areas: improvement in the tutor's writing or attitude toward writing, confidence about instructional content, and self-knowledge about interpersonal skills. Furthermore, two graduating tutors have been accepted into prestigious PhD programs, one in comparative literature and the other in English. A sophomore tutor has received the prestigious Luard Scholarship for study abroad.

■ PRODUCTIVITY

Usage Rates for LRC and CWP

Both LRC and CWP record the numbers of client visits. LRC recorded an increase in the number of regular student-clients for the peer tutoring program from 33 in fall 1998 to 54 in spring 1999. CWP reflected a decline from fall 1998 (179 client visits) to fall 1999 (148 client visits);

however, the staff believes this shift reflects omissions from the record rather than decreased usage, a belief that helped trigger the current focus on improving record-keeping methods. The records reflect a decline in visits from upperclassmen but an increase in visits from first-year students from 89 in fall 1998 to 98 in fall 1999. These figures were gratifying as they reflect an increase in usage by the target group for retention goals, first-year students. High satisfaction expressed in client evaluations of tutors in both LRC and CWP also reflects the effectiveness of the programs. In CWP, 46% of the visits were return visits, suggesting a substantial success in satisfaction. In the CWP evaluations, which ask for five different ratings, each with the highest score as 1 and the lowest as 5, almost all tutors earned consistent 1 ratings.

Faculty Productivity

Particularly in the first-year writing intensive courses, "The African Diaspora and the World" and "First-Year Composition," faculty are strongly encouraged to refer students in their classes to CWP. When referred students do use CWP, tutors send a memo back to the instructor summarizing what happened in the tutorial. In CWP, the tutor-client conferences that involved memos to instructors amounted to 80 visits or 54% of the total client visits in fall 1999; 49 visits or 61% in spring 1999; and 99 visits or 55% in fall 1998. If each faculty referral consists of one hour of work by a CWP tutor instead of a faculty member, it represents a faculty savings of an average of 76 hours per semester. LRC does not keep records of the specific duration of tutor conferences, so figures are not available for savings in faculty time for repeated visits.

The CWP budget for peer tutor wages covering almost 40 hours per week is approximately $5,000 per year, with most tutors receiving minimum wage for their tutoring activities. To hire a full-time professor to provide the same work might cost $34,000 per year, so this represents substantial monetary savings as well.

Value of Two Spelman Programs, LRC and CWP

An analysis of the overall cost of the peer tutorial programs has shown that the total cost to the program of the peer tutorial sessions is about one-half the cost of similar sessions by full-time faculty, or about one-third, if faculty benefits are added in. Efforts at cost analysis feed vital information into program planning and demonstrate the need to make efficient use of tutor time. The CWP and LRC seek to increase participation from student-clients, to build the programs for maximum impact on the community, and to use resources more efficiently. The very core of these programs, the expressed goals for student-client empowerment and academic success, increased faculty productivity, and enhanced learning for undergraduate peer tutors have been affirmed by our participants and appear well on the way toward being met.

SUGGESTIONS FOR REPLICATION

After working with tutors for a number of years, we have assembled a few practical suggestions for those who might be thinking of creating a peer tutoring program on their campuses.

First, if you are thinking of creating a program on your campus similar to the LRC model with connections to national organizations, we would suggest that you contact The National Tutoring Association and the College Reading and Learning Association. They will provide guidelines on adherence to their instructional methods, ethical standards, training techniques, and assessment procedures. We also suggest that you consult web sites of institutions with outstanding writing centers or peer tutorial activities, both to learn from those sources and to establish links on your web site once you create a program.

Second, since it is important for program statistics to be as comprehensive as possible, we suggest that a procedure for collecting program data be established before tutor training begins. Then, in the training programs, coordinators can discuss the importance of gathering data and train peer tutors to record it accurately. We have found that having tutors record data directly into a computer program is an efficient way to collect data and create reports.

Third, we have found that course credit (pass/fail) and ongoing peer tutor meetings with faculty not only provide support for tutors, but also reinforce the concept that working as a tutor requires a training in methodology and theory and is a serious academic endeavor.

Fourth, we feel that thinking of peer tutors as collaborators or catalysts for student learning (rather than proofreaders, editors, or teachers) is essential for student empowerment and ethical practice.

Fifth, setting up the tutorial facility as part of a larger spectrum of services for students and faculty can reduce the stigma of remediation often associated with such centers. We have also found it helpful to emphasize and repeat the message that tutorial activities are collaborative endeavors, and that these activities are valuable to both tutors and learners at every level.

Sixth, ongoing program evaluation, especially a cost analysis for tutorial sessions, allows the program directors

important insights for program building and planning—particularly for maximizing the use of peer tutors' time through publicity, electronic enhancement, and scheduling.

CONCLUSION

For long-term effectiveness, a peer tutoring program needs to incorporate both engagement and assessment. The center responsible for the peer tutoring program, and the peer tutors in particular, help with the engagement portion by stressing that the tutor-client conference is an intellectual activity, providing a context for ongoing and diverse learning experiences. Successful assessment must be continuous, be established at the outset, and be deeply engrained in the pattern of the tutor-client conference. Then, not only can necessary reports be more easily assembled, but program adjustments can be more effective as they are based on relevant and authentic data. We have found that a center that is successful at engaging clients and assessing the tutoring process is one that can develop and maintain a successful peer tutoring program.

ACKNOWLEDGMENTS

We would like to acknowledge the Kellogg Foundation, the Lilly Foundation, Pew Charitable Trusts, the Mellon and Bush Foundations, Title III, and the Model Institutions for Excellence Program (a program sponsored by NASA and the National Science Foundation). Without their support, Spelman would have been hard-pressed to create the peer tutoring programs described in this chapter. Of equal importance are the many professionals across the Spelman campus and beyond, whose time and expertise were essential in the creation, maintenance, and improvement these peer tutoring programs.

REFERENCES

MacDonald, R. B. (1994). *The master tutor: A guidebook for more effective tutoring.* New York, NY: Cambridge Stratford.

Murphy, C., & Sherwood, S. (1995). *The St. Martin's sourcebook for writing tutors.* New York, NY: St. Martin's.

Roberts, L. (1998). *Learning resources center tutor handbook.* Atlanta, GA: Spelman College. (Available from Lula Roberts, Learning Resources Center, Spelman College, 350 Spelman Lane SW, Box #269, Atlanta, GA 30314-4399)

■ Authors

ANNE B. WARNER is an Associate Professor of English and the Interim Director of the Comprehensive Writing Program at Spelman College.

CHRISTINE K. FARRIS is an Associate Professor of Education and Coordinator of the Learning Resources Center at Spelman College.

■ Endnotes

[1] The evaluation system represents the combined work of Jacqueline Jones Royster, Mary Hocks, and Daniele Bascelli.

Chapter 12

Students Mentoring Students in Portfolio Development

W. Alan Wright and Bruce Barton

Dalhousie University, founded in 1818, is a mid-sized research university in Atlantic Canada. Its vast array of programs attract highly qualified students from across Canada and internationally. Many students are drawn to Dalhousie by the reputation of its professional schools, yet about one half of Dalhousie's 12,000 students enroll in undergraduate programs in either arts and social sciences or science. The initiative described here primarily addresses the needs of liberal arts students.

In 1997, the university president established the ad hoc Transition to Work task force to explore ways of preparing students for life after college. The task force developed the Dalhousie Career Portfolio with three components. Students who elect classes formally designed and designated to develop transferable skills may have those skills recorded in a skills transcript, which complements the traditional academic transcript. In the experiential learning component, students explore career possibilities and acquire workplace skills. The third component consists of an "Introduction to Career Portfolios" course (hereafter referred to as the "portfolio course") and a "Communication, Group Dynamics and Career Development" course (hereafter referred to as the "mentors course"). The portfolio course allows first and second year students to create portfolios with a career orientation. The mentors course affords juniors and seniors the opportunity to learn communication and leadership skills to mentor the students enrolled in the portfolio course, and to create or revise their own portfolios.

A portfolio is a reflective self-portrait of the learner, featuring a narrative introduction to a purposeful collection of student work in written, visual, electronic, musical, or symbolic format. It documents growth and achievement, encourages reflection and self-evaluation, requires the integration of understanding and evidence from a variety of sources, and provides evidence of the process as well as the products of learning (Arter & Spandel, 1992; Gordon, 1994). The career portfolio, distinguished by its focus on career-related skills and experiences, can enhance goal setting, improve academic planning, and encourage career preparation (Knight, 1995; Wright, Knight & Pomerleau, 1999).

The principal designers of the portfolio and mentors courses, Jeanette Hung and Elizabeth Yeo, proposed a model that would promote student buy-in, development of portfolio-writing skills, and adoption of best practices in implementing the concept and assessing the product. Students would receive academic credit for successful completion of the courses. The mentors, once trained in the mentors course, would both coach and act as role models for their junior colleagues in the portfolio course. The senior students, it was hoped, could capitalize on their psychological proximity to the portfolio writers while offering focused, friendly, and informed comment, observation, and advice.

■ MODEL

The model described below has evolved over the academic years 1998-1999 and 1999-2000. In the one-semester portfolio course, students attend four-and-one-half hours of class weekly, including a three-hour lecture by the instructors and a one-and-one-half-hour lab facilitated by the mentors. The lecture component involves the study of a wide range of career development theories, both historical and contemporary, made available in a course pack of readings, and takes the form of presentations and structured discussion. Lab activities facilitate the application of the theoretical knowledge, with specific attention to student portfolios, by such means as structured discussions; skills, interest, and values exercises; a site visit to the Lawson Career Information Centre at Dalhousie University; and a student-organized portfolio conference. The career portfolios produced are evaluated by the professors according to established criteria (Figure 12.1). The mentors do not directly utilize these criteria in their facilitation, however, and participate in the labs as nonjudgmental and supportive advocates. But they are responsible for checking and reporting lab attendance, as well as for verifying that the portfolio writers have done their assignments.

Students in the two-semester mentors course attend four hours of class weekly for the full academic year. In the first semester, three hours weekly are devoted to communication concepts and mentoring skills, and one hour to career development theory. The mentoring students complete or revise their own career portfolios. Instructors consciously model the delivery and facilitation modes that students will be expected to carry into their work as peer mentors. Exercises such as role playing encourage the mentoring students to analyze experiences from beyond the classroom. Models of conflict resolution, e.g., Thomas-Kilmann Conflict Mode Instrument (Thomas, 1976), are explored in relation to potential situations in the portfolio course.

The second semester consists of two hours weekly on group dynamics and leadership skills (Cragan & Wright, 1999), and two hours on preparing for and debriefing the lab facilitation periods. In addition, mentors facilitate the weekly one-and-one-half-hour portfolio course lab, at a ratio of two mentors for up to ten students. The labs are structured as workshops, with distinct introductions, exercises, and debriefing. The mentors establish student groups and maintain productive group dynamics, and they facilitate activities such as composition of personal philosophy statements, role playing, discussion, and self-assessment activities. They act as resources for portfolio preparation, applying the career development theory which they learned in the previous semester and which the portfolio course students are currently studying. Foremost among the peer mentors' acquired skills, and one of the greatest challenges for students accustomed to occupying positions of leadership, is active listening. The mentors receive ongoing feedback from the instructors and from other mentors, who observe lab sessions.

Entrance into the mentors course is by application, submission of letters of reference, and a personal interview. The course attracts students with demonstrated leadership experience, such as work with student governments, community organizations or volunteer agencies, or as research or resident assistants. During the interview, in-

structors look for good communication skills, clear expression of personal reflection, a sense of responsibility, commitment to personal development, and openness to learning about individual and group interaction. There are no specific academic requirements, including prior enrollment in the portfolio course, although the students, by virtue of their leadership aspirations and experience, have generally been strong academically.

Thirty percent of the grade in the mentors course is based upon a detailed self-analysis of the peer mentoring experience. This written analysis must incorporate a formal peer assessment by a lab coleader, feedback from the portfolio course students, and a formal self-assessment. This input must then be interpreted in writing in light of the course readings on interpersonal communication and leadership assessment. Reliable mentoring of the portfolio course students, based on regular attendance and active participation, is a requirement for passing the senior level course.

The academic rigor of the career development theory aspect of both courses is important to the success of the program. We cannot overemphasize the absolute necessity of thorough preparation and training for student mentors. The preparation includes development of knowledge in the area of career orientations as well as knowledge of the communications process.

◼ OUTCOMES

Portfolio Student Outcomes
In March 1999, 39% of the 65 students in the first offering of the portfolio course responded to an anonymous survey investigating student perceptions of organization, content, presentation, rapport, and interaction. The students praised their professors for clarity, enthusiasm, course content, and active learning techniques. Students felt that participation was encouraged and that their questions were taken seriously and answered in a clear and precise manner. Class members appreciated the multiple perspectives to which they were exposed, as well as the opportunities to give and receive feedback.

When asked what they liked best about the course, students identified the production of the portfolio itself, the opportunity for self-reflection and growth, and the interaction with the professors and their peers. The students identified five key skills learned in the class: personal reflection, goal setting, teamwork, effective listening, and time management (Table 12.1).

One student stated that he had learned how to assess himself "in a constructive way" and how to "recognize and

Figure 12.1 PORTFOLIO EVALUATION RUBRIC (HUNG, 1999)

Portfolio Evaluation

	Purpose Statement	Philosophy Statement	1.	2.	3.	4.	5.				Comments
Excellent											
Commentary reflects theoretical application(s).											
Statements reflect in-depth synthesis and foundation for continuing professional development.											
Evidence of gap analysis.											
Commentary reflects new actions/perceptions.											
Continuity between purpose and documentation.											
Consistent quality, aesthetically pleasing.											
Selection of material consistent with stated intent.											
Materials presented in an organized, logical sequence.											
Good											
Evidence of analysis, synthesis (insight into meaning).											
Implies gap analysis and learning/growth needs.											
Some continuity between purpose and documents.											
Some editing needed.											
Some inconsistency with selections and stated intent.											
Approaching excellence.											
Fair											
Reflective comments restricted to descriptions, chronology, labels, etc.											
Gap analysis missing.											
Purpose and documents are inconsistent.											
Draft format.											
Problems with content and presentation.											
Significant gaps.											
Has potential.											
Unacceptable											
Reflection missing.											
No evidence of connection to purpose.											Mark

market" his "skills and interests." The impact of the skills development aspect of the course appears to be significant. One student stated that the course had "made me more in touch with my beliefs, goals, and aspirations and has helped me pick a new career path." Another student wrote that "[I have become] more open. More comfortable. More familiar with myself."

It is difficult to attribute these outcomes directly to the mentoring formula, as mentoring was only one aspect of the course. Class members were asked to comment directly on the mentoring component, however. One student exclaimed, "Mentors were always helpful, down to earth, and prepared for the labs!" The comments of the portfolio course students concerning the student mentors can be grouped as described in Table 12.2.

The portfolio class students identified the mentors class students as providing support for learning through generous feedback and encouragement. They noted that the mentors class students provided clarification of course material by making the theories relevant, providing clear, step-by-step instruction, and expanding on the ideas covered in the lectures. The portfolio class students cited the excellent rapport (mentor/mentee) established by the mentoring students, who provided a comfortable environment for discussion, who treated the portfolio course students as equals, whose close proximity in age contributed to excellent communication, and who "made the

Table 12.1 SKILLS IDENTIFIED BY PORTFOLIO CLASS MEMBERS

Outcome Identified	Percentage of Reporting Students
Personal reflection	74%
Goal setting	32%
Effective listening	21%
Teamwork	11%
Time management	11%

Table 12.2 MENTOR ASSISTANCE IDENTIFIED BY PORTFOLIO CLASS MEMBERS

Nature of Assistance	Percentage of Reporting Students
Support for learning	53%
Clarification of course material	47%
Rapport (Mentor/Mentee)	29%
Leadership and facilitation	24%

labs fun!" And the portfolio class students stressed the leadership and facilitation skills of the mentors class students, describing them as models for decision-making and attributing to them many helpful exercises.

Portfolio course students also had suggestions to improve the labs and the role of the mentors. Some wanted more resources for portfolio creation, and others wanted more lab time. Students wanted the mentors to be very familiar with the material discussed in class, and they wanted to be assured that the mentors had completed their own portfolios (in the second year of this new program this last problem was overcome as the mentors completed their portfolios in the first semester and coached the portfolio class only in the second semester). Some class members had difficulty with the theoretical components of the course, and the open-ended nature of some instructions they received and questions they were asked.

Mentor Results

One of the most useful assessment methods was a structured group interview adapted from a process described by Tiberius (1995). Each spring, the authors met with students enrolled in the mentors course (17/20 in 1999, and 12/14 in 2000). A structured exercise led to the formulation of a ranked list of course strengths and a separate list of suggestions for improvement. The facilitators reported to the instructors, who in turn discussed the findings with the class.

This activity suggested five major conditions leading to positive student learning outcomes.

1) The teachers were seen as knowledgeable, committed, well prepared, interested in developing a strong rapport with the students, and working well together.

2) Students felt that the selection process for the course led to the creation of a community of learners, and to each student feeling important to the functioning of the class.

3) The positive atmosphere, the safe, open environment, the trust and support of the teachers in carrying out their duties as mentors, and even the tradition of a weekly refreshment break contributed to the friendly learning climate.

4) Students reported that writing their own portfolios, and mentoring portfolio students in the labs, represented a golden opportunity to apply the knowledge gained in the mentors course.

5) Finally, students appreciated that the course content gave them the opportunity to develop and practice

leadership skills, to participate in peer learning, and to delve into materials which they judged pertinent.

Mentors' suggestions (from 1999) regarding possible course modifications concerned what they perceived as their lack of authority in the labs they offered. In common with typical comments about regular college course offerings, some students found the course workload unusually high, a few of the readings only marginally useful, and the evaluation scheme somewhat inadequate. In the mentors course, students have more opportunity than they would in a typical undergraduate course to effect changes in policy. This reality should allow the mentors course to evolve in a healthy manner that meets the needs of the students and satisfies the goals set by the instructors. In fact, the focus group conducted with students in April 2000 showed that many of the concerns expressed at the end of the first offering of the mentors course were addressed effectively during the 1999-2000 academic year.

■ PRODUCTIVITY

The initial work to establish the career portfolio program was done by volunteer committee members who added to their workloads as they deliberated, researched, formulated text, made presentations, and wrote reports. University authorities realized that the implementation of the plans, and ensuring the future of the program, would require special funding, so they sought and obtained a significant grant from Human Resource Development Canada. The funds subsidized materials development, instructional costs, support staff, and assessment. Although it may have been possible to introduce a modest version of the portfolio program without external funding, we believe that the project would not have enjoyed its present and projected scope without this financial support. A second grant, from the J. W. McConnell Family Foundation, has been obtained to help support the innovation for an additional two years. Those responsible for the career portfolio activities will seek ways to pursue program activities in anticipation of moving from external funding to regular internal sources of support.

Teaching the portfolio and mentors courses required an extraordinary commitment of instructor time at the development stage. The ongoing offerings also involve a significant effort in terms of class time and preparation, visiting the labs to verify the work of the mentors, offering feedback to mentors, and meeting with the coinstructor. Having both courses taught by the same instructors makes sense because their content is intertwined,

team teaching is a model for team mentoring, workload is shared, and both courses benefit from the strengths of both team members. As the two courses did not belong to any given department, the academic departments providing the teaching personnel needed financial compensation from project funds to cover the costs of hiring replacements.

The student mentoring model was adopted in part because of the educational benefits to the mentors and the mentees, and in part because the alternative of mobilizing full-time faculty to handle all aspects of portfolio development was simply not economically feasible. Without mentors, even at this pilot scale, at least two additional faculty would be needed to guide portfolio development. Alternatively, we estimate that a minimum of three graduate teaching assistants could have replaced the mentors. Even if this expense had been met, however, we are committed to the notion of mentoring as an extension of the undergraduate academic and career preparation experience. Although firm plans have yet to be developed, Dalhousie University is exploring means of adding to its repertoire of courses and noncredit activities designed to develop student skills and abilities in preparation for the world of work and lifelong learning.

The Dalhousie Career Portfolio program is designed to enhance student retention, ability to reflect on academic and career choices, acquisition of transferable skills, self-assessment capacity, and overall satisfaction. All of these potential benefits can have a huge positive impact on productivity, but they will be realized only if the project expands to include more students, and they must be documented by careful assessment over several years.

■ SUGGESTIONS FOR REPLICATION

The use of peer mentors, the growing interest in student portfolio models, and the push to define learning outcomes in terms of transferable skills development all make the Dalhousie initiative attractive to institutions seeking to add value to the educational experience. We can offer the following practical advice to those looking to initiate similar programs.

- Establish a broad-based task force to discuss implementation of career portfolio development, and seek early input from all potential stakeholders.

- Seek early support from academic administrators such as deans and department heads. Include at least one dean on the committee and keep department chairs informed.

- Consider the possibility that providing the teaching resources may be easier if the courses in question have a clear, logical home in an academic department.

- Look to the instructional development center (or committee) on campus for resources. This could take the form of presence on the committee, information on mentoring and portfolio development, active involvement in development, or assistance with assessment.

- Survey faculty to discover who might have already used peer mentoring or student portfolios in their classrooms. Invite them to join the committee or to make presentations on their experiences.

- Seek out expertise in the student services department regarding career development, portfolio writing, and student mentoring.

- Seek early input from the registrar's office and public relations, both of which can help a project to become established. Check on publication deadlines for maximum public exposure and early notice to students.

- Be prepared to patiently explain the peer mentoring concept so that the community supports the project. It will take more discussion and written documentation than you might expect to win support for the project.

- Do not limit mentor selection criteria to past academic performance. Motivation, communication skills, the ability to work well with others, and selflessness are essential qualities not easily reflected in academic transcripts.

- Assume that university teachers require preparation to train student mentors, but also be open to the idea that interested faculty will come from a variety of disciplines.

- If academic credit for portfolio writing and mentoring is not provided, devise some other form of recognition or compensation in order to attract students.

CONCLUSION

The Dalhousie Career Portfolio program has the potential to effect major change in the undergraduate liberal arts program. At the center of this initiative lies the career portfolio, the creation of which the student tackles with the advice of a professor and the guidance of a peer men-

tor. The process can provide major educational and career orientation benefits for both the portfolio writer and the mentor. It eloquently demonstrates the power of peer learning.

ACKNOWLEDGMENTS

The authors acknowledge the developmental and course design efforts of Elizabeth Yeo, Jeanette Hung, and Colleen Hood, regarding the career portfolio courses. We are indebted to Professors Hood, Hung, and Patricia DeMéo for providing us access to their classes. We also thank Professors Hung and DeMéo for their insights into the courses described in this chapter, and Eric McKee (Vice President, Student Services) for his helpful comments.

REFERENCES

Arter, J. A., & Spandel, V. (1992). Using portfolios of student work in instruction and assessment. *Educational Measurement: Issues and Practices, 11* (1), 36-44.

Cragan, J. F., & Wright, D. W. (1999). *Communication in small groups: Theory, process, skills* (5th ed.). Belmont, CA: Wadsworth.

Gordon, R. (1994). Keeping students at the center: Portfolio assessment at the college level. *Journal of Experiential Education, 17* (1), 23-27.

Hung, J. (1999). *Portfolio evaluation: Theory, process, and product* (Course materials). Halifax, Nova Scotia: Dalhousie University.

Knight, P. (1995). *Records of achievement in higher and further education.* Lancaster, UK: The Framework Press.

Tiberius, R. (1995). From shaping performances to dynamic interaction: The quiet revolution in teaching improvement programs. In W. A. Wright and Associates, *Teaching improvement practices: Successful strategies for higher education* (pp. 180-205). Bolton, MA: Anker.

Thomas, K. (1976). Conflict and conflict management. In M. Dunnette (Ed.), *The handbook of industrial and organizational psychology* (pp. 889-931). Chicago, IL: Rand McNally.

Wright, W. A., Knight, P. T., & Pomerleau, N. (1999). Portfolio people: Teaching and learning dossiers and innovation in higher education. *Innovative Higher Education, 24* (2), 89-102.

■ AUTHORS

W. ALAN WRIGHT is Associate Professor and Executive Director of the Office of Instructional Development and Technology at Dalhousie University, Halifax, Nova Scotia.

BRUCE BARTON is Director of Instructional Development Services at the Office of Instructional Development and Technology at Dalhousie University, Halifax, Nova Scotia.

Part II

Undergraduate Students Assisting with Difficult Courses

Chapter 13

The Experimental Study Group: An Alternative First-Year Program at MIT

David Custer and Peter Dourmashkin

A visitor to the Experimental Study Group (ESG) at The Massachusetts Institute of Technology (MIT) gets off the elevator on the sixth floor of building 24, passes through swinging wooden doors and immediately is struck by a most unusual sight (Figure 13.1): a big commons room filled with students clustered together in groups at tables talking together, sleeping on couches, or nosing about the kitchen at the end of the room. In the center is a hammock hanging from pipes. Anyone in this hammock can see what the place is about: first-year students, upper-class folk, graduate students, and staff busy eating, napping, talking, reading, working problems, studying, emailing, teaching, building Lego robots. The place hops!

ESG is an alternative first-year program characterized by small group learning and flexibility in place, pace, emphasis, and style. Approximately 50 first-year students, out of an entering class of 1,100, choose to participate in ESG each year. Additionally, a number of students return as upper-class students to enroll in advanced science courses, humanities courses, and seminars. ESG offers all of MIT's core freshman courses as well as special seminars. Faculty, graduate students, and a selected number of upper-class students who were former ESG first-year students teach these courses. The combination of many levels of learners and teachers in a flexible environment connects first-year students to the academic communities that make up the university. Undergraduate instructors (UGIs) are an important link connecting first-year students to their academic and professional careers, and ESG's success would be impossible without them.

ESG's founder, George Valley, set out to address the high number of students who left technical studies during the first two years of college (Valley, 1974). He also noted that MIT students perceived themselves to lack creativity, aesthetic judgement, and self-reflection, and he identified a variety of factors that promoted this alienation of the best and brightest: rigid syllabi, lack of active student participation, disconnection between the technology curriculum and that in other sciences or the humanities, and the swiftness with which technical knowledge becomes obsolete.

Figure 13.1 FLOOR PLAN OF THE EXPERIMENTAL STUDY GROUP

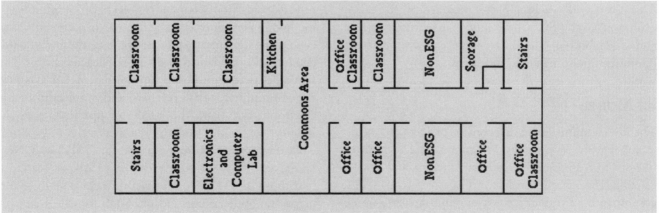

Valley started ESG with the goal of providing an "option for intellectual autonomy" (Valley, 1968, p. 1), and designed it for a category of unconventional, creative students, who might be intellectually stifled by MIT's existing educational program. The goal was to create an educational environment in which the students would control their own education and design a concentrated study program under the auspices of a faculty member, engage in self-study, and attend seminars, lectures, or regular institute courses. Staff would act as "elder learners" (Valley, 1974, p. 17), advising students during biweekly meetings and engaging students in the learning process. Students were expected to acquire the same mastery of basic core concepts as were covered in the traditional curriculum. Responsibility to learn was placed in the learner's hands; staff was on call should assistance be necessary.

The program's first year differed from expectations. Students expressed little interest in traditional core subjects, leaving teaching staff uncertain on how to assist them with nontraditional subjects. Also, students were overwhelmed by their intellectual freedom and only a few highly motivated students were able to pursue advanced topics in an unstructured environment lacking guidance or oversight (Levensky, 1973).

The UGIs were underutilized and faculty were highly critical of the chaotic atmosphere and of students who were perceived as ignoring their studies. Pressure both from within ESG and from MIT administration led to more structure in curriculum design and role of UGIs.

The amount of undergraduate teaching increased in two ways. First, the study of nontraditional subjects was continued as UGI-run seminars. Second, as core science instruction became more formal, staff needed more help with instruction (problem-set grading, problem solving sessions, and tutorials), and all became the responsibility of the UGIs. Soon UGIs moved from running nontraditional seminars to teaching core science courses. Today, UGIs occupy a range of teaching niches from unofficial, unpaid mentor to course designer, teacher, and grader. This diversity of teaching niches provided by 30 years of evolution gives ESG a flexibility that benefits students and UGIs, both of whom have a range of abilities, backgrounds, time constraints, and styles.

■ MODEL

The ESG administrative staff consists of a tenured faculty member who serves as director, an associate administrative director, an associate academic director, and a financial officer/program coordinator. The six academic staff (a combination of regular faculty, emeritus faculty, and lecturers recruited from various MIT departments) teach physics, mathematics, humanities, chemistry, and biology. Administrative staff are also involved in teaching and course innovation.

Most UGIs were ESG first-year students and thus are members of a community in which undergraduate instructors are role models. Prospective UGIs make their intention known just before summer break and go over likely teaching opportunities with a staff member. While there is no formal selection process, UGIs are selected based on academic record, communication skills, and interest in teaching. They can teach a class entirely by themselves, coteach with a staff member, or work with a staff member by leading a problem solving group or grading homework. There are on average about 20 UGIs each term teaching math, physics, chemistry, and biology, supervised by academic staff from that discipline.

Just before the start of the fall semester, UGIs typically attend two meetings, one for all ESG staff and instructors, and one subject specific. These meetings introduce staff and UGIs to each other, allow the dissemination of administrative information, provide an overview of the coming week, and solidify a plan for the coming semester. Often, tentative choices are made concerning textbook and syllabi by the UGIs, with supervision by staff members.

UGIs avoid formal lecturing because such lectures discourage active student participation, require much time to prepare, and are readily available in the regular curriculum at MIT. New UGIs often teach in a manner similar to a conventional recitation; this style is relatively easy because both students and instructors are familiar with it. As UGIs become more experienced, they tend to emphasize the skills and approaches that work best for them, perhaps hands-on projects or modeling how they learned the subject material.

All new UGIs attend the fall ESG teaching seminar. Each week, different teaching concerns are discussed, such as how to structure the class, evaluate and test, communicate difficult concepts, teach problem solving methodologies, encourage active participation in class, encourage students to present work at the blackboard, and improve problematic student-teacher match-ups. The seminar has two purposes: to introduce new UGIs into the community of ESG teachers, and to introduce basic classroom skills and the results of teaching research. Homework for the teaching seminar is the preparation work that new instructors must do for their classes. New UGIs start at $8/hr with raises of $1/hr per year to a maximum of $11/hr for contact time, plus grading and preparation time, minus the four hours for which they get the equivalent of one course of general elective credit toward their undergraduate degree. UGIs average about six to seven hours/week of paid time; 10–11 hours/week total time.

ESG staff members carefully supervise UGIs throughout the semester, approving exam construction and grading procedures and review exam results. Final grades are certified by the UGI and are submitted to the appropriate staff member for review and approval. During finals week, each discipline has staff meetings in which the performances of students are discussed and evaluated together by UGIs and ESG staff.

New students learn about ESG through word-of-mouth recommendations from former students, spring visits, summer mailings, or orientation meetings before September registration. Each fall, approximately 50 first-year students are chosen by lottery from the 60 students who apply. Students can select from all first-year core science and elective subjects but must take at least two of their core subjects within ESG. Often, novel seminars (e.g., robotics, digital electronics design, art of color) are also available. Shortly after students register and form learning groups, a contract is signed between the student, the UGI, and a staff member, explicitly stating material to be covered, required assignments, and exam dates.

Classes meet between one and five hours a week and the structure and purpose of these meetings varies depending on subject and UGI. Class size usually ranges from three to five students; some are one-on-one and some, especially humanities courses (rarely taught by undergraduates), meet in larger sections of up to 15 students. While most classes are taught fully within ESG some subjects, especially sophomore level subjects, are offered as ESG recitation sections within regular MIT lecture formats.

ESG subjects are taught using problem solving methods, and, because of small class size, ESG can provide its students with immediate feedback about their problem solving abilities. ESG officially encourages students to work together on problem sets in the form of "grindstone nights," when ESG provides freshly baked desserts and an instructor in each of the core subjects. Impromptu study groups also coalesce, and students discover that someone at ESG can probably help with any academic question. Time spent in nonclass learning environments makes up a fair portion of the ESG student's learning time.

Ultimately, problem solving ability is tested on written, proctored exams in a fashion comparable with regular curriculum exams. At the end of the semester, a student's test grades, problem set performance, and in-class participation are evaluated to produce a letter grade.

■ OUTCOMES

Impact on Student Performance

First-year students at MIT are assessed on a pass/no pass basis. From 1995-1999, the no pass rate of ESG students was approximately 2%. For the same period, the no pass rate of students in comparable courses (biology, physics, chemistry, and mathematics) in the regular curriculum averaged approximately 12%.

From 1995–1999, the grade point average (GPA) of ESG students (N = 253) during their sophomore year was 4.19 (out of a possible 5.00) while all second year MIT students (N = 5,170) had a GPA of 4.12. Although this difference is not statistically significant, it does suggest that ESG students have no difficulty adapting to the regular curriculum (I. Romano, personal communication, July 25, 1999).

For seniors who received a bachelor of science degree in spring 1999, the average overall grade point average of ESG students (N = 46) was 4.4, while nonESG students (N = 912) had a GPA of 4.3. Once again, ESG students are comparable to nonESG students (I. Romano, personal communication, July 25, 1999).

ESG has been most successful in encouraging students to enter science majors. From the classes of 1992-2003, 34% of ESG students (N = 505) have chosen to major in chemistry, biology, physics, brain and cognitive sciences, earth and planetary science, and mathematics, compared to 25% of all MIT students (N = 10,870).

When some first-year students enter ESG, they are skeptical that UGIs can teach as well the academic staff and faculty teachers. At the end of each semester, all ESG students assess their courses. The qualitative evaluations indicate that ESG students rank their UGIs as those best attuned to their learning needs, and they rate them favorably with respect to both their ESG staff teachers and regular curriculum teachers.

ESG provides a supportive social environment for students who see themselves as alternative in attitudes and lifestyle, facilitating their integration into the greater MIT culture. ESG also provides an academic meshing that international and disabled students find particularly helpful. ESG's ability to deliver individual attention and flexibility in scheduling allows students to match their needs with MIT's demands.

Impact on UGIs

Each year, approximately 20 undergraduates are involved in teaching at ESG. Almost all of these students have indicated that teaching at ESG has enabled them to have a better appreciation and understanding of their other subjects. About 20% of the UGIs spend time immediately after graduation teaching in high schools or special teaching programs.

Impact of ESG upon the Larger Community

ESG has initiated activities to interact with the larger academic community, which in turn has increased MIT acceptance of ESG and has led to adoption of many ESG components. ESG has developed a number of seminars that have been exported to the regular curriculum, resources for traditional core courses, and materials for teacher training workshops for the Department of Physics. ESG students have developed a very popular Lego Robotics Seminar and founded a late night crisis telephone hotline. One of the original founders of ESG initiated an undergraduate research program at MIT. The ESG model for small group learning has been adopted by the Office of Minority Education. In addition, ESG has begun a collaborative institute-wide project to encourage and prepare undergraduate teachers both at MIT and in the wider academic community.

The best measure of ESG's success may be that after 30 years, through good times and bad, through changes in educational philosophy and administrations, the program continues to thrive and to attract students, undergraduate instructors, and professional staff.

■ PRODUCTIVITY

Enrollment at ESG has averaged 50 first-year students and 15 upper-class students for the past five years. The budget for ESG has averaged $425,000 for this same time period. The ESG budget for the fiscal year 2000 is shown in Table 13.1.

Over the past five years, ESG has taught an equivalent of 3,100 credit units per year, corresponding to approximately 260 core science subjects per year. The total budget divided by the number of credit units at ESG has

Table 13.1 ESG BUDGET FISCAL YEAR 2000

Category	Expenditures
Faculty	$48,695
Academic staff	180,516
Graduate student staff	27,272
Student teachers	40,562
Admin. staff with benefits	108,793
Total operating expenses	29,634
Total budget	$435,472

a five-year average of $137/credit unit (H. Sweet, personal communication, November 18, 1999). The biology, physics, chemistry, and mathematics departments at MIT (teaching comparable courses taken by ESG students) averaged $163/credit unit for the same period (L. Snover, personal communication, January 4, 2000). (This figure includes all undergraduate and graduate credit units and there is no standard mechanism for separating strictly teaching costs from other administrative costs. In addition, some faculty salaries are not included in the departmental teaching costs.) Therefore and conservatively, the costs of operating ESG are 16% less than the costs of teaching the standard MIT curriculum.

The 2% failure/no pass rate of ESG students corresponds to 60 credit units. This means that on average it costs approximately $8,000 dollars to teach those students who need to repeat a subject at ESG. The 12% failure/no pass rate (about 370 credit units) for the core biology, physics, chemistry, and mathematics subjects in the regular curriculum equals an additional cost of about $60,000 (this number was calculated by using the regular curriculum failure/no pass rate of 12% on ESG's total credit units. The total cost was determined using the regular curriculum cost per credit unit).

UGIs are paid on average between $10 and $12/hour based on their teaching experience. Graduate TAs (nonstaff) are paid $15/hour. Over the past five years, faculty and academic staff account for about 50% of the teaching, graduate TAs 20%, and UGIs the remaining 30%. The teaching budget costs are as follows: faculty 15%, academic staff 60%, graduate TAs 15%, and UGIs 10%. Undergraduate teachers are cost effective.

This analysis shows ESG compares favorably in cost to the regular curriculum, primarily due to the use of UGIs rather than graduate instructors or faculty, even though the ESG teacher-student ratio is substantially lower than the regular curriculum.

■ SUGGESTIONS FOR REPLICATION

One key to ESG's success has been its ability to create a unique academic community that is not isolated from the parent institution. Other key elements of ESG's effectiveness have been the commitment of the School of Science to support the program, a large physical space for both academic and nonacademic community activities, a dedicated teaching staff consisting of faculty, academic staff, and undergraduate teachers, an interested undergraduate student body, and a supportive administrative staff. It is recommend to those interested in replicating this type of program that they make sure these support pillars are in place.

Preliminary steps in creating a program similar to ESG might include identifying a core student base with specific educational objectives to generate support for the start-up, secure an institutional commitment for an initial development phase that should last at least three years, create an effective faculty advisory/oversight committee to evaluate the program's successes and failures, build in flexibility to adapt to any unanticipated developments, secure sufficient funding to ensure that instructors are not overloaded, and pursue external funding from alumni and grants to support continued development of new courses and educational initiatives.

The program should be centrally located on campus, making it easily accessible. The physical plant contributes to the viability of the program and sufficient space should be available to serve a multitude of roles: communal space, academic space, libraries or reading rooms, computer rooms, and a kitchen. The physical space was designed to create an open community where student, instructor, and staff interaction is encouraged. If a new program is fitted into a preexisting space, effort should be made to ensure that the architectural constraints do not overwhelm the program.

To ensure program success and continuity, an active director to serve as an effective advocate is essential. This individual must publicize the purpose and effectiveness of the program to counterbalance potentially negative community perceptions of alternative, nontraditional, or unsuccessful students.

An alternative program that relies on peer learning such as ESG must create an attractive environment supporting students during the ups and downs of first-year adjustments to college. It must develop techniques for creating a sense of community and participation for new students at the very start of the academic year to connect immediately with those students who may only marginally participate. Activities to emphasize community responsibility and generate an inclusive social environment are essential.

The hardest part of establishing and maintaining a new program is attracting a dedicated teaching staff which may include individuals who do not follow traditional academic career tracks. Such programs do not need to have tenured faculty but they do need to maintain continuity. Teachers can be drawn from a variety of sources: retired professors, new PhDs, graduate students, and undergraduates. The program continually and actively needs to recruit UGIs, for while students enjoy teaching, they often will do so for only one or two years. Because of the constant influx of new teaching staff, the program must establish training programs. The teaching staff and UGIs must be committed to developing new educational initiatives and fine-tuning the methods of teaching to changing student needs.

◼ CONCLUSION

ESG serves many different functions for its parent institution: providing alternative learning methods for first-year students who may not function well in the regular curriculum, providing an opportunity for undergraduates to teach, and providing a place for experimentation with new teaching/learning techniques. The collective experience of the ESG community has given birth to an ESG culture, a diverse group of individuals who are united by a vision of open-mindedness and an eclectic range of intellectual interests, that continues to evolve and grow.

◼ REFERENCES

Levensky, M. (1973). The Experimental Study Group: A new undergraduate program at MIT. *Interchange, 4* (1), 49-63.

Valley, G. (1968). *An option for intellectual autonomy.* Unpublished manuscript, Massachusetts Institute of Technology, Cambridge.

Valley, G. (1974). *My years in the MIT Experimental Study Group: Some old facts and new myths.* Unpublished manuscript, Massachusetts Institute of Technology, Cambridge.

Watkins, C. (1999). *Teaching at ESG* [Online]. Available: http://web.mit.edu/esg/www/teaching/main.html

◼ AUTHORS

DAVID CUSTER has been at ESG since his first undergraduate year at MIT, where he now teaches for both the Experimental Study Group and the Writing and Humanistic Studies Program.

PETER DOURMASHKIN is a lecturer in the Department of Physics and the Integrated Studies Program, and is the Associate Academic Director of the Experimental Study Group at MIT.

Chapter 14

MASH (Math and Science Help): Supplemental Instruction at a Technical University

Ann Garvin and Dale Snyder

Worcester Polytechnic Institute (WPI) is the nation's third oldest private engineering college, and was established by New England industrialists in 1865 to create and convey the latest science and engineering knowledge in ways that would be useful to society. In 1970, WPI adopted a revolutionary new undergraduate project program known as the WPI Plan. The plan replaced the conventional, rigidly-prescribed engineering curriculum with a flexible and academically challenging program aimed at helping students learn how to learn. The heart of the plan is a projects program that prepares graduates for their future professional lives by helping them learn how to identify, investigate, and report on open-ended problems. Students must complete three projects to graduate: a major qualifying project to solve problems typical of those to be encountered in their disciplines, an interactive qualifying project that integrates science, technology, and culture, and a sufficiency that integrates humanities or arts courses.

The current undergraduate enrollment of 2,700 includes students from 44 states and 64 nations. The typical student is in the top 20% of his or her high school class and the average SAT composite score is 1280 (620 verbal, 660 math). These students do not need remedial courses, but many need help with study skills and self-discipline, as we discovered when a significant number of these good students began failing first-year courses.

In the fall of 1987, we enrolled the "best class we've ever admitted to WPI," according to the director of admissions. Class ranks and SAT scores indicated that this class was significantly better than previous ones. So, we were shocked when this class doubled previous failure rates in the first-year courses of calculus, physics, and chemistry. At WPI, these courses are the building blocks for engineering, not weed-out courses, and, with our admissions procedures, every student admitted should suc-

ceed in them. We researched the problem, conducted interviews with students, and concluded that the students were indeed very bright, but were coming with underdeveloped study habits because they had not had to work hard in high school.

Our research for a solution to students' underdeveloped study skills led us to supplemental instruction (SI), developed by the University of Missouri-Kansas City. We developed our version of SI from the UMKC model more than a decade ago, and called it MASH, for Math and Science Help, because we thought the name would generate more attention and be easier to sell than "SI." Like SI at UMKC and hundreds of institutions, the program effectively fills the gaps for new students until they develop good study habits and group support. One difference is that MASH is available to every student enrolled in calculus I and II, physics I and II, and chemistry I and II. By applying support services to all students in "killer courses," we could reach students who needed help, but without labeling anyone as at-risk or offering remedial courses.

■ MODEL

MASH leaders are the key to the success of the program. New leaders are recruited from the undergraduate student population near the end of each academic year. The selection process is highly competitive, and consists of a written application, transcript submission, and an interview with the program supervisor. Finally, to certify the student's skill in subject content, approval of the respective departments is required. We have five leaders each for chemistry and physics, and six for mathematics, for a total of 16 leaders per year. Leaders not only need superior academic records, but also must have outgoing personalities, good communication skills, and positive attitudes toward WPI and the MASH program.

The MASH leader-training program is internationally certified by the College Reading and Learning Association.[1] The purpose of having a certified training program is twofold. First, it provides outside recognition and reinforcement for the MASH leaders' successful work; second, certification ensures that all MASH leaders have met the same standard of skill level and training. Training lasts one full day in August, just before the first term begins. Much of the training focuses on proper study skills and work habits, information which leaders pass to freshmen during MASH sessions. MASH leaders also learn how to integrate study skills with course content and practice the instructional strategies they will use in MASH sessions. Leaders receive handbooks with information on responsibilities, instructional strategies, and tips for conducting successful MASH sessions. Training also includes meeting with faculty for content-specific training.

Each leader is responsible for holding at least three MASH sessions per week. Before each exam, MASH leaders usually conduct Mega-MASH sessions, which consist of all MASH leaders for a subject running a two- or even three-hour review session.

The leaders coordinate the timing of the sessions, so that they are held at various times during the day and are available to as many students as possible. We have found that evening sessions, even as late as 10 p.m. or 11 p.m. are the most popular since most freshmen live on campus. This year, MASH leaders were paired with peer tutors from the new Academic Resources Center. This pairing was a welcome addition because MASH leaders were able to refer students who were struggling with course content to peer tutors for more individualized assistance. Moreover, peer tutors were also available to help leaders with MASH sessions, especially at the end of the term when attendance significantly increased with the approach of final exams.

The typical MASH session starts with a student asking a question about how to do a particular homework problem. The MASH leader responds by asking a group of students to work through the problem together. By having students work together on the problems, the leader can provide problem solving strategies, rather than answers. The students learn by doing and by helping each other, the goal of student assisted learning. The leader also models good student behavior by giving messages such as, "When I took this course I found it helpful to . . ." or "You'd find these sessions more helpful if you did the homework problems before coming to the session."

Because the subjects of calculus, physics, and chemistry require problem solving, most MASH sessions center on homework problems. The leader's main role is to provide structure to the study session; she or he is a facilitator, not a miniprofessor. Leaders are instructed not to lecture or to introduce new material, but to facilitate a collaborative learning environment. Leaders focus on process as well as content and integrate learning and study strategies (organization, note taking, test preparation) into course content, thereby providing immediate practice and reinforcement of academic skills. See Figure 14.1 for a complete list of MASH leaders' responsibilities.

In addition to presemester training, MASH leaders meet with their supervisors and the other MASH leaders in a large group meeting at least twice per term. These meetings tend to focus on problems that occur during the MASH sessions and brainstorming how to deal with the problems. Sharing of success stories occurs as well. Supervisors also schedule individual meetings with leaders to address specific concerns or problems, and follow up with observations of sessions as needed.

As soon as they arrive at WPI, freshmen begin to hear about the MASH program. A flyer is given to all new students and MASH leaders who take part in new student orientation. During orientation and the first MASH sessions, leaders wear special T-shirts and distribute ball-

Figure 14.1 MASH LEADERS' RESPONSIBILITIES

MASH leaders must:

- attend training sessions prior to the beginning of the academic year.
- attend all class meetings (except labs) of their assigned course. They must take notes, read selected material, and do assigned problems.
- attend all scheduled meetings with the supervisor and fellow MASH leaders.
- meet with faculty as needed.
- conduct at least three 50-minute sessions a week throughout the term.
- provide supplemental one-on-one tutoring and extra MASH sessions as needed.
- collect attendance data for all sessions and turn in the sheets to the supervisor.
- administer surveys in their assigned courses at the end of each term
- prepare handouts for study sessions as necessary.
- assist the supervisor with end-of-term surveys and other reports as needed.

point pens and miniature highlighters. MASH schedules are distributed in each class during the first few days and are posted on the campus web site.

■ OUTCOMES

After more than ten years of operation at WPI, MASH has been integrated into our campus culture. Faculty incorporate MASH schedules in their course web pages. The new faculty orientation contains information about MASH and why a MASH leader might be part of a course. Resident advisors post MASH schedules in the resident halls. Parents are aware of the program and encourage their sons and daughters to attend sessions. MASH has been widely recognized as an effective and indispensable student study aid.

Because courses supported by MASH are fundamental freshman courses, the program is a powerful retention service. MASH encourages teamwork among students while developing critical thinking, problem solving, and discussion skills. Our retention rates are impressive: 91% of last year's freshmen returned for the sophomore year, compared with 85% before MASH was introduced. The MASH program is considered a critical element in this success.

The program is continually evaluated using some of UMKC's methodology for SI evaluation (Arendale & Martin, 1998). MASH leaders keep attendance sheets, and at the end of the term, comparisons are made between grades of those who attend MASH sessions and those who do not. Surveys are distributed at the end of the term and students are asked to comment on the effectiveness of the MASH program if they attended, or to indicate why they chose not to attend (Appendix D-5). The research includes anticipated grades as self-reported by the students, which are then compared to the actual grades. Over the years, WPI has shown similar benefits for the MASH program as UMKC has for their SI program (Martin & Arendale, 1994).

We have determined that MASH attendance increases the course grade by about half of a letter grade. The chart below is an example of this effect. In a "Calculus I" course, which was taught in fall 1999 to198 students, exactly one-half (99) attended at least one MASH session and one-half did not attend any sessions. Grades for each group illustrate the effect of MASH sessions (Table 14.1). The "Calculus I" GPA for MASH attendees was 2.55, while nonattendees' GPA was 2.13, for a difference of .42 or almost half of a letter grade. (For this analysis, GPA was calculated as 4.0 for A, 3.0 for B, 2.0 for C. and 1.0 for D/F.) This effect on GPA is a conser-

vative assessment since an attendee is defined as being a student who has attended only one session. We have found consistent results each time we have conducted similar studies over the last decade.

Several factors have been credited with MASH's effectiveness in influencing higher levels of student academic performance.

- MASH is not a remedial program. It is open to any student who wants to perform better and is available in math and science courses that are critical to first-year success.

- MASH schedules are set during the first week of class, allowing students to obtain assistance before they encounter serious academic difficulty. This is especially important at WPI since our terms are only seven weeks long.

- MASH sessions are widely available, both in location and time of day offered.

- MASH leaders attend class and therefore stay current on course content.

- MASH promotes a high degree of student interaction that leads to formation of peer study groups, a concept which students continue to utilize throughout their four years at WPI.

Current MASH leaders were surveyed regarding the importance of the program at WPI and the rewards they receive as MASH leaders. The leaders' views can be divided into three categories. First is the opportunity—for both undergraduates and themselves—to extensively review the basic material and clarify what was learned in previous classes. The manner in which this is done, explaining material to others, forces a better understanding of that material. Second is the personal gratification from

Table 14.1 COMPARISON OF AVERAGE GRADES FOR CALCULUS I STUDENTS WHO DID AND DID NOT ATTEND MASH SESSIONS IN FALL 1999.

	MASH Attendees (n = 99)	Nonattendees (n = 99)
Grade of A	18	8
Grade of B	35	24
Grade of C	30	37
Grade of D/F*	16	30

*WPI groups D and F together and calls them "NR," as they are not recorded on the transcript.

helping other students and knowing they have made a difference for other students. Being thanked for helping is a reward as well. Finally, because of the nature of the job, MASH leaders have the opportunity to build closer relationships with faculty, improve their own communication skills, and test teaching as a career option.

The success of the MASH program depends in large measure on our special students, the MASH leaders. Being a MASH leader is considered one of the best jobs at WPI and only the top students are selected. Over the years, about 80% of the leaders have gone on to graduate work at such universities as Stanford, Brown, Cornell, MIT, and Boston University. They report that they are often tapped to teach freshmen courses during the first year of graduate work because of their MASH experience. Of the nearly 150 graduates who have served as MASH leaders, a large number have entered the teaching profession at all levels. We have observed that MASH has helped leaders develop confidence and leadership abilities.

Faculty surveys show us that MASH receives strong faculty support. They view it as a resource for faculty as well as students because they know that without MASH, not only would student performance be lower, but also, more students would be seeking their help. Faculty understand and support the group approach in the sessions and view MASH leaders as good role models for freshmen. For these reasons, many have enthusiastically taken on the role of mentoring MASH leaders.

■ PRODUCTIVITY

The original budget for MASH, developed in 1988, was $20,000 to support 22 leaders for the first two seven-week terms. Over the years, the budget has increased to

$24,000 and supports 16 leaders for the first two terms and 10-12 leaders for the third term. If faculty identify a need for the program to continue (i.e., lower than expected performance in the third term), the administration funds the program for a fourth term. About $1,000 per year is spent for supplies, primarily printing, advertising, duplicating, and books. The remaining $23,000 is spent for salaries, with beginning leaders receiving $5.25 per hour or $735 per semester, and returning leaders receiving yearly raises.

The MASH program is cost effective by several measures. Out of a total of approximately 675 freshman, at least 400, or 59%, attend MASH sessions during the first term, 400 during the second term, and 200 during the third term. This means that MASH leaders help a total of 1,000 students per year. (Some students attend MASH sessions for multiple terms, so the total number of students helped exceeds the freshman population.) Since our budget is $24,000, the total cost of helping each of the 1,000 students is $24. To put this figure in perspective, we received a report from UMKC in 1994, in which the budget for their SI program was reported at $58,800 and 1,287 students were served for a cost of $45.69 per student (Martin & Arendale, 1994). (Both UMKC and WPI calculate usage in the same way.) Another way to look at cost effectiveness is to compare costs with course failure numbers. With tuition of over $20,000 (not including room and board), WPI stands to lose $20,000 per student

Figure 14.2 PRODUCTIVITY EXAMPLE #1 FROM A FRESHMAN CALCULUS CLASS

Jon (not his real name), a sophomore math major, was assigned as leader for "Calculus II" during the second term. Jon ran 20 MASH sessions during the seven-week term for a total of 74 students. Of these, 43 attended more than one MASH session and were Jon's "regulars."

Jon was paid $367.50 during this term, and the productivity can be calculated as follows: Each session cost $18.38, so Jon helped 43 students at a cost of $8.55 each. For those 43 students, grades were distributed as follows: 12 (28%) received A; 15 (35%) received B, 11 (25%) received C; and 5 (12%) received D/F (both are failing grades at WPI). The D/F rate for the class as a whole was 24%; thus the failure rate for Jon's students was exactly one-half that of the class as a whole.

Figure 14.3 PRODUCTIVITY EXAMPLE #2 FROM A SOPHOMORE CHEMISTRY COURSE

"Organic Chemistry" is a sophomore course with a high failure rate and little student support. At the request of the department, MASH was offered to students, with Beth (not her real name), a senior chemistry major, as leader.

End-of-term surveys were filled out by only 39 of the 68 students in the class, but of the 39 students, 22 had attended MASH sessions. All 22 knew Beth's name, an indication that some good interaction took place in the sessions. On a 1 to 5 scale (with 5 as top); all 22 gave a 4 or 5 for both Beth as a leader and for the helpfulness of the sessions. When asked how many sessions they attended, seven had attended one to two sessions, 11 had attended three to ten sessions, and four had attended more than ten sessions. Six students indicated that they might fail the course; in reality, five of the six passed.

Beth was paid $437.50 for seven weeks of work at ten hours per week. She ran three help sessions per week, attended all lectures, and prepared for her sessions. It cost WPI $21.88 for each session, or $19.87 for each of the 22 students she helped who also filled out the survey.

who drops out of school. MASH leaders need to help retain only 1.2 students in order to pay for the program. Two MASH leaders were selected for a closer analysis of productivity (Figures 14.2 and 14.3).

■ SUGGESTIONS FOR REPLICATION

Our number one suggestion to any institution considering implementing a program similar to MASH is to contact UMKC Center for Academic Development to learn more about their SI program (www.umkc.edu/cad/si). They provide workshops and training material for supervisors as well as ongoing support to institutions. This model was created in 1973 at UMKC and they have an US Department of Education grant for dissemination of the model to institutions across the nation. The small fee for attending the workshop is well worth the investment.

Second, we would recommend careful planning to determine projected costs. The institution will need to determine if new or existing personnel will supervise the program, whether the supervisor will need assistance, and how leaders will be compensated, among other considerations. At WPI, we use the work-study model and pay the leaders minimum wage for ten hours of work per week.

Third, identifying the courses to support is critical. Criteria we used and recommend are to target 1) courses with more than 30% D/F grades, 2) large courses that are taught in a lecture format with little opportunity for student questions, or 3) "gatekeeper" courses that must be passed in order to progress in an academic degree program.

Fourth, faculty who teach the targeted courses need to be supportive and involved. One way to get support is to have faculty evaluate tentative leaders for content knowledge and train leaders who will be working with students in their course. Faculty should not receive information about who attends sessions because attendance or nonattendance should not be a factor in grading. Students should be free to attend or not attend as they see fit.

Finally, the program should avoid being viewed as remedial and students should not receive extra credit for attending sessions. The incentive for participation should be increased academic performance. The way we do that at WPI is that the MASH leaders create a friendly, helpful environment where students feel comfortable asking questions and obtaining help.

■ CONCLUSION

The goals of WPI's MASH program include the improvement of student course grades, reduction of attrition rates in traditionally difficult courses, and student persistence toward graduation. We accomplish these goals by using collaborative learning to integrate learning and reasoning skill development with a review of course content. There is no remedial stigma attached to MASH since high-risk courses (i.e., calculus, chemistry, and physics) rather than high-risk students are targeted. While MASH does not meet every student's needs, it is an academic assistance system that is flexible enough to meet the needs of many.

■ REFERENCES

Arendale, D., & Martin, D. C. (1998). *Review of research concerning the effectiveness of supplemental instruction from the University of Missouri-Kansas City and other institutions* [Online]. Available: http://www.umkc.edu/cad/si/sidocs/sidata97.htm

Martin, D. C., & Arendale, D. (1994, January). *Review of research concerning the effectiveness of SI from the University of Missouri-Kansas City and other institutions from across the United States.* Paper presented at the annual conference of the Freshman Year Experience, Columbia, SC. (ERIC Document Reproductive Service No. ED 370 502)

■ AUTHORS

ANN GARVIN is the Director of Academic Advising at Worcester Polytechnic Institute.

DALE SNYDER is the Director of the Academic Resources Center at Worcester Polytechnic Institute.

■ ENDNOTES

[1] For more information, please contact CRLA International Tutor Certification Program, University of Texas at El Paso, Tutor and Learning Center, 300 Library, El Paso, TX 79968.

Chapter 15

Undergraduate Peer Mentors
in Mathematics

Miguel Paredes, Paul Pontius, Rene Torres, and Joseph Chance

The University of Texas-Pan American (UTPA) is a public, coeducational, comprehensive institution located in Edinburg, Texas, near the Mexican border. The name reflects both the institution's position as a bridge between the cultures of North and South America and the cultural and ethnic diversity of the region. Beginning as a two-year community college, the institution grew steadily and, in 1989, merged with The University of Texas system. UTPA has one of the largest enrollments of Hispanic students among four-year colleges and universities in the United States: about 86% of the 12,500 undergraduate students enrolled in fall 1999 are Mexican American. The university offers associate's, bachelor's, master's, and doctoral degrees in six academic colleges—arts and humanities, business administration, education, health sciences and human services, science and engineering, and social and behavioral sciences.

The dropout rate among minority students in science, mathematics, engineering and technology (SMET) is a concern both at UTPA and nationally. To address this problem, UTPA has actively supported programs in the College of Science and Engineering to increase student success and retention rates, and to improve the quality of teaching. We define the success rate in a particular course as the ratio of the number of students enrolled in that course who earn an A, B, or C to the total number of students enrolled on the 12th class day. We define the retention rate as the ratio of the number of students who earn A, B, C, D, or F to the total number enrolled on the 12th class day. One of the programs that UTPA is using to increase success and retention rates is the Louis Stokes Alliance for Minority Participation (LSAMP), which has offered an Undergraduate Peer Mentors Program (UPMP) since the fall of 1993.

UPMP provides academic support for SMET students enrolled in mathematics courses. Calculus students have first priority, while second priority goes to students taking trigonometry and college algebra. Many students declaring a SMET major start with trigonometry and college algebra, which is also a general education requirement. In fall 1992, the retention rate in these courses ranged from 59% to 90% (average 74 %), and the success rate from 31% to 75% (average 47%). These averages were computed over the total number (326) of students taking calculus in that semester.

Mathematics faculty participate in the mentor program in part because of their experience with the self-paced lab instruction in developmental mathematics that existed at UTPA from 1974 to 1989. Most of the mathematics faculty taught in the lab room using both individual and group instructional techniques and undergraduate assistants. The role of student assistants in the self-paced lab was rather minimal, but its precedent led to the creation of the present peer mentorship program. Faculty and student experience with the Learning Assistance Center (LAC), a tutoring program independent of the mathematics department, has also helped motivate participation in UPMP. LAC personnel cooperate with UPMP by tracking students in their courses, monitoring the syllabi of each instructor, and providing tutoring consistent with the methods employed by mathematics faculty.

■ MODEL

Mentors in UPMP provide a variety of services from their base in the math lab.

Math lab. Outside of class time, students come to the math lab, where peer mentors assist with homework or explain material covered in the classroom.

Academic support materials. Peer mentors issue books, student manuals, sample tests, graphing calculators, and computer software to students, and cooperate with faculty to determine current student needs for academic support materials. A part of the program's budget is used to purchase these resources.

Record keeping. All student users of the UPMP are required to sign in and out of the lab, and must identify both the course and section of their mathematics class. These data are reported monthly to the classroom instructors, and reflect the number of hours each student has participated in the lab.

Homework graders. Peer mentors may grade homework or quizzes in some courses. This service is limited because math lab is given first priority for resources. However, it is popular with faculty because it allows for the daily collection of student work and the rapid return of graded papers to students who are always eager to measure their progress in a course.

A student visiting the math lab is first greeted by a peer mentor who inquires whether the student is familiar with the available services. The peer mentor decides whether the student needs individual help or would benefit by joining an existing group. If peer mentors discern the need to form a new group, they play a leadership role in doing so. Information about the various study groups is interchanged at peer mentor coordination meetings, which are conducted by the director of the program.

The study groups vary in size from two to eight students. In most cases, a session is motivated by a homework assignment. The session starts with questions from a peer mentor to determine how she/he can best serve the study group: Is everyone in class assigned the same problems? Are the homework reports required to be individual or in groups? If groups are allowed by the course instructor, are there any rules for forming the groups? Did the instructor say anything about who can help and what kind of help is allowed? Once the peer mentor is aware of these details, he or she asks a set of questions inquiring whether the students in the study group know the definitions and theorems involved in the problem. If not all students in the group answer in the affirmative, then those who know this critical information are encouraged to explain their understanding to the group. Peer mentors often need to request help from faculty or graduate students to clarify some questions. Once the required concepts and theorems have been clarified, the peer mentor leads a Socratic dialog. What exactly the peer mentor does depends on the experience and quality of the group, but the goal is to challenge the students to identify the unknown or what must be proved, and to isolate what is given. The next set of questions may lead to the translation of a theorem from the language of mathematics to the more familiar vocabulary of the street.

During the first week of classes each semester, and later in the semester if a priority class is without study groups, peer mentors visit priority classes to explain how the program will aid students. With the permission of the instructor, mentors distribute information about the services provided by the program, together with a math lab schedule specifying the times each mentor works and the course in which each is prepared to help. An active recruiting session generally results in increased math lab attendance. Peer mentors who have demonstrated an ability to form study groups are paired with the newer peer mentors on these recruitment visits.

Selection and Training of Peer Mentors

Peer mentors are required to have a GPA of 3.0 or higher in their mathematics courses, and 2.8 overall. Any student who has completed the trigonometry course can apply to be a peer mentor. The selection of peer mentors is made by a committee of three faculty appointed by the director of the program.

Training consists of three one-hour sessions and includes a description of the UPMP, an overview of pedagogical methods in the various components of the program, the role of peer mentors as support to the faculty, methods of self-evaluation, and the evaluation of peer mentors by students. For those with prior experience as peer mentors or as tutors, the training period is reduced. Training is followed up with weekly sessions between the peer mentors and the director and staff assistant.

Mathematics faculty also play an important role in the training of peer mentors. A relationship between a faculty member and a peer mentor may be developed either because the peer mentor grades homework for the faculty member, or because he or she is a student in one of the faculty member's classes. Peer mentors are encouraged to discuss with faculty the difficulties their students are encountering, and to ask faculty questions about the best way to help their students. Many faculty like to instruct peer mentors about homework or projects assigned to students, especially if they involve graphing calculators or computer software.

Peer mentors are hired for a minimum of eight and a maximum of 19 hours per week. The exact number of hours worked depends on the mentor's availability, and is negotiated between the director and the mentor. The policy of the program is to make all reasonable efforts to meet the peer mentors' need to work, so that they can stay in school and complete their degree requirements. In this way, UPMP has proved to be an effective program for retaining good but economically challenged students.

The Role of Faculty in UPMP

Because most mathematics faculty have experience with previous peer mentoring programs, or have mentored students directly through the LSAMP undergraduate research program, it has not been necessary to train faculty for participation in UPMP. In fact, mathematics faculty took an active role in the design of the program, and remain eager to participate, knowing that the success of the program will enhance their students' learning. Individual faculty train peer mentors and students in the use of graphing calculators. Other faculty write handouts and other materials for use in the math lab. These handouts are often of such high quality that other instructors incorporate them into their own course materials. To sustain the high level of cooperation between UPMP and the faculty, the program director reports twice annually to the faculty on the status of the program.

◼ OUTCOMES

The following data are collected during the semester.

- Sign in and sign out sheets, by class and section, for all students attending the math lab.

- The number of hours worked by student assistants on each of the four program components.

- Class histories on all students in the program, listing all math classes taken and grades earned in those courses.

- End-of-semester student evaluations of UPMP, requested in class by mentors from all students who have participated even minimally.

- Evaluation by faculty of the mentor's performance as a grader.

The student participation rate increased steadily through fall 1997, then began to decline in the spring of 1998. This drop may be a result of personnel changes in LSAMP that affected the number and quality of some services. Nevertheless, the average number of hours attended per student has been increasing (Figure 15.1). The total attendance in hours, however, is a number that we would like to see increasing. Even if students attend a small number of hours, they may obtain useful information or motivation to increase their participation in the lab. In fall 1999, the retention rate for calculus students attending the math lab ranged among courses from 52% to 85.3% (average 67.2%), and the success rate ranged from 43.2% to 58.8% (average 50.9%). These averages were computed over the 116 calculus students who attended the math lab, representing approximately 22% of the total calculus student population. The average retention rate for students attending the lab was slightly better than for the population of calculus students (67%) but the average success rate for calculus students attending the math lab (58.8%) was much higher than for the population of calculus students (48%).

From 1994 to 1996, students from precalculus and calculus courses accounted for 89% of the total student

Figure 15.1 MATH LAB PARTICIPATION

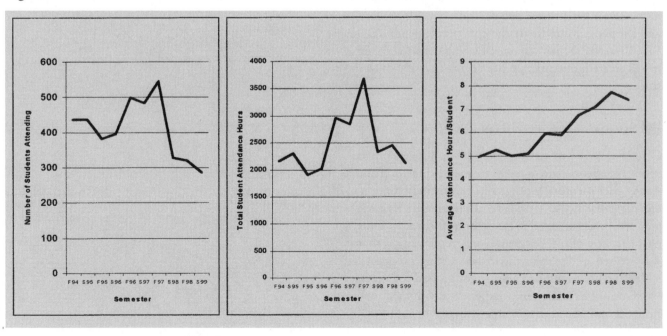

use of the math lab, and students from college algebra and trigonometry accounted for about 9% of the use. This usage is consistent with the emphasis of the UPMP on students in the calculus sequence. Since 1996, student use from college algebra and trigonometry classes has increased to 25%. This change may result from the decrease in the number of students in calculus courses that followed the establishment of South Texas Community College in the neighboring city of McAllen.

Students have expressed their satisfaction, and even enthusiasm, about the mentorship program by rating lab assistants, lab materials, lab access, and the learning environment as good, very good, and excellent over 80% of the time.

■ PRODUCTIVITY

UPMP is directed by a full-time faculty member who receives one course release from his/her instructional duties. One staff member provides part-time clerical support. The number of peer mentors has varied from eight to 14 at a time, and the total number of hours worked per semester has varied from 810 to 1,960. The budget contains $6,000 for peer mentors each semester. Since some peer mentors are also in the work-study program, the resulting cost sharing makes it possible to hire more mentors than allowed by our budget.

The actual cost of the program is difficult to estimate because there are no full-time employees and faculty have mostly volunteered their time. The actual cost of the undergraduate peer mentor program is about $30,000 per year. This figure does not count the large in-kind contribution by the faculty and a small amount by students, but it does cover part-time secretarial staff, wages for mentors, and supplies. We estimate the cost per student at about $10.00 to $12.00 per semester. During the six years since it was created, the program has been a free service to the students.

■ SUGGESTIONS FOR REPLICATION

One of UPMP's main objectives was to harness our faculty's experience and interest in mentoring to create a strong peer mentoring program. An existing program to encourage faculty to serve as research mentors for undergraduates was extended to teaching mentorships. Thus, a characteristic of our program worth replicating is that it was created under the wing of an existing program for which the university had already committed resources.

Given the faculty's prior experience with mentorship projects, UPMP did not organize any formal faculty training. However, for institutions without this prior faculty involvement, we recommend the development of a structured faculty training program.

Perhaps the most special aspect of our program is that it started as an experimental program and it continues to be open to all points of view, approaches, and techniques. We believe that others should strive to replicate this spirit of experimentation.

■ CONCLUSION

At institutions with high minority enrollments, a mentoring program can be an effective vehicle to promote student persistence in disciplines such as mathematics, which do not seem to attract underrepresented populations.

■ AUTHORS

MIGUEL PAREDES is a Professor in the Department of Mathematics at the University of Texas-Pan American.

PAUL PONTIUS is an Assistant Professor in the Department of Mathematics at the University of Texas-Pan American.

RENE TORRES is a Lecturer in the Department of Mathematics at the University of Texas-Pan American.

JOSEPH CHANCE is a Professor in the Department of Mathematics at the University of Texas-Pan American.

Chapter 16

A Model for Integrating Technical Preceptors into the Classroom

Mary Poulton and John Kemeny

The University of Arizona is the state's land-grant institution with an enrollment of approximately 35,000 undergraduate and graduate students in 14 colleges and eight schools. In 1994, as part of a major reform effort to improve the quality of undergraduate instruction, the university adopted a series of seven goals and 36 measures referred to as the Hurwitz Goals (Gottfredson, 1999). The university must report to the Board of Regents each year on progress toward completing each measure. The seven goals are:

1) Students can obtain necessary classes each semester.

2) Students receive adequate advising.

3) Classrooms are adequately equipped.

4) Lower-division courses are taught by ranked faculty.

5) Graduates are prepared to enter the workforce.

6) Students have out-of-class contact with ranked faculty.

7) Students have the opportunity to conduct research with faculty.

Hurwitz Goal 3 is most relevant to this chapter and requires the university to ensure that classrooms are multimedia equipped, support computer-based instruction, provide all students with access to the Internet, provide all faculty with in-office Internet access, train faculty in the use of technology, and create an centralized "information commons" for student access to computers. As a result of this goal, the university embarked on a five-year, $10 million classroom renovation project, with an additional $1.2 million earmarked for adding technology. Since 1994, the number of classrooms equipped with multimedia resources (computer/data projection, VCR, laserdisc, and audio system) has risen from 38 to 185 (out of 328 classrooms on campus). The number of classrooms equipped with Internet access necessary for computer-based instruction has risen from 46 to 93. All students have access to the Internet in their residence hall rooms and 97% of faculty have such access in their offices. The number of faculty trained in the use of new teaching technology has risen from 150 to over 550 (out of 1,576 full-time instructional faculty).

The increase in technology brings an expectation that students have skills necessary to learn from the high-tech environment, and to complete assignments that utilize computer technology. A freshmen class often includes students who are highly skilled with computers and others who have had almost no computer experience. These latter students often come to such modern classrooms with a great deal of anxiety. Increased use of technology is inevitable, and it is important to develop strategies to deal with the wide range of student computing competence.

This chapter presents a model for the use of undergraduate technical preceptors to help students learn computer skills. The model has been successfully implemented in a freshmen general education course for three semesters (fall 1998, spring 1999, and fall 1999). The computer skills taught (web page development, composing web papers, email, etc.) expand pedagogical options and are valuable tools for students in future courses and employment. This model allows technologically skilled students to become technical preceptors who teach others in the class. The technical preceptors take a major burden off the other members of the teaching team (professors and graduate teaching assistants) since they provide out-of-class assistance to students during office hours. At the same time, the technical preceptors get many benefits from the experience, including the opportunity to teach, to improve their communication skills, to improve their technical skills, and to spend time with the professors and more experienced preceptors.

The class that is the focus of this chapter ("Natural Sciences 101" or NATS 101) has been team-taught by the authors since 1989. The use of technology in this course has continually evolved (Table 16.1). Preceptors were first added to the course in the fall 1997 semester. Enrollment between 1989 and 1997 was approximately 35 students per semester.

Initially, the course utilized only traditional classroom facilities. As part of a technology component added in 1995, students were taught to use the Macromedia program Director along with associated software for sound editing, graphics editing, and 3D rendering. This technology development was supported by university grants of nearly $29,000 to purchase computers and a computer projector. Students thoroughly enjoyed this part of the course, and many of the computer projects developed by the students approached professional quality. Some of the students went on to use their newly acquired multimedia skills in other courses, in spite of the lack of multimedia software on campus computers and the high price of purchasing their own copies of the software.

In 1998, as part of the new general education curriculum, 150 students per semester enrolled in NATS 101. The technology component of the course was modified to have students develop web skills (including html and animation programming) rather than the multimedia skills taught previously. We made this change because we felt that being able to comfortably utilize the web would be invaluable to students in future courses. We also found web-based projects and papers to be superior in quality to traditional projects and papers, due in part to the fact that others (peers and even parents) have access to student work. The transition to web-based delivery of the course was supported by university computer grants totaling approximately $22,000.

◼ MODEL

Course Model

The course model and technical preceptor model are tightly coupled. The course was developed with the role of technical preceptors in mind, and the preceptor model is based on the course design. The technology component is a weekly five-hour computer lab session utilizing 45 PCs, each having web access and a variety of software. Students in the class pick any 50-minute slot during that five-hour lab period to work on computer assignments.

During the first year the course was taught with this model (AY 1998–1999), we used the same approach to teaching the computer lab as we had used in teaching multimedia programming. That is, students were taught specific programming skills each week, and by the end of the semester they had to demonstrate proficiency in all skills by completing a capstone project, integrating computer programming with mastery of the course content. Prior to fall 1998, students majoring in engineering and science dominated course enrollments. However, under the new general education guidelines natural sciences courses may not enroll science or engineering majors. Many of these nonscience or engineering students lacked computing experience ("I know nothing about computers and want to learn") or expressed resistance to technology ("I don't have a computer or like using them. I would rather simply get information in class like you are

Table 16.1 EVOLUTION OF TECHNOLOGY IN NATS 101

Year	Technology Used in the Classroom	Class Computer Facilities	Technology Taught to Students	Student Project
1989–1994	Overheads Videos	None	None	Oral or poster presentation
1995–1997	Powerpoint lectures Videos Director tutorials	Multimedia lab with four computers	Director Scanning Sound program 3D program	Multimedia computer project using Director
1998–1999	Powerpoint lectures Html lectures Web access in class Digital videos Flash animation Class web page	Computer lab with 45 computers	Dreamweaver (html) Flash (web animation) Excel and Word Email Caucus (conference)	Experiment and results (including photo and animation) posted to students' home web page

supposed to"). Comments at the end of the semester indicated that some students felt they were learning computer science instead of earth science.

Starting in fall1999, the computer lab was integrated more closely with the course content and focused on fewer programs and more reinforcement of skills. The course featured a lecture on Monday, a hands-on activity on Wednesday to reinforce the lecture topic, and a computer lab on Friday to solidify the concepts and allow students to reflect on the course material and demonstrate understanding. The computer lab replaced the usual discussion section offered by many other courses of this size. The advantage of this course model is that students first hear the weekly topic explained via lecture, they read about the topic, they experiment with the topic, and finally, they integrate what they have learned into a web page that reinforces both the topic and the use of technology, all in the span of one week. Students ask more questions about course content than computer skills after the third week of the semester. The disadvantage of this model is that it is labor intensive because teaching computer skills requires a lot of one-on-one interaction. The current lab assignments are listed in Table 16.2.

The computer assignments are located on the course web site and consist of five parts: 1) about the lab, 2) procedure, 3) skills, 4) FYI, and 5) advanced skills. The procedure section provides the step-by-step instructions to complete the lab, and the skills section contains online tutorials that explain the particular web programming skills to be used for the lab. The FYI section explains different aspects of the web such as tips on good design. The advanced skills section allows students who are ready to explore more sophisticated designs. All labs are designed to be completed within a 50-minute time period, provided the student comes prepared and has done the required reading or calculations. Several students, however, will take two or three times the expected amount of time to complete an assignment, and must finish the assignment during preceptor office hours.

Technical Preceptor Model

Students who received an A or B grade in the course in a previous semester are invited to serve as preceptors for our course through written invitations from the authors. We also ask for volunteers from students currently enrolled in the course during the first week of each semester. The

Table 16.2 INTEGRATION OF COMPUTER SKILLS WITH COURSE CONTENT IN THE FALL 1999 SEMESTER

Week	Assignment	Skill	Content Topic
1	Introduction to course web site	Use of browser	Syllabus
2	Make a homepage	Dreamweaver: site management, FTP, text formatting	Course overview
3	Formation of elements	Dreamweaver: tables, importing images	Atomic structure
4	Uses of copper	Dreamweaver: links, tables	Minerals
5	Velocity, acceleration, and force	Dreamweaver: importing movies, links, tables	Newton's Laws
6	Potential and kinetic energy	Dreamweaver: dynamic html, layers, behaviors, links	Conservation of energy
7	Constructing histograms	Dreamweaver: tables, links	Rock strength
8	Mineral processing flow diagram	Dreamweaver: image maps, links	Mining and mineral processing
9	Evaluation of study habits	Use of forms	Midsemester evaluation
10	Heat capacity of fluids	Excel: making graphs Dreamweaver: importing images, links	Thermodynamics
11	Home energy consumption	Excel: equations, copying and pasting data Dreamweaver: tables, links	Nonrenewable energy
12	Energy in my community	Excel: equations, graphs Dreamweaver: tables, links	Renewable energy

number of preceptors each semester is highly variable, and only 10% to 20% of students invited to serve as preceptors will agree to do so. Approximately 5% of the students currently enrolled will sign up for a preceptorship, and as many as half of those students will drop the preceptorship in the first three weeks. Most students who do complete the preceptorship, however, return for a second semester of preceptoring. Several students complete the maximum of nine units of credit for preceptoring the course. We have a goal of trying to provide a ratio of ten enrolled students per member of the teaching team (faculty, graduate assistants, and preceptors). Table 16.3 lists the number of preceptors each semester and whether they returned the following semester for another preceptorship.

Students are interviewed to determine why they want to be preceptors and what they hope to gain from the experience, in addition to what skills they have that are applicable to the course needs. Students may decide to discontinue their preceptorship during the first three weeks of the semester. First-time preceptors must register for two units of UNVR 197a, which is the university-wide course for beginning preceptors. Participating faculty members have their own section of the course. Returning preceptors must register for two or three units of UNVR 397a.

Rather than leading in-class discussions or doing peer writing review, preceptors assist with the technology components of the course. All preceptors are required to complete the weekly computer assignments ahead of time and have a number of responsibilities:

1) Assist in the weekly computer labs for one to two hours per week.

2) Hold office hours for one to two hours per week.

Table 16.3 NUMBER OF PRECEPTORS CONCURRENTLY ENROLLED IN THE NATS 101 COURSE VERSUS THOSE THAT HAVE PREVIOUSLY TAKEN THE COURSE AND RETURN TO SERVE AS PRECEPTORS

Semester	Total Number of Preceptors	Preceptors Concurrently Enrolled in NATS 101	Preceptors with Prior Experience in Course
Fall 1997	1	0	1
Spring 1998	5	0	5
Fall 1998	8	1	7
Spring 1999	12	6	6
Fall 1999	6	2	4

3) Attend weekly team meetings with faculty and graduate teaching assistant.

4) Attend university-wide training workshops.

5) Complete an independent project that makes a contribution to the course web site.

6) Attend the end-of-semester showcase event for the teaching teams program.

The weekly computer lab is a highly dynamic and interesting environment for the technical preceptor. At any given time during the five hour lab, there might be four or five preceptors and as many as 45 students working at computers. The computer assignments are challenging and involve web page development with text, graphics, pictures, and animation. Students raise their hands when they need assistance, and seeing seven or eight hands raised at any given time is common, especially during the first half of the semester. The preceptor, therefore, has to think fast and be able to analyze a student's problem and come up with a solution quickly so he or she can get on to the next student needing assistance. In an average two hour time period, a preceptor might help as many as 30 students. During preceptor office hours, on the other hand, there are typically only five or six students each hour, enabling preceptors to spend more time with each student at a slower pace. When not helping individual students, office hours also allow preceptors to learn more advanced skills from each other.

Each preceptor selects a project to work on throughout the semester. The projects generally involve the improvement of some aspect of the course, either the course web page or the weekly computer assignments. Through these projects, preceptors play a major role in the design, implementation, and improvement of the course web page (Poulton & Kemeny, 1999). Thus, our technical preceptors have an opportunity to leave a legacy to the course.

Preceptors are treated as equal partners on the teaching team. They provide feedback during the weekly team meetings on what problems students are having with the course material and computer skills, and this feedback enables us to continually improve the course. They help plan changes to assignments, make suggestions on improving lectures, and help plan review sessions. Preceptors are not allowed to grade any assignment, view student grades, or be present when exams are discussed.

Preceptors receive a letter grade for their work. They may receive financial compensation for assisting in some aspect of the course over and above their preceptor duties. For example, one preceptor is usually hired as the course webmaster and is compensated for that work. Preceptors are hired over the summer to help rewrite or improve some aspects of the course. Grades are based on performance of their duties, attendance at training workshops, attitude, and quality of their semester projects. The preceptorship has been a springboard to tutoring jobs on campus for many of our students. We have been able to provide letters of recommendation for employment and graduate school for other preceptors, and those letters are more informative than we could provide for students who had merely taken the course.

Faculty Model

As faculty, we approach the role of undergraduate preceptors in our course the same way we would approach undergraduates working in our research laboratories. We realize student limitations and we recognize that working in a lab and preceptoring a course are both learning experiences. We also see the preceptorship as an important vehicle for getting to know students outside our department. We learn a great deal about technology from our preceptors since they often learn more about web programming than we do.

The introduction of preceptors has allowed us to offer more content-related out-of-class assistance to students than would be possible with faculty or graduate assistants because of cost and availability. Prior to the incorporation of technical preceptors, students working on computer assignments would come to our offices seeking assistance several times each day. Before an assignment due date we might each spend as much as three or four hours each day answering programming questions. We had very little feedback on the course until the semester was over, students seldom made comments on the evaluation forms, and our office hours were under utilized for other than technology related issues.

In the current model, a weekly team meeting is used to set the agenda for the week, discuss the work each preceptor will do that week, and exchange information and suggestions about past and upcoming assignments. We observe the preceptors in action during the lab sessions, and provide feedback individually or make suggestions during the team meeting. In total, we each spend about three hours a week in individual or group instruction with the preceptors.

■ OUTCOMES

Course Outcomes

The purpose of creating the technical preceptor model was to more actively engage students' interest in the course content through the use of web programming skills. The technical preceptors created a highly effective environment for students to learn new computer skills. Preceptors are their peers, and therefore, students could relate and interact with the preceptors in a way not possible for the graduate students and the faculty. With assistance from the technical preceptors, most students were able to complete the weekly computer assignments in one hour or less, and those that could not had many opportunities for additional help during office hours. Preceptor and faculty office hours are more fully utilized, and we receive frequent email and feedback from students on course content, lectures, and assignments, implying increased engagement and accessibility.

A more conventional course model for a NATS 101 course at the University of Arizona is two 50-minute lectures each week, and a 50-minute discussion section run by a graduate teaching assistant. Attendance in large lectures is often as low as 50% and seldom higher than 80% on a typical day. While we have not been able to conduct a controlled experiment to demonstrate that our course model and preceptor model improve learning, we are able to compare spring and fall 1999 midterm scores to determine if the revised computer labs might have had an impact on learning outcomes. The exam questions were similar between the two semesters but since most students are first semester freshmen and few have access to course files at fraternity and sorority houses, we feel the grade differences can be attributed primarily to the course changes and not prior exposure to the questions. The average midterm grade for the spring 1999 semester, prior to the new model, was 58 out of 100. After revision of the computer labs in the fall of 1999, the average improved to 73 out of 100. The fall 1999 students were able to provide more detailed answers to the questions that were common between the two semesters.

Technical preceptors also contributed to student computer use and to the learning of web skills. At the start of the semester, 83% of students reported that they had used a word processing program, 46% had used email frequently, 29% had used computer tutorials, and only 9% had created a web page. By the first month of the semester, nearly every student in the course had email communication with a member of the teaching team, 100% had used computer tutorials for course content and to learn programming skills, and 100% had created web pages. The number of questions in the Friday lab regarding computer operations diminished, and more questions were asked pertaining to course content. In our opinion, teaching web skills to a large-enrollment general education course would not have been possible without the technical preceptors. Our experience showed that the most preferred and least frustrating way for students to learn web skills was for them to ask frequent questions while they were in the process of developing web pages and posting assignments. Without technical preceptors, graduate students and faculty would have to take this responsibility, and this would not be feasible for large classes.

Preceptor Outcomes

There were a number of additional benefits for the preceptors in addition to those described above. Preceptors attended workshops during the semester on learning styles, cooperative learning, and dealing with difficult students. From these workshops and the time spent with students in the weekly lab and office hours, preceptors were able to improve communication and interpersonal skills. The preceptors also gained experience in course design and made important contributions to the infrastructure of the course. In the weekly meetings, preceptors often made insightful suggestions for course improvement (not just the technical component), and many of these suggestions have been incorporated into the course.

We asked preceptors to write an essay about why they became preceptors and what they gained from the experience at the end of the semester. One preceptor wrote, "I don't think I would have moved from just knowing that people learn differently, to understanding this fact, and knowing how to deal with it without the experience of this class." Another student became a preceptor because of a positive experience with a preceptor the previous semester and wrote, "I felt the help I received by them was unmatched by any other and I wanted to be a part of that." An older student wrote, "Though I am not going to school to be a teacher I think a person's life is teaching and communicating. So, I knew to take advantage of that."

End-of-semester evaluations indicated that the preceptors unanimously felt that their experiences as a preceptor were rewarding and educational.

■ Productivity

At large institutions where introductory courses typically enroll 150 students or more, cost-effective ways to provide the personal instruction necessary to effectively teach computer skills must be found. Undergraduate technical preceptors are our solution to the problem. Each preceptor provides approximately six hours of assistance weekly for 15 weeks, for a total of 90 hours per preceptor per semester. Preceptor office hours are fully utilized by students, and preceptors are all busy during the lab, so the 90 hours truly represents instructional time that teaching as-

sistants or faculty would have to cover (or ignore). If undergraduate students were hired for this work at $7 per hour, we would require a budget of approximately $4,000 per semester for six assistants, and we would still need to provide training and supervision. If graduate students had to be hired at a minimal rate of $16 per hour to cover the same number of hours as the preceptors, we would need an additional budget of nearly $9,000 for graduate teaching assistant support. It would be impossible for faculty to provide the out-of-class contact with existing research, teaching, and service workloads. The cost of having preceptors in the classroom is the supervision time, the training workshops, and the individual contact. Preceptors and graduate assistants do most of the teaching in the weekly computer lab, and deal with almost 100% of the problems that students have related to the computer component of the class. We attend university-wide training workshops every semester, with our preceptors accounting for approximately 12 hours of additional work each semester. Training workshop costs are distributed across the university so the cost per preceptor remains very low. The benefits of technical preceptors far outweigh the costs. Total faculty time spent working with preceptors for each of the authors is 60 hours per semester, representing a total cost of approximately $6,000 per semester. We note that this cost is for training and supervision and much of it would be spent even if we used paid assistants.

■ Suggestions for Replication

Our best technical preceptors have been those with a strong work ethic, good computer skills, excellent communication ability, an ability to think on their feet, and a strong motivation to learn, not necessarily the brightest students in class. End-of-semester evaluations by students in the class showed that they did not rate all preceptors equally, and felt that some of the preceptors were rude (making them feel dumb) or poorly trained (they did not know their stuff). These were generally the preceptors that did not show up to the weekly meetings, did not prepare for the Friday lab ahead of time, or had poor people skills. Therefore, it is essential to ensure regular attendance, preparation, and communication skill training. Some preceptors fall into a habit of demonstrating how to complete an assignment rather than eliciting questions from the student and finding a way to explain a concept or skill. Such habits are really a matter of lack of experience with effective questioning and suggest additional training in this area. The issue of misinformation given out by preceptors still exists, and the best approach to deal with it is through training and discussion during the team meetings.

One of the keys to providing a successful experience for the preceptors without increasing the faculty workload too much, has been the selection of preceptors that require little technical training. This allows the focus of training to be on the educational and interpersonal topics covered for all preceptors by the university-wide workshops. Students who have already taken our course generally make the best preceptors since they tend to provide more accurate information and have already gained all the skills required in the course.

Active faculty and graduate student participation on the teaching team is vital to the success of the preceptors. Weekly team meetings are essential to keep the lines of communication open and to ensure that the preceptors are not put into situations for which they are unprepared. The teaching team must function as a team and everyone must feel that their voice is heard and that they are valued members. We have most enjoyed the semesters when our preceptors were very vocal during the meetings and freely offered their suggestions. Such teaming may mean that the conventional lines of authority must be somewhat blurred, or even reversed, during the meetings.

The preceptors must be provided with worthwhile training and must fully understand what their commitment to the course is and how they will be graded. Detailed contracts stipulating what work is expected, what quality of effort to strive for, and what will determine the final grade prevent misunderstandings and give the student more motivation for doing a good job.

Perhaps the most important advice for replicating this model is to always keep in mind that you are providing an educational opportunity for the preceptors. Do not ask or expect more of them than they have the ability to deliver.

CONCLUSION

We have developed a model for incorporating undergraduate students as technical preceptors into a large enrollment, general education science course that emphasizes computer skills. Our model helps ensure that students of all abilities gain the necessary skills to learn in a technology-rich environment. The technical preceptors provide the one-on-one instruction that is necessary to teach computer and web development skills, and in return learn valuable communication, teaching, teamwork, and leadership skills.

REFERENCES

Gottfredson, M. (1999). *Report on meeting Hurwitz Goals* [Online]. Available: http://w3.arizona.edu/~uge/hurwitz/hurwitz99.htm

Poulton, M., & Kemeny, J. (1999). *Improvements of course web page* [Online]. Available: www.fcii.arizona.edu/poulton/nats101

AUTHORS

MARY POULTON is an Associate Professor in the Department of Mining and Geological Engineering at the University of Arizona.

JOHN KEMENY is an Associate Professor in the Department of Mining and Geological Engineering at the University of Arizona.

Chapter 17

Academic Excellence Workshops:
Boosting Success in Technical Courses

Ruth A. Streveler

The Colorado School of Mines (CSM), a science and engineering school with an undergraduate population of about 2,400, began offering Academic Excellence Workshops (AEWs) in 1994 as part of its Student Support Services Program. The target population for the first AEWs was low-income, first-generation students who were eligible for services under a Student Support Services grant. However, the general population of CSM students saw the success of the AEWs and wanted the opportunity to attend as well. In 1998, AEWs became fully funded by CSM rather than by Student Support Services and are now available to all students.

A form of supplemental instruction developed by Treisman (1985), AEWs have been extensively used by minority engineering programs (Hiemenz & Hudspeth, 1993). Students enroll in a noncredit workshop that supplements a beginning course in math or science. The AEWs are led by undergraduate facilitators who assist workshop participants in collaboratively solving a worksheet of problems. The workshops have a dual purpose: to assist students in mastering math and science concepts, and to create a sense of community among students in the workshop.

Because CSM is a science and engineering school, all students are required to successfully complete calculus I, II, and III, differential equations, chemistry I and II, and physics I and II. Of these, calculus I and II, chemistry I and II, and physics I and II are generally the most difficult, and AEWs are offered to supplement these courses. AEWs could also be used in upper division courses, although we have not done this at CSM. Workshops are offered as supplements to four or five courses in calculus, chemistry, and physics each semester. In order to limit enrollment in each workshop section, some courses have multiple sections, so a total of eight or nine workshops are offered each semester.

■ MODEL

AEW Format

Each AEW meets for two hours each week. In the AEW sessions, students ask questions about homework and work on problems supplied by the undergraduate facilitator. Some facilitators field homework questions before the worksheet problems are attempted; others prefer to discuss the worksheet first.

Whether homework or worksheet problems are the topic, facilitators have students work together in groups of three to four to solve problems. Students can choose their group members. One student in each group assumes the role of problem solver, working through the problem at the board and discussing the steps for solving it. Other group members ask for clarification and elaboration. The problem solver role is informally rotated among students in the group. A solution sheet is provided to students at the end of the workshop.

We have somewhat modified the Treisman model, in which students focus on the worksheet of problems presented to them by their facilitator and are not allowed to ask questions about homework problems. At CSM, we found this practice to be a barrier to student participation in workshops, and in our AEWs, homework may be discussed.

Facilitators are expected to:

- Foster a climate of success within the workshop through their enthusiasm for and encouragement of students.

- Be clear about what homework is assigned to the course for which the workshop is a supplement.

- Be familiar with how to solve the assigned homework problems.

- Create challenging worksheets with accurate solutions in a timely manner, leaving adequate time for approval by the professor, duplication of worksheets, and sharing the worksheets with cofacilitators.

- Assure that worksheets reflect the course professor's emphasis through regular meetings with the professor and, in some cases, by attending selected classes.

- Guide workshop attendees in working collaboratively.

AEW Worksheets

Each week the undergraduate facilitators create a worksheet of problems and a solution set. Worksheets consist of three to ten problems that illustrate important topics covered during that week's instruction.

If more than one workshop section is offered for a particular course, the cofacilitators rotate the duty of creating the worksheet. If more than one method may be used to solve a problem, professors may direct facilitators to solve the problems in a way that is consistent with their instruction. Other professors prefer that facilitators point out multiple ways to solve a particular problem.

Worksheets and solutions are duplicated by the Office of Student Development and Academic Services (SDAS). Facilitators bring worksheet and solution sets to the SDAS office by 10 a.m. on Monday morning and they are copied and ready for pickup by facilitators later that afternoon. Copies of all worksheets and solutions are archived in a binder and kept for reference for future semesters.

Though the full benefit of the AEW is not achieved unless students attend the workshops, the worksheets and solutions are also valuable study guides. The worksheets have been so sought after that they are now placed on reserve in the CSM library and may be photocopied by students who cannot or do not want to attend the workshops.

Recruiting and Training AEW Facilitators

New facilitators have come primarily from three sources: referral from professors, SDAS tutors, and past AEW participants. In the Treisman model, both undergraduate and graduate students serve as facilitators, but at CSM, facilitators have been almost exclusively undergraduates. Turnover of facilitators at CSM has been low, and generally there is a waiting list of prospective facilitators.

Before their first session, new facilitators attend a 90-minute training meeting and are encouraged to attend an experienced facilitator's workshop. Training for new facilitators includes discussion of job expectations, a suggested agenda for the workshop, guidelines for creating AEW worksheets, and an introductory discussion of workshop group dynamics. Since AEW participants attend workshops voluntarily, few discipline problems have ever arisen, and so classroom management issues are only briefly mentioned in the facilitator training.

AEW facilitators are guides in the collaborative learning process, and are not expected to be the teacher at the front of the room providing the answers. Through role playing and discussion of possible workshop scenarios, facilitators are trained to encourage collaborative problem solving. Students are encouraged to discuss problems with one another before looking to the facilitator for help. During facilitator training, we discuss possible scenarios with particular focus on ways to encourage students to work in groups and to solve problems on the board in front of the other students.

Ongoing training of new and experienced facilitators occurs weekly. All facilitators meet as a group with the coordinator of the AEWs, who at CSM is the director of Academic Services, each Friday to discuss how their workshop went that week. If problems or questions arise as the semester progresses they can be dealt with in a timely manner. By meeting together, facilitators also get a sense of what is going on in other facilitators' workshops. It is also an opportunity for facilitators working with the same course (for example, "Calculus I") to discuss the upcoming workshop.

In addition to these weekly meetings, facilitators also meet weekly with the course professor to discuss the content for the upcoming week, and the kinds of problems the professor would like the worksheet to cover. Professors often provide facilitators with supplemental texts that can be used to create worksheet problems and generally check the facilitator's draft of the worksheet before it is duplicated and distributed.

Recruiting Students for AEWs

AEWs are advertised during the second week of instruction via a short announcement in the class by either the Director of Academic Services or the course professor. The purpose and format of the workshop is explained and students are asked to complete an application (Appendix C-1) if they wish to participate. Making the announcement in class is very important because supportive comments by the instructor about the workshop increase its credibility, and therefore, increase student attendance.

Record Keeping

Each facilitator is given the list of students who have signed up for his or her workshop, and attendance is taken each week. Students may be added to the workshop as the semester progresses if space allows. The ideal size for a workshop is about 12-15 students with 25 students as an absolute maximum. At the end of each semester, the grades of students attending the workshop are recorded, and the average grade of attendees is compared with the average grade for all students in the course. Student evaluations of each workshop section are summarized and shared with the facilitators.

■ OUTCOMES

AEWs at CSM have been assessed using participants' grades and student evaluations. The average grade of regular workshop attendees has been higher than the class average for 12 of 15 workshops offered from fall 1997 through spring 1999 (Table 17.1). Using the binomial probability, these results are statistically significant. This data suggests that regularly attending AEWs helps students succeed in these key classes and supports the finding that working in small groups improves student learning in undergraduate science and mathematics courses (Springer, Stanne, & Donovan, 1999).

At the end of each semester, attendees are asked to evaluate the AEWs and the facilitators (Appendix D-5). From fall 1997 to spring 1999, 136 of 289 students (47%) completed an AEW evaluation. This completion rate is a reflection of the lower attendance at the end of the semester, the time when evaluations are distributed.

Of the 136 students completing an evaluation, 135 (99%) answered yes to the question: "Did attending the workshop help you increase your understanding of the course material?" and 118 (86%) answered yes to the question: "Did attending the workshops increase your ability to work with fellow students?" All but five students rated their facilitator's overall performance as either superior or excellent.

Student comments on evaluations were also used to improve the workshops. For example, one student commented: "There should be more problems that are easier to work and similar to homework or class problems." Facilitators used this information to guide them in their selection of worksheet problems.

Student comments on the good points of the workshops reinforced the dual purpose of the AEWs. For example, one student wrote that: "[the AEWs] are a good review and also you learn new things related to class." Another stated: "[the workshops] really helped me understand physics better. [They] helped to work with other students to get different views of the problems."

AEW facilitators evaluate the workshops in an informal interview with the Director of Academic Services at the end of each semester (Appendix D-8). Information gathered from the interviews with facilitators has been used to continuously improve the workshops. For example, facilitators have recommended that the AEWs be announced several times during the semester. Following this suggestion, professors have reminded their classes about the AEWs, and this has increased workshop attendance.

The experience of being a facilitator is very valuable for undergraduate students. AEWs provide a rare opportunity for undergraduates to work as a partner with a faculty member. Documenting their teaching/leadership skills through student evaluations can be useful for those contemplating graduate school. Since most of our engineering students enter the work force directly after graduation, the experience of leading groups of students in a workshop setting is a very powerful addition to their resume. Some students have changed their career plans after being facilitators. Two of our physics facilitators, for example, decided to become high school physics teachers rather than engineers. Their experience as facilitators helped them to secure teaching positions.

Table 17.1 EFFECT OF AEW ATTENDANCE ON COURSE GRADE

Workshop Subject (Semester)	Average Grade (Number of Students)	
	Entire Class	Regular Workshop Attendees
Calculus I (F97)	2.71 (n = 426)	2.95 (n = 21)
Chemistry I (F97)	2.57 (n = 465)	2.58 (n = 12)
Physics I (F97)	2.49 (n = 228)	3.43 (n = 14)
Physics II (F97)	2.46 (n = 378)	2.85 (n = 13)
Calculus II (S98)	2.68 (n = 335)	2.75 (n = 12)
Chemistry II (S98)	2.49 (n = 444)	2.56 (n = 25)
Physics I (S98)	2.94 (n = 316)	2.64 (n = 22)
Physics II (S98)	1.42 (n = 200)	1.85 (n = 13)
Calculus I (F98)	2.89 (n = 373)	2.94 (n = 16)
Chemistry I (F98)	2.69 (n = 567)	2.83 (n = 23)
Physics I (F98)	2.48 (n = 210)	2.70 (n = 10)
Physics II (F98)	1.94 (n = 366)	2.06 (n = 16)
Chemistry II (S99)	2.71 (n = 492)	2.31 (n = 13)
Physics I (S99)	2.63 (n = 375)	2.38 (n = 21)
Physics II (S99)	1.86 (n = 156)	1.94 (n = 17)

Note: The average grade of all students in the class is compared with the average grade of students who attended at least three workshop sessions (out of a possible 12 or more sessions). Only workshops with ten or more students attending at least three sessions were considered. This criterion eliminated two workshops from the analysis.

■ PRODUCTIVITY

The largest cost of AEWs is facilitator salaries. Since being a facilitator requires mastery of content knowledge and extensive people skills, facilitators are paid at the high end of the undergraduate student pay scale. The rate of pay in 1999 was $8.00 per hour when minimum wage was $5.15. Facilitators usually spend about ten hours per week in preparing and delivering one workshop, so each section of each AEW currently costs $80/week to deliver (as each facilitator handles only one workshop section). Facilitators' salaries totaled about $18,000 for the 1998–1999 academic year. During that same time period, AEW participants logged about 5,000 contact hours for a cost of less than $4 per contact hour.

The loss of one student costs CSM $13,500 in lost tuition revenue per year (H. C. Cheuvront, personal communication, October 13, 1999). If two students are retained because of AEWs, then revenue incurred by tuition savings more than pays for a year of facilitators' salaries. Since the average grade of regular AEW attendees is usually higher than the class average in key core courses, it is reasonable to assume that the AEWs have a positive impact on retention.

At CSM, the Director of Academic Services hires and trains facilitators, meets with facilitators regularly, and acts as a liaison with faculty members. The director devotes as much as 20 hours per week to the AEWs during the first two weeks of each semester. After the AEWs are up and running, one to two hours per week are needed for oversight. More time is required again at the end of the semester when the AEWs are evaluated. An estimated 60 hours per semester are spent by the director to coordinate the workshops.

Faculty involvement is probably the most critical factor in the success of AEWs. Faculty spend only about 15 minutes per week meeting with facilitators, and some faculty view AEWs as a time saver. Students can use workshop time, rather than faculty time, to ask questions about course material. For example, a calculus professor reported that fewer students come to office hours now that the AEWs are available.

■ SUGGESTIONS FOR REPLICATION

- AEWs are designed to supplement science and math courses. When establishing AEWs for the first time on a campus, first decide which science and math courses could benefit most from these workshops.

- Establish rapport with key faculty members in math and science departments. It is key to the success of the program that faculty feel that AEWs are a service to them and their students, not an indictment of their teaching methods.

- Recruit faculty who are interested in having an AEW to supplement their courses, and allow them to have some ownership of the AEWs. Ask faculty to recommend or recruit potential facilitators and give them final control of the hiring decision.

- Advertise workshops by having the AEW coordinator, or perhaps the facilitators themselves, make a short presentation in the classes during the first few days of instruction.

- Create an application process for students wishing to participate in workshops. Students who apply to attend the workshop are more likely to see the AEW as a semester-long commitment, rather than something they attend just before an exam.

- Plan for proper training of facilitators. Since it is not always easy to coax freshmen into studying together, the AEW coordinator must teach collaborative learning techniques to facilitators in training sessions. The facilitators have also found it useful to meet weekly as a group to discuss the workshop. New facilitators found that attending a workshop led by an experienced facilitator was perhaps the richest component of their training.

- Determine the best time and place to hold AEWs on your campus. Through trial and error, we have learned the days and times (Mondays and Wednesdays from 7p.m. to 9 p.m.) that work best for the majority of our students, but these times will differ from campus to campus. Since workshops require abundant board space, we have found classrooms to be the best workshop venue.

- Integrate the AEWs into the fabric of campus resources. Be sure professors, tutors, coaches, advisors, residence hall assistants, readmission committees, and parents all know about AEWs. With a wide array of people familiar with this service, students needing this help can be encouraged repeatedly to participate.

- Work in partnership with faculty, facilitators, and AEW participants to modify the workshop format to best meet the needs of your campus. Keep asking, "What can we do to improve the workshops?" and be willing to implement the suggestions that arise.

CONCLUSION

Academic excellence workshops are a useful form of supplemental instruction for mathematics and science courses. Undergraduate facilitators can gain skills while contributing to the academic success of the students they serve. There is strong research evidence that working in small groups dramatically improves students' learning (Springer, Stanne, & Donovan, 1999), and our results at CSM support this finding. AEWs provide an opportunity for students enrolled in difficult gateway courses to learn collaboratively and, by doing so, increase their performance.

REFERENCES

Hiemenz, P. C., & Hudspeth, M. C. (1993, September/October). Academic excellence workshops for underrepresented students at Cal Poly, Pomona. *Journal of College Science Teaching*, 38-42.

Springer, L., Stanne, M. E., & Donovan, S. S. (1999). Effects of small-group learning on undergraduates in science, mathematics, engineering and technology: A meta-analysis. *Review of Educational Research, 69,* 21-51.

Treisman, P. M. (1985). A study of the mathematics performance of black students at the University of California, Berkeley (Doctoral dissertation, University of California, Berkeley, 1990). *Dissertation Abstracts International, 47* (05A), 1641.

AUTHOR

RUTH A. STREVELER is Director of Academic Services and Director of the Center for Engineering Education at the Colorado School of Mines.

Chapter 18

Supplemental Instruction at an Urban Community College

Joyce Ship Zaritsky

Supplemental Instruction (SI) is an internationally recognized nonremedial academic support program that provides free group peer tutoring to students in difficult courses. Student participation in SI has been shown to significantly reduce course failure, improve course grades, and increase persistence toward graduation (Martin & Arendale, 1990; Martin, Arendale, & Associates, 1993; Martin, Blanc, Debuhr, Garland, & Lewis, 1983). Most institutions report that student performance increases an average of one letter grade due to participation in SI. The results at our college have, for the most part, replicated and sometimes surpassed these national statistics (Zaritsky, 1994, 1998, 1999).

LaGuardia Community College is typical of urban public institutions. Almost 70% of our almost 10,000 full-time commuter students are of minority racial and ethnic origins. Fifty-five percent are foreign born; of these, 44% have been in the US for less than five years. Most work either full- or part-time while attending school; 20% are parents and have childcare responsibilities. Fifty-three percent report an annual household income of less than $16,000. Approximately two-thirds are the first in their families to attend college. About 25% are over the age of 30. Over 90% arrive needing some college preparatory work in reading, writing, mathematics, or English as a second language (LGCC, 1997, 1998). Although we have extensive remedial courses, academic support for students in nonremedial courses is extremely limited.

The majority of institutions with SI programs are four-year institutions. When we first suggested implementing an SI program, the administration was concerned, given the student demographics, that our students would not have time to attend SI study sessions. They were also understandably fearful that we would not be able to recruit enough excellent students to serve as SI

leaders. However, they did agree to a pilot of three courses in spring 1993. Pleased and perhaps surprised with the results, the administration found funding for SI through our institution's annual state funded Carl D. Perkins Vocational and Technical Act grant. Based on our continuing positive results, our funding has increased; in 1998–1999 SI was available in 22 courses, while in 1999–2000, we provided tutoring for 25 courses.

■ MODEL

Targeted Courses

Instead of targeting high-risk or failing students, SI targets high-risk or difficult courses with a failure rate of 25% or more. We have targeted courses in accounting, computer science, natural and applied sciences, mathematics, humanities and the social sciences. Since we do not have the funding to support all high-risk courses, we usually target introductory or gateway courses most critical for entering a major.

SI Leader Responsibilities

SI leaders are required to reattend the course for which they are hired and to take careful notes. In this way, SI leaders get to know the students, become aware of changes that may have occurred in the course since they were enrolled in it, and become cognizant of the problems students experience with the course material. They also have an opportunity to develop a collegial relationship with the course professor.

SI leaders must organize at least three weekly one-hour SI group study sessions, so named so that students understand that SI is not an individual tutoring program. During these study sessions, important concepts and ideas from the course are reviewed and practiced, and students engage in group problem solving with emphasis on getting students to actively engage and process the material. SI leaders are encouraged to get students solving problems at the board or working in groups at their seats. In the best sessions, a stranger entering the room should at first have difficulty differentiating the SI leader from participating students. SI leaders report that the most popular sessions are those in which students, alone or in small groups, complete practice quizzes or examinations. Students share their work, demonstrating problem solutions at the board when applicable. This gives attending students confidence to face the real examination. One SI leader stated that a student happily reported, "After your practice test, the real one was a piece of cake."

Attendance at SI sessions is voluntary. SI leaders' daily presence in the classroom and frequent announcements assure that students are constantly aware that this support program is available to them at any time and at no charge. Attendance is variable but generally grows as the semester progresses. Not surprisingly, it is at its largest before quizzes and examinations.

All students are invited and encouraged to attend SI study sessions. In this way, SI avoids the stigma that is frequently attached to tutoring programs that target failing students, and is known as a program that can help even good students improve their performance. The mix of student ability levels in study sessions means that stronger students assist and provide role models to weaker students, which reduces dependence on the SI leader.

Hiring and Training

SI leaders are most often hired to work with a professor with whom they have successfully completed a course. Most SI leaders are recommended by faculty, who find it reassuring that a former successful student is working with their students. Also, faculty feel pleased that they can provide preprofessional employment to their outstanding students. On occasion, SI leaders have recommended excellent students from their sessions. When this occurs we discuss the candidate with the faculty member to make sure he or she concurs with this recommendation. Only then are these students invited to apply (Appendix A-3).

The ultimate responsibility for hiring SI student leaders remains in the hands of the project director. We interview carefully, check references, and select candidates who combine excellence in course performance with empathy, kindness, enthusiasm, high energy, responsibility, and interest. Once hired, they sign a contract detailing their responsibilities, and remuneration (Appendix A-5).

Although we have occasionally experienced minor problems in recruiting for certain courses, we have generally been successful in hiring excellent students. Some leaders are native born Americans, while others comprise a virtual United Nations. Some are older and a few have even worked as teachers in their own countries. Because of the demographics and nature of our institution, we have made certain minor modifications to the original SI model in the way we hire student leaders. We often overlook students' problems with English syntax and pronunciation as long as language facility is not germane to the course. Our principal hiring criterion is that a student's spoken language is understandable. Also, since we are a two-year institution, our excellent student tutors are usually with us for a very short time, resulting in very high turnover of tutors. We are therefore constantly in a hiring mode. In addition, because of the uncertainty that accompanies registration at our institution, we sometimes have to make last minute changes, and student leaders can end up working with professors or adjunct faculty they don't know. When this occurs, we are sure to communicate with these professors to make sure they understand the nature of our program. We are pleased to report that whenever these last minute changes have occurred, faculty, whether full-time or adjuncts, have welcomed us and our student leaders.

SI leaders are trained in a two-day workshop prior to the semester. We use as a basis the training materials provided by the Center for Supplemental Instruction at the University of Missouri-Kansas City (UMKC), supplementing with materials we have developed ourselves. SI leaders learn how to organize and lead study sessions and how to develop effective lesson plans (Appendix C-2). Specific strategies presented and practiced include questioning and modeling techniques (Bloom, 1956), study skills, and fostering collaborative learning (Bruffee, 1994). The training is conducted with little lecturing and a great deal of peer-led group work, thereby modeling how we wish the leaders to conduct their own sessions. We emphasize that their role is that of a coach or facilitator who helps students solve problems and assume responsibility for their own learning. Lecturing to students, as a professor might do, is strongly discouraged. During training, SI leaders prepare and practice the presentation they will make to their class on the first or second day of class.

Once the semester begins, training continues in weekly meetings in which SI leaders share their successes and problems. Frequently, experienced SI leaders provide better solutions to problems than the project director can. These meetings also build collegiality, and many SI leaders become friends and support each other in ways unrelated to SI or even school. Leaders report that similar collegiality develops among students who regularly attend their study sessions. Often, they tell us that their students have formed their own study groups that meet in addition to the three weekly study sessions they provide. Tinto (1987) showed that learning communities such as this help students feel connected to their institutions and thereby lower attrition

Each SI leader is observed at least twice each semester by the project director or an assistant, often an experienced SI leader (Appendix D-1). Following each observation, the SI leader meets with the observer to review the strengths and weaknesses of the study session. Each semester we try to produce a videotape of at least one study session to use for future training, to show to administrators, and to support our presentations at professional conferences.

Program Promotion

To assure that SI continues to have a firm base of support, we keep in close contact with participating faculty and the administration via memos, professional articles, email and telephone conversations, and end of semester reports. At the end of each academic year, the president or provost presides at a ceremony at which each SI leader is presented with a certificate of appreciation. Faculty, administration, students, friends, family, and former SI leaders are invited. Participating faculty usually attend, as do a surprisingly large number of students who have participated in SI study sessions. It is always a joyful and inspiring event!

Table 18.1 EFFECT OF SI PARTICIPATION ON COURSE GRADES

Course	Section/ Semester	N[1]	Participation in SI%[2]	Mean Final Grade[3]			Successful Grades[5] (%)	
				Attendees[2]	Non attendees[4]	Attendees vs. Non	Attendees	Non attendees
Accounting I	1/F97	73	30	2.80	2.20	.60	88	71
	2/F97	38	63	2.46	2.00	.46	75	64
	3/F97	39	44	2.68	2.35	.33	94	86
	1/S98	39	41	2.30	1.80	.50	73	63
	2/S98	35	29	3.70	1.60	2.10	100	40
	3/S98	34	47	2.86	2.29	.57	71	69
	4/S98	33	55	2.60	1.30	1.30	82	33
Accounting II	1/F97	28	29	3.00	2.64	.36	100	93
Intro. Computer Science	1/S98	41	49	3.25	2.47	.78	100	100
Intro. Philosophy	1/F97	27	44	1.83	.54	1.29	67	15
	1/F98	27	26	2.43	1.20	1.23	86	38
Topics in Biology	1/F97	36	42	2.47	1.73	.74	73	47
	2/F97	33	48	2.13	1.77	.36	87	85
Fund. of Biology	1/F97	73	30	2.50	1.03	1.47	73	18
Microbiology	1/F97	35	37	2.54	1.21	1.33	92	37
	2/S98	22	68	2.20	1.60	.60	80	20
Biological Chemistry	1/F97	44	30	2.77	1.20	1.57	76	42
	1/S98	48	33	2.00	.80	1.20	69	29
	2/S98	44	30	2.23	1.64	.59	77	60
Overall Mean			40	2.75	1.65	.91	82	53

[1]Total number of students in section.
[2]Participated in SI sessions three or more times during the semester.
[3]Grades are calculated as A = 4.0; B = 3.0; C = 2.0; D = 1.0; F = 0. Students who received W or I were excluded from analysis.
[4]Participated in SI two or fewer times during the semester.
[5]Grades of A, B, or C. Again, students who received W or I were excluded from the analysis.

OUTCOMES

Students who attend three or more SI study sessions (attendees) average half a grade to slightly more than one letter grade higher in the supported course than those who attended between zero and two sessions (nonattendees), and attendees are more likely to earn successful grades—grades of A, B, or C—than nonattendees (Table 18.1).

About 40% of eligible students attended three or more SI study sessions during fall 1997 and spring 1998 (Table 18.1). We consider this percentage to be excellent considering the demographics of our students, but we are continually looking for ways to increase attendance at study sessions. One avenue we are presently exploring is adding one or even two scheduled study hours to targeted courses to assure that all students can attend at least some sessions each week. We have also begun selecting participating faculty more carefully, since faculty who actively encourage students to attend sessions achieve far better attendance than those who do not.

A survey (Appendix D-5) administered by SI leaders to all students enrolled in their targeted courses showed that 60% to 100% of attendees in 1997–1998 rated SI sessions as either good or excellent. In fall 1997, 88% of attendee respondents reported that the SI sessions were helpful in improving their grade in the course, and 49% indicated that they would like to see SI expanded to other courses. A more complete report is available (Zaritsky, 1999).

In evaluative essays written at the end of each semester, SI leaders are overwhelmingly positive in describing their experiences, employing phrases such as "extremely rewarding," "unique," "wonderful," "a growing experience," and "challenging." Their most common responses can be grouped into the following categories:

1) SI reinforced and deepened their knowledge of the subject matter.

2) Helping others gave them great satisfaction.

3) Being selected as an SI leader and then realizing they could be a valuable resource to their peers boosted their self confidence.

4) Serving as an SI leader provided them with a unique and valuable opportunity to get to know their professors and form more equal relationships with them.

5) A few SI leaders reported significantly raised educational and career aspirations, including attending graduate school in order to become a college professor.

We also informally poll via email faculty who participate, asking them to evaluate their experience with SI. Comments are unusually enthusiastic. Some representative excerpts: "should be available for every difficult course"; "deepens knowledge"; "indispensable to the development of mathematical maturity"; "a wonderful way to reinforce classroom instruction." In addition, approval can be clearly inferred from the numerous calls we receive from faculty as soon as they receive their future teaching schedules, requesting that they continue to be included in SI in upcoming semesters.

PRODUCTIVITY

Most SI leaders are paid $7.00 (first-time) to $8.00 (experienced) per hour. Some leaders use their SI experience as a for-credit internship, and others have volunteered because their visa status precluded our paying them. Additional expenses include a part time secretary, a statistical assistant, an SI assistant to help with observations, and a small amount of money for supplies and travel (Table 18.2). The project director (the author) is a faculty member who is paid in release time rather than in direct salary. During 1997–1998, we supported 301 students in 24 sections of 19 high-risk courses, at a cost per attendee of $131.00 per semester. These costs are extremely modest considering that for every student (full-time equivalent) that the college loses there is a loss of approximately $2,000 in state aid. Clearly the benefits of retaining students with this program far outweigh the financial loss that results when a student is forced to leave because of poor performance.

SUGGESTIONS FOR REPLICATION

The fact that SI is already in place in over 500 institutions of higher education both here and abroad is one indica-

Table 18.2 SI EXPENSES (1997–1998)

Expense Category	Annual Cost
Project director (released time)	$11,430
SI leaders (19)	$23,616
Part-time secretary	$ 3,024
Statistical assistant	$ 225
Learning assistant	$ 220
Supplies	$ 225
Travel	$ 800
Total	$39,540

tion that it is easily replicable. Despite initial concerns, our experience indicates that a two-year urban institution such as ours is ideal for this academic support program. The following are some suggestions for replication at a community college.

- Designate a professional from your institution to complete the training workshop held at UMKC (University of Missouri-Kansas City, 1999). This workshop is helpful in learning the nuts and bolts of running SI, and provides a substantial amount of invaluable material.

- Join the SInet listserv, accessible through the UMKC web site, to share your concerns and ideas with other professionals involved with SI. Get additional support from the National Association for Developmental Education (NADE, 2000) through its SI Special Professional Interest Network or SPIN. Take advantage of the fact that SI has a degree of standardization and a level of professional support not often available in academic support programs.

- Begin with a pilot. By targeting a small number of courses in the beginning, learn how to administer the program without the complications caused by large numbers.

- Try to work with those faculty regarded as "welcomers" rather than those regarded as "gatekeepers." The former are more likely to actively encourage student attendance at SI sessions and to support their SI leaders.

- Keep accurate and extensive records to provide continual evidence of the success of your program. Continually share the data you collect with all participants, the administration, and anyone else who is interested.

- Communicate, communicate, communicate with the entire college community. Keeping the administration informed is especially important since they are responsible for your funding. During 1999–2000, because of our extensive communication, we were able to get a small amount of funding from student government, enabling us to support five additional courses. We are hopeful that this student government funding will not only continue, but will increase.

■ CONCLUSION

Students at urban two-year colleges need support and encouragement if they are to succeed. Even though they may have completed their remedial courses, they still need support, and SI is an excellent means of providing this support. Our results indicate that with only minor modifications, SI can not only survive, but thrive, at a community college.

■ REFERENCES

Bloom, B. (1956). *Taxonomy of educational objectives.* New York, NY: Longman.

Bruffee, K. A. (1994). *Collaborative learning.* Baltimore, MD: Johns Hopkins Press.

LaGuardia Community College, Office of Information Management and Analysis. (1997). *1997 institutional profile.* New York, NY: LaGuardia Community College, The City University of New York.

LaGuardia Community College, Office of Institutional Research. (1998). *1997 new student survey report.* New York, NY: LaGuardia Community College, The City University of New York, Division of Information Technology.

Martin, D. C., & Arendale, D. R. (1990). *Supplemental instruction: Improving student performance, increasing student persistence.* (ERIC Document Reproduction Service No. ED 327 103)

Martin, D. C., Arendale, D. R., & Associates. (1993). *Review of research on supplemental instruction: Improving first-year student success in high-risk courses* (2nd ed.). Columbia, SC: National Resource Center for the Freshman Year Experience and Students in Transition. (ERIC Document Reproduction Service No. ED 354 839)

Martin, D. C., Blanc, R. A., Debuhr, L. A. H., Garland, M., & Lewis, C. (1983). *Supplemental instruction: A model for student academic support.* Kansas City, MO: University of Missouri and ACT National Center for the Advancement of Educational Practice.

National Association for Developmental Education (NADE). (2000). *National association for developmental education* [Online]. Available: http://nade.net

Tinto, V. (1987). *Leaving college: Rethinking the causes and cures of student attrition.* Chicago, IL: University of Chicago Press.

University of Missouri-Kansas City. (1999). Center for supplemental instruction [Online]. Available: http://www.umkc.edu/cad/SI/

Zaritsky, J. (1994). *Supplemental instruction: A peer tutoring program at LaGuardia Community College.* (ERIC Document Reproduction Service No. ED 373 850)

Zaritsky, J. (1998). Supplemental instruction: What works, what doesn't. In *Selected conference papers, Vol. 4* (pp. 54-56). Atlanta, GA: National Association for Developmental Education. Available: http://nade.net

Zaritsky, J. (1999). *Enhancing supplemental instruction training with techniques from collaborative learning.* (ERIC Clearinghouse for Community Colleges, ERIC number not yet assigned)

■ **AUTHOR**

JOYCE SHIP ZARITSKY is Professor of Communication Skills and Director of Supplemental Instruction at LaGuardia Community College, a member institution of the City University of New York.

Part III

Undergraduate Students Assisting with Special Groups

Chapter 19

Peer-Assisted Teaching and Learning in Distance Education

Judith A. Couchman

ajor changes have occurred in the Australian university sector in the last 20 years, the chief of these being the introduction of mass education. With an increase in high school retention rates and a 36% increase in student numbers in the higher education sector since 1975 (DEET, 1993; NBEET, 1995), the university student body has become more diverse in a number of characteristics. One of these is preparedness for university study. Many enter university ignorant of the "Geneva Conventions of academic battle," the expectations of faculty that students will be independent learners, critical thinkers, and competent writers in academic genres (Nightingale, 1988).

It was into this context that the Office of Preparatory and Continuing Studies (OPACS) in the University of Southern Queensland (USQ) introduced a Supplemental Instruction (SI) program in 1995 (Martin & Arendale, 1993). During 1995–1996, this program was implemented in selected, high-risk courses with on-campus students. Students who participated in SI performed substantially better than their colleagues who elected not to take part (Anderson, 1996; Couchman, 1996; Couchman & Bull, 1996).

However, USQ is a dual mode university; it offers its courses to 4,833 on-campus students, and to 13,873 off-campus students in Australia and over 40 other countries via distance education. Since 1977, all six faculties (arts, business, commerce, education, engineering, and surveying and sciences) have offered a wide range of courses to increasing numbers of off-campus students. The availability of SI for on-campus students raised questions of equity for off-campus students. Subsequently, OPACS modified the SI model for these students by providing a combination of remote-site and technologically-assisted sessions facilitated by graduates of the courses. The re-sultant program was named Distance PALS (Peer-Assisted Learning Strategy).

■ MODEL

The conventional mode of support for distance education students is through the course team and USQ's Distance Education Centre (DEC), working together to design, produce, and deliver a range of multimedia study materials to students. These materials include an introductory book with the course outline, a study schedule, assignment details, and worked past exam papers; a study book presenting the course content in modules; a book of readings, with supplementary journal articles; audio and videotapes; two or three telephone tutorials with faculty; audiographic tutorials (telephone tutorials with the additional benefit of graphic interaction via computer or electronic whiteboard) as required; and a variety of online discussion groups (all USQ students are provided with access to a dedicated, web-based, student intranet). In difficult courses with a history of low pass rates and at the request of the course team, Distance PALS is offered in addition to conventional academic support. Figure 19.1 (adapted from Weedon, 1997) illustrates the relationships between USQ personnel and distance education students and the support systems provided.

The Distance PALS program has implicit in its structure the four phases of action research: planning, action, observation, and reflection to improve future planning and action (Brown, Henry, Henry, & McTaggart, 1982; Grundy & Kemmis, 1981). The stakeholders are the Distance PALS supervisor, the Distance PALS leaders, the course teaching team, and the enrolled students. The supervisor is a learning enhancement academic within the government-funded Academic Learning Support unit who coordinates, plans, implements, and evaluates the program. The Distance PALS leaders are students who have achieved at least a credit pass in the course and have been trained by the supervisors to facilitate the on-campus and off-campus evening workshops. The course instructor (professor) liaises with the supervisor and leaders in regular meetings and leads the course teaching team, which includes other lecturers and tutors (teaching assistants) responsible for teaching the course. The students are most likely to be over 20 years of age, working part- or full-time, undertaking only a part-time academic load each semester, and working and studying for vocationally-related reasons (Taylor, 1997).

The course explained and evaluated here is a first-year core course in economics. Consequently, the enrolled students come from diverse educational backgrounds and are studying either commerce (with majors in accounting, banking, or finance) or business (with majors in marketing, human resource management, or economics).

Planning

The planning stage of Distance PALS begins in the previous semester with the identification of prospective student leaders. Current leaders and faculty nominate as possible PALS leaders students who have performed well and have shown an aptitude for helping fellow students in Distance PALS sessions and tutorials. Training of those selected is conducted by the supervisors and current leaders

over two days, and includes such topics as student needs, the philosophy and structure of PALS, collaborative learning techniques, and practice in planning, implementing, and evaluating PALS segments and entire sessions. At the beginning of the semester, supervisors and Distance PALS leaders meet face-to-face either on-campus or at the Brisbane Study Centre for a day's review of the previous semester and planning for the current one.

The week before the semester begins, the supervisor notifies regional liaison officers and students of the Distance PALS venues and times by email and mail respectively. The regional liaison officers encourage students to attend Distance PALS and take bookings for the audiographic sessions in their beginning of semester telephone calls to students.

Action

During the action phase, Distance PALS leaders facilitate seven two-hour sessions, held every other week. These sessions are delivered either face-to-face with leaders in the two study center locations with the majority of student enrollments, Toowoomba and the State capital, Brisbane; or by audiographics, with the leader in the on-campus Outreach Services studio, and the students at other study centres throughout the state. Leaders encourage students to actively engage difficult study material through providing

Figure 19.1 DISTANCE PALS MODEL

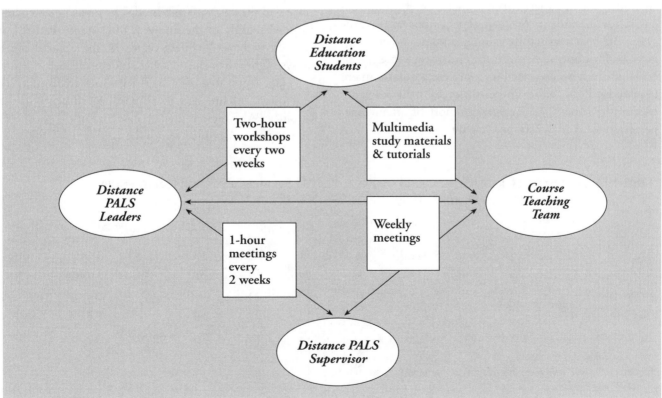

study tips, quizzes, discussions, group activities, competitions, construction of mock examination questions, and implementation of mock tests. The course instructor also makes a brief appearance (10 to 15 minutes) in the first and final sessions. In the first session she/he encourages student participation, outlines the course, and answers questions. In the final session, she/he gives guidance on exam preparation and answers questions.

Leaders and the supervisor prepare for Distance PALS sessions in one-hour debriefing and planning meetings, held every other week, face-to-face on-campus and online. Any additional training of leaders occurs here as well. The supervisor meets weekly with on-campus student leaders and the course instructor for debriefing and planning both the on-campus and Distance PALS programs. Outcomes of these meetings are either emailed to student leaders not able to attend because of geographic distance, or included in the online debriefing and planning meeting between the supervisor and leaders.

Observation

The supervisor observes each Distance PALS session in person at the on-campus venue and the audiographics studio, and twice per semester at the Brisbane Centre. Supervisors and leaders evaluate and discuss leader performance and student involvement as part of the debriefing and planning meetings.

Reflection

At midsemester, supervisors conduct a brief group discussion with students on their expectations of the program, the benefits they are gaining from it, and any suggestions for improvement. At the end of the semester, all enrolled students are asked to complete a questionnaire (Appendix D-5), either in person or by mail. Each semester the supervisor prepares a report of attendance, performance, and questionnaire data.

■ OUTCOMES

Comparisons between Distance PALS attendees and other groups of enrolled students are the basis for ascertaining program outcomes. Data from the first semesters in 1997, 1998, and 1999 have been aggregated and comparisons drawn between 1) attendees (those who attended at least one, two-hour workshop) and those other students who resided in the selected geographic regions and were invited to attend but either chose not to or were unable to, and 2) attendees and all other enrolled distance education students, including those to whom Distance PALS was not available. The positive impact of Distance PALS is evidenced by the superior performance of attendees compared with both other groups with respect to high grades, mean grades, and pass rates (Table 19.1).

When overall course pass rates and mean grades for 1996 (preDistance PALS), 1997, 1998, and 1999 are compared, improvements can be noted (Table 19.2). The course pass rate improved modestly in 1997. The relative inexperience of the leaders and the unexpected challenges (relocation of the off-campus venue, interruptions to telecommunications connections, greater numbers of students attending than would fit into the rooms available, and students' misconceptions of what the program would offer them) in implementing the program at a distance were overcome in the second implementation (1998), and the pass rate improved substantially. In the third year of implementation, 1999, minor curricular changes were made and the pass rate stabilized. The mean course grade dropped slightly in the first year of Distance PALS, but has increased in subsequent years with the attendee mean always higher than the all other student mean.

Data aggregated over the three semesters from a student questionnaire sent to all enrolled students in the Distance PALS regions are also evidence of the success of the program. Attendee respondents (n = 108, for a re-

Table 19.1 AGGREGATE GRADE COMPARISON OF DISTANCE PALS ATTENDEES AND NONATTENDEES IN SEMESTER 1, 1997, 1998, 1999

Student Group	HD[a] %	A %	B %	C %	F %	IDS[b] %	Mean Course Grade[c]	Pass Rate %
Attendees (N = 173)	4	10	27	35	21	3	4.08	76
Nonattendees (N = 340)	1	4	15	28	45	6	3.07	48
All Other Enrolled Students (N = 801)	1	7	14	28	45	5	3.13	50

[a]High distinction, over 90%.
[b]Incomplete with deferred supplementary examination or assignment.
[c]On a 7-point scale.

sponse rate of 62.4%) were demographically typical of USQ's distance education students. The greatest proportion (85%) attended Distance PALS for assistance with the content of the course while 28% were seeking help with revision of the content for the examination and with examination techniques, and 19% wanted to gain a better result than they might have in this difficult unit without the help of Distance PALS. Respondents equally appreciated the student participation and leaders addressing content problems (44%). Also appreciated equally were the informal atmosphere and the friendliness of the leaders (23%). When questioned about their dislikes of the program, 31% did not respond, 10% disliked nothing about the program, and the major dislike (15%) was the limited length of sessions. The main suggestion for improvement (24%) was for more structure and routine in the sessions. Like most adult learners, distance education students are very focused and like to know what to expect during their limited study time. A clear majority of respondents considered that Distance PALS had helped them with revision and examination preparation (68%) and motivation to study (68%). Leader qualities noted were their involvement of students (90%), friendliness and approachability (84%), sharing of appropriate study hints (80%), and sound content knowledge (77%).

Nonattendee respondents (n = 76, for a response rate of 22.4%) had a similar demographic profile to that of attendees. Most were unable to attend because of a time clash (39%) or lack of time (33%).

Leaders from each semester reported that they gained satisfaction from the friendly, informal atmosphere of the sessions, assisting students to become independent learners, using their own experience and expertise to help others, and the stimulus of working with other leaders and faculty. They considered that they benefited from the program because it developed their leadership and commu-nications skills, extended their knowledge of the discipline, and gave them valuable experience in small group management. Faculty commented in a questionnaire on the "high calibre" of the leaders.

Faculty found leader feedback useful in modifying their teaching during the course offering and later, the curriculum itself. The course instructor included additional explanations of difficult content in the lectures and tutorials following such PALS feedback. The difficult content identified in this way was used to inform decision-making in the modification of the curriculum for subsequent semesters. Some of the more tangential material was omitted, allowing time to expand the areas identified as more difficult. Both quantitative and questionnaire data confirm the success of Distance PALS and provide valuable feedback for all stakeholders as the program evolves to meet student needs more flexibly and effectively.

■ PRODUCTIVITY

In addition to the educational attainment aspects of Distance PALS there is, of necessity, a balance sheet aspect to be considered. Retention is a significant contemporary issue, not the least because of its financial impact on higher education institutions. It has been established that at USQ the Supplemental Instruction/PALS on-campus program is cost effective in that future tuition and fees from retained students exceed the sum the school pays for Supplemental Instruction/PALS (Couchman, 1997). The number of additional students retained can be as few as five per semester for all Distance PALS leader costs to be covered for one course in one semester (Table 19.3). The assumption is that those who pass the unit will continue

Table 19.2 EFFECT OF DISTANCE PALS ON COURSE PASS RATE AND COURSE MEAN GRADE

	1996	1997	1998	1999
Course Pass Rate (%) for all Enrolled Distance Learning Students	46	49	57	58
Course Mean Grade	3.08	2.96	3.41	3.60
Distance PALS Attendee Mean Grade (n = 173)	N/A	3.45 (n = 58)	4.38 (n = 54)	4.42 (n = 61)
All Other Enrolled Distance Education Student Mean Grade (n = 801)	N/A	2.87 (n = 296)	3.19 (n = 243)	3.38 (n = 262)

Table 19.3 COST EFFECTIVENESS OF DISTANCE PALS

Item	$AUS	$US
Leaders' salaries (4 leaders x 30 hours x $24.54/hour)	2,890	1,880
Audiographic connection (telecommunication cost for telephone and data link)	2,008	1,305
Miscellaneous (supervisor travel costs, postage)	800	520
Cost of Distance PALS	5,698	3,705
Federal government funding for each course for each enrolled student	1,200	780
Number of additional students needed to be retained to cover program costs	4.75	4.75

studying at least the next semester. When compared with nonDistance PALS 1996 results, in 1997, eight extra students passed the unit, in 1998 it was 26, and in 1999 it was 31.

The cost effectiveness of the program is multiplied when a longer-term view of these 4.75 students is taken. Each subsequent semester when these students, who would have dropped out of their degree courses, re-enroll, they attract additional funding to the university.

Many productivity benefits besides financial gain to the institution are impossible to quantify. Among these are the benefits of success, directly to the student and indirectly to the institutional reputation, and the gain that leaders experience in developing high levels of employment-related skills.

SUGGESTIONS FOR REPLICATION

Although Distance PALS at USQ enjoys the support of an in-house distance education student support department with external study centres, it is possible to replicate the program without such extensive and expensive infrastructure. Two basic models, each having alternative points of delivery, can accomplish this.

In the first model, student leaders can facilitate from the institution using video-conferencing software. Students in a particular geographic area can meet in either a community-based, computer-equipped facility or a home linked by video-conferencing to the institution. For little initial outlay (in 1999, approximately AUS$300) each desktop personal computer can be fitted with a microphone and video camera. NetMeeting can be downloaded free of charge from the Internet. The only costs for the school are for student leader time and Internet connection. If student leaders are available in the centres where enrolled students live, Distance PALS can be held face-to-face in a community-based facility or one of their homes. In both cases, the role of the student leader would expand to include having access to the course roll and student details, making initial contact with students, and organizing Distance PALS meeting times. Video-conferencing has the advantage over email of immediate interaction with the leader and with other students. Also, the facilities of shared files and electronic whiteboards could be used to actively encourage collaboration.

As an alternative, leaders can conduct email discussion groups. These are more loosely organized but can respond readily to student needs. Protocols can be set up so that a global mailing group is defined, but students receive leader emails as if each was the only recipient. The leader would send out a global email at the beginning of the semester welcoming students, explaining the function of Distance PALS and his/her role as leader, providing some content-specific questions or advice, perhaps with the first assignment in mind, and inviting responses. Student responses would be dealt with according to the leader's discretion, either posting replies globally and inviting comment, or responding privately. As email discussion groups have the propensity to be extremely time-consuming, the leader would have to set clear guidelines on when to check mail and respond. The facility to exchange file attachments and interact synchronously or asynchronously, individually or globally could be used to build substantial collaborative learning into this medium.

CONCLUSION

The Distance PALS program was developed and implemented in response to equity issues in USQ's dual mode environment. This program had been successfully implemented with on-campus students, and technological solutions were sought to offer a comparable program to distance education students. In conjunction with the University's Distance Education Centre, such solutions were found and the Distance PALS action research cycle of planning, acting, observing, and reflecting has been in successful operation since 1997.

REFERENCES

Anderson, D. (1996). *Evaluation of supplemental instruction pilot project: Nursing foundations 2, S2, 1995.* Report of The Office of Preparatory and Continuing Studies, USQ, Toowoomba.

Brown, L., Henry, C., Henry, J., & McTaggart, R. (1982). Action research: Notes on the national seminar. *Classroom Action Research Network Bulletin, 5,* 1-16.

Couchman, J. (1996). *Report on the pilot study of the supplemental instruction program: 51103 financial accounting, semester 2, 1996.* Report of The Office of Preparatory and Continuing Studies, USQ, Toowoomba.

Couchman, J. (1997, December). *Supplemental instruction: Peer mentoring and student productivity.* Paper presented at the Australian Association for Research in Education (AARE) Conference, Brisbane, Australia.

Couchman, J., & Bull, D. (1996). *Report on the pilot study of the supplemental instruction program: 51008 business economics, semester 1, 1996*. Report of The Office of Preparatory and Continuing Studies, USQ, Toowoomba.

Department of Employment, Education and Training (DEET). (1993). *National report on Australia's higher education sector*. Canberra, Australia: AGPS.

Grundy, S., & Kemmis, S. (1981, November). *Educational action research in Australia: The state of the art (an overview)*. Paper presented at the Annual Conference of the Australian Association for Research in Education, Adelaide, Australia.

Martin, D. C., & Arendale, D. R. (1993). *Supplemental instruction: Improving first-year student success in high-risk courses* (2nd ed.). Columbia, SC: University of South Carolina, National Resource Center for the Freshman Year Experience.

National Board of Employment, Education and Training (NBEET) (1995). *Charting a course: Students' views of their future*. Canberra: AGPS.

Nightingale, P. (1988). Language and learning: A bibliographical essay. In G. Taylor, B. Ballard, V. Beasley, H. Bock, J. Clanchy, & P. Nightingale (Eds.), *Literacy by degrees* (pp. 65-81). Philadelphia, PA: The Society for Research into Higher Education and Open University Press.

Taylor, J. C. (1997). *A dual mode of distance education: The University of Southern Queensland* [Online]. Available: http://www.usq.edu.au/dec/staff/taylorj/readings/oprax97/oprax97.htm

Weedon, E. (1997). A new framework for conceptualising distance learning. *Open Learning, 12* (1), 40-44.

◼ AUTHOR

JUDITH A. COUCHMAN is Associate Lecturer for Learning Enhancement, and Coordinator of the PALS and Distance PALS programs in the Office of Preparatory and Academic Support at the University of Southern Queensland, Toowoomba, Queensland, Australia.

Chapter 20

Using Structured Study Groups to Create Chemistry Honors Sections

Brian P. Coppola, Douglas S. Daniels, and Jason K. Pontrello

The University of Michigan is a large, public, Research I institution, founded in 1817 in Detroit and relocated to Ann Arbor in 1837. Over 37,000 students on the Ann Arbor campus are enrolled in 19 different colleges, schools, and divisions, including nearly 17,000 enrolled in the largest of these units, the College of Literature, Science, and the Arts, in which the Department of Chemistry is located.

In 1994, the Department of Chemistry introduced an elective honors option, called Structured Study Groups (SSG), within both terms of "Structure and Reactivity," our 1,000-student first-year contemporary organic chemistry course. Students who wish to take this course for honors credit enroll in the SSG option in addition to taking the regular lecture, recitation, and laboratory portions of the course. The SSGs meet two evening hours per week in collaborative learning sessions led by junior or senior undergraduate student leaders.

We developed this modified supplemental instruction option in lieu of a separate honors section of the course because we felt that first-term students could not judge whether taking an honors section of organic chemistry is appropriate for them. Under our format, students can experiment with taking the course for honors credit for three weeks and then drop the SSG sessions if they find them too difficult. Because SSG honors students take the same recitation sections, labs, and exams as nonSSG students, coursework for honors and nonhonors credits can be compared easily. In addition, an SSG honors option saves a faculty teaching assignment that otherwise would be required for a separate honors section. Finally, the SSG option is not restricted to students in the honors program. Any student who elects and completes the SSG option is awarded honors credit.

Approximately 18% of the students in the first-term course, and 16% in the second-term course, enroll in the SSG honors option. About half of second-semester students enrolled in SSGs are in the regular 800-person course; the rest are in a separate, more intensive version of the course where everyone participates in SSGs. Table 20.1 summarizes the scope of the SSG program.

■ MODEL

The concept of reciprocal teaching (Brown & Palincsar, 1989; Palincsar & Brown, 1984;) and the power of explanatory knowledge (Coleman, 1998; Coleman, Brown, & Rivkin, 1997) have informed our design of the SSG model. In reciprocal teaching, instructional tasks are designed by studying the strategies used by successful learners and implementing these to guide novices' learning. In an explanatory framework, tests are seen as an opportunity for students to teach us, to demonstrate their understanding by explaining their ideas, and it proposes that students need opportunities to practice and develop teaching skills before their teaching performance is tested. Research on explanatory knowledge concludes that students need to reflect on their learning and develop interpersonal com-

Table 20.1 THE SCOPE OF THE UNIVERSITY OF MICHIGAN SSG PROGRAM (1998–1999)

Term	Total Enrollment	SSG Enrollment	No. Sections (Leaders)
Structure/Reactivity I (Chem 210)	1,000	175	12
Structure/Reactivity II (Chem 215)	800	175	12
Structure/Reactivity II (Intensive)	65	65	5

munication skills as a part of the learning process. This reflection and skill development will help them understand that true learning comes from discussing the basis for one's answers and conclusions rather than memorizing the answers (Chambers & Abrami, 1991). Effective teaching also involves viewing students' answers as a step in the learning process instead of as being correct or incorrect. An effective teacher can look at students' answers from both the student and teacher perspectives and focus on the assumptions that led to those answers. The challenge that then arises is reconciling inconsistencies between student and teacher perspectives. SSG leaders provide a bridge to help with this reconciliation.

SSG Leader Selection and Training

SSG leaders are juniors and seniors who demonstrated teaching skills when they were SSG students. Deliberately following the analogy of moving students who demonstrate research potential in laboratory courses and to higher level work, SSG tasks permit students to demonstrate their teaching potential with the idea that they might become SSG leaders. SSG leaders identify prospective future leaders from among their students and justify their choices to the faculty coordinator. Identified students submit essays to the coordinator as part of the selection process for SSG leaders. Leaders are not necessarily chemistry majors; of 36 student leaders from 1994 to 1999, 23 have been majors in chemistry, one in biochemistry, three in biology, and nine in cellular and molecular biology.

As former SSG participants, SSG leaders begin with a strong sense of the program. SSG leaders attend weekly lunchtime meetings with the faculty coordinator to reflect on their teaching, anticipate teaching issues, and determine the evaluation criteria for the week. Each week a different leader leads a discussion on teaching and learning, and then records and distributes the outcomes and recommendations for the group. Leaders continue to discuss teaching issues throughout the week on the SSG leaders' listserv.

SSG Leaders in Chemistry 210 ("Structure and Reactivity I")

Because SSG sessions are for honors credit, leaders must go beyond leading group work with problem sets or delivering extra content in a didactic manner. SSG sessions follow a detailed curriculum that encourages discussion and explanation activities that lead to deep mastery of organic chemistry. SSG sessions and homework assignments involve a number of activities that build on each other. In the first session for example, SSG leaders 1) have students go to the blackboard to teach one another how to decode line formulas, 2) take them to the library to explore chemistry journals, and 3) present a short lecture on proper citation format.

For the subsequent homework assignment, SSG leaders have students apply the concepts to new material using a creative task. For their first assignment for example, leaders ask students to pick a molecule with 10-13 carbon atoms from a chemistry journal, construct five new molecules with the same formula, rank the molecules based on selected properties (e.g., magnitude of dipole moment, boiling point, and solubility), and write out rationales for their rankings. The student work for this assignment must include a statement putting the journal article into context, a copy of the journal page from which the example came, and a properly formatted citation. In other assignments, leaders ask students to format an appropriate quiz problem from the new material.

The next SSG session builds on the homework assignment. Students must submit one copy of their homework to their leader and distribute the rest to their classmates for one or two rounds of peer review. SSG leaders create a set of review questions, which for the first assignment might address whether the molecules fit the prescribed criteria, whether the format and information are appropriate to the class level, and whether the citation is formatted correctly. Peer review is a time of in-depth discussions and great learning and the first round can take up to an hour. During this time, the leader circulates, noting common issues that arise, sending students with interesting examples to the board, and otherwise facilitating a sometimes raucous discussion.

In the peer review, students must grapple with ideas in a classmate's homework that conflict with their own and figure out where errors in understanding the material or process have occurred. This grappling gives SSG students the opportunity to make, recognize, and correct their errors before they take an exam. The reviews are returned to the originator, who has a chance to decide whether to make any changes to the original assignment. The SSG leader collects the edited assignments and peer reviews and uses them in evaluating student performance.

The leaders provide feedback to students on their work and participation in the SSG sessions and use this feedback to assign SSG-session grades based on a scale of O (outstanding), S (satisfactory), and U (unsatisfactory). The course grade for an SSG student is determined in the same manner as it is for a nonSSG student (the exam scores). To receive the course grade with an honors designation, students need to receive an S or O grade in their

SSG section. A U in SSG results in the student receiving the honors designation, but the course grade is reduced.

SSG Leaders in Chemistry 215 ("Structure and Reactivity II")

During the second term of "Structure and Reactivity," students have two SSG options. First, they may choose to enroll in the 800-student mainstream course with an SSG option for honors credit. The SSG sessions are similar to those of the first semester with more challenging material and activities appropriate to the higher level course. A second option is taking a separate research-oriented section of the course with about 85 students; SSG sessions are required of all participants who take this option.

In the research-oriented option, there are two layers of SSG assignments. For the first layer, SSG leaders help design and implement a series of tasks that are comparable to those in the SSG sections for the larger course. For the second layer, SSG leaders help students create and carry out projects involving various technological environments. For one of these projects, for example, students constructed a resource on advanced chemical transformations that was incorporated into the course web site. Reading journal articles, understanding the chemical transformations described in them, and then creating animated reaction mechanisms and interactive assignments for their classmates causes the students to think like teachers. The technology project they create is fully owned by the students and they must seek out each other's expertise to understand the material and complete the project.

The SSG leaders in the research-oriented section do a great deal of work that would be impossible for one faculty member to do, including creating lessons on HTML authoring, locating appropriate software, and managing the logistically demanding task of coordinating the efforts of 85 individuals working on a single web site project.

Copies of the complete SSG curricula are available at the CSIE (Chemical Sciences at the Interface of Education) web site (The University of Michigan, 1999) along with representative examples of student work.

■ OUTCOMES

Forms of Assessment

We have collected six forms of assessment data on the SSG program: 1) exam performance for SSG honors students relative to nonSSG honors students and relative to honors students prior to introducing SSG, 2) numerical and narrative survey information from students at the end of their SSG experience, 3) reflections by SSG leaders, 4) performance-based assessments on a counterintuitive task the term after an SSG experience, 5) student reflections on SSG work at least one year following their experience but before they graduate, and 6) annotated student materials (a course portfolio) assembled by SSG leaders.

Exam Performance

We have demonstrated a link between participating in SSGs and better grades (Table 20.2). The average performance of honors college students after the introduction of SSGs *(Hpost)* is higher than the average of those before the introduction of SSGs *(Hpre)*, and the average performance of honors students who enrolled in SSGs *(HSSG)* is higher than honors students who did not enroll in SSGs *(HnSSG)*. We analyzed the results and con-

Table 20.2 COMPARATIVE EXAM PERFORMANCE FOR HONORS AND SSG STUDENTS, 1990–1998

	1990	1991	1992	1993	1994	1995	1996	1997	1998
Hpre	4.0	8.2	7.0	5.2	*(6.10)*	*(6.10)*	*(6.10)*	*(6.10)*	*(6.10)*
Hpost					9.40	7.00	11.00	10.30	11.50
HSSG					10.80	8.33	13.00	15.70	15.10
HnSSG					0.14	2.52	6.61	2.57	3.37
nHSSG						11.90	14.10	10.40	15.92

H(Pre): The 1990–1993 difference scores represent actual differences, and the value of 6.1 between 1994–1998 is a calculated average from the 1990–1993 difference scores. It is used to show the expected difference score if SSGs had not been added to the course.

H(post): Difference scores after adding SSGs to the course. *H(post)* includes both those who participated in SSG *(HSSG)* and those who did not *(HnSSG)*.

HSSG (Honors SSG): Difference scores for honors students who elected SSGs (70-80%).

HnSSG (Honors no SSG): Difference scores for honors students who did not elect SSGs (20-30%).

nHSSG (nonhonors SSG): Difference scores for 25-60 nonhonors students who elected SSGs for honors credit each year.

cluded that the difference in performance between *HSSG* (7.0%–11.5%) and *H(pre)* (4.0%–8.2%, 6.1% average) can be correlated with participating in SSGs rather than that the academically better honors college students were self-selecting into the SSG sections. In practical terms, this difference in performance corresponds to one-third to two-thirds of a letter grade (i.e., B+ or A- instead of B). The procedures we used for that analysis are too detailed for this paper, but are available from the authors.

Numbers in the table are called difference scores, and represent the difference between the average course grade (percentage) for honors students and nonhonors students (e.g., 4.0 in 1990 is the difference between the 65.01% average of 571 nonhonors students and the 69.06% average of 95 honors students).

Numerical and Narrative
Survey Information from SSG Students

We have collected student feedback from each SSG class. The average reply in Chemistry 210 and 215 has become more positive since the first time SSGs were offered. Chemistry 210 students report a high level of satisfaction with SSGs and their SSG leaders, and they are typically neutral on whether they would like to be leaders themselves. While these students support their SSG leaders comparably to those in the research-oriented section, their overall satisfaction with SSGs is not as high. This latter observation is aligned with other information we have about mainstream Chemistry 215, namely, that it is commonly taught in a "fact-heavy" way with less of the con-

ceptual overview that SSGs are designed to support. In Table 20.3, we have listed representative responses from student surveys of Chemistry 210.

These numerical results are coupled with written statements that the students provide. Since 1994, 75%–85% of the written comments in a given year have supported SSG work, 10%–15% of the comments were neutral, and 5%–10% were negative or contradictory. See Table 20.4 for examples of the comments.

Reflective Memos From SSG Leaders

We collect reflective memos from the leaders during their service to monitor their development as teachers. These two brief excerpts are representative samples.

> One could never expect a group of novice learners to precipitate a useful exchange on a topic to which they have just been introduced.... [so] we leaders strive to first deliver a necessary amount of information, assist in its integration, and then facilitate conversation on the topic.... not only to catalyze and focus conversation but also to provide a model of an experienced learner.

> The most important lesson I learned was that the 'teacher' is never just an instructor, but a student as well for the rest of their life. This became evident after going through the program first as a student and then as an instructor.... I believe that my students taught me as much as I taught them.... I hope that [if I teach]...I won't forget that I will always be a student.

Table 20.3 SAMPLE OF STUDENT SURVEY RESPONSES FROM CHEMISTRY 210

	F94/102	F97/130	F98/150
The Chemistry 210 SSG assignments, group work, and participation:			
1) I made a motivated effort to do my best on my written assignments.	4.11 (0.5)	4.41 (0.7)	4.39 (0.7)
5) The in-SSG group work enhanced my understanding of Chem 210 topics.	3.76 (0.7)	4.36 (0.8)	4.17 (0.9)
6) Overall, participating in the SSG sections was of high value to me.	3.34 (0.6)	4.44 (0.9)	4.02 (1.0)
7) If I knew in September what I know now about SSGs, I would still elect it.	3.77 (0.7)	4.58 (0.9)	4.15 (1.0)
My Chemistry 210 SSG section leader:			
9) Overall, my section leader did an excellent job as an instructor.	4.22 (0.6)	4.72 (0.6)	4.50 (0.7)
The future after Chemistry 210:			
15) I would like to be a 210 SSG leader when I am a junior or senior.	2.96 (1.1)	3.09 (1.3)	3.11 (1.4)
17) I intend to participate in Chemistry 215 SSGs next term.	3.72 (1.1)	4.31 (1.2)	3.94 (1.3)

Scale: 1 = strongly disagree, 2 = disagree, 3 = neutral, 4 = agree, 5 = strongly agree

F94/102: fall 1994; average of 102 student replies with standard deviation in parenthesis

F97/130: fall1997; average of 130 student replies with standard deviation in parenthesis

F98/150: fall 1998; average of 150 student replies with standard deviation in parenthesis

Performance-Based Assessments on Counterintuitive Task

SSG students spend two hours per week in sessions that emphasize peer review and analysis of the process of understanding concepts and solving problems, as well as the development of self-assessment skills. One of our expectations is that SSG students will realize that answers to homework problems can be the beginning of meaningful discourse about chemistry, not the end. We performed a study using an interview-based, think-aloud format in order to discover whether SSG sessions had helped students develop advanced problem solving behaviors, including computational chemistry skills.

We created three groups of subjects: an expert group of faculty and graduate students, an experimental group of students from the SSG groups, and a control group of nonSSG groups matched by academic performance in the chemistry course. The subjects were presented with data and asked to make a prediction, with the nature of the data being such that the most likely prediction would be the opposite of experimental results. An interviewer recorded the responses of the subjects as they described their thought processes. Once subjects made a prediction and elaborated on it, they turned to the second page, where they confronted the actual—counterintuitive—results of the experiment. The subjects were instructed to reconcile the actual results with their predictions and suggest a test for their ideas.

The expert group demonstrated the following attributes: 1) restating the problem, 2) taking an inventory of the major factors, making an early prediction, and following up with an extensive, elaborative explanation, 3) adopting a cyclical process of examination of a model, rejection on the basis of a counter argument, and proposal

of a new model, and 4) utilizing primary literature sources, new experiment designs, and computational chemistry methods. About 80% of students who had participated in peer review exercises in the SSG sessions shared the same problem solving behaviors with the experts, while only about 20% of nonSSG utilized these behaviors (Coppola, Daniels, & Lefurgy, 1996).

Reflective Student Responses to SSGs

In January 1999, we collected feedback from 78 of the 390 former SSG students who were at least one year out of the courses. Students received an electronic mail request to reply to three questions. The replies were collected and categorized.

The first question stated that research showed that participation in SSGs strongly correlated with improved performance on Chemistry 210 exams and asked their opinion of this. The vast majority of respondents (93%) reported that this correlation made sense to them. The reasons offered by these students are congruent with benefits from participating in group learning: 1) the content is anchored to the real world because work is based on authentic, primary literature, 2) providing explanations builds confidence, 3) the format provides chances to explore unknown material and lessens tendencies to oversimplify explanations or rules, 4) discussions are guided by mutual respect, not spoon-feeding, 5) the format encourages the asking of questions, and 6) the format provides opportunities for not-so-perfect explanations to develop into better ones.

The second question asked students to consider which aspects of participating in SSG sessions might have impacted their student life beyond their performance in Chemistry 210. All responses were favorable. They said that SSG sessions 1) permitted them to work with others

Table 20.4 SAMPLE COMMENTS ON STUDENT SURVEYS

Type of Comment	Sample Comments
Positive comments (75%-85%)	"It doesn't allow me to convince myself I know something, but forces me to demonstrate and teach that knowledge."
	"SSG made me feel much more confident about my chemistry understanding through extra practice and talking with other students."
	"At first, SSG seemed time consuming and confusing because of the new ideas and information, but very quickly it cleared up any confusion I had in Chem 210 overall and I became confident with my assignments and I started to see them as very interesting."
Neutral Comments (10%-15%)	"There's a lot of work." "It was not as hard as I thought it might be."
Negative or Contradictory Comments (5%-10%)	"I put in a whole lot of work and didn't reap that many benefits."
	"I think a lot of stuff was pointless and busy work, but a good portion helped us out in chemistry."

who have differing points of view, 2) provided a community of people willing to help, whether in class, in the residence hall, or by email, 3) created a smaller space in a large university, a place to call their own, 4) opened their eyes to the possibilities of teaching, and 5) that familiar faces from the SSG session made lab and lecture less intimidating.

The third question asked their opinion of an honors option that deviated from the traditional honors model of offering segregated sections and that used upper-level undergraduates as instructors. Once again, SSG students were unanimous in their support, saying that leaders have "the authority of recent experience" as chemistry students, understand students, are approachable and understanding, and create an environment where fear of doing an imperfect job is reduced.

■ PRODUCTIVITY

The Undergraduate Initiative, a discretionary fund administered by the College of Literature, Science and the Arts (LS&A) provided the initial investment for the SSG experiment from 1994 to 1997. The major cost for running the SSG program is stipends for the SSG leaders, who are paid through the honors office in the College of LS&A. In 1998, the college included SSG as a permanent budget item for the honors office.

SSG leaders are paid at the rate of $1,080 per term, 12 weeks x six hours per week (four hours for preparation and grading, and two contact hours) x $15/hour. In the Fall 1998–1999 term, 12 SSGs served a total of 175 students at a total cost of $12,960. The honors office and the Department of Chemistry supplement this budget by covering the cost for the weekly staff meeting, which is held over lunch. Food expenditure for 1998–1999 was $1,750 (for 13 people for 13 weeks). From a practical standpoint, the cost for the leaders' stipends and meals ($14,710 in fall 1998–1999) is significantly lower than a faculty member's separate course assignment in each of two terms (about $30,000 per term), and six graduate student instructors teaching two SSG sections each (at $12,500 per year per graduate student for a total of $75,000). Based on 175 students in 12 SSGs during the first-term course, the cost for the SSG program is $84 per student in the SSG sections, while a separate course would be $600 per student. Although tuition would be collected for a separate section of the course, this figure does represent an add-on cost, the least cost-effective portion of which would be an increase in the department's teaching load.

■ SUGGESTIONS FOR REPLICATION

Dealing with Initial Resistance
Although our campus has a tradition of using undergraduate students to help with teaching, using them as primary instructors for an honors option was controversial. How did we overcome this resistance? Initially, we argued for an experimental program by citing the benefits of student-centered classrooms and peer-led instruction. Once we began to gather experience, we found that using the assessment data on the program, as well as offering a few well-timed presentations by SSG leaders at the Honors Advisory Board meetings, readily dispelled the resistance.

Selecting Undergraduate Instructors for Demonstrated Potential
We have found that having the SSG leaders nominate the next generation of leaders from among their students is an excellent method of finding the best replacements. Leaders observe their students' nascent teaching skills and can provide highly informed recommendations about who would make a good SSG leader. Also, we ask potential leaders to write an essay describing their interests, abilities, and motivation for becoming SSG leaders. To date, a triangulation of information (leader impressions, faculty impressions, and an essay) has worked successfully for us.

Importance of Faculty-Leader Collaboration
Faculty and student leaders need to fully understand the collaborative responsibility that this system requires. SSG leaders are part of a teaching and learning team, and leadership for the program is shared. Faculty must be willing to develop student leadership and then delegate real responsibility to the leaders. Faculty must also remember their responsibility as mentors because SSG leaders are still students learning to teach and lead. SSG curriculum materials should also be developed collaboratively by faculty members experienced with curriculum design and students with insight into the learning process.

Not Using Traditional Textbook Problems
Each assignment strikes a balance between enough of an open-ended problem to promote creativity ("create and rank five molecules") and enough structure to keep the tasks similar enough for students to encounter the same concepts along the way ("within these specified criteria"). Congruent with the tenets of reciprocal teaching, SSG leaders reflect on their own understanding in order to design tasks that reveal the smaller steps in problem solving that novices need to consider explicitly. A copy of the most recent SSG curriculum materials is available at the CSIE web site (The University of Michigan, 1999).

CONCLUSION

Even more than an effective instructional method, the SSG program is a cornerstone to a broadened vision of scholarly development for future faculty (see the CSIE web site for a detailed discussion). Historically, curricular design has allowed students to demonstrate their potential for research (e.g., in a first-year chemistry laboratory) and be moved into positions of increasing independence and leadership (namely, undergraduate research). So, too, is the design of the SSG program, where the curricular tasks develop students' explanatory knowledge and allow them to demonstrate their potential for teaching. SSG leadership is the position of independence and leadership into which students with these skills can move. The first generation of SSG leaders who have gone to graduate school have carried a strong, positive imprinting experience that has affected their teaching as graduate student instructors and, we predict, their careers as future faculty members.

REFERENCES

Brown, A. L., & Palincsar, A. S. (1989). Guided, cooperative learning and individual knowledge acquisition. In L. B. Resnick (Ed.), *Knowing, learning, and instruction: Essays in honor of Robert Glaser* (pp. 393-451). Hillsdale, NJ: Lawrence Erlbaum Associates.

Chambers, B., & Abrami, P. C. (1991). The relationship between student team learning outcomes and achievement, causal attributions, and affect. *Journal of Educational Psychology, 83*, 140-146.

Coleman, E. B. (1998). Using explanatory knowledge during collaborative problem solving in science. *The Journal of the Learning Sciences, 7* (3&4), 387-427.

Coleman, E. B., Brown, A. L., & Rivkin, I. (1997). The effect of instructional explanations on learning from scientific texts. *Journal of the Learning Sciences, 6* (4), 347-365.

Coppola, B. P., Daniels, D. S., & Lefurgy, S. T. (1996, August). *Integrating computational chemistry into a structured study group program for first-year university honors students.* Paper presented at the 212th national meeting of the American Chemical Society, Orlando, FL.

Gardner, J. B., Coppola, B. P., & Ryder, T. R. (1997, September). *Novel instrument for the self-assessment of laboratory reports: The student laboratory assessment checklist (SLAC).* Paper presented at the 214th national meeting of the American Chemical Society, Las Vegas, NV.

Palincsar, A. S., & Brown, A. L. (1984). Reciprocal teaching of comprehension-fostering and comprehension-monitoring activities. *Cognition and Instruction, 1,* 117-175.

The University of Michigan. (1999). *Chemical sciences at the interface of education* [Online]. Available: http://www.umich.edu/~csie/

AUTHORS

BRIAN P. COPPOLA is an Associate Professor of Chemistry, Faculty Associate at the Center for Research on Learning and Teaching, and Director of the Chemical Sciences at the Interface of Education program at the University of Michigan.

DOUGLAS S. DANIELS is a Macromolecular and Cellular Structure and Chemistry graduate student at The Scripps Research Institute, La Jolla, California.

JASON K. PONTRELLO is a Chemistry graduate student at the University of Wisconsin-Madison.

Chapter 21

Student Mentoring and Community in a University Honors Program

Ronald E. Mickel

The University of Wisconsin-Eau Claire (UW-EC) is a comprehensive liberal arts university also housing various professional and master's degree programs. In 1999, enrollment was approximately 10,500 students, 2,015 of whom were freshmen with an average ACT composite score of 23.6. The university honors program generally enrolls about 4% of those attending UW-EC. New first-year students who are in the top 5% of their high school class and who rank in the top 5% nationally on their ACT or SAT, as well those who complete one semester at UW-EC with at least a 3.67 GPA (and ACT or SAT scores in the top 14%) can participate in the honors program

All but a few courses offered by the honors program satisfy general education requirements. To earn "university honors" at UW-EC, students must graduate with a 3.5 grade point average (out of a possible 4.0) and must complete, in addition to one-credit first-year and senior seminars, four colloquia, interdisciplinary courses specifically for honors students, and four electives, honors sections of regular courses. All honors courses are limited to twenty students and are designed by faculty to be highly interactive and to enhance communication, critical thinking, leadership, and collaborative skills. Tests and exams are rare, and student presentations, group projects, and classroom participation are emphasized.

Five years after the inception of the university honors program, a one-credit senior capstone seminar was added. This mandatory course requires students to review their undergraduate experience, the rationale for the degree requirements, and the value of a liberal education with the aim of providing coherence and integration to their education.

As director of the program, I have taught this senior seminar each semester. Initially, I found myself surprised, disappointed, and frustrated with students' superficial understanding of what was meant by a liberal education, the rationale behind the various requirements for a baccalaureate degree, the differences between humanities and social science courses, and the various methodologies employed by academic disciplines. The course quickly evolved in approach and content to include more in-depth examination of these topics

Students were unanimous in praising the value of the new focus and, no doubt belatedly, understanding the thinking behind the requirements for graduation they had faced, especially in general education. Repeatedly students commented on how the seminar should be a first-year course for they had never before studied such topics, and nowhere in their undergraduate curriculum had they encountered a systematic effort to explore the meaning and worth of a liberal education and the opportunities that the pursuit of a baccalaureate degree provided. Each semester the chorus of student lament grew louder.

A required first-year, one-credit course, however, at that time would have created at least five sections of the seminar each fall and two or three in the spring. Existing program resources and available faculty were insufficient to staff those sections. Gradually, we explored a solution that would have seniors in the honors program teach first-year seminars.

■ MODEL

The University of Wisconsin-Eau Claire publicizes the fact that students officially do not teach other students. The honors program, however, has always been accepted as a laboratory for experimentation in teaching and learning strategies and interdisciplinary course content. So, to escape this caveat we chose the word "mentoring" to describe the actions that student assistants would take in the course. The proposed change breezed through the university honors council without opposition and the university senate adopted the proposal. Two new one-credit courses were established: Honors 100: "First-Year Honors Seminar" and a senior-level Honors 410: "Mentoring in Honors." In the first year, five sections of Honors 100 were offered in the fall of 1996, and two in the spring of 1997. (In the fall of 2000, seven sections will be offered, each with two senior mentors.)

To enroll in the new mentoring course, students need to have taken Honors 400: "Senior Honors Seminar" as well as the new first-year seminar. The content of the senior seminar was revised to build on the work of the first-year seminar and not duplicate it. Mentors meet with me as a group once a week, with some additional reading required, to plan the assignments and activities of their weekly classes with the first-year students, and to discuss their experiences in mentoring from week to week. These class sessions include discussions of how to guide first-year student learning. To keep the honors requirement needed for university honors to 24 credits (20% of total credits required for graduation), mentors can substitute the mentoring course for one of the four required three-credit colloquia.

The first-year seminars have successfully introduced to students topics that the honors program had previously only offered to seniors. In addition, we added an introduction to campus learning resources and Myers-Briggs Type Indicator assessment to assist students in their self-understanding and in academic and career choices.

Mentors, in teams of two, lead weekly one-hour discussions. We emphasize to mentors their roles as "big siblings" who assist new students in learning the ropes of such things as online degree audits, registration procedures, graduation requirements, email, and to whom new students can turn for help. We insist that mentors join their students in attending at least one campus forum, concert, or theatre production in hopes of encouraging regular participation by honors students in the rich opportunities available outside the classroom.

Mentor selection for first-year seminars has been easy, as it has been all self-selection. Seniors who wish to be involved have had the personalities, background, and talents to teach their sections of the course, and having two seniors work as a team has ensured that if one should prove to be weak or less effective, the other could pick up the slack. So far each semester, twice as many seniors than we can use have wished to mentor. We first selected seniors on the basis of the first to sign up, but since have used published criteria including graduation date, number of honors courses completed, and GPA.

■ OUTCOMES

The new first-year seminar in itself increased the honors program's educational impact on students as well as its student credit-hours production. First-year students gain an understanding of the justifications for a liberal education, the nature of academic disciplines, their own learning styles, and responsibility for their own education. Mentors have their own understandings clarified and reinforced, further develop their interpersonal, communication, and leadership skills, and add a significant experience to their résumés.

From its onset, the university honors program has tried to create a sense of community among its students. This was easy during the first year, 1983–1984, when there were 80 students in the program, all of whom were in their first year and sharing in the process of creating the program. As the program grew (to 332 participants in 1997), with students ranging from first-year to senior, a sense of community did not come so easily. Ten years ago we tried to create a buddy system within the honors program, pairing new incoming students with upper-class students. However, the results were uneven and the effort was quite time-consuming to administer.

The introduction of Honors 100: "First-Year Honors Seminar" in the fall of 1996 quickly proved effective in promoting community by linking upper-class mentors with students just joining the program. The course's benefit to new students, mentors, the honors program, and the university was demonstrated during its first semester. Evaluations by first-year students have been almost unanimous in praising the educational value of the experience. They point to the value of having models of successful seniors working with them during their first semester on campus. They see the importance of examining topics that earlier had not been discussed until the senior-level Honors 400, and they developed an awareness of the implications of their own learning styles as a result of the Myers-Briggs assessment. Meanwhile, with no exceptions, mentors have described their experiences in handling the course as one of the most, if not the most, valuable single experience of their undergraduate careers. I have been pleased with the almost unanimous positive and enthusiastic formal and informal evaluations of the seminars by the students, both first-year and mentors.

This new mentor-led first-year seminar has had a positive impact upon the number of students completing the honors program requirements and on doing so earlier. Since the inception of the new course, the number of students finishing the basic honors requirements by the end of sophomore year has increased by one third, and those doing so by the end of junior year by more than 50%. Fewer seniors now are still in need of taking honors courses. In the past, one section each semester of Honors 400, the senior capstone seminar, of no more than 20 students, provided enough space for the students completing the program. Now we need two sections each semester. Enrollment in Honors 400 has increased over 50% since the creation of the first-year honors seminar. It currently appears that the number completing the program and graduating with university honors is likewise increasing by at least 50%.

Another consequence of the first-year seminar is improved retention. At present, approximately 100 students join the program each fall and only eight, on average, transfer each year to other colleges and universities. Total program enrollment has grown from 332 in the fall of 1997 to 354 in the fall of 1998 to 375 in the fall of 1999, mostly the result of improved retention. Students clearly have a better sense of being part of a community of learners. The only change made during this time was the introduction of the first-year seminars with senior mentors.

The university has borrowed from the university honors program for its "first-year experience" courses now available, but not required, for all new first-year students at UW-EC. In the fall of 1999, 86 sections, each limited to 20 students, enrolled 1,700 of the 2,015 new first-year students. Faculty teaching these courses, which are regular general education courses, are assisted by an upper-class student mentor whose responsibilities include leading group discussions, tutoring, and assisting the professor in paperwork. Budgetary support for these university first-year experience courses came from UW-EC students voting overwhelmingly to accept a $50 increase in tuition each semester. This differential tuition beyond that imposed by the state, provides support for courses such as the first-year experience and senior capstone and provides additional funding for student-faculty research collaboration.

Final evidence of the effectiveness of the mentoring program is the interest that seniors show in participating. With more seniors wishing to mentor than can be accommodated, and given the success of the mentoring course, we introduced another one-credit senior course in the fall of 1999, Honors 420: "Tutoring in Honors." Students are not permitted to enroll in both the mentoring and tutoring course. Tutors assist instructors in an honors elective course that they have previously completed. Instructors of courses using tutors are involved in the selection of students. Tutors have responsibilities such as leading review sessions, tutoring individual students, taking over in an instructor's absence, and joining in group dis-

cussions. This course was approved and scheduled after most students had registered for fall 1999 courses so only two changed their schedules to enroll in Honors 420. More are expected for spring 2000 as the opportunity becomes better known. We will be monitoring the effectiveness of this tutoring course, hoping that it will enhance student learning and further develop the sense of community among students in the honors program.

■ PRODUCTIVITY

The only financial cost associated with the introduction of the first-year honors seminar was the duplication of materials distributed in classes. Since a classroom was available, needed instructional technology existed, and student mentors received one credit in Honors 410: "Mentoring in Honors" instead of pay, creating the course had no monetary impact on our program. The course did, however, have a time cost since I increased my teaching load, selectively curtailed my involvement with university committees, and decreased my time for research. The university gained in productivity in that I, the official instructor in each section of the seminar, was now teaching nine or more additional credits each academic year (seven or more first-year seminars, plus a section of the mentoring course each academic year).

Productivity also improved in another way. The number of students participating in the honors program has been steadily increasing. Ten years ago approximately 70 to 80 students enrolled each fall. Since then, more honors-eligible students have been choosing to attend UW-EC, with 105 enrolling for the fall of 1999. As noted, more students are finishing the program and earning university honors. This has put increasing enrollment pressure on the 20 to 24 colloquia and elective courses the program offers each semester. Most have closed (at 20 students) by the end of registration, causing difficulty for students to register in the required number of honors courses in order to finish the program. Given the recent budget constraints imposed by the State of Wisconsin on the University of Wisconsin System, the likelihood of the honors program being allocated additional resources has been slim. For the honors program to be able to offer more courses, other programs would have to offer fewer, and, of course, everyone is convinced that their department, unit, or college needs more. The mentoring course, which substitutes for one of the four required colloquia, has reduced enrollment pressure on the colloquia offered each semester, with now 18 mentors each academic year needing one fewer colloquia.

SUGGESTIONS FOR REPLICATION

The model of using talented seniors who are well informed in the subject matter to teach first-year students in one-credit, first-year experience courses should not be difficult to replicate. For example, the Department of History, my tenure home, could develop a first-year experience course for history majors that would be mentored by seniors majoring in history. The mentors would need to be carefully selected and specially trained in pedagogy as well as on the issues involving a liberal education today, perhaps in a one- or two-credit senior course. Such a "mentored" first-year course could introduce new college students to the department and the discipline of history, the requirements (and reasons for them) of the major, the nature of historical research, and career possibilities. It would also be an opportunity to introduce incoming history majors to the university, to the justifications underlying the university requirements for graduation, to the value of a liberal education, as well as to the many resources on campus that support student learning and provide guidance in the pursuit of a career. Such a course, mentored by seniors, would enhance the sense of community and belonging among students majoring in history.

CONCLUSION

Successful innovations in an academic program sometimes emerge not from brainstorming, not from a thor-ough review of the relevant literature, nor from careful empirical analysis of how to be more effective, but from the inner dynamics of the program itself. Recent changes in the university honors program at the UW-EC have enhanced student motivation to learn, improved their understanding of the value of a liberal education, and promoted a better sense of community among those participating. Although these changes came amid continued national discussions in higher education of the value of first-year experience courses and of students helping other students, the immediate impetus came from within the program and in large measure from students themselves.

The experience of the university honors program at the UW-EC suggests that such a course as Honors 100, mentored by able seniors, could be added to programs with negligible financial costs but with significant educational gains for all involved.

AUTHOR

RONALD E. MICKEL is Professor of History, Director of the University Honors Program, and Coordinator of the Network for Excellence in Teaching at the University of Wisconsin-Eau Claire.

Chapter 22

Where Undergraduates Are the Experts: Peer-Based Instruction in the Writing Center

Dennis Paoli and Eric Hobson

From their often overlooked inception early in the 20th century, through higher profiles with the open-admissions movement of the 1970s, writing centers and their primarily undergraduate staff have become an integral part of higher education, and discussion of issues surrounding the use of peer undergraduate tutors as primary instructional resources has become commonplace (Murphy, Law, & Sherwood, 1996). Despite writing centers' longstanding use of undergraduate peer tutors and the intuitively familiar picture of peers huddled together discussing assignments, describing peer tutoring in writing centers is a problem. Each writing center is site-specific, making it difficult to describe a generic peer tutoring system. At the same time, certain features are common to writing center tutorials: 1) the agenda is determined through negotiation, 2) the interaction relies heavily on a series of exchanges to assess needs and establish goals, and 3) the focus is more macro than micro, attending first to global issues, such as audience, organization and revision, and second to sentence-level issues. This mix of features is consistent with the overarching goal of longitudinal ability development—the tutor's mission is to create a better writer, not necessarily a better paper.

To describe how we see undergraduate peer tutoring in a writing center setting, the discussion in this chapter is situated within a specific learning environment, Hunter College. This institution is an open admissions college of approximately 19,000 students, 500 full-time faculty and 700 adjunct faculty, and is the largest of the ten senior colleges in the City University of New York (CUNY) system. Undergraduate writing tutors serve the whole school, so Hunter's mission statement is theirs, and the college's commitment "to excellence and access" drives and defines the tutorial experience. The nature of the writing center has been shaped by the ever-changing demands of the curriculum and student body. A 1989 college-wide study determined that over 80% of Hunter College courses used writing as a means of testing. This may mean an additional challenge for the 60% Hunter's undergraduate population who speak English as a second language (ESL), or to the 56%-58% who are older than 23. Many in this second category are returning to Hunter from the working world of New York City and are unsure about the quality of their academic writing skills after a hiatus from academia. In these circumstances, Hunter College Writing Center has developed an array of tutoring and outreach programs, many of which may be recognizable to those in smaller urban and rural liberal arts colleges, as well as at larger urban multicollege universities.

■ MODEL

Founded in 1976, the Hunter College Writing Center offers peer tutoring to student writers at every level, remedial to graduate, across the curriculum. The center's services are free and voluntary; even referred students are not required to come to tutoring sessions. Begun as a peer tutoring program providing primarily one-to-one tutorials and a few workshops on term papers and essay exams, the center has evolved in response to student needs and changing budgetary and academic policies. In the process, undergraduate tutors have taken on more significant responsibilities in delivering and developing tutorial help. They tutor, supervise other tutors, train new tutors, and generate support materials for every service the center offers: pair and small group tutoring, drop-in service, various in-center and classroom workshops, classroom tutoring, special-case instruction (e.g., for students with disabilities or multiple repeaters of basic writing courses), web site development, email tutoring, and interactive self-paced learning programs. From going over a paper for organization problems, to leading a group discussion on documentation styles, to creating web-based instruction on outlining, undergraduate writing center tutors participate in every category of pedagogy short of teaching assigned courses and labs. Students benefit from working with peers who have faced similar writing challenges. Because undergraduate tutors are more likely to have greater familiarity and more recent acquaintance with undergraduate writing, they are indispensable to a writing center's performance and fundamental to its pedagogy.

On average, 25–35 tutors fill a six-day, 67-hour-per-week schedule. About 75% are undergraduates representing a dozen different majors, with about 50% being English majors. Primarily juniors and seniors, the staff also includes several sophomores, an occasional freshman, and several graduate students from the English master's program or the School of Education.

Recruitment and Selection of Tutors

The center attracts tutors by reputation and referrals from targeted faculty in the English department, the honors program, the School of Education, and various writing intensive courses and programs. Applicants interview with the coordinator, who inquires into their academic writing experience, explains the responsibilities of the job and the principles of peer tutoring, and provides written information on those principles and procedures. At a second interview, potential tutors furnish a copy of a graded essay they have written for a Hunter College course, analyze a sample of student writing and outline a tutoring strategy they would use if working with the writer, and write an extemporaneous essay on a tutoring-related topic. The coordinator hires the tutors on the basis of the interviews and written submissions. Tutors work five to 20 hours a week and are paid as college assistants. All tutors are paid and professional work habits are expected. The center does not accept volunteers because staff positions require a semester-long commitment for agreed-upon hours. First-term tutors are limited to five to eight hours a week to ensure that they can handle the demands of the work without hurting their academic studies.

Tutor Training

Newly hired tutors attend a one-hour orientation, at which they learn about the center's resources and record keeping procedures. Next, each new tutor observes a tutoring session to see the principles of tutoring in practice. First-year tutors attend weekly one-hour training sessions, where staff demonstrate and analyze tutoring techniques and share problems and methods particular to specific modes of tutoring (e.g., pairs and drop-ins) and special

populations (e.g., ESL and learning disabled students). The training sometimes features guest presenters (faculty with expertise in writing development or administrators of programs such as the Office for Students with Disabilities), but most sessions are led by experienced undergraduate tutors in the writing center.

In a weekly tutor training memo distributed via email to all tutors, the coordinator updates the calendar, provides logistic information (e.g., the photocopier is working again), and discusses tutoring issues. Tutors use a discussion list to talk about issues introduced by the coordinator memo or raised in training sessions, ask for advice with tutoring problems, and share solutions, insights, and afterthoughts.

Within the first month of service, new tutors observe a second tutoring session or a workshop, this time focusing on specific points of interest or problems encountered in the first few weeks on the job. Near the end of a tutor's first semester at the center, the coordinator observes one of the tutor's regularly scheduled tutorials and makes a written record of the session, without making assessment comments. The tutor and coordinator discuss the session, referring to the written record and paying particular attention to the techniques employed and choices made by the tutor. At the end of every semester, the coordinator meets with each tutor to review and evaluate the term's work, highlighting the most successful and most problematic tutoring experiences and the professional lessons learned. The review process includes a self-evaluation and also student evaluations, if they are available.

Individualized and Small Group Tutorials

The majority of tutorials at the writing center are, and have always been, regularly scheduled one-hour sessions of one-to-one or paired (two-to-one) tutoring in 12 scheduled sessions over a 15-week semester. Students are only paired in a session if they are from the same disciplinary course or the same level of basic writing; learning disabled and physically challenged students are not paired. Having 12 scheduled sessions helps students focus on developing as writers instead of focusing on last-minute improvements on individual assignments.

Drop-in service, offered for 44 hours over a six-day week, is available for half-hour, individual sessions on a first-come, first-served basis. Students who cannot get or do not need a weekly hour can receive as many drop-in sessions as they need or want, though they must sign-in for each session and wait, if necessary, until a drop-in tutor becomes available. Drop-in sessions challenge tutors. The limited time often leads the student to pressure the tutor to focus on fixing a particular paper instead of helping them develop as writers. Therefore, experienced tutors provide most of the drop-in service.

The sole exception to the center policy of voluntary participation is special case instruction, when the Developmental English Program determines that a student who has repeated a basic writing course multiple times but has not passed the exit exam would be better served by studying with a tutor in the writing center than by taking the course again. The student must attend a minimum of 12 hours of tutoring focused on the writing and test-taking skills necessary to pass the exit exam that demonstrates writing competency. The English department administers and grades the exam. These cases are rare but demonstrate academic departments' authorization of the center to use undergraduate tutors to provide required instruction.

In-Center and In-Class Workshops

Undergraduate tutors are included among the leaders of up to120 one-hour workshops a semester, on classic topics, such as writing documented essays and writing exam essays, and on a broadening field of issues including sentence structure and the verb system, writing about art, and writing assessment test preparation. Workshops accommodate up to 15 students, and it is the workshop leader's job to get all the students to participate: to speak to the issue, do exercises, or apply the workshop lessons to their individual assignments. Extending tutoring techniques to a small group is difficult and is the focus of extra training sessions for tutors who will become workshop leaders.

Tutors also lead in-class workshops, tailored to specific class writing assignments. In these cases, undergraduate tutors are responsible for teaching all or part of a class period. The core content of these workshops is helping students apply the writing process to the assignment in question (e.g., a book report or a discipline-specific research paper). The challenge, as with in-center workshops, is to get students actively involved, motivating them to ask and answer questions, offer examples, and debate issues. In addition to working with classes during the regular semester, tutors also work in three- and six-week prefreshman and intensive intersession training programs for the Writing Assessment Test, where they instruct small groups of students in peer-editing techniques and lead discussions on writing and test-taking skills. Tutors in these programs must coordinate with faculty and adapt writing center pedagogy to the classroom, serving the teacher's syllabus while maintaining the principles of peer tutoring. This situation can be daunting because tutors are still students in classrooms themselves. The training usually involves two tutors doing the in-class workshops, with an experienced tutor mentoring a tutor in training.

Online Tutoring

While the proliferation of OWLs (online writing labs) and tutoring by email has extended writing centers' reach worldwide, it has fueled profound debate on its efficacy and its effect on writing center principles (Hobson, 1998). Like most others, Hunter's OWL (Reading/Writing Center Page, 2000) describes the center, promoting its services, stating its policies, and offering access to its handouts and exercises. Most undergraduate tutors enter Hunter College with computing skills or gain them in their first year. They use these skills to produce computer-generated texts, tables, and images that support regular tutoring sessions and that also can be made available through the OWL.

E-tutoring (tutoring via email) allows students at Hunter College's separate campuses and those who have difficulty attending tutorial sessions (e.g., due to scheduling problems, family responsibilities, or physical challenges) to access the center's tutoring service. Tutors who provide e-tutoring must be trained in the use of email programs, especially those program features that support tutoring (e.g., interpolating questions within the student's original text in a reply message). Because the interpersonal dimension of the tutoring process is absent online, tutors must be trained to resist the potential for e-tutoring to devolve into mere editing (Monroe, 1998; Rickly, 1998). Still, adapting tutoring methodology to email by carefully analyzing the student text, determining a hierarchy of concern, and guiding the writer's attention to those areas of concern is crucial for those who would otherwise be unable to access tutoring services.

Peer e-tutoring is the primary interactive component in the center's self-paced program for education students who are preparing for the essay writing components of the state teacher certification exams. This program is accessible on the center's web site and provides information on the exams and writing process as it applies to the required essays, quizzes on key steps in that application, and the opportunity to submit practice outlines, theses, summaries, and drafts to the center's e-tutoring staff. Undergraduate tutors helped design the program and will furnish the critical email tutorials.

■ OUTCOMES

Hunter College's Writing Center conducted a study in fall 1988 comparing pass rates of students in remedial ESL and freshman composition courses who received regularly scheduled tutoring at the writing center with pass rates of those who did not. Statistics were tabulated from writing center records and pass rates provided by the registrar's office. In every case, students who came to a minimum of seven tutorial sessions had a higher pass rate—by 9% in freshman composition and up to 27% in introductory ESL classes—than those who did not attend tutorials (Table 22.1).

These outcomes replicate Lerner's findings (1997) that tutoring improves performance at a significant rate in composition courses generally, and in the ESL student population specifically. The studies also reflect the collective wisdom of the students themselves; from 1990 to 1999, 74.3% of registrants for weekly tutorials were students who spoke and wrote English as their second language.

Evidence from writing center evaluation surveys show student satisfaction with the writing center and improved self-image as a result of tutoring sessions. Over the last decade, 99% of students responding said they would recommend the center to other students, and over 85% rated their tutor "excellent" or "very good." Satisfaction was also reflected by attendance. In fall 1998, the average number of regularly scheduled weekly tutoring sessions attended was 11.2 out of 12. Over the years, answers to a question on the effect of the writing center on self-image ("Has the writing center helped you feel more comfortable and/or confident as a Hunter student?") has produced an average positive response of 95%. This evidence of program satisfaction and improved self-image, in conjunction with Lerner's contention that the higher success rates effected by tutoring contribute to improved retention, makes a compelling case for the role of writing centers in retaining students at an institution or in a course of study (Lerner, 1998).

While most centers collect raw data, such as attendance figures, and tabulate results of satisfaction surveys, assessing outcomes (i.e., improvement in writing skills) is often problematic. Many writing centers do not grade or quantify performance, and the nonjudgmental nature of tutoring seems inimical to quantitative outcome assessment. The desired end product of the tutoring process is helping a student become a better, more confident academic writer. While a passing or improved grade may suggest tutor and center success with a student, it does not measure that success.

■ PRODUCTIVITY

In fall 1998, 4,774 Hunter College students used the writing center in some capacity, approximately 25% of the student population. Students who attend writing center tutoring on a regular basis develop academic writing and critical thinking skills, and change their attitude toward writing and learning from anxiety and frustration to at least relative enthusiasm. Growing demand for the center's services among students (seeking extended hours), faculty (requesting more workshops), and programs (soliciting consultation, e.g., for a CUNY-wide writing-across-the-curriculum initiative) argues persuasively for the effectiveness of writing center pedagogy and undergraduate tutors.

Weekly hour-long tutoring is the service most in demand: all available tutorial hours fill within several hours of opening registration. It is also expensive; the format of sessions varies and available hours grow or diminish with budgetary vagaries. When necessary, the center offers four-person one-hour weekly study groups of students from the same level writing course. These sessions are run as small workshops on specific problem

Table 22.1 PASS RATES, FALL 1988, IN REMEDIAL ESL AND FRESHMAN COMPOSITION COURSES (COMPARING STUDENTS WHO ATTENDED SEVEN OR MORE WEEKLY TUTORING SESSIONS AND THOSE WHO RECEIVED NO REGULAR TUTORING)

	Weekly Tutorials	No. of Students	No. Who Passed	% Who Passed
Eng 003 (Remedial ESL–Introductory Level)	With	8	7	88%
	Without	31	19	61%
Eng 004 (Remedial ESL–Intermediate)	With	13	11	85%
	Without	92	60	65%
Eng 005 (Remedial ESL–Upper Level)	With	58	24	41%
	Without	234	92	39%
Eng 120 (Freshman Composition)	With	86	72	84%
	Without	1121	846	75%

areas as they appear in the students' written work, with an emphasis on providing practical methods for addressing those problems.

Budgets for writing centers range widely, depending on the center's role in its institution and the status of its staff, who might be adjunct faculty, volunteers, or student interns. At Hunter in spring 2000, undergraduate tutors were paid $8.75 per hour and graduate student tutors received $9.50 per hour. We hire 15 to 20 new tutors every year. The costs per student served for standard in-center tutorial services in a recent semester are calculated in the Table 22.2.

Since 1996, the writing center has been part of a larger learning center, the Hunter College Reading/Writing Center, and shares administrative staff with the English department-run reading center and a computer facility, so administrative costs are complicated to determine. However, within CUNY, a program director receives a salary of $40,00–$55,000, and supervisory staff (two to four in any given term) are paid at a rate of $25,000–$35,000 per year or $20–$30 per hour. Clerical staff comes from the Federal Work Study Program, and tutors perform clerical tasks as part of their responsibilities, so the writing center has no budget for clerical support.

An even more important aspect of productivity that is not measured by cost analysis is the benefits accrued by the undergraduate tutors. Regularly weekly tutorials provide a profound educational experience for the tutors as well as the student writers. Tutors learn to create nonjudgmental relationships with students in which writing problems are discussed, assessed, and worked through, and in which all parties build confidence and gain ability. Undergraduate tutors develop strategies to apply to more challenging tutorial formats, becoming more versatile and valuable instructors. They also become better academic writers themselves. Several programs in the School of Ed-

ucation request that their students gain experience at the writing center, evidence of the efficacy of writing center pedagogy in teacher education.

■ SUGGESTIONS FOR REPLICATION

The success of writing centers that use undergraduate tutors testifies to the reproducibility of their methods and policies. As long as there are bright, committed undergraduates to perform the tutoring, writing centers will provide impressive educational results for students, courses, programs, and schools. We would like to share three pieces of advice for those thinking of starting a writing center that utilizes undergraduate tutors.

- Ongoing training is necessary to make the most of and extend the capabilities of student tutors. This can be done efficiently by giving the tutors, whenever possible, training responsibilities, for example in mentoring programs or in leading weekly discussion sessions for training new tutors.

- With the rapid expansion of writing center services over the Internet, it is advisable to hire staff with computing skills or to have tutors trained by the college's instructional computing department if the center cannot provide equivalent training.

- Although it requires a considerable investment of time, careful and extensive record keeping is important in evaluating the success of a writing center, identifying areas to upgrade, and justifying budget requests.

For more information on using undergraduate tutors in writing centers, look at the National Writing Centers Association (1998) web site.

Table 22.2 COSTS FOR IN-CENTER TUTORIAL SERVICES, HUNTER COLLEGE, FALL 1999

Tutorial Service	# Hours	Cost per Hour	# Students Served	Total Cost	Cost per Student Served
Regular weekly tutoring	179/week for 12 weeks	$9/hour (average)	257	$19,332	$75.22
Drop-in tutoring	64/week for 15 weeks	$9/hour (average)	1737	$8,640	$4.97
In-center workshops	65	$9/hour (average)	250	$585	$2.35
Tutor training	1/week/tutor for 13 weeks	$9/hour (average)	2,261 (2,244 students who received in-center services plus 17 tutors)	$2,142	$0.95
Total			2,261	$30,699	$13.68

CONCLUSION

Writing centers have helped drive curricular change in higher education, particularly through their advocacy for continuous reflection on educational practice and writing instruction, for proactive approaches to teacher training and apprenticeship, and for expanding awareness of the large available pool from which institutions can draw for excellence in teaching—their undergraduate population. Writing center commitments have included making higher education an equitable and effective environment for expanding student populations, and encouraging curricular initiatives and innovative pedagogies such as writing-across-the-curriculum, collaborative and active learning, one-to-one and small group peer instruction, and online delivery of services. The result is a sophisticated understanding of the benefits that accrue to students, staff, and institutions through carefully constructed, administered, and evaluated uses of undergraduate students in collegiate writing instruction and support (Bruffee, 1984, 1993; Harris, 1986, 1995; Hobson, 1992; Trimbur, 1983, 1987).

REFERENCES

Bruffee, K. A. (1984). Peer tutoring and the 'conversation of mankind'. In G. A. Olson (Ed.), *Writing centers: Theory and administration* (pp. 77-84). Urbana, IL: NCTE.

Bruffee, K. A. (1993). *Collaborative learning: Higher education, interdependence, and the authority of knowledge*. Baltimore, MD: Johns Hopkins University Press.

Harris, M. (1986). *Teaching one-to-one: The writing conference*. Urbana, IL: NCTE.

Harris, M. (1995). Talking in the middle: Why writers need writing tutors. *College English, 57*, 27-42.

Hobson, E. H. (1992). Maintaining our balance: Walking the tightrope of competing epistemologies. *The Writing Center Journal, 13* (1), 65-75.

Hobson, E. H. (1998). Straddling the virtual fence. In E. H. Hobson (Ed.), *Wiring the writing center* (pp. ix-xxvi). Logan, UT: Utah State University Press.

Lerner, N. (1997). Counting beans and making beans count. *Writing Lab Newsletter, 23* (1), 1-4.

Lerner, N. (1998). Research in the writing center. In B. B. Silk (Ed.), *The writing center resource manual* (pp. 1-11). Emmitsburg, MD: NWCA Press.

Monroe, B. (1998). The look and feel of the OWL conference. In E. H. Hobson (Ed.), *Wiring the writing center* (pp. 3-24). Logan UT: Utah State University Press.

Murphy, C., Law, J., & Sherwood, S. (1996). *Writing centers: An annotated bibliography*. Westport, CT: Garland.

National Writing Centers Association. (1998). *Colgate University* [Online]. Available: http://departments.colgate.edu/diw/NWCA.html

Reading/Writing Center Page. (2000). *Hunter College* [Online]. Available: http://www.rwc.hunter.cuny.edu.

Rickly, R. (1998). Reflection and responsibility in (cyber)tutor training: Seeing ourselves clearly on and off the screen. In E. H. Hobson (Ed.), *Wiring the writing center* (pp. 44-61). Logan, UT: Utah State University Press.

Trimbur, J. (1983). Peer tutoring and the benefits of collaborative learning. *Writing Lab Newsletter, 7* (9), 1-3.

Trimbur, J. (1987). Peer tutoring: A contradiction in terms. *The Writing Center Journal, 7* (2), 21-28.

AUTHORS

DENNIS PAOLI is Coordinator of the Hunter College Writing Center at Hunter College, City University of New York.

ERIC HOBSON is Director of the Center for Teaching and Learning, Albany College of Pharmacy.

Part IV

Undergraduate Students Assisting in Courses and Programs for All Students

Chapter 23

Peer Facilitators of In-Class Groups: Adapting Problem-Based Learning to the Undergraduate Setting

Deborah E. Allen and Harold B. White, III

Problem-based learning (PBL) was introduced to the University of Delaware in a three-day workshop to prepare faculty to teach in a new medical scholars program. A number of faculty recognized the potential of the method to improve undergraduate instruction (Allen, Duch, & Groh, 1996; White, 1996a), and decided to adapt it to their introductory science courses.

In implementing PBL at the University of Delaware (a medium-sized, privately-controlled research university with 15,000 full-time undergraduates in 123 degree programs) we faced not only the challenges confronted by the early adopters of PBL in the medical school setting (Engel, 1997), but also challenges intrinsic to the undergraduate setting, with its large class sizes and less intellectually mature learners. Particular concerns were how a single instructor could support multiple groups working through complex problems, and how students would adjust to such a radical departure from traditional teaching and learning formats.

Since fall 1993, a number of faculty have used undergraduate peer group facilitators (PGFs) to address these concerns. As our experience grew, we developed a centralized program with discipline-independent elements for boosting the group facilitation skills of the PGFs. The PGF program now includes PBL courses with both large and small enrollments; for students who are majors and nonmajors; and in advanced and introductory subjects in the basic and applied sciences (biology, physics, biochemistry, geology, agricultural biotechnology, nursing pathology, dietetics), social sciences (political science), and humanities (philosophy, medical ethics, art history). Since its formalization in 1996, the program has impacted 12 courses, 75 facilitators, and over 1,200 undergraduates.

■ MODEL

The Facilitator's Role in the PBL Cycle

The PBL cycle starts with a complex, real-life problem (e.g., large-scale solutions to global warming, plea negotiation in the criminal justice system, the design of exhibits in an art museum) that motivates interest in learning (Allen & Duch, 1998, contains biology examples). Students work in small groups to define the problem. As they brainstorm initial hypotheses, they inevitably identify conceptual holes, called learning issues. The students assign responsibility for researching learning issues, and discuss the best resources (textbook, library, Internet, etc.) for finding the needed information. When students reconvene, they give informal oral presentations to their group on the results of their out-of-class research, and integrate it into their existing knowledge base. Students continue to define and prioritize new learning issues as they home in on their group's resolution of the problem. The PBL cycle thus challenges students to learn concepts in the context of their applications, think critically, communicate effectively, find and process new information, and become influential members of productive teams (Barrows & Tamblyn, 1980).

Two PBL courses taught by the authors, "Introductory Biology" and "Introduction to Biochemistry," provide examples of the dedicated facilitator model. PBL is the predominant teaching/learning strategy, and the small enrollment (20–40 students, in four to eight groups) makes a 1:1 facilitator: group model feasible. Approximately 85% of class time is spent on group discussions of PBL problems, and during the remaining class time the instructor leads class discussions or gives short lectures that concern the ongoing problem. PGFs are expected to attend every class session in order to guide a single group through all phases of the PBL cycle. They are asked to function in the same way as the PBL tutoring role was first envisioned in the medical school setting (Barrows, 1988): to guide, probe, and support students' initiatives, not to lecture, direct, or provide answers. The PGFs thus must monitor both the quality of the information and arguments, and the quality of group interactions, a tall order for even the most experienced faculty members.

Medium-sized to large enrollment classes (70-200 students) using PGFs generally have only one PBL session per week, mixed with other class activities such as lectures that do not necessarily concern the PBL problems. The problems are typically started and completed within one class session, and the resources needed are accessible in the classroom. Courses of this size would require a large number of PGFs to achieve a dedicated model. Therefore these courses often use a roving facilitator model, in which the PGF works with the same two to six PBL groups throughout the semester. The facilitator rotates among groups to guide their progress, spending about 10-15 minutes total time with each group. The PGF in this model must be attuned to the needs of all his or her groups, and thus avoid being too drawn into the discussion of any single group. In the roving facilitator model, the PGF attends only the class sessions that feature PBL activities.

In both the dedicated and roving facilitator models, the well-prepared facilitator need not be a content expert, but should have an understanding of the fundamental concepts whose understanding are among the problem's objectives. They also should come to class with a repertoire of "canned" questions that might help students to dig deeper into a topic ("What is the evidence for your opinion?" "Are there other mechanisms that could explain that?" "Should this be a new learning issue?") or encourage a silent student to participate ("Could you summarize in a few sentences what Jennifer just said?" "Bob, how does this relate to the topic that you investigated?"). The PGFs do not grade assignments or exams, because it might constrain the students' willingness to voice uncertainties and reveal ignorance, the starting points for progress in PBL. They do evaluate their students' performance as group members, typically twice per semester, and this evaluation contributes to the students' grade in the course.

Selection and Training
Faculty recruit PGFs through recommendations from other faculty and former facilitators, by posting flyers, and by encouraging students in introductory level PBL courses to consider this role. Prospective facilitators should have strong interpersonal and communication skills (as assessed subjectively in an interview, or from group evaluations if

the facilitator was previously a student in the instructor's PBL course) and a good background in the subject of the course, and should be mature and responsible. If we have a chance to preview them in a PBL course, we seek facilitators who can in addition ask questions that move the group discussion forward, and who willingly take on the most challenging learning issues.

Our training program begins by addressing the anxieties that PGFs face in their first experience working with groups. A presentation on the mismatch between student expectations and their needs, and on the particular challenges that active learning strategies offer, leads to a group discussion of how to support students while challenging them intellectually. We brainstorm about the roles and responsibilities of facilitators and faculty, to help PGFs negotiate the difficult role of middleman in a multilayered teaching and learning scheme.

Next, the in-service course "Tutorial Methods of Instruction," taught by the authors on a rotating basis, helps unify and consolidate the efforts of PGFs and their faculty mentors across campus. This course meets weekly in eight to ten, two-hour sessions. Among the topics included are the intellectual development of undergraduates, how to involve all students in the group process, diagnosis and therapy for behaviors that undermine the group process, strategies for assessment, questioning techniques and the role of questions in PBL, and how to deal with conflicts (Lewis, 1992; University of Delaware, 2000). The course also provides a forum for discussion of common concerns of the facilitators. Faculty sponsors are welcome to attend, and often do. All course sessions use a blend of short orientation lectures, group brainstorming, whole class discussions, and reflections on the facilitators' recent classroom experiences, followed by class suggestions for resolving any problems. In several "fish bowl" exercises, some facilitators role play a student group working on a problem, and others are observers. Their observations form the basis for a discussion. The last two sessions of the course focus on discussion of teaching cases that the facilitators write based on critical incidents from their experiences with groups. The nearly one hundred cases they have written give us insights into their perceptions of the challenges they face. With permission, we have rewritten some of these as scripts for trigger tapes that we have produced for use in the course. The authors are compiling these cases along with teaching notes into a manual that we plan to make available for distribution.

Finally, facilitators meet weekly with their respective course instructors to review and preview class activities. Meetings start with comments on the last week's sessions. In rotation, PGFs lead a discussion of strategies for the upcoming week, and write and distribute a plan for the next problem. The plan includes timing issues (how to intertwine the group activities led by facilitators with whole class activities led by the instructor), anticipated learning issues, potential conceptual pitfalls, tips for facilitator preparation in content background, and a stockpile of questions that PGFs can draw from when stumped about ways to stimulate discussion and dig for deeper understanding.

Facilitators receive two academic credits for enrolling in "Tutorial Methods of Instruction," and also a stipend that varies from $300 to $585 per semester, depending on how many PBL sessions the facilitator leads and on prior experience.

■ OUTCOMES

Results from the Introductory Biology Course

The "Introductory Biology" course for majors (Allen, 1997) has used PGFs since changing to a PBL format in 1993. Student responses on a survey of facilitators' performance (Appendix D-3) are summarized by the instructor, then discussed in a one-on-one meeting with each PGF. The students back up their ratings choices with specific comments. The average overall rating of facilitator performance on end-of-semester course evaluations is routinely higher than that of the instructor (in response to the same question and on the same scale). In a recent offering of the course, the average rating of five PGFs by 22 students was 1.3 ± 0.1, on a 5-point Likert scale on which 1 is "excellent" and 5 is "poor." When asked how much their PGF benefited their learning of biology, the average response was also 1.3 ± 0.1, on a 5-point scale on which 1 indicated "strong agreement" and 5, "weak agreement."

Most student comments about the value of facilitators in this class are either "comfort" statements ("I have become more comfortable talking in a group and presenting my information confidently") or "PBL buy-in" statements ("My facilitator prompts me to think instead of just giving me the answers"). Student responses to specific items reinforce these comments. Consistently since 1993, the most highly rated skills (responses of 4 to 5 on a 5-point scale on which 1 is "strongly disagree" and 5 is "strongly agree") have related to how friendly and interested the facilitators are in their groups, and how well they foster participation, provide information when needed, keep the group on track, and support good interpersonal relationships. Students also rate their facilitators' questioning skills highly, the one rating with which faculty disagree, not because we think they ask poorly framed or in-

adequate questions, but because we observe missed opportunities for asking questions that might stimulate higher level thinking about problem-related issues. This skill in questioning is one we continually strive to find ways to hone in the "Tutorial Methods of Instruction" course. Facilitation skills that students do not rate as highly (3 to 3.5 on the same rating scale) include helping to identify and appraise the relevancy of learning resources, prioritize learning issues, make connections between old and new problems, give verbal feedback about presentations, and identify ways that they can improve their group's functioning. Because these skills arise from disciplinary content expertise and from experience in providing constructive and nonthreatening feedback, we interpret these ratings as confirmation that there are still important roles for the instructor in a classroom using undergraduate facilitators.

Results from an Introduction to Biochemistry Course

"Introduction to Biochemistry" for sophomore biochemistry majors adopted PBL in 1993. In this course students read and discuss about ten connected research articles (each considered a PBL "problem") in historical sequence (White, 1996a). Initially, the course did not use facilitators. When enrollment exceeded 25 students and five groups in 1995, both instructor and students became frustrated. The instructor felt unable to supervise and monitor each group effectively while the underclassmen felt adrift without frequent instructor guidance.

The employment of facilitators transformed the course. Whereas before it had taken students about a month to become comfortable with their groups and the PBL format, with PGFs groups worked effectively from the start. A large part of the change seemed to come from having experienced peers present in the group at all times to provide reassurance, enthusiasm for the PBL format, encouragement, and personal attention. As in "Introductory Biology," student responses on course evaluations often refer to the "comfort" provided by the PGFs, and almost half said that facilitators kept the groups focused and on track. Here, too, the average rating of PGF performance on end-of-semester course evaluations is routinely better than that of the instructor.

Because the first set of facilitators had taken the course when there were no facilitators, we wondered if the second generation of PGFs, having had role models, would do even better. Based on instructor observations and end-of-course evaluations, the second generation of facilitators performed as well as the first, but not better. This suggests that the beneficial effects of PGFs were due to their presence and their preparation in the "Tutorial Methods of Instruction" course, rather than to any prior experience in facilitator-led groups.

Attendance, which had always been good with PBL, improved slightly with the use of facilitators. In the first three years using PBL, attendance averaged 91.1% (in a class that meets at the unpopular hour of 8:00 a.m.). That has increased to 94.1% in the four subsequent years using facilitators. While this difference may seem small, it corresponds to a 32% reduction in absences, which, in turn, significantly increased the number of groups with full attendance. Furthermore, students reported spending an average of 25% more time (6.0 versus 4.8 hours per week) outside of class on course work after the introduction of facilitators. Parallel with these outcomes has been a more positive response to most items on the end-of-course evaluations. From a list of 11 skills and behaviors, students identified those that were more important for success in "Introduction to Biochemistry" than in their other science courses. Over one-third of the students each year select the six listed in Table 23.1. However, the student perception of how important these six items were for success in the class improved significantly when PGFs were part of the course.

Benefits to PGFs

While the main purpose of using facilitators in undergraduate PBL courses is to improve group dynamics and learning in larger classes, one of the most exciting outcomes is the effect on the facilitators themselves. Regardless of the challenges and difficulties encountered, virtually every facilitator values the experience (Table 23.2). Most report that it has increased their understanding of their discipline, confirming our hope that this could serve as a capstone experience by providing a final overview from the perspective of heightened content knowledge (Boyer Commission Report, 1998). By working closely with one or more faculty members, the facilitators think about the educational process and reflect on how they and others learn. A senior facilitator said, "One thing you come away with is how to learn and this is invaluable."

■ PRODUCTIVITY

Faculty whose educational experiences and teaching styles are teacher-centered perceive many barriers and risks in the current movement toward student-centered educational approaches (White, 1996b). A common faculty concern is how to implement PBL in medium-to-large enrollment classes. The use of facilitators provides a means to handle larger classes, but also adds another barrier if, in addition

Table 23.1 EFFECT OF FACILITATORS ON END-OF-COURSE STUDENT RATINGS OF THE IMPORTANCE OF VARIOUS SKILLS AND BEHAVIORS TO SUCCESS IN INTRODUCTION TO BIOCHEMISTRY

Skill or Behavior	Pre-facilitator Semester 32/33[2]	Post-facilitator Semesters[3] 56/58
Personal initiative	1.65 ± 0.59[1]	1.52 ± 0.66
Library research skills	2.34 ± 0.81	1.77 ± 0.71[4]
Writing skills	2.13 ± 0.74	1.75 ± 0.84[4]
Collaboration with classmates	1.75 ± 0.83	1.38 ± 0.68[4]
Oral communication skills	1.78 ± 0.86	1.32 ± 0.47[4]
Problem solving skills	2.03 ± 1.02	1.55 ± 0.78[4]

[1]Ratings are reported as means ± standard deviation, using the following 5-point Likert scale: 1 = extremely important to 5 = not important.

[2]Number of responses/number of students enrolled.

[3]Values reported are combined for the two semesters immediately following the pre-facilitator year.

[4]Significantly different from rating response in pre-facilitator semester (Mann-Whitney U test p<0.05).

Table 23.2 FACILITATORS' RESPONSES TO SELECTED END-OF-COURSE EVALUATION ITEMS FOR TUTORIAL METHODS OF INSTRUCTION

Course Evaluation Item	Response[1]
I feel that I have benefited from the process of being a facilitator.	1.2 ± 0.1
I would recommend the facilitating experience to others.	1.3 ± 0.1
I think that my understanding of my major field of study has improved as the result of being a facilitator.	2.1 ± 0.2[2]
I think that my interest in incorporating "teaching" into some aspect of my professional career has been enhanced by this experience.	1.9 ± 0.1
I think that the facilitating experience has helped me to better understand the way that I and other people think and learn.	1.2 ± 0.1

[1]Responses are reported as the mean ± SEM of 32 individual ratings, using a 5-point Likert scale where 1 = strongly agree and 5 = strongly disagree.

[2]Includes responses of facilitators working in courses outside their major field of study.

to preparing for classes, instructors also have to prepare facilitators for those classes. The "Tutorial Methods of Instruction" course attempts to lower barriers and decrease risks by providing pedagogical instruction to facilitators. These benefits do not come without some cost. The authors teach the tutorial methods course in addition to regular disciplinary teaching. The added preparation time and effort often is significant and it is not yet clear whether other faculty will be willing to teach the course. On the other hand, within the context of a university working to increase active learning in the classroom through use of PGFs, the "Tutorial Methods of Instruction" course provides a time and cost effective approach to involve more faculty. It relieves most faculty of the significant time and responsibility for PGF training and permits them to focus on implementing PBL in their courses.

■ SUGGESTIONS FOR REPLICATION

We are fortunate in having had grant support from the National Science Foundation, the Fund for the Improvement of Post-Secondary Education, and the Howard Hughes Medical Institute to fund facilitators in our PBL classes. Although financial incentive helps recruit facilitators, many found the experience so rewarding they claimed they would have worked without pay or course credit; this offers promise to us as we look ahead to sustaining the program in the absence of external funding. The addition of service-learning and capstone components to the general education requirements may also provide a viable means for sustaining our program in the long term. Working as a PGF could ultimately be an option for satisfying either of these requirements for graduation.

It is important to provide pedagogical support to the facilitators so that they can be effective. We needed substantial firsthand knowledge of the issues faced in PBL classrooms, and of the resources and literature available in the educational community in order to creatively adapt materials for the "Tutorial Methods of Instruction" course. Without this knowledge and experience, we would have been stumped on many occasions by the questions posed by PGFs seeking our advice about how to handle problems with their PBL groups.

University of Delaware supports the implementation of PBL in undergraduate education through its PBL web site (University of Delaware, 2000). There visitors can find articles, problems, and syllabi of courses in a variety of disciplines, and of the "Tutorial Methods of Instruction" course.

■ CONCLUSION

Our experience and that of many others reported in this volume attest to how powerful peers can be in facilitating learning. Our particular approach is different from many in that we use the peers as facilitators of group inquiry in class, and that we provide an in-service course that serves facilitators working in a variety of courses across campus. By using this approach, we think we have created a multilayered learning community that works well for each layer of the community—for the students in PBL classes, for the undergraduate facilitators who return to an introductory course for a final overview before graduation, and for the faculty instructors who want to use PBL effectively in introductory or large enrollment courses.

■ REFERENCES

Allen, D. E. (1997). Bringing PBL to the introductory biology classroom. In A. P. McNeal & C. D'Avanzo (Eds.), *Student-active science* (pp. 259-278). Philadelphia, PA: Saunders.

Allen, D., & Duch, B. (1998). *Thinking toward solutions: Problem-based learning activities for general biology.* Philadelphia, PA: Saunders.

Allen, D. E., Duch, B. J., & Groh, S. E. (1996). The power of problem-based learning in teaching introductory science courses. In L. Wilkerson & W. H. Gijselaers (Eds.), *Bringing problem-based learning to higher education: theory and practice* (pp. 43-52). New Directions in Teaching and Learning in Higher Education, No. 68. San Francisco, CA: Jossey-Bass.

Barrows, H. S., & Tamblyn, R. E. (1980). *Problem-based learning: An approach to medical education.* New York, NY: Springer-Verlag.

Barrows, H. S. (1988). *The tutorial process.* Springfield, IL: Southern Illinois University School of Medicine.

Boyer Commission on Educating Undergraduates in the Research University. (1998). *Reinventing undergraduate education: A blueprint for America's research universities.* Princeton, NJ: Carnegie Foundation for the Advancement of Teaching.

Engel, C. E. (1997). Not just a method but a way of learning. In D. Boud & G. Feletti (Eds.), *The challenge of problem-based learning* (pp. 23-33). London, England: Kogan Page.

Lewis, K. G. (Ed.). (1992). *Teaching pedagogy to teaching assistants: A handbook for 398T instructors.* Austin, TX: University of Texas.

White, H. B., III. (1996a). Addressing content in problem-based courses: The learning issue matrix. *Biochemical Education, 24,* 41-45.

White, H. B., III. (1996b). Dan tries problem-based learning: A case study. *To Improve the Academy, 15,* 75–9. (Also available at http://www.udel.edu/pbl/dancase3.html)

White, H. B., III. (in press). Research articles as problems for problem-based learning: Stokes' 1864 spectroscopic study of the 'redox' behavior of hemoglobin. *Journal of College Science Teaching.*

University of Delaware. (2000). *Problem based learning* [Online]. Available: http://www.udel.edu/pbl

■ AUTHORS

DEBORAH E. ALLEN is Associate Professor and Undergraduate Programs Director in the Department of Biological Sciences at the University of Delaware, and a member of the faculty of the University Honors Program.

HAROLD B. WHITE, III is Professor of Biochemistry in the Department of Chemistry and Biochemistry at the University of Delaware.

Chapter 24

Student-Directed Instruction in an Undergraduate Psychopathology Course

Cheryl Golden and Calverta McMorris

Historically Black LeMoyne-Owen College offers three undergraduate degrees in 17 majors. The student population is two-thirds female and 95% African American, and its international students represent 17 countries. Its core curriculum has received numerous national awards for its design and implementation. The college has, at the heart of its mission, a commitment to community service; its "Real Men" program was the recipient of one of President George Bush's Thousand Points of Light awards for its exemplary motivational intervention to reach young African American men and promote family unity. LeMoyne-Owen enjoys a distinguished, multicultural faculty and a reputation for teaching excellence and innovation. Notable graduates include historian and author C. Eric Lincoln, linguist Juanita Williamson, former NAACP executive director Benjamin Hooks, and W. W. Herenton, former schools superintendent and current mayor of Memphis.

In contrast to traditional instructional models that are usually teacher-centered, -focused, and -driven, shifts in the teaching/learning paradigm have instructors moving from their position in the front of the classroom, as the key component in the learning process, to the back, as experienced observers. Grabe and Grabe (1998) noted that, as students move into an active role in the learning process, instructors shift from being dispensers to facilitators of learning. They advocated that instructors provide and guide learning experiences in which students become independent learners. In this model, students take responsibility for what and how they learn, and learning is a cooperative endeavor. Interaction and feedback allow instructors to hear students process, apply, and synthesize. Problem solving, research, and communication skills are a natural outgrowth of the teacher/student relationship. Students learn to critically analyze situations, use creative thinking skills, support ideas with research, and value the opinions of others, especially when they differ (Tinzmann et al., 1990).

The course described in this chapter is a junior-level offering in psychology, a minor program of study within the college's Division of Social and Behavioral Sciences. The course has been offered in both traditional and student-directed formats; seemingly, the latter has produced more favorable results.

■ MODEL

Author Cheryl Golden introduced student-directed instruction in a junior level psychopathology course whose subject matter was the diagnosis, assessment, and treatment of mental disorder. This course was first offered in 1993 as a traditionally taught lecture-seminar for students majoring in social and behavior sciences. When fall 1996 registration closed with an enrollment of ten, the class consisted of extremely bright, highly motivated students. Golden gave the students the syllabus that had originally been designed for the lecture version of the course. She explained that since the class was small and she respected their academic abilities, they would be responsible for the development of the new syllabus, complete with assignments, ancillary exercises, and grading standards, and for course instruction. If the group met the standard of shared responsibility for the conduct of the class, the entire group would receive a grade of A. The students chose multiple presentations over multiple examinations. They decided to use the textbook as the primary resource for preparing student lectures on each of the diagnostic categories, but they accepted the instructor's suggestion that they also use a variety of supplementary materials. Students were required to integrate multiple delivery methods; often class sessions were conducted in computer labs where access to PowerPoint and the Internet was available. In the first two sessions, the instructor advanced an introduction to the discipline, but by the end of the second class, the students had prepared the schedule for the remainder of the course.

The class developed a system of group accountability involving equally shared loads for development and presentation of course content, consistent attendance, and a requirement that an absentee student had to call at least one member of the group prior to absence. Students organized the course content around themes of diagnosis, assessment, and treatment of disorders. Small groups prepared class presentations, and each student had a day to lead the class discussion. Students pointed out difficulties they had with the assignment. The class brainstormed and analyzed until the difficulties were resolved. The instructor did not enter the discussion until students had completed their discussion or to ask if they had considered a particular point. The group selected two additional books to supplement the textbook, and since one of the readings concerned an inpatient mental health facility not far from Memphis, they elected to include a field trip to the site. Their oral report assignments consisted of six videotaped psychological autopsies. They also completed two written assessments for which they had to learn various models of psychosocial development.

In this student-directed instruction model, Golden's role was to define the course objectives, and the students' was to delve into them in creative ways. For example, Golden defined the objective of "using assessment skills to determine disorder" and suggested the psychological autopsy, a tool used for diagnosis when the subject is unavailable for interview or input. The students determined the quality and quantity of assignments, and one student immediately saw an application of the autopsy to the assessment of mental disorder in certain well known rap artists. Students analyzed the lyrics, reviewed the historical background of the artists' families, viewed video recordings of musical presentations to analyze their mental statuses, and developed class presentations of their findings. Golden would not accept a psychological autopsy unless the group presenting agreed upon the complete diagnosis. Thus, those with different opinions attempted to convince other group members with substantiated arguments. Later, when students were challenged to analyze traditional case studies, they met the challenge with little difficulty due to their high levels of understanding and prior preparation.

Students applied information learned from their respective majors to the assignment at hand. For example, the biology major in the group might address genetic or physiological aspects of a particular disorder, while the sociology and social work majors gave perspectives from their disciplines on assessment and treatment.

Generally, the student-directed instruction model required creativity and initiative from both faculty and students. Since students initiated course activities, students had to understand the concepts; examine, evaluate, and solve problems; and demonstrate the competencies required to pass the course. Since Golden was more knowledgeable about the competencies and tools needed for successful completion, she was responsible for collecting resource materials (e.g., video clips, news articles, journals, books, music/art selections) and having ready a selection of acceptable assignments. She had to be knowledgeable about community resources and connected with individuals who might serve as consultants or guest lecturers to provide alternatives for course delivery should students not be able to conceptualize the appropriate medium for instruction. Because students were relatively inexperienced in the process of instruction, Golden had to be vigilant about course delivery issues such as student motivation, quality and quantity of materials, pace of instruction, individual and group learning styles, and progress in learning.

In view of the course philosophy of shared responsibility and accountability, the failure of one of the students to attend the required field trip presented a challenge for both the instructor and the students. In order to respect the established course structure, Golden had to refrain from moving ahead of the students in making decisions regarding consequences for the student's behavior. It became the students' task to problem solve this unexpected development. They held a judiciary council in which they elected a judge, seated a jury, and appointed prosecution and defense attorneys. After deliberations, the class determined that the student's grade would be lowered to a B; the student had to arrange to visit the site himself and report findings to the class; the grade could be revisited once the assignment was completed; and if the assignment was not completed, the grade could be lowered to "F." The instructor had final authority over procedures and outcome of the process, in order to ensure fairness for all, but her intervention was unnecessary. Interestingly, when the recommendations were presented, some students believed that group accountability also meant there should have been group penalties for the failure of the individual student who did not attend the field trip. By the time they completed the judgment process, students had learned to operate in a real world setting and to step outside of themselves to make a judgement, and had formed strong bonds within the group.

The course attracted attention from other students who were not enrolled. One of the two books selected by the students to support their discussion of the psychogenic aspects of personality disorder gained such attention beyond the classroom that the class had regular visitors who began to read with them and attend the discussions. The students had actually begun a forum for which they would receive course credit!

The model is not limited to psychology: Golden has used a modified version in a junior-level introductory statistics course. After students had been introduced to the course objectives, they determined the pace and delivered instruction, making use of group homework assignments, tests, and laboratory experiences including computer-assisted instruction. The main issue was that some students approached the course content with a degree of "phobia." However, students learned more about their abilities in the context of interacting with their peers. As they worked math problems and looked for solutions, they discovered that everyone has strengths and weaknesses, and that even the weakest math student is able to teach. This latter finding is perhaps the greatest strength of a model that requires students to initiate instruction.

■ OUTCOMES

Outcomes were compared for this course offered in a traditional seminar format in 1993 and in the student directed format in 1996. Quantifiable outcomes included improved attendance, class participation, quantity and variety of assignments, course completion, grade performance, and on-time graduation (Table 24.1). Perceptible improvements were noted in motivation and original thought, active initiation rather than passive acceptance of class content, level of cognitive processing (analysis and synthesis levels rather than mere knowledge and application levels) relative to Bloom's taxonomy (Bloom, 1956), and out of class contact between students and faculty.

Students in the student-directed class were surveyed, with a 60% response rate. When asked to describe their experiences in the class, students used terms such as "unforgettable," "challenging," "different," and "self-directed." Other student comments included, "This course clearly gave students opportunities to identify their individual learning needs...It also fostered a learning environment that had a strong give and take component between students," and "The instructor provided the boundaries within which students could receive knowledge...We received knowledge from the students."

When asked whether they would recommend the course to others, the answer was unanimously positive. Students commented that "This class gives students a chance to understand how they are ultimately responsible for their own education," and that "This class introduced me to the investigative skills required for graduate school." Students identified the strengths of the course as the small class size, the challenge presented by being in a group of academically enhanced students, different perspectives of multiple disciplines represented in the class, group work, class discussions, flexibility, use of nontraditional materials, the fact that it was student directed, variety of learning opportunities, no lectures from the instructor, and the use of field trips and library books to gain in-depth knowledge. Students identified weaknesses as insufficient class time, possible unsuitability for students who need direction and structure, and the group projects when not everyone operated responsibly.

When asked what they learned from this course that helped them in other areas of study or career, students replied that the class helped them to learn "my individual learning style," "how to be a better critical thinker," "better organization and planning skills," "responsibility for my learning in graduate school," "to ask instructors for what I needed," "to do research on my own," "to look for evidence to support decisions," "to work with others, although I may not agree with what they are saying," "to present my ideas without being intimidated," "to negotiate...a difference in opinion," and "to organize my thoughts so that others would understand my point." Other comments included, "Everyone worked very hard ...and everyone had a voice. When we got stuck and

Table 24.1 PSYCHOPATHOLOGY COURSE OUTCOMES IN TRADITIONAL AND STUDENT-DIRECTED FORMATS

Outcome	Traditional (1993)	Student-Directed (1996)
Enrolled students	10	10
Attendance	76%	82%
Estimated average class participation	30%	90%
Assignments/tests	3	10
Course completion rate	60%	100%
Early warnings for poor performance	30%	0%
Pass with C or better	50%	100%
On-time graduation	60%	100%
Graduate school acceptance	unknown	100%

could not come to a consensus, we would also discuss it in class. Each person reported his/her point of view, giving supporting data. We worked as hard outside of class as we did in the class to get things done... We really had to work as a team."

The outcomes of this work extended to the students' academic preparation for later tasks. Two students made presentations of psychological autopsies in an honors conference. One used the research skills learned in this class to complete a senior capstone project on perceptions of parenting styles among African American adolescents, and presented the paper at a national conference. Her superior research was a factor in her acceptance to an internship program at the Centers for Disease Control, and later to graduate school and a postgraduate fellowship.

PRODUCTIVITY

The student-directed instruction model seems to be less costly than instruction delivered through traditional methods. Because students were internally driven to learn and to achieve, they provided direction for the class and required less input from the instructor. However, the faculty member who chooses the student-directed instruction model should be prepared for an increased grading load. The traditional course depended heavily upon "objective" testing (multiple choice, true-false, and short answer) that was inappropriate for the student-directed style of delivery. In keeping with the student-initiated dynamic, the students shared in the development of the instruments used to evaluate their videotaped assignments and other oral presentations. This process of developing and implementing new assessments required more time and effort on the part of the instructor, but the outcome was well worth it.

Generally, the student-directed model does not require more work from the instructor, but it does require different work and a different set of teaching skills. The instructor has to remain aware of course objectives and to think about how they can be met as the course evolves. Since the direction of the course is highly dependent on the character and motivation of the class and the delivery is out of the instructor's control, the instructor has to listen for achievement of course objectives at various Bloom's levels (acquisition, comprehension, and application of course content, in this case). Furthermore, the instructor must be aware of appropriate application of known resources and be open to the use of nontraditional materials.

SUGGESTIONS FOR REPLICATION

Replication of this model is dependent upon the size and composition of the class. Larger class sizes would require modification of the number and type of assignments, because of time constraints on presentations within and on preparation outside of class. For lower levels of student ability, creativity would be needed to develop assignments that would promote inclusion regardless of preparation or ability. The model works best with small class sizes of less than 20. But larger classes could incorporate small group activities and presentations to satisfy at least partially the goals of the model.

To prepare to teach in the student-directed model, the faculty member needs to assemble a variety of resources that are appropriate both with respect to meeting the course objectives and with respect to the class' ability to use the resource to meet the objectives.

As the course survives several generations of delivery, student assistants recruited from previous courses could be useful as facilitators. This is especially true for larger classes.

Discussions with colleagues are useful in identifying additional resources. Some of our best suggestions for materials came from staff members who heard about our class. Likewise, attendance at teaching conferences or other events where there is an opportunity to discuss ideas with faculty is useful. However, the strength of the model comes from the recognition that the students themselves are their own best teachers, and so it is important to listen to their ideas as well.

CONCLUSION

The key to the success of student-directed instruction is that everyone has different learning and teaching styles. When the teacher is the sole instructor, the likelihood is that only one style is presented. However, when the entire class teaches, the entire class benefits from exposure to a variety of styles.

◼ REFERENCES

Bloom, B. S. (Ed.). (1956). *Taxonomy of educational objectives, handbook 1: Cognitive domain.* New York, NY: David McKay.

Grabe, M., & Grabe, C. (1998). *Integrating technology for meaningful learning* (2nd ed.). Boston, MA: Houghton Mifflin Company.

Tinzmann, M. B., Jones, B. F., Fennimore, T. F., Bakker, J., Fine, C., & Pierce, J. (1990). *What is the collaborative classroom?* [Online]. Available: http://www.ncrel.org/sdrs/areas/rpl_esys/collab.htm

◼ AUTHORS

CHERYL GOLDEN is Director of Academic Support and Associate Professor of Psychology at LeMoyne-Owen College.

CALVERTA MCMORRIS is Associate Professor of Education at LeMoyne-Owen College.

Chapter 25

Peer Writing Tutors

Lisa Lebduska

At Worcester Polytechnic Institute (WPI), the nation's third oldest engineering college, peer tutors offer writing consultations for a population of approximately 2,700 undergraduate and 1,100 graduate students (including 340 international students). This service began with the writing center in 1988. As student assignments have begun to reflect an increasing demand for global awareness and oral proficiency, the writing center evolved into a Center for Communication Across the Curriculum, where students can also receive peer assistance in oral presentations and Spanish language (Center for Communication Across the Curriculum, 1999). The majority of the tutorials, however, still involve writing, and are administered through the center's writing workshop and a group of 23 undergraduates and one graduate peer tutor. These tutors offer nearly 800 one-hour tutorials each year.

Approximately half of the 800 tutorials relate to WPI's project system, which requires students to complete three projects in order to graduate: one is a synthesis of five humanities courses, another is a group analysis of a problem involving technology and society, and the third is a group project with a thesis-like analysis of a problem in the students' major field. Although WPI does not require writing classes, these projects generate a significant need for writing support, from the drafting stages to the finished products, which often include original research and may be 15–200 pages in length.

◼ MODEL

Writing consultations occur through two vehicles: the writing workshop, open weekdays from 10:00 to 5:00, and designated tutoring, in which tutors are assigned to a specific course. The workshop is developing an online writing lab (OWL). OWL now has a web site with links to various aspects of writing (e.g., documentation, invention heuristics, transition words) and an email address for student questions. In January 2001, we will test shareware that will allow off-campus students to receive electronic feedback on their writing.

Workshop Tutoring

Our writing model draws on Kenneth Bruffee's (1978) "Brooklyn Plan," which describes writing labs as spaces of alternative learning where tutee and tutor alike benefit from a collaborative exchange. During this collaboration, tutee and tutor articulate the writer's goals for and the reader's questions about a draft. Our program is based on the premise that peer writing tutors are not miniteachers; their job is not to correct but to become colearners. John Trimbur (1998) notes that such collaboration "redefines learning as an event produced by the social interaction of the learners—and not a body of information passed down from expert to novice" (p. 188). In our model, which employs tutors with no background in the content area for which they are tutoring, colearning occurs in the subject area as well as in the rhetorical process.

Tutors without background in the content area benefit the writer in two ways. First, the writer has better feedback on which explanations in the paper are not clear enough to the reader. Second, tutors who lack background knowledge often teach their tutees the value of using discussion and explanation to really understand a subject. While writing a paper about the fillers used to make grinding wheels, for example, a chemical engineering student may need to explain hydrolysis to her computer science writing tutor. The explanation may seem to be a digression, a move away from the goal of a completed paragraph. Ultimately, however, this process of explanation is productive. In struggling to explain a concept that she or he intuits but has never explained, the writer will often come to understand the concept better. The tutee discovers that explaining a concept to another is an excellent method of understanding a concept better. Then, the writer must decide if the reading audience will need that explanation or not, and, if it does, where that explanation should be placed.

In order to initiate such a collaboration with their tutees, our writing tutors must be careful readers who can clearly articulate the kinds of confusions a text produces (Bouquet, 1999). They are not editors, nor do they write papers for their peers; instead, they read portions of the paper aloud, asking for clarification. Tutors usually begin with global concerns such as clarifying the writing assignment, thesis, and overall focus, and move on to grammar, punctuation, and word choice. They may also assist with grammatical constructions by correcting and explaining a specific type of error such as subject/verb agreement and then asking the writer to check for agreement in an entire paragraph. Such modeling is more often necessary for students whose first language is not English, as they may not have the same ear for error that native speakers possess.

Implementation

Our workshop, a converted conference room, is an ideal place for tutors to offer their one-hour sessions. Readily available are writing resources such as reference books, handouts, a computer, a phone, and even other students. The setting may help students improve their writing habits by associating writing with the regularity and consistency of a fixed place. Also, it may help them voice questions that a classroom often silences.

Students may make tutoring appointments electronically or try to drop in without an appointment. Having students schedule appointments maximizes use of tutor time. Scheduling also helps students plan out the writing process, which means that students may be more likely to come in early enough to do a real revision, instead of looking for a quick fix just before a paper is due. Because of budget constraints, we have one tutor on duty at a time, so students who wait until the last minute also risk losing help entirely. When we are training interns, we can double up on sessions by using interns to tutor under supervision.

Designated Tutoring

In designated tutoring, instructors have a team of tutors assigned to their course. These tutors generally receive additional training on course content and objectives. Designated tutors are either "on-call," meaning they may be contacted as needed, or are assigned to a group of students who are required to meet with them on a regular basis. The advantage to designated tutoring is that tutors get to know their tutees and the assignments better because they work with the same students and material all term.

The disadvantages of designated tutoring are that it may threaten the collaborative nature of tutorials and the tutor may be seen as a designated miniteacher, particularly if the instructor requires that students meet with the tutor. The tutor tries to correct these misperceptions and move to a more collaborative relationship, but such negotiations sometimes fail. If students do not keep their designated appointments, for example, the tutor must report nonattendance, which is a very noncollaborative action. Similarly, a student who feels coerced into attending a tutorial is not always willing to engage in the dialog necessary for revision. Nevertheless, instructors who request designated tutoring (approximately five yearly) report that students' papers are better after tutor consultations, and that students seem to have fewer questions and less anxiety about their written work. Because of these advantages and disadvantages, we continue to debate the place of the designated tutoring program.

Tutor Selection, Roles, and Training

Training for those interested in becoming tutors consists of a one-term, credit-bearing course. Before they can begin the course, interested students must complete a three-part application that includes the name of a faculty reference, a writing sample, and a statement of intent. To date, all applicants have received admission to the course, because of the feeling that students who want to help their peers should have the opportunity to learn how to do so. Besides, the course itself has been a better means for selecting those who will be good tutors.

The tutoring course is designed to hone both writing and tutoring skills. Students write assignments of varying lengths, practice tutoring one another, observe peer writing tutorials, and intern (tutor under observation). As interns, they keep journals recording and reflecting on their tutoring experiences, review observed tutorials with the instructor and/or a tutor, and audiotape and review at least one of their tutorials. The audiotape has been both a confidence booster and gentle corrective. For example, interns who over-talk a tutorial often do not realize the extent of the problem. A few minutes of listening to one's monologic exchange, however, makes the point effectively.

During training, tutors are encouraged to think of themselves as ambassadors of writing. One assignment, for example, includes interviewing a nonwriting faculty member about his or her relationship to writing. Invariably, these interviews lead to discussions about the tutoring program, which increases workshop visibility and generally increases goodwill among the faculty.

After successfully completing the course (receiving a B or higher), students are eligible to become paid peer tutors the following term. (Approximately 90% successfully complete the course.) Ongoing professional development continues in the form of regular meetings and discussions with the director. In these meetings, we discuss each tutor's best and most problematic tutorial of the week, or a particular tutoring challenge, such as tutoring students who are writing large projects.

■ OUTCOMES

Unlike content tutors, writing tutors tutor a process, which complicates assessment considerably. Our writing tutors strive to "produce better writers, not better writing" (North, 1984, p. 237). This means that a writing tutor does not simply "clean up" a paper for a student. Instead, she or he actually models a means for the student to read a text in order to elicit re-vision or re-seeing. Consequently, our assessment measures attempt to evaluate the extent to which students are becoming better writers and their attitude toward writing has improved.

Increasingly students are seeking help from the writing tutors, which suggests at least an appearance of success. In 1997–1998, we had 339 tutorials, and in 1999–2000, we expect to complete almost 800. Designated tutoring has experienced similar growth with four faculty working with the designated tutoring program in 1997–1998 and 12 in 1999–2000. The number of tutors has grown as well, from eight in 1997 to 23 in the spring of 2000. The increased interest from students, faculty, and tutors suggests higher visibility for the tutoring program and a corresponding increased interest in writing development.

When questioned informally, faculty generally report that papers of students who meet with tutors have greater development and fewer errors. One humanities instructor also noted that the tutorial reports taught him something about writing. Two faculty pointed out, however, that tutors do not reduce their workload. One of these commented that although her workload had not decreased, her students were more confident about how to approach a writing task, so tutoring was worthwhile.

A survey of 11 history students who had received designated tutoring elicited positive responses. Of the five respondents, three found the tutorials "useful," and two "very useful." Written comments included the following: "The tutor helped me gain a better understanding of the organizational work involved in writing a paper"; "the

focus of my paper changed as he helped me find a good thesis"; "work with my tutor helped me to make my sufficiency writing easier and kept me from having too much stress." These responses indicate more than student satisfaction with the tutoring process because they speak of a fuller understanding of the writing process that categorizes experienced writers (Sommers, 1998).

Last year, graduating tutors were asked to write about the impact tutoring had on them, if any. Four of the five tutors responded, offering a range of comments. One civil engineering major saw the experience in terms of career advancement: "The peer tutoring position has helped develop the skills necessary to effectively communicate my ideas to fellow students; a skill that is priceless as I exit the world of academia and enter a professional world where communication is essential for a successful career." Another tutor expressed dissatisfaction with campus perceptions: "Too often, we are simply thought of as proofreaders and receive very little credit from a community that is not quite aware of our role on campus." This same student later elaborated: "As writers ourselves, we are constantly questioning our effectiveness, wondering whether or not our efforts are being well-received and making any impact. It is not until a chance meeting around campus, where the student expresses their gratitude, that we fully acknowledge the notion that, as a writing tutor, we did make a difference." The tutor's comments here indicate to me a heightened metacognition that I detect in many of our tutor meetings. The tutors' abilities to write and speak about writing—its complexities and its challenges—testify to an improved climate of writing on campus.

■ PRODUCTIVITY

Until the 1999–2000 academic year, the Center for Communication Across the Curriculum (of which the writing workshop is a part) lacked its own budget, and the director's salary and the tutors' wages were apportioned from the humanities and arts department, while all other funding (e.g., publicity, supplies, equipment, and travel) was acquired on an ad hoc basis from a variety of sources. Beginning with the 1999–2000 academic year, however, the center received its own budget, while remaining in the humanities and arts department.

For the 1999–2000 academic year, we will spend approximately $8,000 on student wages, which should provide us with approximately 900 undergraduate tutoring hours, 300 graduate tutoring hours, two meetings per term, and a supplemental training seminar in oral presentation. The pay scale for writing tutors is comparable to that of other student tutors: in Spring 2000, first- and second-year tutors received $6.00 per hour (Massachusetts minimum wage), third-year tutors, $6.25, and the graduate tutor, $8.00. Attracting skilled, dedicated tutors is difficult in a market where competition for their talent runs high, especially off campus where they can often earn up to $10 per hour. Designated tutoring, which pays $7.50 per hour, is funded by the department whose instructors request designated tutoring. This arrangement recognizes writing improvement as a communal responsibility.

The training costs of this program are minimal because the students pay for a credit-bearing course. The writing workshop director is compensated for teaching a single course, which takes about 40 hours per week for preparation, response, observations, and writing consultations. Faculty who request designated tutoring usually devote an additional five hours per course per term in consultation with the director establishing parameters for tutorials, reviewing assignments and scheduling, and discussing performance.

We have not measured, and perhaps cannot measure, the long-term impact of improving writing skills for students who have used the writing workshop. As Edward M. White (1994) laments, "Unfortunately for those of us who have had to confront the behaviorist perspective, we have yet to come up with writing tests sensitive enough to measure the value added to individual writing skill (out of a lifetime of language use) by a single writing course" (p. 7). At WPI, we also have not measured, and again may not be able to measure accurately, the impact of the writing workshop on the WPI community. Finally, it is difficult to measure the value or cost of alliances created among departments, or the benefit to students who do not sign up for official tutorials but who work with tutors in unofficial ways. For all of these reasons, I am reluctant to construct a strict cost-benefit analysis of the program. We can say from the data that we have gathered that a need for improving writing exists at WPI, and that the writing workshop seems to be filling that need—and, in the process, providing WPI students with a lifelong benefit—at a reasonable cost in terms of both money and time.

■ SUGGESTIONS FOR REPLICATION

Establishing or expanding a peer writing tutorial program requires informed action, and I would recommend *The Writing Center Resource Manual* (Silk, 1998) as a starting point, supplemented with *Writing Lab Newsletter*, the *Writing Center Journal*, and the National Writing Centers Association's homepage (National Writing Centers Association, 1998). In addition to providing useful

information about writing resources, this homepage provides a list of electronic discussion groups, one of the most useful places for exchanges about writing tutoring. Additionally, *The Harcourt Brace Guide to Peer Tutoring in Writing* (Capossela, 1998) and the *Allyn and Bacon Guide to Peer Tutoring* (Gillespie and Lerner, 2000) make superb tutor training texts.

A good way to introduce the idea of a writing center that uses undergraduate tutors is to collect data on campus perceptions about writing. At WPI, John Trimbur conducted such a survey in 1988 (Trimbur, 1988). The study helped Trimbur obtain a grant from WPI's Educational Development Council, which he used to bring in outside evaluators from the Council of Writing Program Administrators, who, among other suggestions, recommended using peer tutors.

Once a fledgling peer tutor program has begun, data gathering plays a crucial role in its development. We designed a system of tracking tutorials that asks for a nonevaluative summary of the tutorial (date, tutor's name, and tutee's name, year, major, course or project for which help was sought, and instructor or advisor), which is entered into a database. I used the data to identify which groups used the center most and asked tutors to record how many students were turned away from the center because of a lack of available tutors. These statistics let me approach the dean and ultimately get additional funding from our provost.

Another important aspect of developing a writing program is publicity. In my first year as director, I attended functions as if I were running for mayor. Conversations at meetings, seminars, and lunches inevitably led to names of students who would be good tutors, courses that might use designated tutoring, and discipline-specific writing texts. I also deliver presentations about our program whenever I can and have begun to offer faculty workshops about responding to student writing. Each year I also email all faculty asking them to identify students as potential tutors, and I mention my search in every presentation I make. I ask tutors to talk with peers and advertise in the school newspaper.

Additionally, I suggest that a fledgling program not become complacent in the face of growing usage rates and positive comments. For us, there are still shortcomings in the current program, ways to expand the program to better serve WPI's writing needs, new faculty and students to inform about the program, and needed conversations on the process versus the product of good writing. Also, the issue of gathering better data is always there. At WPI, for example, requests for writing tutorials have increased steadily each year, but can we correlate this increase with producing better writers? Looking more closely at initially glowing data can also have a sobering effect. For example, a portion of our increased demand occurs at the very end of the term, indicating that for some students, writing is not an ongoing process (a concept that we hope tutorials would inculcate), but remains a product that may be fixed with last-minute proofreading.

Finally, tutor training varies wildly and includes activities from a one-day presemester workshop to a credit-bearing course. While I believe that a course is the best type of training program to create, I suggest that those creating a writing program consider the extent of administrative support for a credit-bearing course, the willingness of students to enroll in a course, the issue of offering the course for free, and the availability of a qualified instructor.

■ CONCLUSION

The ideal writing program, like the ideal writing classroom, is one in which the director or teacher invests her tutors with increasing independence. A good peer writing program should encourage tutors to exchange their writing with one another, and ask each other for ideas and advice so that they can continue to teach each other how to learn, which I believe is the greatest asset any education can offer.

■ REFERENCES

Bouquet, E. H. (1999, February). 'Our little secret': A history of writing centers, pre- to post-open admissions. *College Composition and Communication, 50,* 463-483.

Bruffee, K. A. (1978). The Brooklyn Plan: Attaining intellectual growth through peer-group tutoring. *Liberal Education, 64,* 447-468.

Capossela, T. L. (Ed.). (1998). *The Harcourt Brace guide to peer tutoring in writing.* Orlando, FL: Harcourt Brace.

Center for Communication Across the Curriculum. (1999). *Worcester Polytechnic Institute* [Online]. Available: http://www.wpi.edu/+writing

Gillespie, P., & Lerner, N. (2000). *The Allyn and Bacon guide to peer tutoring.* Needham Heights, MA: Allyn and Bacon.

National Writing Centers Association. (1998). *Colgate University* [Online]. Available: http://departments.colgate.edu/diw/NWCA.html

North, S. M. (1984, September). The idea of a writing center. *College English, 46,* 433-446.

Silk, B. B. (Ed.). (1998). *The writing center resource manual.* Emmitsburg, MD: National Writing Center Association Press.

Sommers, N. (1998). Revision strategies of student writers and experienced adult writers. In T. L. Capossela (Ed.), *The Harcourt Brace guide to peer tutoring* (pp. 177-187). Orlando, FL: Harcourt Brace.

Trimbur, J. (1988*). Writing and undergraduate education: A self study.* Unpublished manuscript, Worcester Polytechnic Institute, Worcester, MA.

Trimbur, J. (1998). Peer tutoring: A contradiction in terms? In T. L. Capossela (Ed.), *The Harcourt Brace guide to peer tutoring* (pp. 117-123). Orlando, FL: Harcourt Brace.

White, E. M. (1994). *Teaching and assessing writing: Recent advances in understanding, evaluating, and improving student performance.* San Francisco, CA: Jossey-Bass.

■ AUTHOR

LISA LEBDUSKA is an Adjunct Assistant Professor of English and Director of the Center for Communication Across the Curriculum at Worcester Polytechnic Institute.

Chapter 26

The Workshop Project:
Peer-Led Team Learning in Chemistry

**Jerry L. Sarquis, Linda J. Dixon, David K. Gosser, Jack A. Kampmeier,
Vicki Roth, Victor S. Strozak, and Pratibha Varma-Nelson**

The workshop project is organized around a peer-led team learning (PLTL) model of teaching chemistry and other science courses that was developed by a team of faculty, learning specialists, and students with support from the National Science Foundation. New elements of student participation and leadership were first introduced at the City College of New York (Woodward, Weiner, & Gosser, 1993); the development of the model involved New York City Technical College, St. Xavier University, and the University of Rochester. Currently, the model is used by more than 50 faculty at over 30 schools including community colleges, technical colleges, liberal arts colleges, urban commuter campuses, public and private colleges and universities, and research universities. In 1998–1999, these schools engaged over 300 peer leaders and 2,500 students per semester in workshop courses. The model is now spreading to other science disciplines and has been implemented in at least ten different courses: "Bridge Chemistry," "General Chemistry," "General-Organic-Biochemistry," "Organic Chemistry," "Biochemistry," "Principles of Biology," "Genetics," "General Physics," "Principles of Economics," and "Computer Science Data Structures."

Many students in introductory science courses experience frustration, alienation, and withdrawal, at great expense to the student, the institution, and society. The theoretical basis for PLTL is the recognition that learning occurs best when the students are actively engaged with the material and with each other. In the prevalent lecture model, the teacher is active, but the students are relatively passive. The PLTL model provides an active participatory structure, a workshop, to complement the traditional lecture. The workshop is a hands-on, minds-on interactive community of learners—a working support group for beginning students. Because beginning students have to learn how to function in this mode, each workshop has a specially trained peer leader.

■ MODEL

The core of the PLTL model is a weekly two-hour workshop, included in the course schedule, where students come together to solve carefully structured problems. Each workshop includes six to eight students and a trained peer leader. Peer leaders are students who have done well in the course previously and are trained for leadership roles. The role of the peer leader is to guide students to solve challenging problems by cooperative discussion and debate (Gosser et al., 1996; Gosser & Roth, 1998).

Since the inception of workshops, extensive experience has identified six critical components that are necessary for effective workshops.

1) Workshop sessions are integral to the course and coordinated with its other elements.

2) Course faculty are closely involved with workshops and peer leaders.

3) Peer leaders are well trained and closely supervised, with knowledge of workshop problems, teaching/learning strategies, and leadership skills for small groups.

4) Workshop materials are challenging at an appropriate level, integrated with other course components, and designed to encourage active and collaborative learning.

5) Organizational arrangements, including size of group, space, time, noise level, and teaching resources, promote learning.

6) At administrative and departmental levels, the institution encourages innovative teaching and provides sufficient logistical and financial support.

A comprehensive guide to the model is available (Gosser et al., 2001).

Peer Leader Roles

The peer leader assumes key roles in the model. Peer leaders have to know the course material, but are not expected to be answer-giving experts. They are taught not to lapse into lecture mode and not to provide or impose solutions upon the group. Instead, they facilitate discussion and collaborative learning, encouraging and helping the students to interact productively. Peer leaders use well known cooperative group tactics such as round robin problem solving, and subgroup or paired problem solving followed by comparison of results, to help students construct their own answers to problems.

Peer leaders have challenging jobs. They must provide intellectual and social leadership, and understand both content and team work. They need to prevent domination by a few students and create an atmosphere that encourages quiet or less-confident students to contribute. Creating a community of learners is one of the goals of the PLTL model. Peer leaders use readings, learning style assessments, personality inventories, self-reflection activities, group discussions, and role plays in their training sessions to learn to foster an environment that recognizes and appreciates differences in students and cultural backgrounds. As students who have mastered course content, peer leaders also serve as role models, mentors, and cheerleaders for the students.

Typical Workshops and Materials

The essential ideas in the workshop have been introduced in the lecture by the instructor, who provides a carefully structured workshop unit. Students are assigned preliminary readings, homework, and self-test/review questions in preparation for the workshop. Sessions begin with brief discussions of fundamentals and self-test problems and move on to formulation and implementation of tactics for the team attack on the problems.

The special structure of the workshop requires special problems whose construction presents a new and creative challenge for faculty. The problems are constructed with the background of the students in mind, but are challenging enough to require a group effort: they demand thinking about concepts, they cannot be solved by formula or algorithm, and they promote group work to appeal to different modes of learning. Answer keys are not provided for students or peer leaders. The focus is on the process of finding and evaluating answers rather than on the answer itself. Confidence in a solution to the problem comes from the debate. A good workshop promotes brainstorming and discussion, teaches students to communicate scientific concepts verbally, and encourages reflection and diverse methods of problem solving. Field-tested workshop materials are available for general chemistry, for general-organic-biochemistry, and for organic chemistry (Gosser, Strozak, & Cracolice, 2001; Kampmeier, Varma-Nelson, & Wedegaertner, 2001; Varma-Nelson & Cracolice, 2001). An example of a problem is in Figure 26.1.

Leader Selection and Training

The first selection requirement is that the peer leader has been successful in the course. But success as a peer leader requires more than content knowledge, and not all successful peer leaders are A students. A workshop team of faculty, learning specialists, and peer leaders reviews applications from prospective peer leaders. Interviews are conducted workshop-style with a group of applicants making up the workshop group. Applicants are often asked to respond to typical workshop situations (Appendix A-4, 8–12).

At most institutions, the process of team building and peer leader training starts with a one-half to two-day presemester meeting. In addition to content and problem review, peer leaders learn about PLTL philosophy, the leader's role, group behavior, motivation, student development, learning styles, active listening, effective communication, collaborative learning principles and techniques, community building, diversity issues, ethics, and campus resources. A comprehensive guide to peer leader training is available (Roth, Marcus, & Goldstein, in press).

Ongoing training varies with local resources. In one model, peer leaders meet once a week with the instructor who provides guidance in both group leadership and content for the upcoming workshop. A discussion about the previous workshop always provides opportunities for the instructor to introduce ideas about learning and interpersonal interactions. A second model involves a series of meetings throughout the term utilizing the combined resources of the instructor and a learning specialist. The learning specialist focuses on pedagogical issues and group dynamics and can often build bridges between these ideas and the workshop problems. Yet a third model involves a for-credit peer leader training course, often taught collaboratively by the instructor and the learning specialist. Such courses are interactive seminars rather than lecture courses. Using the instructor and learning specialist to team teach sends a powerful message to the peer leaders about their need to understand content, group behavior, and learning theory.

In all models of peer leader training, the peer leaders work on the workshop problems in the same way their students will in the actual workshop. The instructor takes the role of the peer leader, using the same techniques and tactics that the peer leaders are expected to use with the student groups. Peer leaders are encouraged to keep a journal in which they record attendance and comments about specific workshop problems and group dynamics issues. The journals allow the instructor and learning specialist to identify pedagogical issues and group concerns. More often than not, peer leaders will admit to difficulties and openly seek the help of the training group.

Training is essential to ensure a positive experience for peer leaders. Both preparation and practice build peer leaders' understanding of course content and their own leadership and communication skills. Peer leaders also gain a keen appreciation of different learning styles and study habits, including their own, and become more tol-erant and accepting of students who learn differently. The weekly meetings build camaraderie among the members of the workshop team that derives from working together toward a common goal.

Most peer leaders spend four to six hours a week on their workshop obligations, for which they are paid $6.00 to $8.00 per hour. For practical and political reasons, compensation should conform to institutional practice for tutors, laboratory assistants, or other peer mentors. The project's experience is that the stipend is powerfully professionalizing and is required to recruit a full complement of responsible peer leaders.

■ OUTCOMES

Throughout, the workshop project has engaged in action research based on evaluation, in which results have been utilized to refine and improve the model. Data collection methods have included focus groups, surveys, structured phone interviews, reports from faculty on student grades,

Figure 26.1 SAMPLE WORKSHOP PROBLEM ON RATES AND EQUILIBRIA (GOSSER, STROZAK, & CRACOLICE, 2001)

Most presentations of chemical kinetics start out with the definition that the speed of a chemical reaction corresponds to a change in concentration per unit time. This idea is easily digested because of the analogy to familiar ideas about the speed of moving objects such as cars. The next step in the discussion usually builds on qualitative observations about the rates of chemical reactions: "heat it up and it goes faster" or "increase the concentration and it goes faster." And then, suddenly, an equation appears: rate = k[reactant]^m. This workshop problem uses a simulation to bring an intuitive feel to the study of chemical kinetics. Like many good workshop problems, there is something physical and concrete to do; there is a kinesthetic dimension to the problem. There is also something fun to do. There is a game going on and the game is being played with other people. The game is not just a game, of course. It is an experiment in which the students measure (count) concentrations as a function of time. Ultimately, the observable experiences are transformed into analytical descriptions (graphs) of the relationships of concentration to time in the different games.

Work in groups of three,
with two players and one scorekeeper.

1) Consider a simple chemical reaction, A → B, that follows a first-order rate law, rate = k[A]. You will model this reaction with pennies. Start with 100 pennies, which will represent the initial concentration of A, 100 mM. Each penny will therefore represent 1 mM. It may be useful to mix in higher denomination coins such as quarters, nickels, and dimes to make the counting easier.

Student A (SA) will represent the concentration of A, and Student B (SB) will represent the concentration of B. We will represent the reaction of A to form B by passing pennies from SA to SB. Each exchange of pennies will represent one second of time. Student C records the observed results.

We will model a reaction in which 10% of the concentration of A reacts per second. Thus, for each second of time (exchange step), SA should transfer 10% of his/her pennies to SB. Round fractions to the nearest penny. Continue this exchange for 15 seconds.

a) Record concentrations of A and B (number of pennies) each second (after each exchange step) in a table.

b) Plot the concentration of A versus time on a graph. Use a different color to plot the concentration of B versus time on the same graph.

2) Let's apply the modeling technique developed in question 1 to a reversible reaction,

$$A \leftrightarrow B$$

In each second of time (exchange step), allow 10% of A to react to form B, and allow 10% of B to react to form A.

a) Change roles and record the results in a table like the one in question 1.

b) Plot the concentration of A versus time for the 10%/10% reaction on a graph. Compare this graph to the irreversible reaction A → B in question 1.

3) Consider a reversible reaction in which 10% of A reacts to form B and 5% of B reacts to form A. Record, plot, and compare to the results of questions 1 and 2.

site visits, and observations by the project evaluator (Gosser et al., 2001).

A number of faculty have compared the performance of nonworkshop and workshop sections of their classes in a given semester or between semesters. Data across a wide range of courses and institutions demonstrate that students who participate in PLTL workshops perform better than those who do not (and those who may participate in other structures such as traditional recitations) (Table 26.1). In a controlled experiment, grades in first semester organic chemistry at the University of Rochester were followed from 1992 to 1999. The average course grade for workshop students (2.5) was significantly ($p = 0.001$) greater than that for nonworkshop students (2.1).

Focus groups consistently revealed that students were more comfortable in the workshops than in lectures. Students felt free to make mistakes and reported that the personal atmosphere of the workshops allowed them to voice and share ideas. Many of the issues that emerged in the focus groups were later echoed in the more quantitative results of extensive surveys of students and peer leaders. In 1996, 723 students and 75 peer leaders from nine institutions reported their beliefs about the efficacy of workshops. Seventy-five percent of the students reported that workshops were helpful to their learning, while nearly 70% agreed that workshops improved their grade. Eighty-two percent of the students and 100% of the peer leaders would recommend a workshop course to other students. And 97% of the peer leaders agreed that acting as a peer leader improved their knowledge of chemistry.

A formal study of the impact on peer leaders is in progress. Faculty who teach PLTL courses are unanimous in their opinion that peer leaders gain a deeper understanding of chemistry through their experience as a peer leader, as well as enhanced confidence. Peer leaders often cite greater personal and intellectual confidence, gratifying interactions with their students, enhanced understanding of different learning styles, and increased interest in a teaching career as benefits of the experience. Indeed, one of the goals of the workshop project is to facilitate peer leaders' involvement in teacher preparation and certification programs.

The workshop project continues to collect the results of comparison studies, the results of which are posted on the project web page (The Workshop Project, 1999).

■ PRODUCTIVITY

A traditional approach to assessing the productivity of an academic program is to itemize the resource costs per student. However, a better measure of educational productivity is to itemize the resource costs per unit of student learning: This analysis focuses attention on the quality of the instruction. While there are new costs associated with workshop instruction, there are also new gains in student learning.

Most peer leaders are paid $300-$500/semester. Since a typical workshop accommodates eight students, an average cost of $400/leader corresponds to a peer leader stipend cost per student of $50 per semester. In the context of today's tuitions, this is not exorbitant; it is, however, a new cost to the institution. The other major workshop costs are allocations of faculty and staff time. A class

Table 26.1 FINAL GRADE PERFORMANCE[1] FOR NONWORKSHOP AND WORKSHOP CHEMISTRY COURSES

Institution	Nonworkshop % ABC	Workshop % ABC
University of Rochester[2]	66 (n = 1,450)	79 (n = 1,554)
University of Pittsburgh	83 (n = 113)	90 (n = 130)
Saint Xavier University[3]	72 (n = 95)	84 (n = 116)
New York City Technical College	62 (n = 443)	81 (n = 131)
City College	38 (historical)	58 (n = 484)
City College	52 (historical)	66 (n = 137)
University of Kentucky	1st Semester 60 (n = 4,554)	80 (n = 188)
	2nd Semester 58 (n = 2,912)	73 (n = 151)

[1]Percentage of A, B, and C grades obtained as a fraction of the total initially registered class. This measure of performance includes both performance and retention.
[2]Organic Chemistry; the difference is significant ($p = 0.001$).
[3]The organic biochemistry semester of a general-organic-biochemistry course for allied health professions.

of 100 students might use as much as $5,000 in continuing program support costs (Table 26.2). Faculty time to prepare workshop materials is a hidden cost. Fortunately, it is largely a start-up cost.

While it is essential to be honest about the costs associated with the workshop project, the itemization of cost per student does not take into account the benefit to the student. Metrics for analyzing cost per unit of student learning are not available. However, we can catch the spirit of the desired analysis by dividing the cost per student by the grade points earned. If the student learned at the A level (grade points = 4), the resource cost per unit of student learning would be smaller than if the student learned at the C level (grade points = 2). If the student failed or dropped out (grade points = 0), the resource cost per unit of student learning would be infinite. Since workshops improve student learning, as measured by percent success (% ABC) and average grade, the new resource cost is balanced by the learning gain. Using the data from first semester organic chemistry at Rochester, the investment in workshops produced 19% and 20% gains in average grade and percent success, respectively. These gains, per hundred dollar investment per student, provide a basis for comparing educational experiments. Although we do not have comparable data from other experiments, our speculation is that workshops are a relative bargain.

Other dimensions of the cost/benefit analysis are important. Ultimately, increased student satisfaction translates into increased revenue from tuition, alumni giving, and state allocations. Increased student success and satisfaction also lead to a decrease in revenue lost to attrition. The changes in revenue decrease the net cost of workshops. When the educational and personal benefits to the peer leaders are added to benefits to the students, the cost/benefit ratio for PLTL workshops becomes very attractive.

Table 26.2 CONTINUING COSTS FOR A WORKSHOP PROGRAM FOR A CLASS OF 100 STUDENTS

Peer leader salaries ($50/student)	$5000
Release time, learning specialist	2500
Staff support	1500
Supplies	500
Assessment, computing	500
Total for Class	$10,000
Per Student Cost	$100

SUGGESTIONS FOR REPLICATION

We advise those who are adapting the model to consider the central tenet of the workshop project—that teams are often the best way to tackle big ideas. To get started, we recommend assembling a small team of interested faculty, two or three students with previous success in the course, and a learning specialist. Talented graduates of the course serve as expert sources of information about how students experience the course; they often make good workshop peer leaders, and they know other potential peer leaders. Learning specialists bring expertise in how people learn and how peer groups function, and often have considerable experience in training peer leaders, initiating and maintaining program innovations, and program evaluation.

Institutions wishing to develop workshop courses can consult the workshop project web site (The Workshop Project, 1999). This site offers an introduction to the concept of peer-led team learning, a description of the workshop model, tips for training of peer leaders, a student page, information about upcoming presentations and workshops, useful references, and a personnel contact list. It also has an application form for the workshop project associate program, which provides funds to help faculty and learning specialists start workshop courses at their institutions.

To help newcomers gain a deeper understanding of the model, two- to three-day short courses are offered by project faculty, learning specialists, and peer leaders. We advise that a team attend one of these courses before attempting to implement the model. Having a mentor from the project is also beneficial to successful adoption.

CONCLUSION

The PLTL workshop is an effective, proven model for improving student performance in chemistry courses. It provides an active learning experience for students, creates a leadership role for undergraduates, and engages faculty and learning specialists in a creative new dimension of teaching. The model is robust and transferable from institution to institution and, more recently, from discipline to discipline.

ACKNOWLEDGMENTS

The authors gratefully acknowledge the support of the National Science Foundation, NSF/DUE 9450627, NSF/DUE 9455920, NSF/DUE 9972457, and NSF/DUE 9950575.

■ REFERENCES

Gosser, D. K., Cracolice, M. S., Kampmeier, J. A., Roth. V., Strozak, V. S., & Varma-Nelson, P. (2001). *Peer led team learning: A guidebook.* New York, NY: Prentice Hall.

Gosser Jr., D. K., & Roth, V. (1998). The workshop chemistry project: Peer-led team learning. *Journal of Chemical Education, 75* (2), 185-187.

Gosser, D., Roth, V., Gafney, L., Kampmeier, J., Strozak, V., Varma-Nelson, P., Radel, S., & Weiner, M. (1996). Workshop chemistry: Overcoming the barriers to student success. *The Chemical Educator* [Online serial], *1* (1). Available: http://journals.springer-ny.com/chedr/

Gosser, D. K., Strozak, V. S., & Cracolice, M. S. (2001). *Peer led team learning: General chemistry.* New York, NY: Prentice Hall.

Kampmeier, J. A., Varma-Nelson, P., & Wedegaertner, D. (2001). *Peer-led team learning: Organic chemistry.* New York, NY: Prentice Hall.

Roth, V., Marcus, G., & Goldstein, E. (in press). *Peer led team learning: On becoming a peer leader.* Manuscript submitted for publication.

Varma-Nelson, P., & Cracolice, M. S. (2001). *Peer led team learning: General, organic and biological chemistry.* New York, NY: Prentice Hall.

Woodward, A., Weiner, M., & Gosser, D. (1993). Problem solving workshops in general chemistry. *Journal of Chemical Education, 70,* 651.

The Workshop Project. (1999). *The workshop project* [Online]. Available: http://www.sci.ccny.cuny.edu/~chemwksp/

■ AUTHORS

JERRY L. SARQUIS is Professor of Chemistry and Biochemistry at Miami University, Oxford, OH.

LINDA J. DIXON is Assistant Dean of Students for Learning Assistance and Retention Programs at Miami University, Oxford, OH.

DAVID K. GOSSER is Professor of Chemistry and the Project Director of the Workshop Project at the City College of New York.

JACK A. KAMPMEIER is Professor of Chemistry at the University of Rochester.

VICKI ROTH is Assistant Dean of the College and Director of Learning Assistance Services at the University of Rochester.

VICTOR S. STROZAK is at the Center for Advanced Study in Education of the City University of New York and Professor Emeritus at New York City Technical College.

PRATIBHA VARMA-NELSON is Professor of Chemistry at Saint Xavier University.

Chapter 27

An Introductory Psychology Laboratory Designed and Taught by Undergraduate Teaching Interns

Stephen P. Stelzner, Michael G. Livingston, and Thomas Creed

The College of Saint Benedict (CSB) and Saint John's University (SJU) are two Catholic, liberal arts colleges located in central Minnesota. CSB is a women's college and SJU is a men's college, but all academic departments are joint, students attend classes on both campuses, and the schools share faculty, provost, and common graduation requirements. The combined student population of 3,700 is 90% Caucasian-American and 70% Catholic, 85% hail from states in the upper Midwest, and 42% enroll in "Introductory Psychology."

The mission of the psychology department at CSB/SJU, which graduates approximately 60 students a year, is to provide quality education in psychology to foster student communication, as well as analytical and critical thinking skills. "Introductory Psychology," offered in both the fall and spring semesters, is required of all psychology majors and fulfills a general education requirement.

A laboratory component was added to our "Introductory Psychology" course in 1984 to improve student thinking and communication skills, which we felt were not being developed by the traditional lecture format. Furthermore, we wanted to enrich the active learning experience by incorporating simple experiments and simulations. Like many small liberal arts colleges, we do not have graduate teaching assistants. However, we do have a number of majors who, in their senior year, are capable of leading labs as teaching interns (TIs).

The labs provide both our "Introductory Psychology" students and our advanced majors with an opportunity for experiential learning. Introductory students learn by doing: they conduct and analyze experiments, discuss pivotal topics in psychology, and complete ten written assignments. TIs learn by doing: They prepare the activities and content of the labs, and they teach two labs per week.

TIs take part in a psychology internship that includes a seminar on teaching, an apprenticeship with a faculty member in a large lecture section, and supervision with feedback from the faculty coordinator.

Between five and eight sections of "Introductory Psychology" are taught each semester (more in fall than spring), with each section enrolling between 30 and 35 students. Full-time psychology faculty teach each lecture section. Students registering for "Introductory Psychology" must also register for "Introductory Psychology Lab," with approximately ten students per lab section. The labs are designed as stand-alone experiences that complement the lecture sections by enhancing and elaborating on key concepts from the "Introductory Psychology" course. Students from a particular lecture section can register for any lab section. The labs meet approximately once every week for 70 minutes. The first meeting is an orientation to the lab, and the remaining ten meetings are devoted to topics covered in most introductory psychology courses. While topics vary slightly from semester to semester, labs cover topics such as research methods, learning, sensation and perception, memory, cognition, motivation and emotion, developmental psychology, social psychology, gender roles, abnormal psychology, and applied psychology.

■ MODEL

Teaching Internship

Selection of teaching interns. One of the capstone experiences that psychology majors at CSB/SJU may choose is the teaching internship. Faculty rate all junior majors on their potential as teaching interns, and in some instances, the faculty coordinator will encourage students who have been highly rated to apply for the teaching internship. Juniors may apply by submitting a letter of interest and a current transcript, which are evaluated by psychology faculty. Occasionally, we have recruited students who are psychology minors, because faculty have brought these students to the attention of the faculty coordinator. On the basis of the applications and faculty ratings or recommendations, the faculty coordinator selects 8-12 students for the teaching internship per semester. Essential qualities for TIs are understanding of psychology, responsibility, good social skills, and the ability to work with others. In our experience, a strong desire to participate in the program and to do a good job can sometimes compensate for a lack of "credentials."

Seminar on teaching. TIs attend a twice-weekly seminar on teaching taught by the faculty coordinator in charge of the labs. The seminar focuses on different elements of the internship, such as teaching and lab design. The TIs receive a syllabus at the first seminar meeting that details their duties, provides guidelines for conducting labs and developing lab topics, and describes the teaching seminar. The syllabus also lists the texts, additional readings on teaching, grading information, and the schedule for both the seminar and the labs. It emphasizes the importance of attending all seminar meetings, and the responsibility they have in teaching their lab sections. If they must miss a lab, they must find a substitute from among the other TIs and notify the faculty coordinator.

One meeting per week of the seminar is usually devoted to learning about and developing teaching skills. Students discuss teaching issues such as building rapport with students, grading, explaining concepts, and fostering discussion. The second seminar meeting is devoted to preparing for upcoming labs. TIs conduct a lab dry run to ensure they can explain essential concepts, carry out experiments, and lead discussions. During the dry runs, TIs make lesson and activity modifications and talk about potential problems and different ways to approach the material.

A goal of the teaching internship is that TIs learn to design and develop the labs. The faculty coordinator designs the first three labs, since preparation occurs prior to the beginning of the semester, and TIs use these as models for lab design. Working in teams of two or three, TIs design the remaining eight labs. They select readings, develop and type up prelab written assignments, develop activities and discussion topics, and prepare any additional handouts, overheads, or lab materials.

To help in lab development, TIs are provided with access to labs prepared in previous years, which are maintained and updated each semester. TIs also have access to various texts published by the American Psychological Association (Benjamin & Lowman, 1981; Benjamin, No-

dine, Ernst, & Broeker, 1999; Makosky, Sileo, & Whittemore, 1990; Makosky, Whittemore, & Rogers, 1988), instructor's manuals, and guides to teaching (e.g., McKeachie, 1999), to assist with lab preparation and the teaching of "Introductory Psychology."

In addition to designing and teaching labs, and attending the teaching seminar, TIs function as instructional apprentices. At least one TI is assigned to each professor teaching one of the introductory psychology lectures. Apprentice responsibilities vary and include some of the following tasks: proctoring exams, grading exams or homework, facilitating class discussions or activities, conducting review sessions, developing test questions, and on rare occasions, giving a lecture.

Feedback to interns. TIs are encouraged to learn from each other. For example, to help each other grade consistently, TIs pair up, check the grading of each other's students, and add additional written feedback on prelab assignments. TIs also visit each other's labs once or twice each semester to observe how their peers teach, meeting afterward to discuss their observations. TIs use an observation form to structure their observations and provide feedback to their peers (Appendix D-1).

TIs also get coaching and feedback from the faculty coordinator. Two of their labs are videotaped, usually the fourth and eighth out of the ten graded labs. The first lab observation occurs early enough for the TI to use the feedback to make adjustments, but not so early as to create unnecessary anxiety. The second observation occurs late enough to see development, while still allowing time for further adjustments. The TI and faculty coordinator consult on feedback and teaching improvement suggestions. Occasionally, a peer also reviews and critiques the videotape, providing further feedback.

Finally, the faculty coordinator meets with TIs as they develop each lab to give guidance and feedback on lab design and TIs' grasp of important concepts. The coordinator provides advice and coaching on teaching skills during the teaching seminar, and visits labs upon TI request if there is a particular concern, such as getting quiet people to participate or dealing with a disruptive student.

Evaluation of the teaching interns. TIs are not paid. They participate in the teaching internship as part of a capstone course that, in the last six years, has been graded in two ways. In one system, the faculty coordinator determines 80% of the grade (including student lab evaluations), and 10% each is determined by peer evaluation and the lecture professor. In the second system, the faculty coordinator determines 60% of the grade and 20% each is determined by peer evaluations and the lecture professor. Under both systems, the faculty coordinator uses multiple sources of information to determine TI grades, including student lab evaluations, seminar participation, video reviews, lab designs, peer evaluations, and evaluations from lecture professors.

Introductory Psychology Labs

The TI's primary responsibility is to teach two lab sections for the entire semester. The TIs teach their lab sections by leading discussions, preparing materials, presenting concepts, directing experiments or demonstrations, and grading students' written work and discussion.

During the first lab (which is ungraded), lab students receive a syllabus detailing lab requirements, grading, texts, and other basic information. Prelab written assignments are due at the beginning of each of the ten subsequent labs, and require students to answer questions based on a reading completed in advance of the lab. To prepare for the lab, students are frequently asked to conduct a short survey or carry out a mini-experiment, observe some aspect of human behavior, or simulate an experience, such as blindfolding oneself to replicate the experience of blindness. TIs facilitate a discussion based on this prelab preparation.

TIs grade prelab written assignments and discussions and provide written feedback at the next lab based on criteria provided by the faculty coordinator. A ten-point grading scale is used, with students earning up to five points each for the written prelab and graded discussion (resulting in 100 points for the entire semester). Final lab grades are distributed to students and to lecture professors at semester's end. Professors determine the value of the lab grades relative to the total course grade. In most cases, professors count the labs as 10% to 20% of the final course grade.

TIs and students spend considerable time during the first lab discussing guidelines for effective lab participation and interaction. These guidelines accompany the lab syllabus and include being prepared, attending class on time, listening, asking questions, and are based, in part, on group behaviors outlined by William Fawcett Hill (Rabow, Charness, Kipperman, & Radcliffe-Vasile, 1994). TIs also conduct a simple mnemonics experiment with students in preparation for the next lab on research methods. This experiment serves as an example of a typical lab activity. Other examples of lab activities during the semester include a simulated experience demonstrating the controversial nature of eyewitness testimony, and the use of a tongue-in-cheek intelligence scale developed by a TI as a means to generate discussion of cultural bias in intelligence testing.

◼ OUTCOMES

The introductory psychology lab taught by undergraduate TIs has been highly beneficial to the psychology program. Introductory students receive additional opportunities to engage in active learning and discussion, which allows them to understand material in greater depth and help develop their writing and discussion skills. TIs develop teaching and group facilitation skills, and consolidate their psychology knowledge. Faculty members who supervise the TIs develop a close working relationship with a group of highly motivated, bright students. In addition, concepts and ideas presented in the lecture section of the "Introductory Psychology" course are reinforced through discussion and active learning in the labs. Evaluations from teaching interns and introductory psychology students have been collected since the inception of the program.

Impact on Lab Students

Introductory students show high levels of satisfaction with the lab experience and with TI performance. Students complete evaluations of the labs at the midpoint and end of each semester. The evaluation form asks students to rank each specific lab on a 5-point scale (5 being high or excellent and 1 being low or poor) in terms of like/dislike (as well as a rationale for their ranking), and to rank the teaching intern on preparation, generation of interest, ability to emphasize important points, enthusiasm, ability to facilitate discussion, and overall performance. The evaluation form also asks students to identify what the TI did particularly well and suggest areas for improvement.

Data from the past 16 years have been very consistent. The average satisfaction score for specific lab sessions is 4.26, with some lab sessions ranking higher or lower depending on the particular semester or topic. For the past six semesters, TIs have received an average student satisfaction rating of 4.53.

While the majority of students like the labs a great deal, some students do not. This minority often includes students who expect psychology labs to be more similar to natural science labs, students who do not want to put much time into a course they are taking to satisfy a general education requirement, and students who had an average or poor TI.

Impact on Teaching Interns

Data from TIs indicate that the teaching internship is a very positive experience as evidenced by an average rating of 4.79 from a sampling of TI evaluations over the past six semesters. Experience over the last 16 years with over 300

TIs has confirmed the research finding that teaching is an effective way to learn material in depth. For example, the most common comment on TI evaluations of their teaching experience is that it consolidates their knowledge of psychology (67% responded this way over the last six semesters). TIs also comment that the internship helps develop interpersonal and group facilitation skills (53%), organizational skills (41%), and general confidence (23%). Informal oral feedback from lecture professors indicates that TIs achieve a high level of skill as discussion leaders and teachers.

■ PRODUCTIVITY

Impact on Introductory Psychology Professors

Our program has had a clear impact on the faculty who teach "Introductory Psychology" by increasing their productivity. TI apprentices reduce the workload of faculty, thus freeing up faculty time for scholarly activity or teaching improvement efforts. TIs also reduce faculty workload by proctoring exams, grading exams or homework, and conducting review sessions. A conservative estimate is that faculty gain one to two hours of time per week as a result of the TI program.

TIs also enable faculty to integrate innovative teaching techniques into their classes. One example of this is the use of TIs as coaches and assistants in a cooperative learning activity known as a structured academic controversy (Johnson, Johnson, & Smith 1991). The structured academic controversy involves small groups of students debating the pros and cons of an issue within a field of study. In a second example of innovation, students answer a survey on gender roles at the start of the class, and while a TI tabulates the results, the professor continues teaching. Later in the class period, the data are presented and discussed in detail, with the TI assisting the professor in facilitating discussion. These kinds of active learning strategies and immediate feedback would be very difficult to carry out without the help of the TIs serving as apprentices to the lecture professors.

Cost/Benefit Issues

The major cost for this program is associated with the faculty member who coordinates the labs, teaches the seminar, and supervises the TIs as part of her or his regular course load. The time needed is comparable to the workload of a regular course. The work is not evenly spaced, however, as the beginning of the semester and the period when the coordinator reviews the TI videos is especially intensive and requires larger blocks of time.

The program saves money in terms of the cost that would be required to hire or assign a faculty member to teach the labs. Using the staffing of labs in the natural sciences as an example, teaching the introductory psychology labs would be equivalent to approximately 83% of a faculty member's normal teaching load during a semester. Thus, the salary savings for the institution would approximate $37,500 for the year, as opposed to the approximate salary cost of $15,000 per year necessary for the lab coordinator (assuming the associate professor level).

The cost to TIs is that they are involved in a capstone course that requires a significant time commitment (an estimated 12–15 hours per week) compared to the standard investment in a typical academic course (an estimated ten hours per week). However, the time commitment is also significant in other capstone experiences, so there may be no real difference compared to similar experiences.

The other major costs associated with the program include photocopying costs for lab materials and time spent scheduling rooms for the labs. The photocopying costs have been absorbed by the psychology department since the inception of the program and have, for the last two semesters, amounted to an average of $513 per semester.

■ SUGGESTIONS FOR REPLICATION

In our opinion, this program would work best at other small liberal arts colleges. It seems less applicable to two-year colleges as senior-level students are needed, or to large universities where graduate students act as teaching assistants or laboratory instructors. It may, however, present an alternative to the use of graduate teaching assistants at large research universities. While our program works well for the social sciences or humanities where both discussion and experiential activities can supplement lectures, this does not preclude the natural sciences from implementing such a program.

It would be difficult to duplicate this program from scratch without the investment of additional preparation time. At CSB/SJU, this was facilitated by support from a small internal grant that provided a one-course release to the faculty coordinator the semester preceding the start of the program. This kind of program could also be developed over the summer. Once established, the program is no more costly or time consuming than a typical college course.

Room scheduling is also an issue that needs particular attention. Labs require small, seminar type rooms with moveable chairs. With as many as 24 labs being taught in a semester, considerable classroom space must be reserved to accommodate instructional needs. Fortunately, each lab is taught only once per week, and the labs are scheduled at different times throughout the day, minimizing the extent of this problem.

■ CONCLUSION

Over the last 16 years, we have found that five factors contribute to a successful program using undergraduate students as teaching interns to enhance student learning in introductory psychology: 1) select high quality undergraduates as teaching interns, 2) provide careful training in pedagogy and content to the TIs, 3) have clear expectations and deadlines for both the TIs and the lab students, 4) give TIs responsibility and authority to develop labs and run lab sections, and 5) regularly assess TIs' performance and give them formative feedback.

Functioning as instructors in active learning-oriented psychology labs, and as apprentices in psychology lectures, TIs have helped reinforce students' basic psychological knowledge, increased their own knowledge and communication skills, and increased faculty productivity. The program has demonstrated the value of students teaching students, and TIs discover the truth to the old expression that "to teach is to learn twice."

■ REFERENCES

Benjamin, L.T., & Lowman, K.D. (1981). *Activities handbook for the teaching of psychology* (Vol. 1). Washington, DC: American Psychological Association.

Benjamin, L.T., Nodine, B. F., Ernst, R. M., & Broeker, C. B. (1999). *Activities handbook for the teaching of psychology* (Vol. 4). Washington, DC: American Psychological Association.

Johnson, D. W., Johnson, R. T., & Smith, K. A. (1991). *Active learning: Cooperation in the college classroom.* Edina, MN: Interaction Book Company.

Makosky, V. P., Sileo, C. C., & Whittemore, L. G. (1990). *Activities handbook for the teaching of psychology* (Vol. 3). Washington, DC: American Psychological Association.

Makosky, V. P., Whittemore, L. G., & Rogers, A. M. (1988). *Activities handbook for the teaching of psychology* (Vol. 2). Washington, DC: American Psychological Association.

McKeachie, W. F. (1999). *Teaching tips: Strategies, research, and theory for college and university teachers.* Boston, MA: Houghton Mifflin.

Rabow, J., Charness, M. A., Kipperman, J., & Radcliffe-Vasile, S. (1994). *William Fawcett Hill's learning through discussion* (3rd ed.). Thousand Oaks, CA: Sage.

■ AUTHORS

STEPHEN P. STELZNER is a Professor of Psychology at the College of St. Benedict and St. John's University.

MICHAEL G. LIVINGSTON is an Associate Professor of Psychology at the College of St. Benedict and St. John's University.

THOMAS CREED (1946–1999) was a Professor of Psychology at the College of St. Benedict and St. John's University.

Chapter 28

Undergraduate Teaching Assistants Bring Active Learning to Class

Melissa A. Thibodeau

Syracuse University (SU) is a research university in Syracuse, New York. Enrollment for the 1998–1999 school year was about 18,000, of which just over 12,000 were undergraduates enrolled in 11 colleges with baccalaureate programs.

This chapter describes Public Affairs 101: "Introduction and Analysis of Public Policy" (PAF 101), a course in the College of Arts and Sciences taught by Professor William Coplin. The course seeks to transform students from self-interested individuals into adults who want to shape government actions to serve both their own needs and the public interest. It is one of more than 100 courses that satisfy the social science distribution in liberal arts requirements at SU. Averaging 125 students a semester, PAF 101 meets three times a week. Throughout the duration of the course, students complete five papers on local, state, or federal public policy problems of their choice. In class, students prepare for their papers by using university problems to help practice their policy skills.

The class is hands-on, focusing on processes and skills rather than on content, and incorporates guest speakers from various public policy professions who speak to the students about career options. There is also a five-hour community service requirement for each student. The most skills-based part of the class activity is the competition exercise that precedes each paper assignment: Students compete against each other to give the best answers to questions that will be dealt with in a given paper. During these competitions, an undergraduate teaching assistant (UTA) calls on two students in the class. One of the students is asked a question (the UTA has predetermined who will be called on, but students themselves do not know) and the second student must critique the first student's answer. One or both of the students can receive extra credit points by giving correct answers or adequate critiques. By the end of the semes-

ter, almost every student in the class has participated in at least one competition exercise.

When this course was developed in 1976, the instructor felt that because of its complexity (five papers per student) and size (125 students per semester), the course could not be run successfully without teaching assistants. Instead of adopting the traditional model of having graduate teaching assistants (TAs), Coplin decided to employ undergraduates as his teaching assistants. He began teaching the course with the help of graduate TAs in 1969, but in 1972 switched to using undergraduates as he needed more help in grading assignments and thought he could maintain more quality control with UTAs. Coplin felt that UTAs understood his viewpoints, course management procedures, and course objectives better than graduate TAs because they had previously taken the course with him.

■ MODEL

Every semester approximately 30 PAF 101 students apply to be UTAs for the following semester (Appendix A-3), and between 12 and 15 are selected. According to interviews with UTAs in 1999, students apply to be UTAs for a combination of six reasons: 1) to build professional relationships with the instructor, 2) to gain positions of prestige, 3) to put an extra activity on their resume, 4) to have an opportunity to work with students as an instructor, 5) to obtain academic credit in an upper-division public affairs course (that also carries honors designation for those in the honors program), and 6) to learn the content of the course better. Since 1976, over 600 UTAs have helped teach PAF 101.

To be selected as a PAF 101 UTA, a student should:

- Have a GPA of at least 3.0 (out of 4.0) and demonstrate knowledge of course material by receiving high paper scores, giving intelligent and confident answers to questions posed in the interview, and performing well in competition exercises.

- Demonstrate a solid grasp of the course's important concepts through course assignments.

- Demonstrate high levels of maturity, enthusiasm, and effective communication skills.

- Demonstrate punctuality and responsibility (e.g., turning assignments in on time, arriving at class on time).

- Show leadership skills and extracurricular involvement.

- Express a desire and ability to work well with others.

While there are very few students who meet all of those expectations, each one selected does have a firm grasp of the course material, is responsible and mature, and has leadership and communication skills.

Both the instructor and current UTAs interview the applicants. During the five-minute interview they are asked why they want to be UTAs and why they think they would be good at it. They are also asked if they think they will have enough time to do the job right, as well as other questions that determine if they have an understanding of the course material. The interview is also used to determine how well the students can communicate to a group, and if they accurately understand the course objectives. While the interview does play a role in determining if a student is selected as a UTA, the reference of each applicant's former UTA is the most important factor.

The PAF 101 UTAs receive a grade and academic credit for their work through enrollment in PAF 409: "Intermediate Public Policy Analysis." PAF 409 is open only to PAF 101 UTAs, is taught by the same instructor as PAF 101, and meets for one hour before every PAF 101 class period. Each UTA's PAF 409 grade depends on how well the assigned PAF 409 tasks are completed.

General tasks required of all UTAs include:

- Attending a lunch meeting with the instructor, providing a schedule of his/her plans, and a description of the specific role he/she will play in the PAF 101 class.

- Participating in the staff meetings (PAF 409 class) prior to each PAF 101 class.

- Keeping one office hour per week.

- Taking attendance, collecting and returning papers, and preparing reports to the instructor on PAF 101 student performance and participation.

- Grading approximately ten module papers within seven days of receiving them. Two UTAs read and grade each paper. Before each paper is due, the PAF 101 teaching assistants go through "grade training" for that particular assignment. The training includes guidelines about where to take off points and an exercise in grading sample papers. UTAs are also given a previously graded version of the sample paper and discrepancies between the sample paper and UTA grading are discussed.

- Conducting regrades and reviews for the instructor's assessment. Regrading is a process where students examine graded papers and request a review if they feel they were graded unfairly. Regrades are encouraged to ensure that UTAs are as accurate as possible when assessing their peers and to minimize student concern about UTA grading ability. The instructor reads that student's paper and determines whether or not the grade should be changed. To encourage regrades, the instructor only adds points and never deducts points, even if he finds the UTA was too generous. The PAF 101 regrade request form is provided in Figure 28.1.

In addition to reducing concern over students grading their peers, regrading is encouraged because it acknowledges that UTAs (like professors and TAs) sometimes make mistakes, it is a good learning experience for students to examine their papers after they've been graded, UTAs take grading more seriously when they know that if they make a mistake the instructor may conduct a regrade, and regrading enables the instructor to improve the wording of the writing assignments or UTA grading practice exercises.

- Monitoring student completion of community service requirement.

- Responding to requests from fellow UTAs.

- Assisting in the selection of UTAs for the next semester.

- Preparing a semester report that documents work done by him/herself, and makes suggestions for improving the course.

- Participating in performance self-evaluations.

UTAs are told to remember one more thing, possibly the most important: Their relationship with students in the class is that of a coach. "A coach is a teacher, a disciplinarian, and a motivator—not a friend or someone on a power trip" (Coplin, 1997, p. 3).

In addition to completing all of the general requirements, each UTA has a specific role assignment for the semester. These role assignments allow each UTA to become an expert in, and take responsibility for, one specific aspect of the course. The PAF 409 role assignments are:

UTA manager: Monitors the productivity and behavior of all the other UTAs. Some of the tasks required are setting up the office hour schedule for each UTA, preparing the agendas for every staff meeting (PAF 409 class), coordinating the UTA mid-semester evaluations, and scheduling the UTA lunches with the instructor.

Competition director: Organizes and runs the competition exercises for each unit (described in the opening section of this chapter). This UTA briefs PAF 101 students on the competition exercises, prepares the overhead slides for the competitions, and awards points to the students who give appropriate answers.

Extra credit speaker coordinator: Keeps an updated list of all the speakers across campus that deal with public policy issues during the semester. This UTA also collects and grades all papers that students write about the extra credit speeches they attend.

Outside speaker coordinator: Makes arrangements with numerous guest lecturers from the Syracuse community. This UTA also designs surveys that students use to evaluate each speaker, tabulates the results of the surveys, and writes a report of the results.

Module (paper) directors: Five UTAs, one for each module (paper) that students are required to write, train the other UTAs on grading by providing sample modules; distribute tip sheets on grading procedures and review the grading and regrading processes.

Newsletter editor: Designs the five different newsletters distributed to PAF 101 students throughout the semester. The newsletters provide helpful hints for each module as well as other information about the class.

Computing and web director: Devises a plan to increase the use of computers in PAF 101. The computing and web director creates ways of introducing Microsoft Word and Microsoft Excel to students, and the use of email as a communication and instructional device for the class.

Honors director: Takes attendance at, and arranges activities for students in PAF 101 who are members of Syracuse University's Honors Program (a special section of PAF 101 for students in the honors program meets once a week).

Community service director: Provides an updated list of all community service opportunities that meet the five-hour PAF 101 community service requirement. This UTA also keeps an updated list of all students who have completed their community service and what service each student did. At the end of the semester, the UTA prepares

Figure 28.1 REGRADE REQUEST FORM

I am formally requesting that Professor Coplin look at the sections listed below to reevaluate the paper. I understand that his decision is final, and that I must take this form and my paper to a UTA in Room 113, where the UTA will sign and date this request.

Signature by Student: _____ Date: _____

UTA Signature: _____ Date: _____

** All regrade requests must be made no more than **one week** after the papers were returned in class.
(Note: If you run out of room, you can use another form.)

Exercise #	Student's Justification for Change in Grade	Reviewer's Comments	Coplin's Comments

New Grade: _____ Original Grader: _____ Student's UTA Name: _____

Reviewer: _____

Comments to Original Grader:

a report of the pattern of student community service activity for the semester.

UTAs are viewed as employees whose livelihood depends on performance reviews. Six weeks into the course, each UTA attends a ten-minute interview with the instructor. During the interview, the UTA's individual contributions to the class, performance, and areas of improvement are discussed. That interview evaluation helps to assure that each UTA is graded fairly (Appendix D-2). Eighty percent of the final grade each UTA receives (for PAF 409) is based on how well each UTA performs the tasks listed above (which are described in a 30-page manual provided to each UTA), and 20% on a written final report each UTA must write about their experience.

◼ OUTCOMES

No research has been undertaken to determine the impact of the PAF 101 model on student learning or satisfaction. The only available means of assessing the model's impact is the feedback given by students on UTA evaluations (Appendix D-4) or in conversations with the instructor. Based on that feedback, many students feel UTAs are a very positive aspect of the course. Others feel there are changes that need to be made in order to improve the model.

In PAF 101 course evaluations from the spring and fall 1999 semesters, students said:

- "I thought the UTAs were one of the greatest strengths of this course."

- "The UTAs were very helpful."

- "I felt less intimidated by the undergraduate TAs then I would have by graduate TAs—it's easier to get help from someone your own age."

- "The undergraduate TAs were more approachable than graduate TAs."

- "I thought the grading of papers was one of the major weaknesses of the course—No TA graded the same, which made it quite difficult for the students."

Other faculty members have expressed opposition to allowing UTAs to grade other undergraduates' papers. Some think undergraduates are unreliable, while others are afraid that letting undergraduates grade would undermine the professor's authority in the class. This issue is the most problematic aspect of the UTA model; however, the instructor feels that the regrade policy and the fact that all papers are graded by two UTAs provides a degree

of grading consistency that exceeds that of traditionally taught courses.

UTAs benefit from their work just as much, if not more, than the PAF 101 students. In interviews during the 1999 spring semester, UTAs said that they learned a lot about responsibility, and got a much better understanding of the PAF 101 course material. UTAs over the years have given the instructor consistent feedback that they learn teamwork, collaboration, and evaluation skills. Learning evaluation skills helps UTAs to understand criteria and standards so that in future courses they will more clearly understand how they are graded. Possibly the greatest benefit to UTAs is that through working closely with the faculty they become prepared for relationships with supervisors in their career field.

◼ PRODUCTIVITY

PAF 101 would not be as effective without UTAs; however, as with almost anything, there are costs that come with benefits. The major cost is increased instructor time: The instructor must spend an extra two to three hours each week working with, preparing and training the UTAs. Regrades take a lot of time and numerous UTA training materials must be developed.

There is also a cost that is difficult, if not impossible to calculate: the impact of the UTA model on the instructor's reputation among colleagues. Over the years of the program, it has become evident that some faculty think the instructor gives too much attention and authority to undergraduates.

It is felt, however, that the benefits of using UTAs far outweigh the costs. UTAs are not paid, so the only monetary costs (excluding instructor time) involved with using UTAs in PAF 101 are the costs of printing UTA manuals—the 30-page books that describe all the responsibilities of being a UTA (Coplin, 1997).

The UTA model increases the learning productivity of students by bringing small class advantages to a large class as each UTA works with and monitors class participation of no more than ten students per class. This level of attention would not be possible with a single instructor or with the use of a traditional graduate TA model.

Without UTAs to assist in grading the required five papers per student, the class would need to be limited to 25 students or reverted back to traditional large class procedures of fewer written assignments and multiple-choice examinations. One professor and a couple of graduate TAs could not read over 600 papers each semester, be available to help the students outside of class each day, and keep track of community service requirements and extra credit points. Allowing the class to stay so large and hands-on is the greatest benefit of the UTA model.

The use of UTAs has increased the instructor's productivity by assisting with various aspects of course development and improvement. UTAs are responsible for infusing a spirit of innovation into the course. New ideas are proposed and pilot tested as a result of UTA involvement and interest. For example, as UTAs became more technologically knowledgeable, a course web site was developed and integrated into the course (Schultz, 2000).

UTAs are responsible for conducting weekly evaluations of certain aspects of the class, and the results of these evaluations are fed back into course improvement. UTAs add their opinions about their own previous class experience and critique lectures and exercises, often resulting in revision of assignments and classroom activities.

The UTA model delivers direct benefits to both the undergraduates who are selected to perform this instructional role and to the public policy department. Excellent students are recruited to the policy studies major through their experience of being UTAs. In fact, 40% of all policy studies majors have been PAF 101 UTAs.

The use of UTAs has proven to be an excellent way to recruit students to the course by telling them about both the class and the opportunity to become UTAs. UTAs form networks that they use throughout their college career and beyond. For students in the course, as well as the UTAs, the perception of absolute authority of college professors is challenged because someone just like them also has authority.

■ SUGGESTIONS FOR REPLICATION

The PAF 101 UTA model may not be appropriate for every professor or in every class. The model seems to make most sense for those instructors who offer their course at least every year—or every semester—because UTAs remember more of the course information and concepts if they took the course recently. However, I believe that the model will work for any course in any subject where active learning is employed and students learn by doing. This is because there is not much for a UTA to do in a lecture-based course. There need to be activities for the UTAs to plan and run, and opportunities to assist students. This may mean that papers replace multiple-choice tests as the main means of assessment. If so, there need to be very clear grading guidelines that undergraduates can follow.

A critical aspect of the model is that the UTAs help to continuously improve the course because they have moved from student to instructor and understand what needs to be changed. Not only do the UTAs observe the class, but they also talk to students in it and get their feedback on what could be improved. The instructor has to be willing to listen to the UTAs and be open to change. An important constraint is that the instructor must spend time prior to each class with the UTAs to ensure training and coordination.

Another very important issue to be considered if the UTA model is to be adopted is the impact of students grading students. The risk of UTAs breaching ethics, rating friends who are in the class higher than others, or revealing students' grades must be safeguarded against through added training and a procedure such as regrading. Regrading is recommended as it also helps prevent inconsistencies in grading as some UTAs grade easy, others grade very tough.

Although the model was developed as a total course package, many of the principles and ideas could be applied, in part, to any course. For example, an instructor might have one or two UTAs to conduct mini-evaluations or classroom assessment activities with students throughout the course, and prepare a report on how to improve the course for the following semester. The utilization of former students in this way, as a potential source of support for you as an instructor, is a revolutionary component of the UTA model worth replicating. The model could be a starting point for more sweeping instructional change.

■ CONCLUSION

This model demonstrates the ability of one instructor, without added institutional support, to make significant changes in the delivery and outcome of his/her course. By sharing authority with students, the instructor is able to increase his/her impact upon students and student learning.

Undergraduate teaching assistants increase the productivity and effectiveness of faculty by providing human resources to interact directly with students in and out of the classroom. With the demand for more active hands-on learning, fewer large lectures, faculty downsizing, and fewer graduate students, UTAs are a solution to a very serious squeeze on available teaching resources. Even if there were ample graduate assistants, UTAs, as a result of recently having mastered the material as students, have a distinct advantage over graduate students, especially in the more mechanical teaching activities required to help students master material. Student evaluations tell us that undergraduates perform as well as or better than graduate students do.

The use of UTAs in this model should not be construed as an argument that they can replace graduate assistants. The practice does not itself require fewer graduate assistants, just a different and more professional use of them for tasks such as researching lecture materials, conducting lectures, or writing course exams (Coplin, 1998).

■ REFERENCES

Coplin, W. D. (1997). *Teaching assistants manual: PAF 101*. Syracuse, NY: Syracuse University.

Coplin, W. D. (1998). *Improving undergraduate education at Syracuse University through more student-faculty collaboration*. Unpublished manuscript, Syracuse University, New York.

Schultz, F. (2000). *Maxwell school of citizenship and public affairs* [Online]. Available: www.maxwell.syr.edu/paf/

■ AUTHOR

MELISSA A. THIBODEAU is an undergraduate Policy Studies and Newspaper Journalism major at Syracuse University.

Part V

Undergraduate Students
Assisting in
Faculty Development

Chapter 29

Student-Faculty Partnerships to Develop Teaching and Enhance Learning

Milton D. Cox

Student learning communities are increasingly attractive as curricular structures that provide coherence across disciplines while building community for students (Cross, 1998; Lenning & Ebbers, 1999; Shapiro & Levine, 1999). Among other things, these student communities increase the learning, intellectual development, and retention of students (Gabelnick, MacGregor, Matthews, & Smith, 1990). Faculty learning communities (FLCs) are now beginning to hold attraction because they produce similar learning and community-building effects for faculty (Cox, 2001).

Over twenty years ago, FLCs were initiated by Miami University, a state-assisted Doctoral I institution with 14,500 undergraduates, 1,500 graduate students, and 750 full-time faculty on the Oxford campus, plus 4,000 students and 100 faculty on two regional campuses. At Miami, an FLC is a year-long program involving about ten faculty. The program curriculum is designed to stimulate interest in teaching and learning, build community, foster civic responsibility, and develop scholarship of teaching. Miami's FLCs are designed and coordinated through our Teaching Effectiveness Programs (TEP) office, which currently supports six FLCs for approximately 50 faculty each year.

◼ MODELS

At Miami, we have developed two ways for students to become involved in TEP efforts to improve teaching and learning: 1) as student associates in FLCs, and 2) as participants and hosts in faculty development seminars and conferences.

Faculty Learning Communities and the Introduction of Student Associates

FLCs at Miami are either cohort- or issue-focused. Cohort-focused communities address the needs of faculty who have felt isolated, while issue-focused FLCs address specific teaching issues and are open to all faculty. Miami's two cohort-focused communities are the Teaching Scholars Community for Junior Faculty, in place for 22 years, and the Senior Faculty Community for Teaching Excellence, in place for ten years. The 2000–2001 issue-focused communities are the Faculty Community Using Difference to Enhance Teaching and Learning, in its fourth year; and three communities in their first year, focusing on problem-based learning, technology, and team teaching.

Each community selects seminar topics and presenters, conducts an off-campus retreat to foster bonding, and helps participants design teaching projects as a first step in developing a scholarship of teaching. During the first semester, seminars and readings introduce participants to literature on higher education pedagogy; in the second semester, participants present their projects at a campus teaching retreat and a national teaching conference.

Student associates were introduced into Miami's FLCs three years ago when we realized that we were missing a key component—the insights of students. Faculty in the learning communities realized that students provide feedback: as observers in the classroom, as consultants on teaching projects, and as consultants about student life outside the classroom. The faculty-student connection is two-way, with students learning about teaching at the college level and about life in academe.

Selection of Student Associates

Each FLC member selects one or two student associates to work with her or him for the FLC membership year. Students can be of any class standing or major. In selecting student associates, faculty need to consider if they would like to involve different students each semester, and whether to choose associates from students in their current classes. While a class member can provide more information on current class activities, most faculty choose former students as associates because of ethical considerations.

Compensation of Student Associates

To ensure participation throughout the semester, student associates receive some form of compensation. Juniors and seniors with strong academic records may receive a notation on their transcript that they served as an "undergraduate associate." To earn that notation, students work with their faculty partner, assisting with many tasks associated with academics (e.g., teaching, grading, and engaging in research) and write a report summarizing the significance of the experience. Students may also receive one to five hours of independent study credit per semester for working with a faculty member; however, the independent study must be approved by the faculty member's department chair.

If an FLC teaching project involves a student associate to observe an instructor's class or work with students in the class, the instructor can pay the associate from FLC funds. Students who work as hosts for faculty development seminars and conferences are rewarded similarly. Many faculty also thank their student associates with gifts of books and software purchased with FLC funds.

Student Associate Activities in FLCs and Faculty Development Seminars

Student associates are involved in FLCs in numerous ways. First, the faculty member and student associates meet for twice-a-month discussions of issues raised in learning community seminars, short articles they have read, the faculty member's teaching project, innovations the faculty member is testing in class or considering for future classes, and ways associates can assist with teaching (e.g., participating in cooperative learning activities in class and giving feedback on how the process worked and students reacted).

A second way that students can serve in the FLCs is as seminar partners. Early in the year, all student associates and faculty in a learning community participate in a community seminar to share perspectives on teaching and learning. This provides an opportunity for faculty and associate pairs to get to know each other and other faculty and associates in the FLC. To prepare for the seminar, faculty are asked to list their five most important "keys" to effective teaching and learning, plus a metaphor for teaching and two questions they wish to ask students about learning. Students are also asked for their "keys": a metaphor, and two questions to ask faculty about teaching. The responses are compiled and distributed to participants before the seminar. At the seminar, a lively discussion arises about the differences between what faculty and students consider important for effective teaching. For example, in the November 25, 1999 seminar, two faculty identified knowing first names as being a key to building rapport, while no students indicated that as key. On the other hand, two students indicated being approachable as key to building rapport, something which no faculty listed. Some keys, such as enthusiasm and knowledge of the subject, were high on both faculty and student lists. After the discussion, faculty and students take turns asking their questions, exploring issues that arise. To provide an opportunity for informal discussion and to extend an appreciative gesture to all participants, dinner is included in the seminar.

A third type of FLC involvement for student associates is to work with TEP as session hosts during teaching retreats or conferences. Student associates meet and introduce session presenters and contribute student perspectives during the session they host. In a one-hour training session, students who have worked as hosts describe various scenarios and lead role plays. As many as 30 students serve as session hosts at Miami's Lilly Conference on College Teaching; these include FLC associates, members of student service organizations, and students who are completing optional course assignments. Students who are hosting as part of a course assignment write one-page reaction papers, while FLC associates and service organization students are paid, with the latter usually donating their wages to their organization.

Finally, we are currently encouraging FLC faculty members to team teach with their student associates (Gray & Hulbert, 1998). In team teaching with a student, the instructor is in charge of course design, while the student associate helps with the daily delivery of the course and performs most of the administrative duties associated with the course. The student associate must have completed the course with an above average understanding of content and processes, and the instructor and associate must be compatible enough to work together.

OUTCOMES

Faculty in FLCs complete a questionnaire to report the impact of various FLC components on their learning, one of which is student associates. In the senior faculty FLC, the impact of student associates over the years has ranked third, with an impact of 7.7 (on a scale from a low of 1 to a high of 10). In the junior faculty community, however, the student associates component ranks last, at 5.4. In open-ended questions, junior faculty reported difficulty identifying students as associates and keeping them committed to the partnership. Perhaps junior faculty have problems because they have not been teaching long or are not experienced enough to identify qualified students and work with them comfortably.

When the faculty rank the dozen or so seminars they attend in their year in the Miami FLCs, the seminar where faculty and student associates share their views on keys to effective teaching and learning has often been ranked as the most interesting. Faculty say this seminar strengthens faculty-student partnerships, builds trust, and increases understanding and respect for "the other side."

Student papers on their involvement in the faculty development seminars show that they gain perspectives on teaching and learning from their experiences. For example, in a reaction paper to a play on the shift from an instructor-centered classroom to a student-centered one, a student wrote that the play helped him realize that different teaching styles could affect his learning.

Student session hosts gain skills and experience that contribute later to their interest in forming teaching partnerships with faculty. Also, the faculty presenting or attending the seminars report in open-ended evaluation comments that they appreciate and welcome the student perspectives.

PRODUCTIVITY

Even before we added the student component, FLCs contributed effectively to the development of participants and the institution. For example, a 1995 study showed that junior faculty who participated were tenured at a significantly higher rate than those who did not (Cox, 1995). Adding student associates enhanced FLCs at a negligible cost: The annual cost of each learning community is about $30,000, and the student component cost only $200. Weighing the benefits accrued from adding student associates—student perspectives and suggestions about teaching and learning—against the costs involved, using associates for this program is highly productive.

Involving students as participants in campus-wide faculty development seminars incurs no additional cost because students write reaction papers as part of the courses in which they are enrolled rather than receive pay.

The students hosting sessions at the Lilly Conference receive wages totaling $1,000, which is only 1% of the total conference budget. The benefits that students provide, namely sharing student insights about teaching and learning plus helping the conference run smoothly, far outweigh the additional costs.

SUGGESTIONS FOR REPLICATION

The suggestions below are from an article on issues teaching centers should consider when thinking of using students to enhance faculty development efforts (Cox & Sorenson, 2000).

- Determine faculty development goals to which students can contribute and roles that students can assume (e.g., as associates or seminar participants).

- Determine qualifications for student participants and decide how they will be identified, selected, and rewarded for participating.

- Plan how to initiate student involvement (e.g., from honors program or student affairs division) and develop joint efforts with other programs.

- Establish ways to assess the effectiveness of student involvement and monitor how faculty and students react to joint projects.

- Discuss whether or under what circumstances faculty may engage students currently in their classes.

CONCLUSION

The models described in this chapter provide examples that have led to successful faculty-student partnerships at Miami University. I recommend that interested faculty visit the teaching center on their campus and explore additional ways that student-faculty partnerships can be developed.

■ REFERENCES

Cox, M. D. (1995). The development of new and junior faculty. In W. A. Wright & Associates (Eds.), *Teaching improvement practices: Successful strategies for higher education* (pp. 283-310). Bolton, MA: Anker.

Cox, M. D. (2001). Faculty learning communities: Change agents for transforming institutions into learning organizations. Lieberman, D. & Whelburg, C. (Eds.), *To Improve the Academy, Vol 19*. Bolton, MA: Anker.

Cox, M. D., & Sorenson, D. L. (2000). Student consultation in faculty development: Connecting directly to the learning revolution. *To Improve the Academy, 18*, 97-127.

Cross, K. P. (1998, July-August). Why learning communities? Why now? *About Campus, 3* (3), 4-11.

Gabelnick, F., MacGregor, J., Matthews, R. S., & Smith, B. L. (1990). *Learning communities: Creating connections among students, faculty, and disciplines.* New Directions for Teaching and Learning, No. 41. San Francisco, CA: Jossey-Bass.

Gray, T., & Hulbert, S. (1998, Fall). Team teach with a student. *College Teaching, 46* (4), 150-153.

Lenning, O. T., & Ebbers, L. H. (1999). The powerful potential of learning communities: Improving education for the future. [Monograph]. *ASHE-ERIC Higher Education Report, 26*, 6.

Shapiro, N. S., & Levine, J. H. (1999). *Creating learning communities: A practical guide to winning support, organizing for change, and implementing programs.* San Francisco, CA: Jossey-Bass.

■ AUTHOR

MILTON D. COX is the University Director for Teaching Effectiveness Programs in the Office for Advancement of Scholarship and Teaching at Miami University, Oxford, OH.

Chapter 30

Educating the Critic:
Student-Driven Quality

**Elizabeth Kinland, Lisa Firing Lenze, Lynn Melander Moore,
and Larry D. Spence**

Josie discovered student quality teams in a statistics course when a student came into the room one day and asked for volunteers to help assess and improve the course. Her professor added that the concept, sponsored by the Schreyer Institute for Innovation in Learning (a campus unit dedicated to shifting the focus in undergraduate education from teaching to learning), based its approach on quality improvement methods used in corporations like Ford Motor Company. While Josie did not understand the link between building cars and learning statistics, the call for volunteers interested her. She realized that this might be a chance to have some control over her college education, but did not know that becoming a team member would change her approach to learning.

Founded in 1855 as a land grant college, Penn State became known for its research and learning in agriculture and engineering. Today it is one of the leading public research universities, ranking number two nationally in industry-sponsored research. It enrolls 40,000 students at the main campus and another 40,000 at 23 other locations. In her freshman year, Josie learned her way around a campus the size of a small city, did what she was told, and tried not to gain the notorious fifteen pounds. She completed tedious assignments and attended boring lectures without complaint. Still, it seemed that there should be more to learning than what she was getting.

The offering in her statistics course intrigued Josie—this professor wanted feedback. Josie became part of the course quality team, and with her teammates discussed class problems, constructed survey questions to investigate those problems, and developed suggestions for improvement. Then, the team leader met with the professor to report the findings and suggestions, and the professor listened!

The experience opened her eyes. Josie learned that although professors genuinely wanted to help her learn,

they often did not know how. She learned that data on the extent of a problem is better than complaints, and that specific ideas for change make change more likely. Above all, Josie realized that professors do not make students learn, but that learning was the students' job, and that she had to learn how to be a better learner.

Josie learned that the continuous quality improvement (CQI) concept came to Penn State in 1991, at a time when many colleges and universities were noticing how industry had successfully used CQI to reduce costs and improve quality. In most universities, quality efforts were instituted in the business side of the university; however, the Schreyer Institute proposed that it be used in the classroom to help improve teaching and learning. Josie is hooked—and so are the 130 students who have helped advance the student quality team program at Penn State. In this chapter, we will provide a description of our model, a discussion of program outcomes from our pilot study, an account of costs and benefits, and some lessons we learned in the process.

■ MODEL

Participants in the Quality Team Effort
Many members make up a quality team effort: team members, team leader, team coordinator, sponsor, and of course, the students and instructor in the course (Figure 30.1).

A student quality team is a group of four to six students in a course who investigate ways to improve it. Students volunteer to participate on the quality team and receive one independent study credit for their efforts for each semester they participate. The course instructor assigns the independent study grades, usually giving the entire team the same grade. In weekly meetings, team members discuss course problems, construct surveys to determine the cause and scope of these problems, analyze survey results, prepare presentations on the results for the entire class, and suggest changes for the instructor and for students in the course.

The team leader, an undergraduate who has participated on at least one quality team, recruits team members from the course, facilitates meetings, and meets with the instructor to debrief her/him on the team's progress. At Penn State, team leaders are paid $250–$350 per semester by the Schreyer Institute, and may or may not be enrolled in the course. During the semester, team coordinators and leaders identify team members who show potential to become team leaders, and those who are interested complete a training session emphasizing meeting management skills and techniques for negotiating with instructors. After the training, which takes place at the beginning of each semester, new team leaders begin working with their own teams.

Team leaders report to a team coordinator, an undergraduate student hired by the Schreyer Institute to coordinate assignments for team leaders. The coordinator works with course professors before the start of the semester to plan what the quality team will be doing in a particular course. After the start of the semester, the co-ordinator advises the team leaders as needed and evaluates the teams' efforts.

Another supervisory member is the advisor (also the sponsoring unit at Penn), a Penn State faculty or staff member who supervises the whole process, provides training as needed, and ensures the continuity of the program as trained students leave and new ones come in. The advisor's time commitment is greater at the beginning of the semester. Right now, because of the skill level of our team coordinator and the five teams per semester we have had to this point, the advisor averages less than three hours per week; however, if the number of teams increases, or if team coordinators and leaders are less experienced, the advisor's time commitment will grow.

The final members in the quality team effort are, of course, the students in the course and the instructor.

Setting Up a Quality Team

The process begins with an instructor expressing interest in creating a quality team in a course. The instructor meets with the team coordinator to explain course goals and requests that the team focus on one or two of those. The instructor and team coordinator also identify a team leader, determine how many students will serve on the

Figure 30.1 PARTICIPANT ROLES AND RELATIONSHIPS AMONG THEM

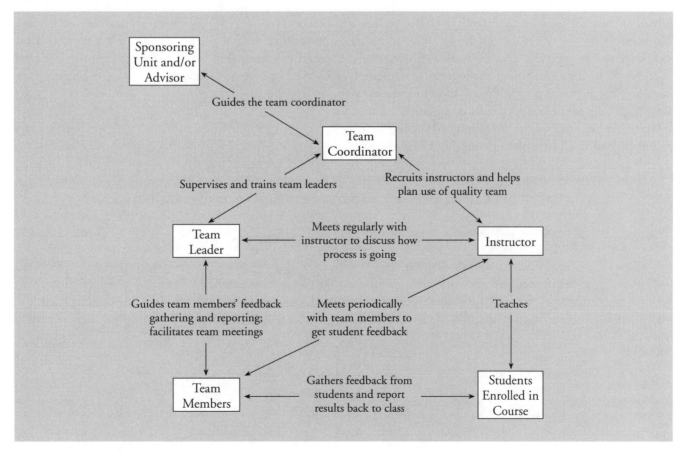

team, strategize for recruiting team members, plan the number and style of surveys to be distributed to the class, and discuss what to do should part of the process fail. At the conclusion of the meeting, the team coordinator drafts a timeline (Table 30.1).

The team leader comes to the class sometime during the first week to explain the concept and recruit team members. Team members may be selected through an application process or by asking for volunteers. During the second or third week of the semester, quality team members and leaders participate in a two-hour workshop, led by the team coordinator. The workshop helps students think critically about learning and provides an opportunity to develop skills in question writing and data analysis. The workshop begins with students discussing courses they have taken and the qualities that made those courses good or poor learning experiences. The team coordinator explains the difference between rote and meaningful learning (Ausubel, 1963; Novak, 1998) and asks students to generate examples of both. Students then read a case study of a troubled course, create survey questions for students in this course, and, with the help of a question-writing guide, critique those questions. Finally, students examine feedback charts and graphs created by previous teams, and practice editing a confusing graph or chart to make it clearer.

After the training, the team writes and administers surveys in accordance with the established schedule, usually about every two weeks. During the ten to 20 minutes that instructors typically allot to quality teams, team members distribute and collect new surveys and present results of the previous survey. Presentation of the survey results gets the entire class involved in the improvement process. At the end of the presentation, quality team members and the instructor discuss the data presented and the instructor responds to the suggestions, explaining what she/he can or cannot do differently. Students also discuss what they can do differently to alter the learning outcomes in the course.

Instructors choose the amount of time they want to devote to the quality team effort. Some meet with the team several times a semester, while others wait until the end of the semester. Instructors also choose the amount of time committed to in-class presentations, from long presentations every two weeks to two to three short presentations per semester. Most instructors spend about 15 hours per semester (including time spent both inside and outside of class) on quality team efforts.

The team coordinator monitors the teams and works with team leaders throughout the semester. The coordinator observes at least one team meeting, gives the leader a written critique of the meeting and, if necessary, discusses the critique with him or her. The team coordinator is also available to the instructor, team leader, and team members throughout the semester as a troubleshooter and resource. The team coordinator spends no more than 20 hours per week managing a maximum of ten teams.

The team members, leader, coordinator, and instructor meet at the end of the semester to discuss what was successful and what could be improved in the quality team process. They review the changes that were made to the course and whether these changes improved the course. They also identify changes that could not be made during the semester (e.g., requests for a new text) but could be changed in future semesters. Finally, the team coordinator invites students to apply to become team leaders and coordinators.

Table 30.1 The Process Timeline
(This schedule, based on a 15-week semester describes the quality team process.)

Presemester	• Instructor expresses a desire to use a quality team for a course • Team coordinator and instructor select team leader • Team coordinator meets with instructor and team leader to plan team expectations, size, structure, and schedule
Week 1	• Team leader visits class to describe quality team and recruit team members • Instructor and team leader meet to select team members
Weeks 2–3	• Team members attend two-hour training workshop and begin weekly one-hour meetings
Weeks 4–14	• Teams meet weekly to create and analyze surveys, distribute four to six surveys to class, analyze these results, and create recommendations • Team leader reports team recommendations to instructor every one to two weeks • Team coordinator observes one to two team meetings and gives team feedback on their performance
Week 15	• Team coordinator facilitates a meeting with the instructor and team members to discuss the process and suggestions for improvement

OUTCOMES

Since its creation in fall 1998, the student quality team program has worked with 20 teams in courses ranging from "Introductory Statistics" to "Upper-Level Communication," involving a total of more than 2,500 students. In two years of piloting our student quality team program, we have observed changes in students, in faculty-student relationships, and in instruction. While most of our data is case-based in nature, we are beginning to see trends, especially in terms of student engagement in learning, the practical skills team members gain, and the quality of communication between instructor and students.

Becoming Engaged Learners

The most profound impact of the quality team program has been students' recognition of their responsibility in the learning process. In one course using quality teams, for example, survey responses indicated that two thirds of the students recognized that to improve their learning, they needed to change how they interacted with course material. They reported specific ways they modified out-of-class study habits and class preparation habits (e.g., reviewing mistakes on tests to improve understanding).

As team members learned more about the learning process, their survey questions improved. At the beginning of the semester, quality teams wrote survey questions unconnected with student involvement in learning, but after discussions about meaningful and rote learning, the same teams designed questions that helped students reflect on the part they play in the learning process (Table 30.2). At end-of-course debriefings, one third to one half of the quality teams recounted debates on crafting questions that would encourage meaningful learning.

Developing Practical Skills

Because of the training and commitment to quality that the program offers, team members developed practical

Table 30.2 EXAMPLES OF SURVEY QUESTIONS BEFORE AND AFTER QUALITY TEAM DISCUSSIONS ABOUT MEANINGFUL LEARNING

September 1998	November 1998
Please rate the quality of this class. 1 2 3 4 5 6 7	I can apply statistics concepts to my other courses. Strongly agree Agree Disagree Strongly disagree

skills in survey question writing and data analysis. Each quality team wrote approximately five surveys in a semester, and successive surveys showed improved question design. For example, surveys at the beginning of the semester often contained straight yes/no questions (e.g., "Are you comfortable with the pace of lectures?"), while those at the end contained questions asking respondents to make distinctions and elaborations (e.g., "When you have difficulty understanding a concept, homework, or have other questions, who do you go to for help, and why?"). The written survey analyses for instructors reflected changes in team ability to make conclusions and recommendations. At the end of a semester, team members were more likely to provide multiple reasons for survey results, and more likely to recommend changes in both faculty and student behavior than to advocate changes in faculty behavior only.

Team leaders developed even more skills. Their additional time-on-task, enriched by the mentoring of an experienced coordinator, enabled them to become better facilitators, project managers, communicators, question writers, and data analyzers. They also developed a greater understanding of the distinction between rote and meaningful learning. Team leaders gained a remarkable education in the process of doing their jobs.

Improving the Quality of Communication

In courses with quality teams, communication between the instructor and students improved substantially. The data from students helped instructors recognize where key concepts were being misunderstood, and suggested ways for clearing up confusion and ideas for helping students prepare better for class. Better communication also helped faculty and students gain respect for each other's roles. By shifting emphasis from whom to blame to how to change (Moore, Kinland, Lenze, & Spence, 1999), instructors and students worked together to improve the learning experience. As one instructor stated, "The use of student quality teams has reminded me that students really do care about their courses. They want to provide input and suggestions. I have been impressed with both the thoroughness and professionalism of the student quality teams." A student from this professor's course added, "In such a large learning environment, the student quality team serves as a forum through which other students can express their questions and concerns, which makes the classroom more accessible and less intimidating."

Influencing Instruction

Feedback from quality teams clearly led to suggestions for changes in instruction. Many were simple technical improvements, such as enlarging overhead transparencies and presenting material at a slower pace. However, teams also suggested more complex changes, such as adding more realistic examples and providing class time to work on group projects. In the most advanced cases, students even suggested changes in their own study habits that would improve their learning. As student quality teams progress through these stages of providing feedback, it can be frustrating for faculty at the beginning, but becomes exciting as students move into engaged learning (Spence & Lenze, in press).

■ PRODUCTIVITY

This revolutionary learning tool has costs in three major areas: money, time, and emotions.

Financial Investment

The newness of the program and its inherent flexibility complicate calculating the financial cost. However, our expenditures for fall 1999 covered team leader stipends, team coordinator wages, and supplies (for pizza and other incidentals). Most team leaders receive a small stipend ($250-$350 a semester). A few team leaders and all of the team members receive one credit of independent study rather than pay. We currently pay an undergraduate team coordinator $7 per hour for approximately 20 hours of work each week for managing a maximum of ten teams. This position extends beyond the semester for several weeks of planning, preparing training materials, conducting training, and debriefing.

The monetary cost of the program depends on whether team leaders and members are paid or given course credit, and on the number of teams and courses involved. We do not compensate instructors or advisors, but

some institutions might consider adding this incentive. However, even when participants are paid, the real costs lie more in time and emotional investment.

Time Investment

As previously described, the amount of time involved in quality teams reflects the goals and preferences of the instructor. The estimates in Table 30.3 represent the most vigorous schedules with which we have been involved. On average, the cumulative time per course invested by the instructor, team members, team leader, coordinator, and advisor in the quality team project is approximately 105 hours.

Emotional Investment

Negative feedback can be painful and disheartening. One faculty member spoke candidly, "I must admit I was a little naive when I first signed up to use quality teams. I didn't prepare for the amount of criticism that would be brought my way.... One must look to the long-term gains and not dwell on the short-term 'negative moments'." A good team and leader can mitigate some of the instructor stress by writing questions that address changeable elements of the course and presenting the material sensitively, including culling excessively sharp comments.

Despite the emotional stress involved with receiving criticism, the five instructors who used quality teams in spring 1999 used them again in fall 1999 (with the exception of one who took sabbatical leave). They felt that knowing what helped students learn and seeing students take ownership of their learning, as well as the improved communication, compensated for an occasional depressing survey. A veteran instructor explained the rewards as "the satisfaction that comes from making changes . . . that seem to work, the positive feedback that a good team

Table 30.3 MAXIMUM TIME REQUIRED FOR STUDENT QUALITY TEAMS

	Frequency	Semester Total
Class	10-20 minutes every two weeks	1½-3
Instructor	1 hour every one to two weeks	8-16 hours
Team member	2 hours of initial training 1 hour meeting/week 1-2 hours/week of additional work	25-40 hours per team
Team leader	2 hours of initial training 1-3 hours each week working with team and on specific tasks 1 hour each one to two weeks for meeting with instructor	30-45 hours per team
Team coordinator	Approximately 20 hours/week, including a few weeks before and after the semester	Up to 380 hours
Advisor	0-3 hours per week	Up to 30 hours

Student-Assisted Teaching

provides," and "knowing that you are doing the right thing (or trying to) by taking steps to improve student learning."

Like the instructors, most team leaders, once they experienced leading a team, wanted to continue working with quality teams. For example, all nongraduating spring 1999 team leaders led another team in fall 1999. Instructors and students state that the benefits of becoming more engaged learners, developing practical and communication skills, and improving courses are their reasons for returning. And, while time commitment and emotional costs cause some grumbling, by the end-of-semester debriefing session, most participants state that the benefits outweighed the costs.

■ SUGGESTIONS FOR REPLICATION

Our quality team's emphasis on students, one of its greatest strengths, also presents the greatest challenge for replication. Students have to juggle activities and employment with their courses, and eventually they graduate. We offer the following lessons that we have learned about using students in quality teams.

Developing a Solid Structure with Clearly Defined Roles

Because the quality team experience places undergraduates in new roles, they need to have a clear understanding of those roles before they begin. Expectations of team members need to be developed by the team leader, coordinator, and instructor before the semester begins, and need to be clearly communicated to the students who are considering volunteering for the team. Students need to understand that they will receive a credit of independent study for the team activities, and that they will be graded on performance. Role definition and accountability measures need to be in place for team leaders as well. At Penn State, leaders sign a contract listing job expectations and stating that, if the leader does not fulfill these duties, the stipend may be reduced or withheld.

Finding Students and Capturing Their Insights

Recruiting students presents a challenge. Team coordinators and team leaders must have an avid interest in improving teaching and learning, and must demonstrate leadership and facilitation skills. They must be willing to participate in training to develop the skills they will need for their roles. The best sources for team leaders and coordinators are team members who found the experience particularly rewarding.

Given the transient nature of the student population, a quality team program can lose a great deal of practical knowledge that students experience on the teams. We found that having teams submit a report (that includes a presemester plan, meeting minutes, surveys, results, charts and graphs developed for in-class presentations, and debriefing minutes) reduces the need for the following semester's teams to completely reinvent the wheel.

Necessity of a Sponsoring Unit or Advisor

A quality team effort requires a sponsoring unit or advisor, both to advise coordinators and leaders in carrying out their duties and to ensure that the program does not end when a group of students graduates. This role is difficult because the advisor needs to provide enough guidance without becoming an overbearing presence. Initially, the team coordinator will need more supervision, especially when recruiting faculty, developing a training program, and troubleshooting team difficulties. As the coordinator and leaders acquire experience, the need for supervision decreases substantially. Most importantly, the sponsor needs to know when to guide and when to allow the team coordinator and leaders the freedom to make mistakes and to learn from those mistakes.

■ CONCLUSION

As a teaching tool, and more importantly as learning tool, student quality teams can transform learning in a university. Students on the quality teams not only help instructors in improving their teaching, but also educate their peers in ways to think about learning that transcend a specific course and even the collegiate experience.

■ REFERENCES

Ausubel, D. P. (1963). *The psychology of meaningful verbal learning: An introduction to school learning.* New York, NY: Grune & Stratton.

Moore, L. M., Kinland, E., Lenze, L. F., & Spence, L. D. (1999, March). *Slackers, dictators, and jerks: Making learning teams effective.* Paper presented at the annual conference of the American Association of Higher Education, Washington, DC.

Novak, J. D. (1998). *Learning, creating and using knowledge.* Hillsdale, NJ: Lawrence Erlbaum & Associates.

Spence, L. D., & Lenze, L. F. (in press). Taking student criticism seriously: Student quality teams. In K. Lewis (Ed.), *New Directions for Teaching and Learning*. San Francisco, CA: Jossey-Bass.

■ AUTHORS

ELIZABETH KINLAND is a senior majoring in Political Science in the Schreyer Honors College at Pennsylvania State University.

LISA FIRING LENZE is the Associate Director of the Schreyer Institute for Innovation and Learning at Pennsylvania State University.

LYNN MELANDER MOORE is the Outreach Coordinator of the Schreyer Institute for Innovation in Learning at Pennsylvania State University

LARRY D. SPENCE is the Director of the Schreyer Institute for Innovation in Learning and Associate Professor of Political Science at Pennsylvania State University.

Chapter 31

College Teachers and Student Consultants: Collaborating about Teaching and Learning

D. Lynn Sorenson

In the 1990s, the emphasis on student learning and critically reflective teaching led to the formation of faculty-student partnerships. Brigham Young University implemented several faculty development initiatives to foster this kind of teacher-student collaboration. Students Consulting on Teaching (SCOT), which links a college teacher and a student in a consultative process, was one of those initiatives and is the focus of this chapter.

Brigham Young University (BYU), a Carnegie Doctoral/Research I institution, is an undergraduate teaching university with both a research and a religious orientation. This nonprofit university, owned and operated by The Church of Jesus Christ of Latter-day Saints, is located 50 miles south of Salt Lake City in Provo, Utah. Founded in 1875, BYU is the largest private university in the US, offering bachelor's degrees in more than 125 majors and graduate degrees in about 100 programs. About 90% of its 30,000 students are undergraduates and most are Mormon. First-year students enter with a mean high school GPA of 3.7 and an average ACT score of 27. Most BYU undergraduates are traditional college age (although nearly a quarter are married), and more than half come from Utah, California, and Idaho; the rest hail from all 50 states and more than 100 countries. About 10% are people of color.

An Overview of Student Consultant Programs

Students consulting with faculty members on teaching is one way to initiate dialog about teaching, classroom climate, course design, and other important learning issues. In student consultant programs, college teachers invite trained students who are not members of their classes to consult on course learning. Like traditional faculty development programs, student consultant programs can help "change the status of teaching from private to community property" (Shulman, 1993, p. 6). Faculty come to view student consultants as peers who provide valuable perspectives that can catalyze improvements in teaching and learning.

Critics sometimes raise objections to the idea of student consultants: "They are just students; how can they help faculty?" They are students, and that is exactly their strength. They are not experts on content. But as experienced students, they are experts about sitting in classes, understanding new concepts, and creating their own learning. They have developed a strong sense about activities that are conducive to their learning, and their voices and perspectives merit attention.

■ MODEL

Evolving from service-learning activities in a 1991 honors education course, the Classroom Student Observer Program was initiated in 1992 and has continued under the name of Students Consulting on Teaching. Since that time, the SCOT program has developed a wide range of services from simple data-gathering to continuous quality consultation.

SCOT Services

Recorder/observer. The SCOT observer creates a chronology of classroom activities—observing, not evaluating what is happening—and gives it to the instructor (Figure 31.1).

Faux student. The SCOT takes notes as if she or he were a student in the class and shares them with the instructor. This helps the teacher understand what points were perceived as important in the lecture.

Videotaper. The SCOT videotapes the class and gives the videotape to the teacher. Occasionally the instructor and student consultant watch and discuss it together.

Interviewer. The instructor leaves the classroom for about 20 minutes while the SCOT interviews class members about their learning in the course, using a method adapted from Small Group Instructional Diagnosis (Appendix C-4) developed at the University of Washington in the 1970s (Redmond & Clark, 1982). The interviewer coordinates small group discussions and notes students' responses to questions on major strengths of the course and changes that might assist with learning (Black, 1998). Afterwards, the SCOT writes a report highlighting the strengths and concerns expressed by students (Table 31.1), and the SCOT and instructor discuss the report and strategize about course issues. At BYU, the interviewer option is by far the most popular SCOT service.

Primed student. The professor meets with the SCOT before class to discuss what aspects to observe, for example, clarity of a media presentation, facilitation of class discussion, student activities in group work, and frequency of responses by students in various categories (e.g., women/men, minority/majority, traditional/nontraditional).

Student consultant. The student consultant combines several SCOT services to provide the instructor with feedback and suggestions. The SCOT gathers resources for the teacher from the faculty center or other academic support units. Together they plan interventions and innovations, which the instructor implements. The student consultant continues to observe and provide feedback throughout the process.

Managing the Program and Inviting Faculty Participation

A student consultant program needs one person to oversee logistics and train student consultants. At BYU, the SCOT program is overseen by a faculty developer and assisted by a student coordinator. The director or someone who has influence with faculty (e.g., vice provost, dean, faculty senate president) invites faculty to participate via email, flyers, or letters. Recruitment efforts are informational only; participation is completely voluntary and confidential. When faculty members decide to participate in SCOT, they receive the SCOT faculty handbook

Figure 31.1 14-MINUTE EXCERPT FROM EXAMPLE OBSERVER'S REPORT

Ann Student, Observer
Prof. Juan S. Feedback
Jan. 3, 2000, 11:00-12:15

25 Students in Class in 210 TNRB,
Business Management 401

11:55 Professor lectures on stats of different countries and exports and imports. One student in back reading other textbook. One male student in front asks question and short discussion occurs between professor and students in front. Students in back whispering.

12:00 Back to overhead. "Who do we trade with?" professor asks. He answers question by reading from the overhead and restating the countries named on first overhead. New overhead. Professor explains MNCs. He asks three connected questions beginning with "Is this significant in any way? Can anyone tell me what this means to Europe?" Three male students answer and discuss. Most students listen as professor asks questions and discusses with students. One student in back sleeping. A few take notes.

12:05 One male student tells about his company's hub in Europe. Professor asks student to explain to class. Professor listens, looking at overheads in hands, and restates student's comments and explains more about concept. Professor then asks, "What are a few other reasons companies expand overseas?" He lists reasons.

12:09 New overhead on direct foreign investments and portfolio investments

Table 31.1 EXCERPT FROM INTERVIEW REPORT WRITTEN BY SALLY SMILEY FOR PROFESSOR I. M. GREAT, FEBRUARY 15, 2000, FOR LINGUISTICS 2222 WITH 25 STUDENTS

Things That Help Students Learn in the Class	# Making Response
Class discussions	15
Applying material through games, videos, songs	10
Concrete examples to illustrate principles	10
Group work	5
Willingness to answer questions	3
Things that Hinder Student Learning in the Class	
When discussion goes off on tangents	9
Vague assignments (especially papers and written assignments)	6
Too much material causing lack of focus	2
Suggestions for Improving the Class	
Study guide for tests (i.e., list of terms to know)	6
More homework problems to focus on important information	5
More organized, structured, goal-oriented agenda	4
Keep class discussion on topic	4

Student-Assisted Teaching

which introduces the program and contains references and a program evaluation form (Sorenson, 2000a).

Recruiting and Hiring SCOTs

The BYU Faculty Center recruits students for SCOT at the beginning of fall and winter semesters. During the first week of a semester, the SCOT student coordinator visits classes and student organizations and provides a press release to the campus newspaper. In addition, the SCOT director asks past faculty participants to recommend students with interest in teaching and learning. Word of mouth has provided the best recruitment; many new SCOTs are roommates, relatives, or classmates of experienced SCOTs.

SCOTs must have at least a 3.0 GPA and provide two references, including one from an instructor. After a brief informational meeting, each applicant performs a practice observation and writes a report on that classroom visit. The director and student coordinator check the references, review the observation and class visit report, and make the hiring decisions. Usually about 80% of the applicants become SCOTs. This process has provided increasingly large numbers of SCOTs, from six in 1992 to nearly 30 in 2000.

Campuses compensate student consultants for their participation in different ways. In some places, they are volunteers, much like community service tutors or student government participants. At other institutions, students enroll in a credit-bearing class, and their work is part of the service-learning component of that class. The most common model, and the one employed at BYU, is paying hourly wages through student employment services or work-study programs. The annual budget for the BYU SCOT program is $10,000, most of which is student wages. The program director's costs in time or salary are not reflected in that amount.

Training and Supporting SCOTs

The training of students in SCOT-type roles varies by university, ranging from a semester-long, credit-bearing course before or during consultative work to a two-hour orientation before beginning. Those initiating a student observer/consultant program need not be overly concerned about extensive training. At BYU, an introductory meeting provides students with a program overview and an opportunity to determine if SCOT is appropriate for them. Then, if a prospective SCOT performs the practice observation, writes a report, and role plays a follow-up consultation, she or he is usually ready for the first assignment. Once they begin working, SCOTs participate in bimonthly, hour-long seminars, are mentored by ex-

perienced SCOTs, and consult with the campus faculty developer. SCOTs also receive the SCOT student handbook, which outlines the program and provides training materials emphasizing student responsibilities (Sorenson, 2000b).

Topics addressed in the bimonthly, two-hour training meetings include observation techniques, one-on-one consultations, and articles on teaching and learning. One training session is devoted to interviewing, with SCOTs being introduced to SGID techniques and writing follow-up reports. Sessions on preparing written feedback include examples of well-written student consultants' reports. Often the most successful ongoing training sessions include discussions of situations that have originated in current SCOT consultations. The SCOTs raise issues, and their peers explore options and solutions. A faculty developer or a professor facilitates the discussion and serves as a resource to the student consultants.

The fact that student consultants are not experts on pedagogy is not a hindrance; the SCOT contribution is the student perspective. Nevertheless, SCOTs who are going to work as student consultants (observing a faculty member and working to change teaching) need training in peer consultation. For this type of training, experienced SCOTs role play a follow-up consultation. Then, each new SCOT practices the role of being a peer consultant, and a veteran SCOT plays the part of an instructor. New SCOTs use the reports they wrote for their trial observations before they were hired.

Past and current student coordinators have encouraged SCOTs' affable, business-like professionalism. This includes making suggestions tactfully—or assertively, as appropriate—and practicing effective communication skills, such as active listening and good eye contact. In addition, SCOTs should be reliable (e.g., arriving on time, performing their duties discreetly, and providing reports and tapes in a timely manner).

■ OUTCOMES

Since the BYU program's inception in 1991, nearly 250 students have served in the SCOT program, some for multiple semesters. The typical workload for SCOTs is five to ten hours per week. Each semester 25-30 instructors use SCOT services, totaling nearly 400 instructors, or approximately 20% of the teaching faculty, in nine years. About 450 classes have been observed, videotaped, or interviewed, affecting thousands of students. Nearly a quarter of the faculty using the program are repeat users, and about half are on their way to tenure. Since the program began in 1991, the numbers of participating faculty have increased each semester.

Faculty, Student-Consultant, and Enrolled Student Comments

At the conclusion of their consultation process, both instructors and SCOTs evaluate their collaboration through questionnaires in which they reflect on the strengths and limitations of the program and on their own consultations. A decade of evaluation data about the BYU program reveals consistently positive attitudes, interactions, and outcomes.

One faculty participant described SCOT as adding "a new dimension to the evaluation process" that is "conducive to improving the quality of teaching." Others were impressed with the "great feedback and encouragement" which was "almost priceless." One professor noted that it helped him "learn from mistakes and build on strengths as a teacher."

Through their training sessions and their relationships with faculty in the SCOT program, student consultants develop interpersonal skills, and they learn to give constructive feedback. For example, one SCOT stated, "Professor X was extremely interested in my ideas which was a valuable experience for me." Another said, "I learned a lot about effective teaching and communication between a teacher and his or her students." For some SCOTs, the experience may affect life plans. Perhaps the inside view of professorial life they gained through their consultations has been what has encouraged several to go on to graduate school with the goal of becoming professors.

When faculty invite SCOTs to work with them on their classes, the enrolled students comment about the teachers' interest: "I'm impressed that he cares enough about us and our learning to do something about it." Another said, "She really cares about her teaching." When the faculty participants implement changes as a result of student consultations, enrolled students report more positive feelings about the teacher, the course, and their learning.

Student consultant programs afford faculty and students an opportunity to listen to one another, and in the process understand better how they are seen by the other. This narrows the hierarchical distance between professors and students, encouraging partnership as "a shared responsibility between different, and potentially conflicting partners. The students are regarded as active participants, . . . [and] are invited to participate in the process of transforming higher education" (Havnes, 1998, p. 1).

Transforming instruction progresses incrementally as a result of student consultants' feedback on teaching. Some instructors may make modifications as simple as speaking louder or writing more legibly. Others implement more significant innovations such as initiating role plays. A physiology professor made a list of behaviors his students said intimidated them and worked at expunging them. After SCOT participation, one teacher of Portuguese wrote about his pedagogical improvements:

> I developed a system wherein I include student presentations along with a teaching cycle that involves a practice session after every . . . concept. The time I spend giving instruction decreased to under 20 minutes, while the students' practice time increased to 30+ minutes. My students [learn at] a higher mastery level. I [intend to] continue [this] in the future.

◼ SUGGESTIONS FOR REPLICATION

For those thinking of creating a program similar to SCOT, the following issues and suggestions may be of interest.

Ensuring Confidentiality

The assurance of confidentiality is important to faculty and promotes the likelihood of developing a productive partnership. SCOTs are counseled in the student handbook:

> It is absolutely critical for you to keep the entire consultation process confidential. You may have access to sensitive information that could affect the instructor's reputation, retention, salary, etc. Be sure that you share your findings ONLY with your instructor and/or in confidential student consultant seminars—even if friends or other students ask you about the instructor or course. (Sorenson, 2000a)

Publicizing the Program

A person initiating a student observer/consultant program will do well to start with a small number of consultants and a large dose of advertising zeal because a program is of no value if faculty do not use it. One good way to begin is to ask faculty friends or colleagues to allow students to consult with them. When participating faculty see the value, they will help spread the word.

Promoting the program is also important. In addition to flyers distributed by campus mail and email, offering to discuss the program at faculty meetings, resource fairs, and other venues gets the attention of potential participants. Eventually the best recruiters are experienced consultants; their enthusiasm and sincerity attracts faculty and clearly sells the program.

Implementing an "Unofficial" Program

In a school with no consultant program, a faculty member interested in developing a one-on-one partnership could invite a former student to perform any of the SCOT functions. This would require discipline on both parts to follow through, explore options, and initiate changes. Nevertheless it is "doable." Student consultants working as peers with faculty allows an opportunity for personal growth that is rare at most colleges and universities. SCOTs at BYU seem to value these intrinsic rewards as highly as the monetary ones—perhaps even more—and are interested in this kind of partnership to explore academia, to network, and to develop a résumé. Advisees, service club members, education majors, TAs, RAs, graders, or students performing similar functions might be interested in serving as volunteer consultants. A viable option for those on constrained budgets is initiating a consultant program staffed entirely by student volunteers.

Investigating Other Models

A number of campuses have initiated student observer/consultant programs and provide alternative models. These include Carleton College, St. Olaf College, Penn State, Worcester Polytechnic Institute, and University of Georgia. For more information about these and other models see Cox and Sorenson (2000). Details about SCOT appear on the BYU faculty center web site.

CONCLUSION

Student consultant programs honor both the student voice and faculty desire to improve teaching. For professors, the program provides a source of feedback on teaching and a stimulus to focus on students and their learning. For student consultants, peer relationships with faculty afford the opportunity to explore the teaching and learning process from new perspectives, to develop observation and consultation skills, and to contribute to the campus learning environment. Student consultant programs not only improve the quality of teaching and enhance learning, they also build a campus-wide community of peers dedicated to supporting one another's educational endeavors.

REFERENCES

Black, B. (1998). Using the SGID method for a variety of purposes. *To Improve the Academy, 17*, 245-262.

Cox, M. D., & Sorenson, D. L. (2000). Student collaboration in faculty development: Connecting directly to the learning revolution. *To Improve the Academy, 18*, 97-106.

Havnes, A. (1998, April). *Students as partners in educational development: Practice, policy, and theory.* Paper presented at the 4th International Consortium for Educational Development Conference, Austin, TX.

Redmond, M. V., & Clark, D. J. (1982). A practical approach to improving teaching. *AAHE Bulletin, 34* (6), 8-10.

Shulman, L. S. (1993, November/December). Teaching as community property: Putting an end to pedagogical solitude. *Change, 25* (6), 6-7.

Sorenson, D. L. (1994). Valuing the student voice: Student observer/consultant programs. *To Improve the Academy, 13*, 97-108.

Sorenson, D. L. (2000a). *Students consulting on teaching: Faculty handbook.* (Available from BYU Faculty Center, 4450 WSC, Provo, UT 84602, (801) 378-7419, faculty_center@byu.edu).

Sorenson, D. L. (2000b). *Students consulting on teaching: Student handbook.* (Available from BYU Faculty Center, 4450 WSC, Provo, UT 84602, (801) 378-7419, faculty_center@byu.edu).

AUTHOR

D. LYNN SORENSON is the Assistant Director of the Faculty Center at Brigham Young University.

Conclusion: Issues to Consider in Implementing a Student-Assisted Teaching Model

As amply demonstrated by the array of models in this book, the student-assisted teaching approach has the potential to yield benefits for all the participants in the higher education enterprise, and is adaptable to virtually any institutional, disciplinary, or classroom context.

Those who wish to introduce such a model at their own institution will find a rich array of specific suggestions in the individual chapters. Some aspiring adopters have succeeded by building a small local program, perhaps within a single course, and perhaps (but not necessarily) expanding the program later. Others have started at the institutional level by building a constituency of interested individuals, linking the project to existing institutional priorities, and procuring internal or external funding. Most have found it to be important to plan, in advance, for the collection of assessment data adequate for internal demonstration of program efficacy. Such data collection, if done well, can additionally constitute the basis of professional presentations and publications that will contribute to faculty and staff scholarly credentials, as evidenced by this volume and the many publications of its contributors. Aspiring adopters are strongly advised to avail themselves of the resources that are available on campus (in their teaching and learning, counseling, or student affairs offices), in the form of local and national colleagues (including those whose models are described in this volume), and in national professional organizations (cited in the individual chapters). Contributors have stressed time and again the need for careful selection, training, and monitoring of undergraduate students and their faculty supervisors, as well as the importance of clarity and appropriateness of undergraduate roles. Many have also mentioned the need for good public relations efforts, both to advertise the program and to disseminate the evidence of success to administrators and potential participants.

Most of the chapters included in this book describe the cost effectiveness of student-assisted teaching programs. In combination with the positive impact on educational quality, the productivity aspects of these approaches are quite compelling. Student-assisted teaching may be especially attractive for schools with financial pressures and institutions with limited resources such as those in developing countries. However, where resources are limited, it is tempting to allow the brunt of the resource cost in the form of faculty time to be borne by a small number of dedicated and visionary individuals in the form of an overload to their usual job responsibilities. Ultimately, in order for such innovations to be self-sustaining, they must be designed with an eye to maximizing productivity. But the burden should not rest entirely with faculty; we urge that institutions adopt personnel loading models and cost accounting rubrics that recognize the value of such innovative approaches and ensure their long-term survival.

Contributors to this volume have identified some thorny issues in the implementation of learning models that involve undergraduate students. We have selected for discussion here some of the issues that we feel should be considered in the planning stages of establishing a student-assisted teaching model on your campus. Since many approaches to student-assisted teaching are in their infancy, other issues undoubtedly have yet to be identified.

The decision whether to pay undergraduate students, to award them academic credit, or to accept their help on a volunteer basis has important practical and philosophical implications. An attractive feature of for-credit and volunteer models is that program cost is minimized when undergraduate students are not paid. Compared with the cost of faculty and graduate teaching assistants (TAs), however, the cost of undergraduate students is extremely small. Most programs that can afford to pay peer assistants have found the financial compensation, even if relatively low, to be powerfully professionalizing, and as a paying job, the experience is a strong asset to the student's résumé.

When undergraduate students receive academic credit in addition to their normal course load, the institution may collect additional tuition revenue as a result of their teaching activities. Effects of teaching activities on tuition revenue, though not large in any case, will vary depending on the financial situation of the individual institution with respect to state tuition reimbursement and financial aid. In some cases, potential peer assistants might be deterred from applying for the position if they can't afford to pay for the extra credit, or don't wish to adversely affect their academic program or time to graduation. Depending on institutional policy on reenrollment for duplicate academic activity, a for-credit model may preclude a peer assistant from serving in that capacity more than once, thus depriving faculty of the benefits of working with experienced peer assistants. However, some programs have argued that having undergraduate students take a class is professionalizing, by adding rigor to the program and by providing students with an opportunity to learn the theory as well as the practice of teaching. Additionally, they receive recognition in the form of credit on their transcript, and a grade for the teaching activity can be a motivating factor.

The major advantage of a volunteer model is its neutral effect on program cost and on peer assistant tuition cost and academic load. On the other hand, because the time required of undergraduate students is not recognized in any formal way, commitment to these teaching responsibilities may wane at busy times of the school year. Qualified potential peer assistants might also be deterred from applying by their financial need for a paying job. A volunteer model might be good for the planning or pilot stage of a new program, in which a few dedicated students might work hard for the intrinsic reward of helping to create a program for which they see a need.

New programs might also consider combining or allowing for flexibility in compensation methods. For example, students could receive credit for the training portion of the program, plus pay for the hours they work; or, they might take a training course for credit, but with tuition waived. Some programs have established pay as the method of compensation, but allow students to participate as volunteers to meet service-learning components of a course they are taking.

An additional complication of the compensation decision is its effect on the power relationship between faculty and undergraduate students. One repeatedly articulated goal of the student-assisted teaching approach is for faculty to establish a "junior colleague" relationship with peer assistants. But that relationship is very different depending on whether the individual is an employee, a student, or a volunteer.

As discussed in the introduction to this volume, student-assisted teaching models have the potential to facilitate the creation of a true cooperative community of scholars, where students and faculty share responsibility for teaching and learning processes and outcomes, and traditional hierarchical structures are replaced with a greater sense of mentoring and equality between faculty and peer teacher. But on a pragmatic level, such power redistribution has barely begun to be addressed. Since most faculty and students are accustomed to the idea that professors have absolute power in the classroom, programs will need to make an explicit effort to work with faculty on their willingness to relinquish some power and the structures by which they will do so. The best-intentioned faculty resolve to share power will be tested when peer assistants do, as they inevitably will, make mistakes. Such mistakes can be minimized and quickly corrected by careful selection, training, and mentoring of students. Nevertheless, they need enough freedom and power to make mistakes, and to learn from them, if their learning is to be meaningful.

Another aspect of the power issue is the type of tasks to which students are assigned. Major mistakes on the part of peer assistants—and, at the same time, meaningful power sharing—can be avoided by using them only for menial tasks such as photocopying and class observation. At the other end of the spectrum are tasks such as grading that many may consider to represent too heavy a burden of authority for a student. In the middle of the range are meaningful teaching tasks of course management, peer support, peer facilitation, and content development and delivery. The challenge for these teaching programs is to find a balance between menial and meaningful tasks, and to define an institutionally appropriate dividing line between student and faculty responsibilities. When faculty do inadvertently overburden or underutilize peer assistants or assign them to inappropriate tasks, the assistants may be placed in an awkward or ethically questionable situation that they may feel uncomfortable discussing with their faculty supervisors because of the unequal power balance. Ideally, these programs should have safeguards in place—clear policies, and a third party program director—to prevent these situations from occurring, and to resolve them when they do.

Research institutions have recently come under fire (The Boyer Commission, 1998) for inadequate contact between senior faculty and undergraduate students. Critics who interpret these programs as yet another way to get senior faculty out of the classroom overlook the fact that student-assisted teaching approaches are a quintessential example of the desired new paradigm of learning-centered institutions (Barr & Tagg, 1995). But even when innovative faculty are willing to share power, and for the right reasons, they may inadvertently run afoul of the written regulations and the unwritten culture of the institution or the academy. Institutional policy or other faculty may frown on allowing undergraduate students to have access to personal or grade information about, or even to grade, their peers. Other faculty not involved in the program may feel threatened by the culture change implied by the actions of colleagues who share power with their undergraduate students. For both students and faculty, confusion and misunderstanding may result when some faculty in an institution share power with undergraduates and others do not: Certainly undergraduates who have been empowered in one setting are unlikely to abandon the skills they have learned in dealing with other faculty. Students in peer-assisted courses may suspect that assistants have an unfair academic advantage and privileged access to the professor if they simultaneously take a course and assist in it. Long-cherished traditional conceptions of education will not disappear overnight, and extensive and mutually respectful communication between program staff and other stakeholders is absolutely essential in allaying concerns and working out difficulties. Those who embrace peer-assisted learning are, perhaps unintentionally, agents of change of institutional and academic culture. They need to realize that the culture change process will be slow and will be accomplished only by extensive communication about the benefits of change.

Whether planned or not, the role of the TA inevitably changes when undergraduate students take on roles that were the TAs' traditional domain. Driven by cost pressures, one approach is to simply replace TAs with undergraduate students. Certainly these programs can be successful in the absence of TAs, but this approach has serious implications for the financial aid structure of an institution's graduate program. Even if TAs are not replaced, such change can be destructive if, in the excitement surrounding the introduction of undergraduate peer assistants, the traditionally somewhat routine role of TAs, as graders and holders of office hours, is further marginalized. Institutions that have graduate programs have in peer teaching programs an opportunity to enhance the education of both their undergraduate and graduate students by implementing a teaching team approach. In order for such an approach to be successful, these programs should carefully negotiate and define roles with all stakeholders, including TAs. Specific issues to be discussed include the division of responsibilities among faculty, TAs, and undergraduate students; how TAs and undergraduate students can work together and help one another; and how the course staff can build a real team, with all working to better students' learning. In a true team approach to teaching, the new role of TAs can expand from support staff to faculty apprentice, contributing significantly to course development and delivery. The academy stands to benefit from current movements (Preparing Future Faculty, 1999) to rethink the education of future faculty, and a good place to start is by involving TAs in educationally innovative student-centered teaching and learning teams. TAs who experience firsthand multiple student-centered approaches to education will be far more likely to employ, in their own faculty careers, a broader range of educational strategies than those who have simply assisted in traditional lecture-based, teacher-centered delivery systems.

The models in this book illustrate how it is possible to truly revitalize undergraduate education by capitalizing on an underutilized renewable resource—the students themselves. When adequately selected, trained, and mentored, student assistants can provide the vehicle for putting the responsibility for learning where it belongs, onto students themselves. We invite our readers to keep us informed of existing programs that we may have overlooked, or new programs as they emerge, in which undergraduate students take on partnership roles in teaching and learning environments. We hope that this volume will be the start of an ongoing international dialog on the use of student-assisted teaching models, and on the role of this approach in the larger context of higher education reform.

▪ REFERENCES

Barr, R. B., & Tagg, J. (1995, November/December). From teaching to learning: A new paradigm for undergraduate education. *Change*, 12-25.

The Boyer Commission on Educating Undergraduates in a Research University. (1998). *Reinventing undergraduate education: A blueprint for American research universities* [Online]. Available: http://notes.cc.sunysb.edu/Pres/boyer.nsf

Preparing Future Faculty. (1999). *Preparing future faculty home page* [Online]. Available: http://www.preparing-faculty.org/

Appendix A

Hiring Documents

Letter of Invitation to Prospective Peer Mentors

(contributed by Chidister, Bell, & Earnest)

Dear (First Name),

I am writing to invite you to apply to become one of a select group—the peer mentors for the College of Design's learning community, the Design Exchange. The position offers great leadership experience, peer mentor training, and help with your college expenses.

The College of Design and Department of Residence are seeking qualified applicants for four peer mentor positions—two women and two men. Each mentor will help approximately 25 new design students make the transition to college life. The mentor is an extremely important community builder and academic resource; therefore, we want to select the most capable and committed staff possible. Peer mentors provide information and advice as well as plan, market, and facilitate programs in areas of personal and academic development. They are also responsible for linking residents to appropriate academic support resources and conducting monthly interviews with design students.

Qualifications for being a peer mentor include:

- a strong desire to help other students
- a strong interest in living and working in a diverse learning community
- a willingness to get involved

- strong listening and communication skills
- experience living in the residence halls
- knowledge of the College of Design and its varied course offerings
- knowledge of basic computer applications (MS Office and email)
- a cumulative GPA of 2.25 or better at Iowa State
- availability both fall and spring semesters

Compensation includes 100% room (single room) and board (20 meals a week) for fall and spring semesters as well as training in peer mentoring, study skills, and time and money management.

If you are interested, please pick up a position description and application in the Student Services Office, Room 297 College of Design. If you would like to receive an electronic copy of the application materials, contact me at markc@iastate.edu. Completed applications and two letters of reference are due on March 10. Successful applicants who are studying abroad will be interviewed via telephone or email.

Sincerely,
Mark Chidister
Associate Dean

Peer Assistant Job Description

(compiled from contributions by Chidister, Bell, & Earnest; Thibodeau)

Qualifications

- Strong desire to help other students and willingness to get involved
- Strong interest in working in a diverse learning community
- Strong listening and communication skills
- Knowledge of the course
- Knowledge of basic computer applications
- History of strong academic performance and GPA
- Must have received an A in course previously

Responsibilities

- Spend 18 hours per week in class related activities
- Participate in mentor training the week before the beginning of fall semester and throughout the year as needed
- Assist residents in the transition from high school to college-level academic expectations, responsibilities, and social life
- Design, post, and distribute publicity advertising class events
- Participate in the required meetings

- Post and maintain consistent office hours (two per week) and be available to residents for informal and formal conversation

- Collaborate with staff to create a seamless learning environment

- Intercede, as a concerned student and staff member, when there is a violation of rules

- As needs arise, advise and refer residents to appropriate department resources

- Make personal contact with each of the students placed in your care at least once every two weeks. Keep a journal of your observations to be summarized in quarterly reports on the status of each student

- Submit regular reports to your supervisor on meetings with students

- Check equipment in the computer lab periodically and report any problems to your supervisor

- DO NOT schedule any classes that would conflict with your requirements for this job

- Grade papers on time and complete all other duties delegated to you

Employment and Extracurricular Activities

Demands on a peer mentor's time are many. After academics, the mentor position takes next priority; therefore, mentors are not to accept additional employment.

All extracurricular activities must be approved. Requests for extracurricular activities should include the approximate amounts of time required each week. When conflicts arise between mentor duties and other activities, mentor responsibilities take priority.

Appendix A-3

Peer Assistant Job Application

(compiled from contributions from Adams, Brown, & Cook; Thibodeau; Zaritsky)

Name _____

Address _____

Phone_____ Email _____

Current Class Year   Freshman _____   Sophomore _____

                         Junior _____   Senior _____

College: _____

Major: _____

Previous universities attended: _____

Grade Point Average: _____

Describe your work experience(s).

Describe your involvement in campus activities.

Describe your involvement in community activities.

Why should we select you to be a peer educator?

How will being a peer educator enhance your career plans?

What appeals to you about being a peer educator?

What skills/experience do you have that would make you a successful peer educator?

What is the BEST feature of the class you wish to be a peer educator for?

What is the WORST feature of the class you wish to be a peer educator for?

Suggest one major improvement for the class you wish to be a peer educator for.

Attach your schedule for the upcoming semester.

List two references, preferably one from school and one outside. No relatives please!

Appendix A-4

Peer Assistant Interview Questions

(compiled from contributions from Adams, Brown, & Cook; Miller, DiBiasio, Minasian, & Catterall; Sarquis, Dixon, Gosser, Kampmeier, Roth, Strozak, & Varma-Nelson)

1) Why did you apply for this position?

2) Based on your own first-year experience, what do you think is important for first-year students to know?

3) Please describe your study skills.

4) Describe an experience you've had working in a group.

5) What are your career objectives?

6) Think of a group you have been in that did not function optimally.

   a) Pick the perspective of one particular individual in that group, and describe what the group was like.

   b) What could have been done to improve the group's functioning?

7) Describe any public speaking, tutoring, or mentoring experience you've had.

8) This is your first meeting as a study group leader, so you are still a little nervous. Wouldn't you know it, one of the first things that happens in your session is that a students asks you a question you can't answer. All eyes turn to you. How will you handle this?

9) You have seven students in your workshop, one of whom monopolizes the group. The other students are getting annoyed. What will you do about this?

10) You meet your workshop group for the first time. Students are very anxious because they've heard this is a killer course. Their future career goals depend upon how they do in this course. How will you handle this?

11) We've just had the second exam in organic chemistry. Students come to you and say that they did everything humanly possible to prepare for this test—they studied hard, they changed their approach from the first exam, and they still received Cs. The students want to know what they should do now. How do you respond?

12) Here we are at the third or fourth week of the semester, and the students are still clamoring for an answer key to the workshop problems. You are absolutely certain that the professor doesn't intend to distribute a key, to you or to the students. How will you field these requests from the students?

13) Do you have any questions for me?

Appendix A-5

SI Leader Contract

(compiled from contributions from Murray; Zaritsky)

As a leader appointed by the school to conduct supplemental instruction (SI) sessions, I hereby contract with the school to undertake the following duties throughout the semester.

1) Attend the SI training sessions.

2) Attend all sessions of the course that pertain to my SI sessions.

3) Provide a minimum of three SI study sessions per week.

4) Meet with the SI supervisor for one hour a week.

5) Complete all required paperwork.

6) Complete all other requirements that have been outlined.

7) On fulfillment of these responsibilities I will receive a stipend of $1,008, $420 at the midpoint, $336 after 10 weeks, and $252 after all paperwork has been completed and handed in.

8) I agree that should students' attendance at my SI session drop to eight participants or less repeatedly, then my session may be cancelled. I will receive a pro rata payment to me for the number of sessions I have conducted.

SI Leader Signature_____ Date _____

Appendix B

Training Syllabi

SI Training Program

(contributed by Murray)

Time	SI Leaders	SI Supervisor	Experienced Supervisor	Tutors	Martin
8:35 a.m.	What is SI? How NOT to run a tutorial (video)	Meet together for initial training as supervisors		With leaders in the session on "What is SI? How NOT to run a tutorial"	
9:30 a.m.	Characteristics of a good SI session or tutorial (video, comments from leaders in other programs), SI manual				
10:20 a.m.	Supervisors meet leaders, to know each other and set up rules	Morning tea			
10:40 a.m.	Morning tea	Difference between SI and tutorials			
11:00 a.m.	Supervisors and leaders help four leaders prepare SI session on "I will/won't" from manual.	How to start a tutorial and how to motivate students to participate			
11:20 a.m.	All are divided into two main groups with two of the nominated leaders in each group. They run a 20-minute session each, with a ten-minute discussion after each. First leader does a week 1 opening and part of the "body" of a session. Second leader does the remainder of the week 1 "body" to the session and then closure to the session. Tutors observe and note the leaders and the feedback given. (Supervisors to observe SI sessions, take notes on leaders, give feedback; experienced supervisors do same and watch and take notes on supervisors).				
12:40 p.m.	Lunch (New supervisors to go with leaders to check out SI rooms and arrange meeting time for week 1 of semester)				
1:30 p.m.	Review of pre-lunch sessions. One large group. New supervisors give feedback on how they saw leaders' performance in sessions. Experienced supervisors observe new supervisors, how they give feedback, what they noted in sessions			Tutors finished and gone	Observe, review, and comment on the review session
2:00 p.m.	Four nominated leaders prep SI session on week 6 material; four others on week 7 material	Discussion session on the review process. Experienced supervisors give comment to the new supervisors on how they handled their leaders in the pre-lunch sessions and in the review session just finished; they also comment on the content and style of feedback the new supervisors gave the leaders.			
2:30 p.m.	All are divided into two groups with two of the nominated leaders in each group. They each run 20-minute sessions on week 6 material, with five minutes of feedback after each. First one does opening and body, second one does body and closing. New and experienced supervisors: do same as in pre-lunch sessions				
3:20 p.m.	Afternoon tea				
3:40 p.m.	All are divided into two groups with two of the nominated leaders in each group. They each run 20-minute sessions on week 7 material, with five minutes of feedback after each. First one does opening and body, second one does body and closing. New and experienced supervisors: do same as in pre-lunch sessions				
4:30 p.m.	Administrative matters, wind up				
5:00 p.m.	Depart	Review of day, leaders, problems, ideas			
5:30 p.m.		Clean up and depart			

FIG Leadership Seminar Syllabus

(contributed by Thompson, Westfall, & Reimers)

Staff

Maxwell Hall 050	856-4302
Sarah Westfall	sbwestfa@
Jennifer Berson	jberson@
Franklin Hall 004	855-9023
Christine Reimers	creimers@
Samuel Thompson	samthomp@

Please feel free to contact any staff member at any time. If we are not immediately available, an appointment at a mutually convenient time can always be arranged.

Meeting Time: 9 a.m.–12 noon, Saturday, Maple Room (East End 1st Floor)

Letter to the Peer Instructor

Welcome to an exciting program at IU, a program intended to enhance the academic success and retention rate of freshmen. You will have the chance to make a difference in the success of next year's entering class, and what you do with that opportunity will influence the success and future of the freshman interest groups (FIGS) program. Much is expected of you, but you will be well supported by former peer instructors and program staff. Our intent is to prepare you as well as possible for your important responsibilities. A key element of that preparation is the FIG leadership seminar. In the seminar, we'll ask a lot of you but will also provide you with excellent training, employing the best resources available and state-of-the-art concepts of teaching and learning. The reward for your commitment and effort will be a solid professional grounding for eventual teaching in higher education.

Description of the Seminar

The leadership seminar is to improve your understanding of the goals of the FIGS program and give you the training and resources to achieve those goals. The seminar cannot possibly anticipate every situation you will encounter or prepare you for it. The seminar will attempt to erect a framework—a scaffold, if you will—in which you can make independent decisions toward how the goals may best be achieved in your own FIG. In this vein, the emphasis in the seminar will not be on breadth or depth of content coverage. We'll touch on a lot of topics, try to get quickly to their essence, and then leave them. In leaving them, we'll leave you with a binder full of reading material, people you can contact, and other resources that you can return to later when you must deal with the topic in more detail for your FIG students. You'll be actively involved in discussion and structured tasks much of the time. The staff will always try to model excellent professional practice for you. About a third of the seminar will be devoted to practice teaching, called "microteaching." You'll simulate teaching freshmen in the fall by preparing a microlesson and teaching it to your peers. You'll receive a videotape and constructive feedback from your microteaching which will help your performance in the fall as a leader (and teacher) of the FIGS seminar (X111).

Seminar Schedule

Assignment Due	Activities	Assignments for Next Session
First Session (3 hrs.) Feb. 20, Maple Room		
	• Welcome and orientation • Establish permanent peer instructor (PI) teams • Discussion of syllabus for the leadership seminar • Explicit and implicit syllabi • Building your syllabus I: Critiquing syllabi	• Study materials on getting and giving feedback and active learning • Select tentative time for microteaching
Second Session (3 hrs.) Feb. 27, Maple Room		

Be prepared to select a session for your microteaching	• Getting and giving feedback
	• Active learning
	  a) rationale and survey of methods
	  b) collaborative/cooperative learning
	  c) facilitating discussion
	  d) concept of a learning community: building groups and teams
	• Developing a lesson plan
	• Schedule individual PIs for microteaching sessions
		• Write a welcoming letter to your FIG students telling them your role and why X111 will benefit them
		• Prepare a lesson plan for microteaching (first two to three PIs)
		• Study resource materials on learning styles and levels
		• Complete Learning Styles Inventory (LSI)

Third Session (2 hrs topics/1hr microteaching) Mar. 6, Maple Room

Welcoming letters
Submit LSI
	• Expository teaching
	   a) guest speaker on use of visual aids
	• Constructs for helping freshmen
	   a) learning styles
	   b) cognitive learning levels
	• Syllabus construction templates
	• Microteaching (First two to three PIs)
		• Study assigned sections in Ellis, *Becoming a Master Student*, and resource materials on note-taking, test-taking, study, and time management skills
		• Draft your syllabus (w/o schedule)
		• Prepare a lesson plan for microteaching session

Fourth Session (3 hrs. content + 3 hrs. microteaching) Mar. 27, Maple Room

Make appointment to discuss your lesson plan
Submit draft syllabus
	• Critique of welcoming letters
	• Survival skills for FIG students:
	   a) reading effectively
	   b) note-taking
	   c) test-taking
	   d) using study groups/learning communities
	   e) interacting with faculty
	   f) using other campus resources
	   g) time management skills
	• Microteaching (eight to ten PIs)
		• Prepare a lesson plan for microteaching session
		• Prepare a reflective statement on what has been learned in the leadership seminar and how it will influence your conduct of X111
		• Read material on learning stages

Fifth Session (1½ hrs. content + 1½ hrs. microteaching) Apr. 3, Maple Room

Make appointment to discuss your lesson plan (all remaining PIs)
Submit reflective statements
	• Critique of draft syllabi
	• Other X111 curriculum elements
	   a) term projects
	   b) cultural events (outing of FIG students)
	   c) involvement in campus activities
	   d) chats with faculty
	• Guest speaker: Prof. Craig Nelson on cultivating growth in freshmen
	• Microteaching (four to five PIs)
		• Refine for resubmission the draft X111 syllabus
		• Read material on incivilities
		• Read case studies

Sixth Session (3 hrs. content + 3 hrs. microteaching) Apr. 10, Maple Room

Refine X111 syllabi	• Critique reflective statements • Dealing with disruptive students • Case studies: problematic situations for PIs • Prepare draft lesson for FIG seminar • Microteaching (all remaining PIs) • Evaluation and wrap-up of leadership seminar

Microteaching

Each PI should begin planning early for a ten-minute microteaching session. Microteaching sessions for the remainder of the seminar will be scheduled in the second seminar session. Lesson plans will be submitted by the third seminar session and later. Your lesson plan will describe the microteaching session you plan to conduct. Your microteaching topic must be a topic from the curriculum of the leadership seminar, a topic that you plan to teach your FIG students. Each microteaching session will be videotaped and critiqued in class with peers. In the following week, the session will be critiqued with the staff using the videotape. The videotape will be yours to keep after the critiques.

Expectations

Class attendance and participation are crucial to the experience of being an effective FIG leader. You are expected to participate in all seminar meetings. If an emergency arises and you cannot participate, please prearrange your absence with the FIG coordinator. In addition to participation, you are expected to complete all assignments in the above schedule.

Grading

You will receive no grade for the seminar. No official academic credit is earned. However, much as is done for apprentice professionals, your performance will be unofficially evaluated. Noncompliance with the above expectations is grounds for dismissal from the FIG program.

Resources

You will be provided with ample resources. Materials include a loose-leaf binder to maintain curriculum materials distributed throughout the seminar, and a 3.5" disk for electronic files. Human resources include access to the above staff continuously through the fall 1998 semester.

      Student-Assisted Teaching

Syllabus for UNIV 350 Peer Education

(contributed by Adams, Brown, & Cook)

Instructor:

Office:

Phone:

Course Objectives

- To develop an understanding of the social, emotional, cognitive, and intellectual needs of the first year student.

- To broaden interpersonal skills to include group leadership, listening, and classroom management.

- To discover how teaching and learning styles influence the learning process.

- To learn how to design and implement a presentation/workshop.

- To gain greater knowledge of specific learning and study strategies.

Course Requirements

1) Regular UNIV 350 class attendance and participation is required. The class times include 16 hours of training before the semester begins, and one-hour classes that will meet approximately 12 times during the semester—once a week for the first half of the semester and biweekly for the second half of the semester. (75 points)

2) An initial assessment paper will be due soon after training is over. This self-assessment paper should address the following: What relevant skills and experiences do you bring to the peer educator role? What did you learn about yourself and peer education skills and theory as a result of the training (i.e., training/learning styles, workshop design, ethics, classroom skills)? In what areas would you like to improve or grow? What topics do you feel most comfortable presenting on that are addressed in UNIV 150 courses? Finally, share two or three ideas that you have regarding a specific class activity or assignment for the course in the fall. (25 points)

3) Each student is expected to read any handouts or articles given during UNIV 350, the textbook for the UNIV 150 class, and the undergraduate handbook. In addition, occasional additional assignments will count toward participation points.

4) Regular attendance at your UNIV 150 class is required.

5) A weekly journal must be kept by each student. This will be evaluated by the instructor of UNIV 350. The journal should include a discussion of your current role as a peer educator, your relationship to the students and the instructor, the strengths and weaknesses of the assignments and activities performed by the UNIV 150 students, a general assessment of the classroom community in the UNIV 150 course, and reflection on the content and environment of the UNIV 350 course. (60 points)

6) During the semester you will be given the opportunity to design and implement at least two class periods of the UNIV 150 class to which you are assigned.

   a) The UNIV 350 instructor will observe one class period. (35 points)

   b) One of your UNIV 350 classmates will observe the other class period in order to provide you with feedback. Thus, each student will provide written and verbal feedback to one of their classmates. This peer feedback will be turned in to the instructor. (15 points for the observer)

7) A final assessment paper of at least five pages is due during finals week. This paper should explore what you learned about yourself, your skills, first year-students, and peer education. Further instructions on this paper will be provided in a separate handout. (100 points)

8) The instructor with whom the peer educator is paired will evaluate the peer educator. This evaluation will be based on how helpful the peer educator was in planning course content, arranging speakers, moderating class discussion, presenting information, facilitating in-class activities, and communicating with UNIV 150 students. (100 points)

Students with Disabilities

If you have, or think you have, a disability, you may wish to self-identify. You can do so by providing documentation to Services for Students with Disabilities located in Garcia Annex (646-6840). Appropriate accommodations may then be provided for you.

Grading Scale

A = 369-410   B = 328-368   C = 287-327
D = 246-286   F = 245 and below

Tentative Schedule

Date	Topic	Assignment
8/22	Training	
	• Introductions	
	• Opening exercise	
	• Overview of UNIV 350	
	• Reflections on your first year	
	• Demographics of first-year students	
	• Overview of UNIV 150	
	• Learning and teaching styles	
	• Role of peer educator and role of instructor	
	• How to design a presentation	
	• Overview of CLA resources	
	• Professionalism and ethics	
	• Pair-up and plan presentation	
8/24	Instructor/peer educator conjoint training	
8/26	Question and answer	Initial assessment paper due

Date	Topic	Assignment
9/2	Time management	
9/9	Listening and note-taking	
9/9	Textbook reading	
9/16	Test prep and test taking	
9/23	Open discussion	Journal due
9/30	Cultural diversity	
10/7	Student development theory	
10/21	Open discussion	Journal due
11/4	Open discussion	
11/18	Open discussion	Journal
12/2	Wrap-up	Final assessment paper due

Appendix B-4

Peer Educator/Instructor Conjoint Training Discussion Questions

(contributed by Adams, Brown, & Cook)

Developing a Team Approach to Classroom Communication

1) Where will we sit during the class?

2) Who will open and end each class?

3) How will we present the role difference between the peer educator and instructor?

4) How will we communicate our qualifications for teaching this course?

5) How do we feel about sharing email addresses or phone numbers with students so they can communicate with us outside of class?

6) How do we want to communicate with each other while in class?

7) How should we respond to each of the following:

a) Students talking to each other while the instructor or peer educator is presenting information.

b) Students not interacting or asking questions in class.

c) One of us wants to add to what the other is saying.

d) There is a conflict in class (for example, a student expresses not caring about information being presented or complains about an assignment).

Planning and Feedback

1) When will we meet to plan the class and discuss how things went in the previous class?

2) What will be our roles in planning each class session?

3) What type of feedback will we give to each other?

Appendix C

Teaching Materials

Appendix C-1

Application for Student Participation in Academic Excellence Workshop

(contributed by Streveler)

ACADEMIC EXCELLENCE WORKSHOP
Application for Participation
Physics II

Workshops for *Physics II* meet for two hours weekly,
beginning the week of September 7 and ending
the week of November 16.

Two workshop sections will be held.

CIRCLE THE WORKSHOP YOU WILL ATTEND

Workshop A: Mondays, 7p.m.-9p.m.
Chris Kelso, Meyer 357

Workshop B: Wednesdays, 7p.m.-9p.m.
Sara Brock, Meyer 353

---

* I wish to participate in the Academic Excellence Workshop for Physics II and plan to attend the workshop regularly.

* I understand that in the workshop I will work with fellow students to solve problems related to course material.

* I authorize the release of my course grades to the workshop facilitator throughout the semester. I understand that this information will be kept confidential and will be used only for research purposes that promote student academic success.

Signature_____ Date _____

Print name _____ SSN _____

Local address _____

Local phone number _____

Space in the workshops is limited. PLEASE RETURN YOUR APPLICATION TO STUDENT DEVELOPMENT AND ACADEMIC SERVICES BY FRIDAY, SEPTEMBER 4.

For more information: Call Student Development and Academic Services, 273-3377.

Appendix C-2

SI Session Planning Log

(contributed by Zaritsky)

Fill out one of these planning logs for every study session you hold and give it to your supervisor at the end of the week.

SI Session Number: **SI Leader:**

Course Instructor: **SI Supervisor:**

Course:

Objective: What do I hope to accomplish during this study session?

Materials to be used:

Plan: How do I plan to achieve my objective? What are my steps? What handout have I prepared? Attach a copy of the handout to this planning log.
   Step 1:
   Step 2:
   Step 3:

Evaluation: How will I know if I have reached my objective? (Quiz, recall, checking for understanding, verbal feedback)

Closure: How will I sum up today's session?

Appendix C-3

UNIV150 Class Feedback and Planning Form

(contributed by Adams, Brown, & Cook)

Weekly meeting date and time: **Today's date:**

Feedback for this week:

Did the students understand the material we presented?

What went well in this class?

What didn't go as well as it could have?
   What can we do about it?

What improvements or adjustments do we need to make?

What's our plan?

Next week's plan:

Topics:

Who's presenting what:

Review before new topic is introduced:

Reading assignments:

Discussion questions:

Guest speakers:

Handouts:

Class assignments to be turned in:

Announcements:

Notes:

Appendix C-4

Interview Procedure for Students Consulting on Teaching*

(contributed by Sorenson)

Interview Procedure

1) Instructor leaves the room for 15-20 minutes. This usually works best at the end of the class. (If the instructor seems to have forgotten about the interview, be assertive and remind the instructor.)

2) Interviewer asks students to individually write down answers to the interview questions. Students write for about five minutes.

3) Interviewer puts students into groups of two or three (or in very large classes, four or five). People in the small groups share what they have written for about five minutes. Ask one person to write "Group Responses" on the back of her/his sheet. There they list the items about which their small group reached consensus. (Small classes of under 20 can skip this step.)

4) Reconvene the whole class. Interviewer asks the class as a whole to respond to the questions and writes responses on the board. (It is helpful to ask one student to write the responses on the board and another to record on paper what is on the board.) Narrow down the responses to determine which responses are most beneficial for the instructor.

5) Interviewer collects all papers from students.

6) Interviewer tallies the results and prepares a report for the instructor.

7) Interviewer meets with the professor to discuss the results and deliver the report.

A Few Helpful Suggestions

1) Mention to the instructor ahead of time that you can add other questions to the interview in order to adapt it to their class (if they would like).

2) Remember that the faculty center has copies of the basic interview questions. You can photocopy them there (4450 WSC).

Sample Interview Form

Class _____(e.g., Bio 100)

Instructor _____

1) What helps you learn in this class?

2) What hinders your learning in this class?

3) What suggestions do you have for improving this class?

* (Modified version of SGID)

Appendix D

Evaluation Procedures

Supplemental Instruction Observation Record

(compiled from contributions from Stelzner, Livingston, & Creed; Zaritsky)

Name of SI leader:

Name of observer:

Date and time of observation:

SI course:

Topic of this session:

Objectives of the study session:

Positives/Things I learned from this leader:

Suggestions for improvement:

Additional comments:

Response of SI leader:

Faculty-UTA Review of UTA

(contributed by Thibodeau)

UTA: **Date:**

Please evaluate on a scale of 1 to 10, with 1 being the lowest score and 10 being the highest.

1) **Public Policy Knowledge:** Shows interest in and factual knowledge of at least one policy issue. Also, shows a general knowledge of many public policy issues.

   Rating:

   Comments:

2) **Public Policy Skills:** Demonstrates a thorough understanding of public policy skills.

   Rating:

   Comments:

3) **Punctuality:** Punctual with respect to attendance at class, meetings, office hours, and turning in assignments.

   Rating:

   Comments:

4) **Standards:** Maintains a high level of work standards. Shows considerable effort in preparing quality written products.

   Rating:

   Comments:

5) **Administration:** Understands duties and material. Able to follow instructions. Completes project assignments on a timely basis.

   Rating:

   Comments:

6) **Commitment:** Demonstrates an aggressive commitment to the success of the students and the teaching program. Shows high level of interest and effort. Participates actively in TA meetings.

   Rating:

   Comments:

7) **People Practices:** Provides a role model for the students at all times. Sets the standard for excellence. Sits with group. Pays attention to lecture.

   Rating:

   Comments:

8) **Planning:** Establishes an action plan for self and others to follow. Completes duties within planned guidelines.

   Rating:

   Comments:

9) **Initiative:** Takes action and responsibility to achieve individual goals. Demonstrates self-starting rather than quiet acceptance. Attempts to influence events to achieve goals. Completes duties without being asked.

   Rating:

   Comments:

10) **Creativity:** Makes suggestions and undertakes activity, through oral and written reports, to improve the class.

   Rating:

   Comments:

11) **Teamwork:** Uses appropriate interpersonal methods to guide students toward accomplishment. Shows correct respect when addressing fellow UTAs during class, office hours, and meetings.

   Rating:

   Comments:

Overall Rating:

Comments:

UTA's Signature: _____

Professor's Signature: _____

Student Evaluation of Peer Facilitator

(contributed by Allen & White)

Your Facilitator's Name: Your Name:

Please use the following form to provide feedback to your facilitator about how he/she can assist your group in working to its optimal level. Indicate with an "X" in the appropriate box the extent to which you agree that each statement describes the way in which your facilitator interacts with you and your group. The form is due at the start of class on the dates provided in the syllabus.

Facilitator Behavior	1 = Strongly Disagree	2 = Disagree	3 = Somewhat Agree	4 = Agree	5 = Agree Strongly
Shows active interest in my group; is honest, friendly and interested in participating in the group process.					
Creates a relaxed and open environment for discussion.					
Listens and responds well to my concerns or problems.					
Is honest about admitting what he/she doesn't know.					
Helps my group to identify the relative importance of learning issues and to relate learning issues to the problem under discussion.					
Guides and intervenes to keep my group on track and progressing through the problem.					
Suggests appropriate resources and helps my group to learn how to find them.					
Provides constructive comments about information presented.					
Shows good judgment about when to provide an answer to a question, and when to deflect it back for others in the group to consider.					
Poses questions that stimulate my thinking and ability to analyze the problem.					
Encourages group members to refine and organize their presentations.					
Guides my group in planning what we can do better next time.					

Please use the back of this form to respond to the following two statements. Be sure to relate your responses to your ratings choices above.

1) Describe the ways in which your facilitator best helps your learning.

2) Describe the ways in which your facilitator could provide additional help with your group's learning.

Appendix D-4

Student Evaluation of UTA

(contributed by Thibodeau)

PAF 101 UTA Evaluation

Please rate your UTA on the following criteria:

	Poor				Excellent
1) Communication skills	1	2	3	4	5
2) Knowledge of material	1	2	3	4	5
3) Ability to help with questions	1	2	3	4	5
4) Organization	1	2	3	4	5
5) Willingness to give extra assistance	1	2	3	4	5
6) Keeps group informed of announcements	1	2	3	4	5

7) What is your UTA's major strength?

8) What is your UTA's major weakness?

9) Do you have any suggestions to help your UTA become more effective?

10) How many times have you visited office hours?

      Never   1 to 4 times   5 or more times

  If you circled "Never," why have you not sought extra help?

  If you have visited office hours, how helpful have you found them to be?

      Very helpful   Somewhat helpful   Not helpful at all

11) Do you have any suggestions to help all UTAs become more effective?

Appendix D-5

Student Evaluation of Supplemental Instruction

(compiled from contributions from Couchman; Garvin & Snyder; Streveler; Zaritsky)

Directions: Please answer all of the questions below on the separate answer sheet. Answer all questions as completely and honestly as you can. Do not give your name.

Part I

1) The SI study sessions that I attended were for the following course:

2) The grade I expect in this course is:
   A B C D F Incomplete

3) The number of SI study sessions I attended this semester was:
   a) 0 to 2
   b) 3 or more

If you answered you attended zero to two sessions, complete Part II ONLY. If you answered you attended three or more study sessions, skip to Part III.

Part II
(Answer this part if you attended two or fewer sessions)

1) I did not attend SI study sessions because:
   a) I had classes when they were scheduled.
   b) I had to go to work.
   c) I did not feel I needed them.
   d) I prefer studying alone.
   e) I went once or twice and did not find them helpful.
   f) I have been to similar kinds of sessions in other courses and did not find them helpful.
   g) Other (please explain)

2) Is this your first attempt at this unit?
   a) Yes
   b) No

3) Would monthly sessions of four hours held on a weekend be preferable?
   a) Yes
   b) No

Part III
(Answer this part if you attended three or more sessions this semester)

1) Is this your first attempt at this unit?
   a) Yes
   b) No

2) For the most part, the SI study sessions I attended were:
   a) Excellent
   b) Good
   c) OK
   d) Poor

3) In the future, I have the following suggestions (pick two):
   a) Expand SI into other difficult courses
   b) Provide more than three hours a week of tutoring
   c) Block in the hours for tutoring so that all students are free to attend study sessions
   d) Offer SI during the six-week semester

4) Overall, SI study sessions helped me to (pick two):
   a) Study better
   b) Understand the course material better
   c) Be a better student generally
   d) Improve my self-concept

5) To what degree was SI helpful in improving your study skills?
   a) Very helpful
   b) Somewhat helpful
   c) Only a little helpful
   d) Not at all helpful

6) To what degree was SI helpful in improving your understanding of how to succeed in this course?
   a) Very helpful
   b) Somewhat helpful
   c) Only a little helpful
   d) Not at all helpful

Student-Assisted Teaching

7) To what degree do you believe SI has been helpful in improving your grade in this course?

   a) Very helpful

   b) Somewhat helpful

   c) Only a little helpful

   d) Not at all helpful

8) To what extent was SI helpful in improving your understanding of course materials and assignments such as homework, handouts, textbooks, or other assigned readings?

   a) Very helpful

   b) Somewhat helpful

   c) Only a little helpful

   d) Not at all helpful

9) To what extent was SI helpful in improving your grades in other courses?

   a) Very helpful

   b) Somewhat helpful

   c) Only a little helpful

   d) Not at all helpful

10) Would you recommend SI to other students?

   a) Yes

   b) No

11) How could SI be improved?

12) What qualities have you seen in your leaders?

   a) were well organized for the sessions

   b) knew the content of the unit

   c) were friendly, approachable

   d) involved students in activities

   e) provided appropriate study hints

   f) were tolerant and understanding of my concerns

   g) created clear worksheets with accurate solutions

   h) other (specify)

Thank you for your cooperation in filling out this questionnaire. You may, if you wish, write comments here.

Appendix D-6
Peer Educator Evaluation of Training

(contributed by Adams, Brown, & Cook)

1) How did the training help prepare you to be a peer educator?

2) What was most challenging about the training?

3) What didn't you like about the training?

4) What did you like about the training?

5) Please comment on the trainer's style.

6) If you were designing this training, what parts (including the amount of time) would you keep as is, leave out, change, or add?

7) How would you describe the atmosphere of training?

8) Other comments?

Peer Educator Evaluation of UNIV 150/UNIV 350

(contributed by Adams, Brown, & Cook)

Please evaluate your UNIV 150/UNIV 350 experience on a scale of 1 = Strongly Agree to 5 = Strongly Disagree.

1 2 3 4 5

1) My UNIV 150 instructor was approachable.

Comments:

2) I had sufficient opportunities to participate as a peer educator in my UNIV 150 class.

Comments:

3) My UNIV 150 instructor seemed comfortable with me in the class.

Comments:

4) It is helpful to have regularly scheduled meetings with the UNIV 150 instructor.

Comments:

5) This experience (UNIV 150/350) was what I expected.

Comments:

6) The information in my UNIV 350 class was helpful.

Comments:

7) The discussions in my UNIV 350 class were helpful.

Comments:

If I could change the UNIV 150 class, I would:

If I could change the UNIV 350 class, I would:

Outside of class attendance in the UNIV 350 and UNIV 150 class, I spent approximately _____ hours each week in outside preparation and _____ hours meeting students.

Peer Facilitator Evaluation of Workshop Experience

(contributed by Streveler)

1) What was your most positive experience this semester?

2) What was your most difficult experience this semester?

3) How would you rate your communication with the course professor this semester?

4) How would you rate the worksheets used in your workshop this semester? Were you satisfied? Did they seem to work well for the students?

5) How would you rate your communication with your co-facilitator?

6) How could the workshops be improved?

Teaching Teams Preceptor Questionnaire

(contributed by Stover, Story, Skousen, Jacks, Logan, & Bush)

M   F

Please circle one: Freshman Sophomore Junior Senior

Age

1) Course you are preceptoring in
   Instructor

2) Is this a course in your major?

   ☐ yes

   ☐ no

3) Have you taken this course before or are you taking it for
   the first time while preceptoring?

   ☐ took course before

   ☐ taking course while preceptoring

   ☐ other

4) Have you preceptored before?

   ☐ yes

   ☐ no

5) Which preceptor course are you taking?

   ☐ UNVR 197A

   ☐ UNVR 397A

   ☐ Other (please fill in)

6) For how many credits?

   ☐ 1 credit

   ☐ 2 credits

   ☐ 3 credits

   ☐ 4 credits

7) The amount of work required to earn these credits was

   ☐ too little

   ☐ too much

   ☐ just right

8) How much of an influence was each of the following in
   your decision to become a preceptor?

	Strong influence	Moderate influence	Some influence	No influence
To gain teaching experience				
To gain insight and knowledge about the teaching process				
To have a career-relevant experience				
To gain experience working as a part of a team				
To work more closely with a faculty member				
To improve my understanding of the course material				
To earn a better grade in the course				
To help me to get to know my classmates better				
To share my knowledge with others/help other students				
Other (please fill in) _____				

9) What are your responsibilities as a preceptor? (mark all
   that apply)

   ☐ attend class

   ☐ attend meetings with instructor(s)/GTA(s)

   ☐ go to teaching workshops

   ☐ do assignments in advance

   ☐ hold office hours

   ☐ hold review sessions

   ☐ help students with assignments/projects/labs

   ☐ help with writing

   ☐ help with math

   ☐ help with in-class activities

   ☐ facilitate/moderate group discussions

   ☐ act as a team leader for student teams

☐ help develop class projects/assignments

☐ help maintain course web site

☐ other

10) In addition to the responsibilities indicated above, what else was required for your preceptor credit(s) (i.e., did you keep a journal, do an extra project, etc.)?

11) Please indicate your agreement with the following statements.

Being a preceptor has…	Strongly agree	Somewhat agree	Somewhat disagree	Strongly disagree
Given me experience teaching others				
Given me insight and knowledge about the teaching process				
Increased my interest in teaching as a profession				
Allowed me to get to know more of my classmates than usual				
Allowed me to get to know the professor better				
Improved my understanding of the course material				
Kept me on top of my work for this class				
Improved my ability to present material in an organized and understandable manner				
Improved my ability to explain complicated ideas to others				
Improved my ability to recognize when students need help				
Developed my reflective listening skills (listening without making judgments about what I hear)				
Improved my ability to give clear, honest, supportive feedback				
Helped me to learn to work effectively with people of different backgrounds and opinions				
Improved my ability to moderate group discussions				
Improved my teamwork skills				
Improved my leadership skills				
Developed my time management skills				

12) Because of my work as a preceptor in this class, I believe I will earn . . .

☐ a better grade

☐ the same grade

☐ a worse grade

13) How often did you feel you had enough knowledge to be able to help students when they asked you questions?

☐ all of the time

☐ most of the time

☐ some of the time

☐ never

14) On average, how frequently have you met with the following people?

	Every week	A few times a month	A few times a semester	Never
Faculty				
GTAs				
One or more preceptors				

15) How satisfied are you with the supervision and guidance given by the instructor(s) and/or GTA(s)?

☐ completely satisfied

☐ somewhat satisfied

☐ somewhat unsatisfied

☐ completely unsatisfied

16) How clear was the instructor(s) in delineating your role as a preceptor from that of the GTA(s)?

☐ completely clear

☐ somewhat clear

☐ somewhat unclear

☐ completely unclear

17) In your teaching team, who is most active in advising and guiding preceptors?

☐ instructor(s)

☐ GTA(s)

☐ Both

☐ Neither

18) How good a descriptor is "team" for describing interactions between the instructor(s), GTA(s), and preceptors in this class?

☐ very good

☐ good

☐ poor

☐ very poor

19) Overall, how satisfied were you with your preceptor experience this semester?

☐ highly satisfied

☐ moderately satisfied

☐ minimally satisfied

☐ not at all satisfied

20) Overall, how satisfied were you with the way the instructor ran the course?

☐ highly satisfied

☐ moderately satisfied

☐ minimally satisfied

☐ not at all satisfied

21) Do you have any suggestions for improving teaching team interactions?

22) Do you have any comments or suggestions for future preceptors?

23) Do you have any suggestions for faculty considering the use of preceptors in their classes?

Please use the back of this sheet to tell us anything else about your preceptor experience that could help us improve the experiences of future preceptors or improve the teaching teams in general.

Appendix D-10

Teaching Teams GTA Questionnaire

(contributed by Wood, Hart, Tollefson, DeToro, & Libarkin)

M F   Age

Course   Instructor

Working toward ☐ MA ☐ MS ☐ PhD ☐ Other

1) How far in advance of the start of classes did you know you had a teaching assistantship in this course?

☐ more than two months

☐ 1–2 months

☐ 1–3 weeks

☐ a few days

☐ after the start of classes

2) At that time, did you know it was a general education class?

☐ yes

☐ no

3) At that time, did you know there would be preceptors for the course?

☐ yes

☐ no

☐ instructor was considering it

4) Did you have any choice in whether you would teach in this course as opposed to some other course?

☐ yes

☐ no

5) If given a choice, would you prefer to teach in an introductory course in your major or in a general education course?

☐ course in my major

☐ general education course

☐ no preference

☐ not applicable

6) Have you been a teaching assistant before now?

☐ yes

semesters _____

☐ no

7) Have you been a teaching assistant for a general education course before now?

☐ yes

semesters _____

☐ no

8) How likely is your career to include teaching in higher education?

☐ very likely

☐ somewhat likely

☐ uncertain

☐ somewhat unlikely

☐ very unlikely

9) In which type of institution would you prefer to teach?

☐ research university

☐ large state college

☐ small liberal arts college

☐ professional school

☐ community college

☐ other _____

☐ no preference

☐ will not be teaching in higher education

10) Before teaching in this course, how familiar to you was the term "preceptor?"

☐ very familiar—knew exactly what it was

☐ somewhat familiar—heard of it and had a general idea of what it was

☐ somewhat familiar—heard of it but didn't know what it was

☐ very unfamiliar—-never heard of it

11) What special skills do GTAs need to be successful teaching general education students?

12) Overall, how prepared did you feel for teaching this general education course?

☐ completely prepared

☐ somewhat prepared

☐ somewhat unprepared

☐ completely unprepared

13) How much preparation (formal or informal) did the instructor(s) provide to you?

☐ a large amount

☐ a moderate amount

☐ a minimal amount

☐ none

14) How clear was the instructor(s) in delineating your role as a GTA from that of the preceptors?

☐ completely clear

☐ somewhat clear

☐ somewhat unclear

☐ completely unclear

15) Which of the following duties did you perform as a GTA? (mark all that apply)

☐ led discussion sessions

☐ led lab sessions

☐ substitute lectured

☐ developed projects or labs

☐ created quizzes

☐ created handouts

☐ graded homework/quizzes/projects

☐ graded exams

☐ conducted help sessions

☐ conducted exam review sessions

☐ supervised preceptors

☐ trained preceptors

☐ other _____

16) In what capacity did you interact with preceptors? (mark all that apply)

☐ held meetings with groups of preceptors

☐ met with individual preceptors

☐ trained preceptors, explained their function and duties

☐ provided preparation and assistance for assignments/projects

☐ debriefed preceptors on finished assignments/projects

☐ provided feedback on how well preceptors were doing

☐ engaged in discussions of teaching and learning

☐ graded preceptor course work

☐ assigned grades for preceptor units (i.e., UNVR 197)

☐ other _____

17) What kind of effect do you think the GTA(s) and preceptors had on each other?

☐ overall positive (i.e., a complementary effect)

☐ neither positive nor negative

☐ overall negative

☐ mixed

18) How did working with preceptors affect your experience as a GTA?

☐ made it better

☐ made no difference

☐ made it worse

☐ made it better in some ways, worse in others

19) If given a choice, would you work with preceptors again?

☐ I definitely would

☐ I probably would

☐ Uncertain

☐ I probably would not

☐ I definitely would not

20) How good a descriptor is "team" for describing the interactions between the instructor(s), GTA(s), and preceptors in this class?

☐ very good

☐ good

☐ poor

☐ very poor

21) How effectively did the instructor(s) facilitate teaching team interactions?

☐ very effectively

☐ somewhat effectively

☐ somewhat ineffectively

☐ very ineffectively

22) Overall, how satisfied were you with your teaching assistantship this semester?

☐ highly satisfied

☐ moderately satisfied

☐ minimally satisfied

☐ not at all satisfied

23) Overall, how satisfied were you with the way the instructor(s) ran the course?

☐ highly satisfied

☐ moderately satisfied

☐ minimally satisfied

☐ not at all satisfied

24) What would you do, or what would you suggest be done, to enhance your GTA experience in the teaching team?

Please use the back of this sheet to tell us anything else about your experience that could help us improve the teaching teams program.

Teaching Teams Instructor Questionnaire

(contributed by Larson, Mencke, Tollefson, Harrison, & Berman)

Instructor

Course

No. of GTAs for class

No. of GTAs who worked with preceptors

Were there separate discussion/activity sections taught by GTAs? yes no

1) How many courses have you used preceptors in (including this one)?

2) Why did you decide to use preceptors in your course? (mark all that apply)

☐ to have extra assistance in the classroom

☐ to have an extra outside resource for students to go to for help

☐ because I wanted to work more closely with some students

☐ to gain insight into student perspectives about my course and my teaching

☐ to gain insight into students' lives and concerns

☐ other

3) Please indicate the number of preceptors in each category.

students taking this course for the first time _____

students who already took this course or a comparable course _____

4) Please indicate the number of students in each category

preceptors you originally wanted to have _____

students who applied for preceptorships _____

students you accepted as preceptors _____

preceptors that remained active _____

preceptors earning honors credit for course _____

honors preceptors earning preceptor credit _____

5) In your course, preceptors are

☐ essential

☐ helpful but not essential

6) Briefly describe your recruitment/selection process.

7) Rate your overall satisfaction with your recruitment process.

☐ highly satisfied

☐ somewhat satisfied

☐ neither satisfied nor dissatisfied

☐ somewhat dissatisfied

☐ highly dissatisfied

8) How did coordination occur in your teaching team? (mark all that apply) *Note: Regularly means at least once every two weeks.

☐ instructors, GTAs, and preceptors met regularly

☐ instructors and preceptors met regularly

☐ instructors and GTAs met regularly

☐ GTAs and preceptors met regularly

☐ preceptors met regularly by themselves

☐ irregular/informal meetings

9) Were you happy with the above arrangement? What changes will you make, if any?

10) How good a descriptor is "team" for describing the interactions between the instructor(s), GTA(s) if any, and preceptors in the class?

☐ very good

☐ good

☐ fair

☐ poor

☐ very poor

11) If any of the GTAs worked with preceptors, how well would you say they worked together?

☐ very well, no problems

☐ moderately well, had some problems

☐ minimally well or not at all well

☐ not sure

12) In working with preceptors, who did what? (mark all that apply)

	Instructor	GTA(s)
Trained preceptors, explained their function and duties____		
Held meetings with preceptors ____		
Provided assistance to preceptors on assignments/projects ____		
Prepared preceptors to work with students ____		
Graded preceptor course work____		
Debriefed preceptors on finished assignments/projects ____		
Provided feedback on how well preceptors were doing their jobs ____		
Assigned grade for preceptor units (i.e., UNVR 197) ____		
Engaged in discussions of teaching and learning with preceptors____		
Other ____		

13) What roles did preceptors play in your class? (mark all that apply)

☐ held office hours

☐ held review sessions

☐ helped students with assignments/projects/labs

☐ helped students with writing

☐ helped students with math

☐ helped with in-class activities

☐ assisted GTAs in discussion sections

☐ facilitated/moderated group discussions

☐ acted as a team leader for student teams

☐ helped develop class projects/assignments

☐ helped maintain course web site

☐ others

14) In addition to the above duties, what was required of the preceptors to earn preceptor credit? (mark all that apply)

☐ attend class

☐ attend meetings with instructor(s)/GTA(s)

☐ go to teaching workshops

☐ do assignments in advance

☐ keep a journal

☐ make a portfolio

☐ other

15) In your work with preceptors, how important are the following goals?

	Very important	Important	Not very important
To prepare them to be able to assist me with the class ____			
To help them understand the course content____			
To help them understand something about teaching and learning____			
To give them teaching/mentoring experience ____			
To help them develop leadership skills____			
To help them develop good communication skills ____			
To give them constructive feedback on how well they are doing their jobs ____			
Other ____			

16) Did the preceptors receive feedback on how well they were doing their jobs?

☐ yes

☐ no   Go to question 19

17) Who provided that feedback? (mark all that apply)

☐ instructor

☐ GTA

☐ students in class

☐ fellow preceptors

18) How often was feedback given to preceptors?

☐ regularly

☐ occasionally

☐ only when a problem arose

☐ only when a superb job was done

☐ only when either a problem arose or a superb job was done

19) Some possible problems encountered with preceptors are listed below. Please indicate the number of preceptors each problem applies to, if any.

____ didn't attend team meetings

____ didn't attend class regularly

____ had trouble getting assignments done ahead of time

____ did not understand the material sufficiently to be able to help others

____ did not have sufficient writing skills to help students with writing

_____ did not have sufficient math skills to help students with math

_____ was unable to distinguish telling from facilitating

_____ was too judgmental or authoritarian

20) Briefly describe any other problems encountered with using preceptors in your class.

21) Briefly describe any positive changes you noticed in your preceptors over the course of the semester.

22) Overall, how satisfied were you with the way the course went this semester?

☐ highly satisfied

☐ moderately satisfied

☐ minimally satisfied

☐ not at all satisfied

23) Will you use preceptors again?

☐ yes

☐ no

24) What changes will you make in the future? (Please use the back if necessary)

Bibliography

Allen, D. E. (1997). Bringing PBL to the introductory biology classroom. In A. P. McNeal & C. D'Avanzo (Eds.), *Student-active science* (pp. 259-278). Philadelphia, PA: Saunders.

Allen, D. E., Duch, B. J., & Groh, S. E. (1996). The power of problem-based learning in teaching introductory science courses. In L. Wilkerson & W. H. Gijselaers (Eds.), *Bringing problem-based learning to higher education: Theory and practice* (pp. 43-52). New Directions in Teaching and Learning in Higher Education, No. 68. San Francisco, CA: Jossey-Bass.

Allen, D., & Duch, B. (1998). *Thinking toward solutions: Problem-based learning activities for general biology.* Philadelphia, PA: Saunders.

Anderson, D. (1996). *Evaluation of supplemental instruction pilot project: Nursing foundations 2, S2, 1995.* Report of The Office of Preparatory and Continuing Studies, USQ, Toowoomba.

Angelo, T. A., & Cross, K. P. (1989). Classroom research for teaching assistants. In J. D. Nyquist, R. D. Abbott, & D. H. Wulff (Eds.), *Teaching assistant training in the 1990s* (pp. 99-108). San Francisco, CA: Jossey-Bass.

Arendale, D., & Martin, D. C. (1998). *Review of research concerning the effectiveness of supplemental instruction from the University of Missouri-Kansas City and other institutions* [Online]. Available: http://www.umkc.edu/cad/si/sidocs/sidata97.htm

Arter, J. A., & Spandel, V. (1992). Using portfolios of student work in instruction and assessment. *Educational Measurement: Issues and Practices, 11* (1), 36-44.

Association of American Colleges. (1985). *Integrity in the college curriculum: A report in the academic community.* Washington, DC: Author.

Astin, A. (1984). Student involvement: A developmental theory for higher education. *Journal of College Student Personnel, 25* (4), 297-308.

Ausubel, D. P. (1963). *The psychology of meaningful verbal learning: An introduction to school learning.* New York, NY: Grune & Stratton.

Bandura, A. (1986). *Social foundations of thought and action: A social cognitive theory.* Englewood Cliffs, NJ: Prentice Hall.

Barr, R. B., & Tagg, J. (1995, November/December). From teaching to learning: A new paradigm for undergraduate education. *Change,* 12-25.

Barrows, H. S. (1988). *The tutorial process.* Springfield, IL: Southern Illinois University School of Medicine.

Barrows, H. S., & Tamblyn, R. E. (1980). *Problem-based learning: An approach to medical education.* New York, NY: Springer-Verlag.

Benjamin, L.T., & Lowman, K.D. (1981). *Activities handbook for the teaching of psychology* (Vol. 1). Washington, DC: American Psychological Association.

Benjamin, L.T., Nodine, B. F., Ernst, R. M., & Broeker, C. B. (1999). *Activities handbook for the teaching of psychology* (Vol. 4). Washington, DC: American Psychological Association.

Berman, D. (1996). University 101 peer leaders program information packet. Unpublished manuscript, University of South Carolina. (Available from National Resource Center for the First-Year Experience and Students in Transition, http://www.sc.edu/fye/, phone: 803-777-6029).

Black, B. (1998). Using the SGID method for a variety of purposes. *To Improve the Academy, 17,* 245-262.

Bloom, B. S. (Ed.). (1956). *Taxonomy of educational objectives*. New York, NY: David McKay.

Bouquet, E. H. (1999, February). 'Our little secret': A history of writing centers, pre- to post-open admissions. *College Composition and Communication, 50,* 463-483.

The Boyer Commission on Educating Undergraduates in the Research University. (1998). *Reinventing undergraduate education: A blueprint for American research universities* [Online]. Available: http://notes.cc.sunysb.edu/Pres/boyer.nsf

Brown, A. L., & Palincsar, A. S. (1989). Guided, cooperative learning and individual knowledge acquisition. In L. B. Resnick (Ed.), *Knowing, learning, and instruction: Essays in honor of Robert Glaser* (pp. 393-451). Hillsdale, NJ: Lawrence Erlbaum Associates.

Brown, L., Henry, C., Henry, J., & McTaggart, R. (1982). Action research: Notes on the national seminar. *Classroom Action Research Network Bulletin, 5,* 1-16.

Bruffee, K. A. (1978). The Brooklyn Plan: Attaining intellectual growth through peer-group tutoring. *Liberal Education, 64,* 447-468.

Bruffee, K. A. (1984). Peer tutoring and the 'conversation of mankind'. In G. A. Olson (Ed.), *Writing centers: Theory and administration* (pp. 77-84). Urbana, IL: NCTE.

Bruffee, K. A. (1993). *Collaborative learning: Higher education, interdependence, and the authority of knowledge*. Baltimore, MD: Johns Hopkins University Press.

Capossela, T. L. (Ed.). (1998). *The Harcourt Brace guide to peer tutoring in writing*. Orlando, FL: Harcourt Brace.

Carns, A. W., Carns, M. R., & Wright, J. (1993). Students as paraprofessionals in four-year colleges and universities: Current practice compared to prior practice. *Journal of College Student Development, 34,* 358-363.

Carpenter, C. R. (1959). *The Penn State pyramid plan: Interdependent student work study grouping for increasing motivation for academic development*. Paper presented at the 14th National Conference on Higher Education, Chicago, IL.

Catterall, J. S. (1998). A cost-effectiveness model for the assessment of educational productivity. In J. E. Groccia & J. E. Miller (Eds.), *Enhancing productivity: Administrative, instructional, and technological strategies* (pp. 61-84). New Directions for Higher Education, No. 103. San Francisco, CA: Jossey-Bass.

Center for Communication Across the Curriculum. (1999). *Worcester Polytechnic Institute* [Online]. Available: http://www.wpi.edu/+writing

Center for SI. (1998). *Review of research concerning the effectiveness of SI from the University of Missouri-Kansas City and other institutions from across the United States* [Online]. Available: http://www.umkc.edu/cad/si/sidocs/sipubindex.htm#overview

Chambers, B., & Abrami, P. C. (1991). The relationship between student team learning outcomes and achievement, causal attributions, and affect. *Journal of Educational Psychology, 83,* 140-146.

Coleman, E. B. (1998). Using explanatory knowledge during collaborative problem solving in science. *The Journal of the Learning Sciences, 7* (3&4), 387-427.

Coleman, E. B., Brown, A. L., & Rivkin, I. (1997). The effect of instructional explanations on learning from scientific texts. *Journal of the Learning Sciences, 6* (4), 347-365.

Cooper, J. L., Prescott, S., Cook, L., Smith, L., Mueck, R., & Cuseo, J. (1990). *Cooperative learning and college instruction: Effective use of student teams*. Carson, CA: California State University Foundation.

Coplin, W. D. (1997). *Teaching assistants manual: PAF 101*. Syracuse, NY: Syracuse University.

Coplin, W. D. (1998). *Improving undergraduate education at Syracuse University through more student-faculty collaboration*. Unpublished manuscript, Syracuse University, New York.

Coppola, B. P., Daniels, D. S., & Lefurgy, S. T. (1996, August). *Integrating computational chemistry into a structured study group program for first-year university honors students*. Paper presented at the 212th national meeting of the American Chemical Society, Orlando, FL.

Couchman, J. (1996). *Report on the pilot study of the supplemental instruction program: 51103 financial accounting, semester 2, 1996*. Report of The Office of Preparatory and Continuing Studies, USQ, Toowoomba.

Couchman, J. (1997, December). *Supplemental instruction: Peer mentoring and student productivity.* Paper presented at the Australian Association for Research in Education (AARE) Conference, Brisbane, Australia.

Couchman, J., & Bull, D. (1996). *Report on the pilot study of the supplemental instruction program: 51008 business economics, semester 1, 1996.* Report of The Office of Preparatory and Continuing Studies, USQ, Toowoomba.

Cox, M. D. (1995). The development of new and junior faculty. In W. A. Wright & Associates (Eds.), *Teaching improvement practices: Successful strategies for higher education* (pp. 283-310). Bolton, MA: Anker.

Cox, M. D. (2001). Faculty learning communities: Change agents for transforming institutions into learning organizations. *To Improve the Academy, 19,* 69-93.

Cox, M. D., & Sorenson, D. L. (2000). Student consultation in faculty development: Connecting directly to the learning revolution. *To Improve the Academy, 18,* 97-127.

Cragan, J. F., & Wright, D. W. (1999). *Communication in small groups: Theory, process, skills* (5th ed.). Belmont, CA: Wadsworth.

Cross, K. P. (1998, July/August). Why learning communities? Why now? *About Campus, 3* (3), 4-11.

Davage, R. H. (1958). *The pyramid plan for the systematic involvement of university students in teaching-learning functions.* University Park, PA: Pennsylvania State University, Division of Academic Research and Services.

Davis, P. (1994). Asking good questions about differential equations. *College Mathematics Journal, 25* (5), 395-400.

Demetry, C., & Groccia, J. E. (1997). A comparative assessment of student experiences in two instructional formats in an introductory materials science course. *Journal of Engineering Education, 86* (3), 203-210.

Department of Employment, Education and Training (DEET). (1993). *National report on Australia's higher education sector.* Canberra, Australia: AGPS.

DiBiasio, D., & Groccia, J. E. (1995). Active and cooperative learning in an introductory chemical engineering course. *Proceedings of the Frontiers in Education 25th Annual Conference, Engineering Education for the 21st Century, Institute of Electrical and Electronics Engineering, USA, 2,* 19-22.

Ehrmann, S. C. (1999). Asking the hard questions about technology use and education. *Change, 31* (2), 25-29.

Engel, C. E. (1997). Not just a method but a way of learning. In D. Boud & G. Feletti (Eds.), *The challenge of problem-based learning* (pp. 23-33). London, England: Kogan Page.

Fago, G. C. (1995). *A scale of cognitive development: Validating Perry's scheme.* Collegeville, PA: Ursinus College. (ERIC Document Reproduction Service No. ED 393 862)

Fry, R., & Kolb, D. (1979). *Experiential learning theory and learning experiences in liberal arts education.* New Directions for Experiential Learning: Enriching the Liberal Arts through Experiential Learning, No. 6. San Francisco, CA: Jossey-Bass.

Gabelnick, F., MacGregor, J., Matthews, R. S., & Smith, B. L. (1990). *Learning communities: Creating connections among students, faculty, and disciplines.* New Directions for Teaching and Learning, No. 41. San Francisco, CA: Jossey-Bass.

Gardner, J. B., Coppola, B. P., & Ryder, T. R. (1997, September). *Novel instrument for the self-assessment of laboratory reports: The student laboratory assessment checklist (SLAC).* Paper presented at the 214th national meeting of the American Chemical Society, Las Vegas, NV.

Gillespie, P., & Lerner, N. (2000). *The Allyn and Bacon guide to peer tutoring.* Needham Heights, MA: Allyn and Bacon.

Gordon, R. (1994). Keeping students at the center: Portfolio assessment at the college level. *Journal of Experiential Education, 17* (1), 23-27.

Gosser, D., Roth, V., Gafney, L., Kampmeier, J., Strozak, V., Varma-Nelson, P., Radel, S., & Weiner, M. (1996). Workshop chemistry: Overcoming the barriers to student success. *The Chemical Educator* [Online serial], *1* (1). Available: http://journals.springer-ny.com/chedr/

Gosser, D. K., Cracolice, M. S., Kampmeier, J. A., Roth. V., Strozak, V. S., & Varma-Nelson, P. (2001). *Peer led team learning: A guidebook.* New York, NY: Prentice Hall.

Gosser, D. K., Strozak, V. S., & Cracolice, M. S. (2001). *Peer led team learning: General chemistry.* New York, NY: Prentice Hall.

Gosser Jr., D. K., & Roth, V. (1998). The workshop chemistry project: Peer-led team learning. *Journal of Chemical Education, 75* (2), 185-187.

Gottfredson, M. (1999). *Report on meeting Hurwitz Goals* [Online]. Available: http://w3.arizona.edu/~uge/hurwitz/hurwitz99.htm

Grabe, M., & Grabe, C. (1998). *Integrating technology for meaningful learning* (2nd ed.). New York, NY: Houghton Mifflin Company.

Gray, T., & Hulbert, S. (1998, Fall). Team teach with a student. *College Teaching, 46* (4), 150-153.

Groccia, J. E., & Miller, J. E. (1996). Collegiality in the classroom: The use of peer learning assistants in cooperative learning in introductory biology. *Innovative Higher Education, 21* (2), 87-100.

Grundy, S., & Kemmis, S. (1981, November). *Educational action research in Australia: The state of the art (an overview).* Paper presented at the Annual Conference of the Australian Association for Research in Education, Adelaide, Australia.

Harris, M. (1986). *Teaching one-to-one: The writing conference.* Urbana, IL: NCTE.

Harris, M. (1995). Talking in the middle: Why writers need writing tutors. *College English, 57,* 27-42.

Hart, F., & Groccia, J. E. (1994). An integrated cooperative learning oriented freshman civil engineering course: Computer analysis in civil engineering. *Proceedings of the 19th International Conference on Improving College Teaching, USA,* 318-327.

Havnes, A. (1998, April). *Students as partners in educational development: Practice, policy, and theory.* Paper presented at the 4th International Consortium for Educational Development Conference, Austin, TX.

Hiemenz, P. C., & Hudspeth, M. C. (1993, September/October). Academic excellence workshops for underrepresented students at Cal Poly, Pomona. *Journal of College Science Teaching,* 38-42.

Hobson, E. H. (1992). Maintaining our balance: Walking the tightrope of competing epistemologies. *The Writing Center Journal, 13* (1), 65-75.

Hobson, E. H. (1998). Straddling the virtual fence. In E. H. Hobson (Ed.), *Wiring the writing center* (pp. ix-xxvi). Logan, UT: Utah State University Press.

Hung, J. (1999). Portfolio evaluation: Theory, process, and product (course materials). Halifax, Nova Scotia: Dalhousie University.

Johnson, D. W., & Johnson, R. T. (1975). *Learning together and alone: Cooperation, competition and individualization.* Englewood Cliffs, NJ: Prentice Hall.

Johnson, D. W., & Johnson R. T. (1989). *Cooperation and competition: Theory and research.* Edina, MN: Interaction Book.

Johnson, D. W., Johnson, R. T., & Smith, K. A. (1991). *Active learning: Cooperation in the college classroom.* Edina, MN: Interaction Book.

Kagan, S. (1994). *Cooperative learning.* San Clemente, CA: Kagan Cooperative Learning.

Kampmeier, J. A., Varma-Nelson, P., & Wedegaertner, D. (2001). *Peer-led team learning: Organic chemistry.* New York, NY: Prentice Hall.

Knight, P. (1995). *Records of achievement in higher and further education.* Lancaster, UK: The Framework Press.

Kolb, D. A. (1976). *Learning style inventory: Technical manual.* Boston, MA: McBer.

Kouzes, J. M., & Posner, B. Z. (1995). *The leadership challenge.* San Francisco, CA: Jossey-Bass.

LaGuardia Community College, Office of Information Management and Analysis. (1997). *1997 institutional profile.* New York, NY: LaGuardia Community College, The City University of New York.

LaGuardia Community College, Office of Institutional Research. (1998). *1997 new student survey report.* New York, NY: LaGuardia Community College, The City University of New York, Division of Information Technology.

Lenning, O. T., & Ebbers, L. H. (1999). The powerful potential of learning communities: Improving education for the future. [Monograph]. *ASHE-ERIC Higher Education Report, 26,* 6.

Lerner, N. (1997). Counting beans and making beans count. *Writing Lab Newsletter, 23* (1), 1-4.

Lerner, N. (1998). Research in the writing center. In B. B. Silk (Ed.), *The writing center resource manual* (pp. 1-11). Emmitsburg, MD: NWCA Press.

Levensky, M. (1973). The Experimental Study Group: A new undergraduate program at MIT. *Interchange, 4* (1), 49-63.

Lewis, K. G. (Ed.). (1992). *Teaching pedagogy to teaching assistants: A handbook for 398T instructors.* Austin, TX: University of Texas at Austin.

MacDonald, R. B. (1994). *The master tutor: A guidebook for more effective tutoring.* New York, NY: Cambridge Stratford.

Makosky, V. P., Sileo, C. C., & Whittemore, L. G. (1990). *Activities handbook for the teaching of psychology* (Vol. 3). Washington, DC: American Psychological Association.

Makosky, V. P., Whittemore, L. G., & Rogers, A. M. (1988). *Activities handbook for the teaching of psychology* (Vol. 2). Washington, DC: American Psychological Association.

Martin, D. C., & Arendale, D. (1994, January). *Review of research concerning the effectiveness of SI from the University of Missouri-Kansas City and other institutions from across the United States.* Paper presented at the annual conference of the Freshman Year Experience, Columbia, SC. (ERIC Document Reproductive Service No. ED 370 502)

Martin, D. C., & Arendale, D. R. (1993). *Supplemental instruction: Improving first-year student success in high-risk courses* (2nd ed.). Columbia, SC: University of South Carolina, National Resource Center for the Freshman Year Experience.

Martin, D. C., & Arendale, D. (Eds.). (1994, Winter). *Supplemental Instruction: Increasing achievement and retention.* New Directions for Teaching and Learning, No. 60. San Francisco, CA: Jossey-Bass.

Martin, D. C., & Arendale, D. R. (1990). *Supplemental instruction: Improving student performance, increasing student persistence.* (ERIC Document Reproduction Service No. ED 327 103)

Martin, D. C., Arendale, D. R., & Associates. (1993). *Review of research on supplemental instruction: Improving first-year student success in high-risk courses* (2nd ed.). Columbia, SC: National Resource Center for the Freshman Year Experience and Students in Transition. (ERIC Document Reproduction Service No. ED 354 839)

Martin, D. C., Blanc, R. A., Debuhr, L. A. H., Garland, M., & Lewis, C. (1983). *Supplemental instruction: A model for student academic support.* Kansas City, MO: University of Missouri and ACT National Center for the Advancement of Educational Practice.

Mazur, E. (1997). *Peer instruction.* Upper Saddle River, NJ: Prentice Hall.

McKeachie, W. F. (1999). *Teaching tips: Strategies, research, and theory for college and university teachers.* Boston, MA: Houghton Mifflin.

Miller, J. E., DiBiasio D., Minasian J., & Catterall, J. (1998). *More student learning, less faculty work? The WPI Davis experiment in educational quality and productivity.* Worcester, MA: Worcester Polytechnical Institute, Center for Educational Development. Retrieved May 18, 2000 from the World Wide Web: http://www/wpi.edu/Academics/CED/reports.html#davis

Miller, J. E., & Groccia, J. E. (1997). Are four heads better than one? A comparison of cooperative and traditional teaching formats in an introductory biology course. *Innovative Higher Education, 21* (4), 253-273.

Monroe, B. (1998). The look and feel of the OWL conference. In E. H. Hobson (Ed.), *Wiring the writing center* (pp. 3-24). Logan, UT: Utah State University Press.

Montaigne, M. E. (1958). The complete works of Montaigne (D. M. Frame, Trans.) Stanford, CA: Stanford University Press.

Moore, L. M., Kinland, E., Lenze, L. F., & Spence, L. D. (1999, March). *Slackers, dictators, and jerks: Making learning teams effective.* Paper presented at the annual conference of the American Association of Higher Education, Washington, DC.

Murphy, C., Law, J., & Sherwood, S. (1996). *Writing centers: An annotated bibliography.* Westport, CT: Garland.

Murphy, C., & Sherwood, S. (1995). *The St. Martin's sourcebook for writing tutors*. New York, NY: St. Martin's.

Murray, M. H. (1994, December). Integrating internal and distance education. *Proceedings of the 6th Annual Conference of the Australian Association of Engineering Education, Sydney, Australia*.

Murray, M. H. (1999, October). Building networks through peer interaction. *ASCE Journal of Professional Issues in Engineering, 125* (4), 1-4.

National Association for Developmental Education (NADE). (2000). *National association for developmental education* [Online]. Available: http://nade.net

National Board of Employment, Education and Training (NBEET). (1995). *Charting a course: Students' views of their future*. Canberra: AGPS.

National Writing Centers Association. (1998). *Colgate University* [Online]. Available: http://departments.colgate.edu/diw/NWCA.html

Nightingale, P. (1988). Language and learning: A bibliographical essay. In G. Taylor, B. Ballard, V. Beasley, H. Bock, J. Clanchy, & P. Nightingale (Eds.), *Literacy by degrees* (pp. 65-81). Philadelphia, PA: The Society for Research into Higher Education and Open University Press.

North, S. M. (1984, September). The idea of a writing center. *College English, 46*, 433-446.

Novak, J. D. (1998). *Learning, creating and using knowledge*. Hillsdale, NJ: Lawrence Erlbaum & Associates.

Nyquist, J. D., Manning, L., Wulff, D. H., Austin, A. E., Sprague, J., Fraser, P. K., Calcagno, C., & Woodford, B. (1999, May/June). On the road to becoming a professor: The graduate student experience. *Change, 31* (3), 18-27.

Pace, C. R. (1990). *College student experiences questionnaire* (3rd ed.). Los Angeles, CA: University of California, Center for the Study of Evaluation. (Available from the Center for Postsecondary Research and Planning, Indiana University.)

Pace, C. R., & Kuh, G. D. (1998). *College student experiences questionnaire* (4th ed.). Bloomington, IN: Indiana University, Center for Postsecondary Research and Planning.

Palincsar, A. S., & Brown, A. L. (1984). Reciprocal teaching of comprehension-fostering and comprehension-monitoring activities. *Cognition and Instruction, 1*, 117-175.

Perry, W. (1970). *Forms of intellectual and ethical development in the college years: A scheme*. New York, NY: Holt, Rinehart, and Winston.

Pfeiffer, J. W., & Ballew, A. C. (1988). *Presentation and evaluation skills in human resource development* (University Associates Training Technologies (UATT) Series, Vol. 7). San Diego, CA: University Associates.

Poulton, M., & Kemeny, J. (1999). *Improvements of course web page* [Online]. Available: www.fcii.arizona.edu/poulton/nats101

Preparing Future Faculty. (1999). *Preparing future faculty home page* [Online]. Available: http://www.preparing-faculty.org/

Rabow, J., Charness, M. A., Kipperman, J., & Radcliffe-Vasile, S. (1994). *William Fawcett Hill's learning through discussion* (3rd ed.). Thousand Oaks, CA: Sage.

Reading/Writing Center Page. (2000). *Hunter College* [Online]. Available: http://www.rwc.hunter.cuny.edu

Redmond, M. V., & Clark, D. J. (1982). A practical approach to improving teaching. *AAHE Bulletin, 34* (6), 8-10.

Rickly, R. (1998). Reflection and responsibility in (cyber)tutor training: Seeing ourselves clearly on and off the screen. In E. H. Hobson (Ed.), *Wiring the writing center* (pp. 44-61). Logan, UT: Utah State University Press.

Roberts, L. (1998). *Learning resources center tutor handbook*. Atlanta, GA: Spelman College. (Available from Lula Roberts, Learning Resources Center, Spelman College, 350 Spelman Lane SW, Box #269, Atlanta, GA 30314-4399).

Roth, V., Marcus, G., & Goldstein, E. (in press). *Peer led team learning: On becoming a peer leader*. Manuscript submitted for publication.

Schultz, F. (2000). *Maxwell school of citizenship and public affairs* [Online]. Available: www.maxwell.syr.edu/paf/

Schwenk, T. L., & Whitman, N. (1984). *Residents as teachers*. Salt Lake City, UT: University of Utah School of Medicine.

Shapiro, N. S., & Levine, J. H. (1999). *Creating learning communities: A practical guide to winning support, organizing for change, and implementing programs.* San Francisco, CA: Jossey-Bass.

Shulman, L. S. (1993, November/December). Teaching as community property: Putting an end to pedagogical solitude. *Change, 25* (6), 6-7.

Silk, B. B. (Ed.). (1998). *The writing center resource manual.* Emmitsburg, MD: National Writing Center Association Press.

Sommers, N. (1998). Revision strategies of student writers and experienced adult writers. In T. L. Capossela (Ed.), *The Harcourt Brace guide to peer tutoring* (pp. 177-187). Orlando, FL: Harcourt Brace.

Sorenson, D. L. (1994). Valuing the student voice: Student observer/consultant programs. *To Improve the Academy, 13,* 97-108.

Sorenson, D. L. (2000a). *Students consulting on teaching: Faculty handbook.* (Available from BYU Faculty Center, 4450 WSC, Provo, UT 84602, (801) 378-7419, faculty_center@byu.edu).

Sorenson, D. L. (2000b). *Students consulting on teaching: Student handbook.* (Available from BYU Faculty Center, 4450 WSC, Provo, UT 84602, (801) 378-7419, faculty_center@byu.edu).

Spence, L. D., & Lenze, L. F. (in press). Taking student criticism seriously: Student quality teams. In K. Lewis (Ed.), *New Directions for Teaching and Learning.* San Francisco, CA: Jossey-Bass.

Springer, L., Stanne, M. E., & Donovan, S. S. (1999). Effects of small-group learning on undergraduates in science, mathematics, engineering and technology: A meta-analysis. *Review of Educational Research, 69,* 21-51.

Taylor, J. C. (1997). *A dual mode of distance education: The University of Southern Queensland* [Online]. Available: http://www.usq.edu.au/dec/staff/taylorj/readings/oprax97/oprax97.htm

Thomas, K. (1976). Conflict and conflict management. In M. Dunnette (Ed.), *The handbook of industrial and organizational psychology* (pp. 889-931). Chicago, IL: Rand McNally.

Tiberius, R. (1995). From shaping performances to dynamic interaction: The quiet revolution in teaching improvement programs. In W. A. Wright and Associates, *Teaching improvement practices: Successful strategies for higher education* (pp. 180-205). Bolton, MA: Anker.

Tinto, V. (1987). *Leaving college: Rethinking the causes and cures of student attrition.* Chicago, IL: University of Chicago Press.

Tinzmann, M. B., Jones, B. F., Fennimore, T. F., Bakker, J., Fine, C., & Pierce, J. (1990). *What is the collaborative classroom?* [Online]. Available: http://www.ncrel.org/sdrs/areas/rpl_esys/collab.htm

Trefethen, L. (1970). *The Trefethen report.* Medford, MA: Tufts University.

Treisman, P. M. (1985). A study of the mathematics performance of black students at the University of California, Berkeley (Doctoral dissertation, University of California, Berkeley, 1990). *Dissertation Abstracts International, 47* (05A), 1641.

Trimbur, J. (1983). Peer tutoring and the benefits of collaborative learning. *Writing Lab Newsletter, 7* (9), 1-3.

Trimbur, J. (1988). *Writing and undergraduate education: A self study.* Unpublished manuscript, Worcester Polytechnic Institute, Worcester, MA.

Trimbur, J. (1998). Peer tutoring: A contradiction in terms? In T. L. Capossela (Ed.), *The Harcourt Brace guide to peer tutoring* (pp. 117-123). Orlando, FL: Harcourt Brace.

TTP. (2000). *Teaching teams program* [Online]. Available: http://www.LPL.arizona.edu/teachingteams

University of Delaware. (2000). *Problem based learning* [Online]. Available: http://www.udel.edu/pbl

The University of Michigan. (1999). *Chemical sciences at the interface of education* [Online]. Available: http://www.umich.edu/~csie/

University of Missouri-Kansas City. (1999). Center for supplemental instruction [Online]. Available: http://www.umkc.edu/cad/SI/

Upcraft, M. L., Gardner, J. N., & Associates. (1989). *The freshman year experience.* San Francisco, CA: Jossey-Bass.

Valley, G. (1968). *An option for intellectual autonomy.* Unpublished manuscript, Massachusetts Institute of Technology, Cambridge.

Valley, G. (1974). *My years in the MIT Experimental Study Group: Some old facts and new myths.* Unpublished manuscript, Massachusetts Institute of Technology, Cambridge.

Varma-Nelson, P., & Cracolice, M. S. (2001). *Peer led team learning: General, organic and biological chemistry.* New York, NY: Prentice Hall.

Watkins, C. (1999). Teaching at ESG [Online]. Available: http://web.mit.edu/esg/www/teaching/main.html

Webb, N. J., & Gribb, T. F. (1967, October). *Teaching process as a learning experience: The experimental use of student-led groups* (Final Report, HE-000-882). Washington, DC: Department of Health, Education and Welfare.

Weedon, E. (1997). A new framework for conceptualising distance learning. *Open Learning, 12* (1), 40-44.

Wheeler, M., & Marshall, J. (1986). Trainer type inventory. In J. W. Pfeiffer & L. D. Goodstein (Eds.), *The 1986 annual: Developing human resources* (pp. 93-97). San Diego, CA: University Associates.

White, E. M. (1994). *Teaching and assessing writing: Recent advances in understanding, evaluating, and improving student performance.* San Francisco, CA: Jossey-Bass.

White, H. B., III. (1996a). Addressing content in problem-based courses: The learning issue matrix. *Biochemical Education, 24,* 41-45.

White, H. B., III. (1996b). Dan tries problem-based learning: A case study. *To Improve the Academy, 15,* 75–91. (Also available at http://www.udel.edu/pbl/dancase3.html).

White, H. B., III. (in press). Research articles as problems for problem-based learning: Stokes' 1864 spectroscopic study of the 'redox' behavior of hemoglobin. *Journal of College Science Teaching.*

Whitman, N. A. (1988). *Peer teaching: To teach is to learn twice* (Report No. 4). College Station, TX: Association for the Study of Higher Education.

Wills, C., & Finkel, D. (1994). Experience with peer learning in an introductory computer science course. *Computer Science Education, 5* (2), 165-187.

Woodward, A., Weiner, M., & Gosser, D. (1993). Problem solving workshops in general chemistry. *Journal of Chemical Education, 70,* 651.

The Workshop Project. (1999). *The workshop project* [Online]. Available: http://www.sci.ccny.cuny.edu/~chemwksp/

Wright, W. A., Knight, P. T., & Pomerleau, N. (1999). Portfolio people: Teaching and learning dossiers and innovation in higher education. *Innovative Higher Education, 24* (2), 89-102.

Wrigley, C. (1973, March). Undergraduate students as teachers: Apprenticeship in the university classroom. *Teaching of Psychology Newsletter,* 5-7.

Zaritsky, J. (1994). *Supplemental instruction: A peer tutoring program at LaGuardia Community College.* (ERIC Document Reproduction Service No. ED 373 850)

Zaritsky, J. (1998). Supplemental instruction: What works, what doesn't. In *Selected conference papers, Vol. 4* (pp. 54-56). Atlanta, GA: National Association for Developmental Education. Available: http://nade.net

Zaritsky, J. (1999). *Enhancing supplemental instruction training with techniques from collaborative learning.* (ERIC Clearinghouse for Community Colleges, ERIC number not yet assigned.)

Index